HAPPINESS, JUSTICE, AND FREEDOM

Happiness, Justice, and Freedom

The Moral and Political Philosophy of John Stuart Mill

Fred R. Berger

UNIVERSITY OF CALIFORNIA PRESS

Berkeley • Los Angeles • London

University of California Press
Berkeley and Los Angeles, California

University of California Press, Ltd.
London, England

Copyright © 1984 by The Regents of the University of California

Library of Congress Cataloging in Publication Data

Berger, Fred R., 1937–
  Happiness, justice, and freedom.

  Bibliography: p. 345
  Includes index.
  1. Mill, John Stuart, 1806–1873—Ethics. 2. Mill,
John Stuart, 1806–1873—Political and social views.
3. Ethics—History—19th century. 4. Political
science—History—19th century. I. Title.
B1608.E8B47 1984   171'.5   83-6502
ISBN 0-520-04867-9

PRINTED IN THE UNITED STATES OF AMERICA

1 2 3 4 5 6 7 8 9

For Audrey, with Love.
You thought it would never get done,
But now I can say:
I told you so!

CONTENTS

ACKNOWLEDGMENTS

A work of this length, requiring years of research and writing, reflects much more than the time and labor of the writer. The contributions of others are numerous, diverse in kind, and sometimes are not apparent even to the author. The direct assistance, training, and encouragement provided by others have certainly played a part in the production of this work. I should like to record my intellectual indebtedness and to thank those who have helped.

My earliest teachers in philosophy—George R. Bartlett, Charles W. Morris, and William T. Blackstone—all were important in my development, and in sharpening my interest in philosophy. The untimely death of Bill Blackstone was a great personal loss, as well as a tragedy for the philosophical community.

At several crucial stages of my career, I received aid and encouragement from H. L. A. Hart, my supervisor at the University of Oxford, Torstein Eckhoff of the University of Oslo, and Richard Wasserstrom, for whose friendship I am additionally grateful.

Several former students of mine were subjected to reading portions of this manuscript at various stages of its writing. Their discussions have been extremely helpful, demonstrating that teaching is a two-way process. Of my former students, I especially appreciate discussions I have had with D. Clayton Hubin, Bruce Russell, and Timothy D. Roche.

A number of persons working on Mill have been kind enough to exchange work in progress with me. At an early stage of my work, D. G. Brown graciously made available to me unpublished work of his on Mill, and met with me for helpful discussion. David Lyons and John

Gray have likewise exchanged manuscript materials with me, and each has been willing to spend hours with me talking about Mill. Though I subject the views of all three to criticism in the text, I believe all have made important contributions to the literature on Mill and I have learned a great deal from each. Gray's views and my own coincide to a remarkable degree (see his book, *Mill on liberty: a defence* [London: Routledge & Kegan Paul, 1983]). This is due to a scholarly coincidence, since we developed our positions independently. As a consequence, however, I believe our books complement each other.

I have also been blessed with critical reviews arranged by the University of California Press that are the sort that gladden the heart of an author. Filled with good critical points, they helped to improve the book a great deal. Richard Arneson provided one of the reviews, while the other reviewer has not been identified to me. I have made a great many changes spurred by each review, and have rewritten an entire chapter at Arneson's urging. I have not made all the changes suggested—in some cases I disagreed, in other cases I simply ran out of steam. The efforts of these reviewers are much appreciated.

The matter of manuscript preparation proved arduous. I received outstanding assistance, however, from Julie Keefer and Charlotte Honeywell, and from Cheryl Hale, who provided special aid at a time of dire need.

I am grateful as well to the editors of the following journals, who have granted permission for me to use materials in this book that I have published in their journals: *American Philosophical Quarterly*, *Canadian Journal of Philosophy*, and *Interpretation*. I am further indebted to the University of Toronto Press and Routledge and Kegan Paul, for permission to quote liberally from Mill's *Collected Works*.

I also want to express my appreciation to the Rockefeller Foundation for a Humanities Fellowship, under which the last three chapters of this book were written.

Finally, I want to thank my copy editor, David P. Shuldiner, and John R. Miles, Laurie J. Taylor, and Shirley Warren of the University of California Press, who, I am sure, will be glad not to have me bugging them any longer.

INTRODUCTION

John Stuart Mill was one of the most respected philosophers of his day. Partly as a consequence of hostile criticism in the early part of this century, his reputation has been in eclipse until quite recently. Over the past fifteen to twenty years, much scholarly work has been done (aided greatly by the continuing publication of Mill's *Collected Works*) that has led to revisionary analyses of his theories. While it cannot be said that these in turn have restored his standing among philosophers to its former position, at least in the area of ethics it is now recognized that he had important things to say, of relevance to problems of moral theory and practice that concern contemporary philosophers.

This book is an attempt to explore Mill's moral and political theories in some detail, with a special emphasis upon recent research. I contend that Mill held a cohesive set of doctrines that are complex, interesting, and philosophically stronger than traditional interpretations have credited him. I believe these doctrines provide the basis for a more defensible form of utilitarianism, and of political liberalism, than has often been previously supposed possible. In demonstrating this, I will concentrate on what I take to be the most central concepts in Mill's theories—the concepts of happiness, justice, and freedom.

There are at least three different sorts of emphasis among writers on the history of philosophy. The first, sometimes referred to as the "history of ideas" approach, is chiefly concerned with what may be thought of as the historical aspects of a philosopher's writings. Attention is directed toward the influences on the thinker, the development of the ideas that occur in his or her work, the relationship of those ideas to the social or political events of the day, and the special understandings that must be given to what the author wrote, in light of concepts used at the time.

The second emphasis, sometimes called simply "history of philosophy," concentrates on the philosopher's *theories*. The concern here is with explicating the concepts used, their interconnections, and the principles or claims that are put forth. Of crucial importance are the *arguments* given, and their relative strengths and weaknesses. The central objective within this tradition is the making of a clear, coherent presentation of the theories of the philosopher and the chief grounds given in support of those theories.

The third emphasis in historical commentaries is what can be called "philosophical reconstruction." In this approach the philosopher's writings are used as a sort of mapping of a theory, the full details and development of which is the job of the commentator. The commentator is concerned with the philosopher's theory as providing basic insights into an interesting or correct philosophical position; but the chief concern is to *reconstruct* the textual position in ways that remove unclarities or ambiguities, and that substitute sound for defective arguments.

These are not different kinds of history of philosophy. The best work of each genre displays features of the others. One cannot adequately trace the historical development of ideas without understanding the logical features of those ideas, and something of their strengths and weaknesses. Similarly, the reconstructive ideal could be thwarted if central themes are best understood in light of the conditions of the time. The present work emphasizes the latter two approaches, though I have explored the historical development of certain themes in the utilitarian tradition. The approaches do require different skills, and mine are not those of the scholar-historian. I have attempted to be as true to the texts, and the intellectual contexts in which they were written, as my expertise permits. But I am fully aware that there is a danger of reshaping Mill's intentions and concerns to those of today, with a consequent distortion of his views.

Mill's psychological theories are crucial to understanding his moral philosophy. Therefore, the first chapter of this book is devoted to a sketch of his views in psychology and their relation to morality, with a special emphasis upon his theory of the moral sentiments and the notion of a moral judgment.

With Mill's psychological theory as background, I elaborate, in chapter 2, his conception of happiness, and his famous "proof" of the Greatest Happiness Principle. I then turn, in chapter 3, to a consideration of the role of rules in his moral theory. This is a topic of consider-able debate among contemporary utilitarians, and recent scholarship has credited Mill with having held most of the variant theories pre-sented by contemporary philosophers. A further reason for the exten-sive treatment of rules is that they play a crucial role in his conception of duties of justice.

In chapter 4, I shall discuss Mill's views on justice, including the principles that make up what I term Mill's "substantive theory of justice," that is, those principles that are to be applied in everyday social, economic, and political life. I will argue that Mill's theory of justice is more defensible than the textbook depictions of it.

Finally, in chapter 5, I shall discuss Mill's theory of freedom, which I take to be an application of his theory of justice. Moreover, I will argue that his most central themes can be fully understood only in terms of his view of happiness. In sum, I will show that the conceptions of happi-ness, justice, and freedom are interrelated, and that Mill's moral and political philosophy can be best understood by seeing those intercon-nections. Throughout, I shall contend that Mill's theories shed light on the possibilities open to utilitarian theory as such, and that, as a conse-quence, they have considerable contemporary import.

Readers will want to know what is special about my interpretation, and why it justifies the very lengthy treatment given here. Deferring ultimate judgment to others, I can indicate what I take to be its chief distinctive features. First, it is a detailed exploration of interconnected doctrines in Mill; I do not think that his moral theories have been so thoroughly explored. Second, I believe that I have brought to light important features of Mill's theories that, for the most part, have not been sufficiently discussed. A brief outline of these will also serve to highlight the primary themes of the book.

First, I shall emphasize that Mill did not define happiness as simply an aggregate of pleasures. He held that human well-being requires some specific elements, especially those associated with what he called our "higher natures"—a sense of freedom or self-determination, a sense of security, and the development and use of our specifically human capaci-ties of intelligence and sociality. Such a theory, I will argue, avoids many of the untoward consequences of the simpleminded hedonism that has been traditionally attributed to him, and it helps to explain his "proof" of the principle of utility.

Following this, I shall point out the great stress he gave to the role of rules in his moral theory. I will explore various recent interpretations of Mill on the subject of his criterion of right and wrong action and its relation to moral rules, and will try to show that none of these interpretations fully accounts for the texts, which display unreconciled features. I shall argue, nonetheless, that Mill provided grounds for utilitarians to adhere to rules in practical moral decision-making. I will also show that Mill's views are to be found in incipient forms in the writings of his teachers, John Austin, Jeremy Bentham, and James Mill.

In the second part of the book, I shall show how the conception of happiness and the stress on moral rules in practical deliberation shed light on Mill's theories of justice and freedom. Mill took duties of justice to be defined by the existence of a right held by the person to whom the duty is owed, but he also held that these rights are tied to interests that society ought *as a matter of rule* to protect. Duties of justice, then, are defined by moral rules. Since the interests protected by rights are ones essential to human well-being, and happiness is best pursued by adherence to rules, Mill could give a strong, consistently utilitarian, justification for rights that can meet certain prevalent criticisms of utilitarianism on this score.

Traditionally, Mill's views on justice have not been taken seriously. Only a few very recent commentators have recognized that they are important to his moral theory. There has been, however, no attempt to pick out the particular principles of justice he maintained, and to systematically trace them through his writings in political and economic theory. I have made such a preliminary exploration, showing how his substantive principles of desert and equality were applied to such questions as punishment, taxation, property, political suffrage and representation, and the status of women. Mill's views on these matters have considerable significance for contemporary theories, and I bring out some important similarities and contrasts.

Finally, I shall argue that the most crucial themes in his theory of freedom are best explained and defended by the principle that everyone has a right to be autonomous; that this implies that everyone has a right to freedom insofar as freedom is requisite to being autonomous; and that it implies that one may interfere with freedom only to protect persons from conduct that threatens harm from which people have a right to be protected. In other words, I shall argue that his theory of liberty is best understood in terms of his theory of justice. I will also stress that much of *On Liberty* is directed at demonstrating the crucial roles that self-development and autonomy play in his conception of human happiness; that, in sum, the central themes of happiness, justice, and freedom are interconnected, and provide support for one another.

In the final chapter, I raise criticisms that seem to me important for Mill's theory, and for utilitarian theories in general. Utilitarianism is very much alive today, and I believe that this detailed exploration of its historical foundations can contribute to its contemporary understanding and development. In the concluding section, I indicate what I take to be the most significant contributions Mill's writings have for present-day moral and political philosophy.

As a final introductory note, I should warn readers that I am using the term *utilitarianism* in the broad manner that has become standard among some philosophers, namely, to designate any moral theory that takes consequences (of acts, rules, and so on) as the criterion of right and wrong action. Many philosophers, and most social choice economists, use the term in a narrower way that more specifically captures Bentham's version of utilitarianism. Though I believe there are some good reasons for this latter usage, I prefer not to limit the term in a way that might rule out Mill as a utilitarian. It seems reasonable to me that, as one of the founders of this theory, and as the author of a work that purports to explain it, his conception of it must carry great weight in our own determinations of what forms utilitarianism may take.

Part I
MILL'S MORAL THEORY

1

PSYCHOLOGY AND MORALITY

Classical English utilitarians closely linked their theories of human nature and their accounts of morality. This was certainly true of Bentham, and of James Mill. The opening sentence of the text of Bentham's *An Introduction to the Principles of Morals and Legislation* is an oft-quoted statement of the basic sources of human motivation. ("Nature has placed mankind under the governance of two sovereign masters, *pain* and *pleasure*.") This psychological theory is crucial to Bentham's theory of value and morality. As a disciple of Bentham, James Mill took over Bentham's views, and elaborated on them at length in his *Analysis of the Phenomena of the Human Mind*. His views in ethics were heavily dependent on this psychological theory. When John Stuart Mill prepared an edition of his father's classic study in psychology, he added selections from his father's writings in ethics, found primarily in the highly polemical *A Fragment on Mackintosh*. J. S. Mill's own views in ethics were similarly wedded to a conception of man's psychological nature.

Utilitarian ethics has traditionally been naturalistic in two important senses. First, utilitarians have viewed morality as a natural outgrowth of man's nature. Moral rules were seen as arising from human needs. Moral sentiments were explained as deriving from basic, natural feelings and emotions. Second, utilitarians in the English tradition tended to explain the bindingness or obligatoriness of morality by reference to ends which people seek by nature. In its weakest (and most defensible) form, this amounts to the claim that nothing can be an obligation for a person to do unless it can be connected with ends people are capable of seeking. As all persons were depicted as seeking happiness or pleasure, no standard of duty could be adopted which could not be shown to promote happiness. Essential to the utilitarian program was a theory of human motivation.

Interestingly, many of the opponents of the classical utilitarians agreed with these two points. The utilitarians insisted, however, that man's moral sentiments were not themselves an "original" element of man's nature. They rejected, in other words, a theory which treats the moral sentiments as part of man's basic apparatus for knowing truths; the moral sentiments do not constitute a moral "sense" which reveals moral truth in the way the physical senses disclose truths about the world of bodies. The so-called "intuitive school" was the chief enemy of the utilitarian camp.

There can be little question that John Stuart Mill's moral philosophy cannot be rightly understood without reference to the psychological framework within which he developed it, and from within which he attempted to explain it. In this chapter, I will outline the most important features of Mill's theory of human psychology, and present a version of the moral theory that it supports.

ASSOCIATIONISM

Mill took over from his father the dominant notion of psychology of British empiricism, deriving from Locke and Hume. Psychology, according to Mill, studies the "laws of the mind," that is, the laws according to which states of mind or consciousness follow, or are caused by one another.[1] There are two general laws that govern mental phenomena:

1. Once a state of consciousness has occurred, it can be reproduced in the mind without the presence of the original cause. Citing Hume, he wrote: "Every mental *impression* has its *idea*."[2]
2. Ideas are caused to occur in the mind by other ideas or impressions according to certain laws of association.

The laws in virtue of which ideas are associated are given in *A System of Logic* as follows:

a. Similar ideas tend to excite one another. (This is referred to as the law of "Resemblance" in "Bain's Psychology.")
b. If two impressions are frequently experienced together or successively, the occurrence of one (or the idea of it) tends to

produce the idea of the other. (This is the law of "Contiguity.")
c. Greater intensity of one or both impressions has the same effect of making them call up one another as does greater frequency of conjunction.[3]

Mill believed that, insofar as human *psychology* is concerned (i.e., the influence of mental phenomena on one another), all states of consciousness can be explained by reference to these laws. No matter how complex, all states of mind—desires, emotions, abstract ideas, judgments, and volitions—obey these laws. It may well be the case that associated with mental phenomena are physical events in the nervous system or brain which have causal relations with mental events; nonetheless, the relations of succession among mental events cannot simply be deduced from a science of physiology, and thus there is an independent science of the Mind.[4]

The account given so far must be supplemented with further discussion before we will be in a position to explain those elements of Mill's psychology which are needed to understand this moral theory—his view of human motivation, the nature of the will, and his conception of human happiness.

Mill often emphasized that ideas may combine to make up more complex ideas in a sort of "chemical union," so that the separate component ideas are not experienced in the new idea. Water is made up of hydrogen and oxygen, but these are blended in such a way that they are not readily recognized. Similarly, impressions which are regularly connected may result in the frequent and instantaneous conjunction of the ideas as a group when any of the impressions are had. Thus, what we experience is one idea (e.g., that of an orange), in which we cannot make out the separate component ideas; they "melt and coalesce into one another."[5]

This latter doctrine of the "chemical union" of complex ideas (which Mill attributed to David Hartley) was employed to explain how complex ideas, which "feel" different from the sum of their alleged constituents, are, nevertheless, really composed of ideas of simple impressions. As we shall see, Mill regarded the moral sentiments, in particular the sentiment of justice, as exhibiting just this sort of union. Moreover, Mill insisted that holding important complex ideas to be composed of simple elements into which they can be analyzed does nothing to detract from the importance of those ideas or their role as real, and important (though not "original"), parts of human nature.[6]

So far, it would appear that the mind is a merely passive faculty, receiving sensations which generate ideas according to regular laws. This would be an inadequate theory of mind for several reasons. For one thing, people exhibit different mental propensities and experience things differently from one another in ways which are not fully explained by their past mental history—their childhood training or education. There are, according to Mill, mental predispositions peculiar to individuals. He is willing to attribute these to differences in "organic constitution," which can cause feelings to be more or less intensely felt, and even generate "different *qualities* of mind, different types of mental character." Moreover, we share with animals a measure of instinctual constitution. Thus, each of us is predisposed to a kind of character. (This point is important for explaining the significance of individuality in *On Liberty*.) Nonetheless, these are not given, unalterable aspects of the human mind; all can be lessened or "overcome" by the influence of education, custom, and other mental influences.[7]

MOTIVES

A passive depiction of mind would be inaccurate for more profound reasons, however. Plainly, the mind "is active as well as passive," and "activity cannot possibly be generated from passive elements; a primitive active element must be found somewhere."[8] Without activity, the mind would be a receptive, contemplative faculty, but it could not be involved in the production of human acts. Central to the views of associationist psychologists, however, was the claim that actions are produced (either immediately or ultimately) by pleasures or pains. Bentham began his text on morals and legislation with this claim. James Mill held that every voluntary act is produced by a motive, and a motive is the idea of a pleasure contemplated as produced by our action.[9] Moreover, the idea of pleasure, he held, is the same thing as a desire; hence, all voluntary acts are done from a desire for anticipated pleasures.[10]

Such statements have led commentators to attribute to the utilitarians two important claims:

1. Persons always act from a desire for pleasure; all voluntary acts are sought only as a means to the end of pleasure.
2. Persons always seek their own pleasure or good in all their voluntary acts.

The first claim (which has been labeled "psychological hedonism") can, with *some* plausibility, be attributed to Bentham and to James Mill. The second statement (a version of "psychological egoism") was probably rejected by both. My concern, however, is with John Stuart Mill, and I want to show that he rejected both claims. As we shall see, these points are of great importance, as one holding the views stated would have great difficulty reconciling them with Mill's concept of happiness in *Utilitarianism*, and with claims he made in that essay concerning human motives, for example, the assertion that utilitarianism insists along with every other theory that people should act from the desire to be virtuous for its own sake. In the remainder of this section, I shall consider psychological hedonism. In the section dealing with sympathy and the social feelings, I will discuss psychological egoism.

It is not difficult to show that Mill rejected the view that all acts are motivated by desires for pleasure as the end or aim of the action. As we shall see, he maintained that pleasure and pain are *causally* linked to all voluntary human acts (though sometimes only indirectly, through past associations of the act with pleasure). He did not hold, however, that all acts are done with the thought of gaining a pleasure by means of them. The first important statement of this theory was given by Mill twenty-eight years prior to the publication of his essay *Utilitarianism*. He wrote a critical study of Bentham's moral and jurisprudential thought entitled "Remarks on Bentham's Philosophy." One of Mill's chief criticisms was that Bentham's conceptions of human nature and human motivation were too narrow:

> That the actions of sentient beings are wholly determined by pleasure and pain, is the fundamental principle from which he starts. . . . Now if this only means what was before asserted, that our actions are determined by pleasure and pain, that simple and unambiguous mode of stating the proposition is preferable. But under cover of the obscurer phrase a meaning creeps in, both to the author's mind and the reader's which goes much farther, and is entirely false: that all our acts are determined by pains and pleasures *in prospect*, pains and pleasures to which we look forward as the *consequences* of our acts. This, as a universal truth, can in no way be maintained. The pain or pleasure which determines our conduct is as frequently one which *precedes* the moment of action as one which follows it. . . . the case *may* be, and is to the full as likely to be, that he [a man] recoils from the very thought of committing the act; the idea of placing himself in such a situation is so painful, that he cannot dwell upon it long enough to have even the physical power of perpetrating the crime. His conduct is determined by pain; but by a pain which precedes the act, not

by one which is expected to follow it. Not only *may* this be so, but unless it be so, the man is not really virtuous. The fear of pain *consequent* upon the act, cannot arise, unless there be *deliberation*. . . . With what propriety shrinking from an action without deliberation, can be called yielding to an *interest*, I cannot see. *Interest* surely conveys, and is intended to convey, the idea of an *end*, to which the conduct (whether it be act or forebearance) is designed as the *means*. Nothing of this sort takes place in the above example. It would be more correct to say that conduct is *sometimes* determined by an *interest*, that is, by a deliberate and conscious aim; and sometimes by an *impulse*, that is by a feeling (call it an association if you think fit) which has no ulterior end, the act or forebearance becoming an end in itself.[11]

Mill went on to hold that Bentham's attempt to list all human motives was misconceived in principle, since "motives are innumerable; there is nothing whatever which may not become an object of desire or of dislike by association."[12] Indeed, Mill went on to claim, Bentham left out such important motives as conscience or the feeling of duty. Men sometimes do or forbear doing acts because they are right or wrong.

In these passages, Mill seems to have been saying that actions are caused by pleasures or pains, either the pleasure or pain anticipated as *resulting* from the act, or the pleasure or pain generated by the very thought of doing the act. In the latter case, that which is desired—the doing or not-doing of an act—is not a pleasure anticipated as resulting from action, and Mill explicitly asserted that in this case there is no ulterior motive beyond the action or forbearance which is sought. The claim that Mill endorsed in these paragraphs, that all actions and forbearances are *caused* by pleasures or pains is not equivalent to the claim that all persons desire or seek only pleasures and the avoidance of pain.

"Remarks on Bentham's Philosophy" was written by Mill for Edward Bulwer, who was preparing his book *England and the English*. Bulwer reprinted part of it as an appendix, though he did not fully acknowledge it for some time.[13] These criticisms of Bentham were not idiosyncratic, however, nor did Mill come to a different position on the matter. In 1838, writing in the *London and Westminster Review*, he echoed the criticisms made in the "Remarks." Bentham failed to recognize, he wrote, that people can pursue "spiritual perfection" or a virtuous character for its own sake. He overlooked the role of conscience, and of such motives as the sense of honor, of personal dignity, the love of beauty, the power of giving effect to our volitions, and so on.[14]

Mill's *A System of Logic* was published in 1843. In it, he maintained the view of human motivation outlined in the essays on Bentham, and went on to explain in associationist terms how we could come to desire things other than pleasures and the avoidance of pains, even if originally that is all we desire. In *Utilitarianism* (first published as a series of articles in 1861), Mill referred the reader to this passage in the *Logic* as expressing his views concerning human motives:

> When the will is said to be determined by motives, a motive does not mean always, or solely, the anticipation of a pleasure or of a pain. I shall not here inquire whether it be true that, in the commencement, all voluntary actions are mere means consciously employed to obtain some pleasure or avoid some pain. It is at least certain that we gradually, through the influence of association, come to desire the means without thinking of the end: the action itself becomes an object of desire, and is performed without reference to any motive beyond itself. Thus far, it may still be objected, that the action having through association become pleasurable, we are, as much as before, moved to act by the anticipation of a pleasure, namely the pleasure of the action itself. But granting this, the matter does not end here. As we proceed in the formation of habits, and become accustomed to will a particular course of conduct because it is pleasurable, we at last continue to will it without any reference to its being pleasurable. Although, from some change in us or in our circumstances, we have ceased to find any pleasure in the action, or perhaps to anticipate any pleasure as the consequence of it, we still continue to desire the action, and consequently to do it. . . . A habit of willing is commonly called a purpose; and among the causes of our volitions, and of the actions which flow from them, must be reckoned not only likings and aversions, but also purposes. It is only when our purposes have become independent of the feelings of pain or pleasure from which they originally took their rise that we are said to have a confirmed character.[15]

Finally, we may note that in 1869 (after the publication of *Utilitarianism*), he published an edition of his father's *Analysis of the Phenomena of the Human Mind*, to which he appended explanatory and (sometimes) critical footnotes. In one of the more important notes, he pointed out (again) how various things that are not themselves pleasures come to be desired "for their own sake, without reference to their consequences," by being closely associated, originally, with pleasure.[16]

We shall return to Mill's discussion of human motives in *Utilitarianism* when we take up his concept of happiness. For present purposes, it will suffice to point out that he there endorsed the theory, given in *Logic*, that acts are not always motivated by desires for pleasures or avoidance of pains. From the passages already cited, we can extract elements of a theory of the will to which Mill was committed.

WILL

James Mill had explained voluntary action by the association of the idea of an act (as cause) with the idea of a pleasure (as effect). For John Stuart Mill, this explanation was insufficient even for those acts which really are motivated by desires for pleasure. The one salient fact the account leaves out is that desire can initiate action. Similarly, aversion initiates action which seeks to avoid pain. The mere idea of a pleasure associated with the idea of an act is not yet a desire. He argued that

> painful states of consciousness, no less than pleasurable ones, tend to form strong associations with their causes or concomitants. The idea, therefore, of a pain, will, no less than that of a pleasure, become associated with the muscular action that would produce it, and with the muscular sensations that accompany the action; and, as a matter of fact, we know that it does so.[17]

What distinguishes desire from aversion is that one stirs toward action which produces pleasure; the other stirs avoidance behavior. "Desire," he concluded, "is the initiatory stage of volition."[18] Now, this does raise difficulties of interpretation, for in *Utilitarianism*, he had contrasted will and desire, describing the former as "the active phenomenon," and desire as "the state of passive sensibility." We are also left unclear about the status of habitual willings. In these cases, "instead of willing the thing because we desire it, we often desire it only because we will it."[19] Some of the language Mill used in discussing habitual willings carries the suggestion that there is in them no true desire. If, indeed, a desire always includes an idea of a pleasure (along with a tendency to action), it is hard to see that desires are always present in habitual willings.[20]

Fortunately, the details here are not crucial to the points I wish to make concerning Mill's theory of the will. Sometimes, it is clear, the will is activated by a desire for pleasure. At other times our acts derive from habit, and if a desire is involved at all, it is a desire to do the act. Mill did distinguish three forms that habitual willings may take.[21] First, we may unconsciously act from habit. This appears to be more or less mechanical behavior of which we are barely even conscious. If there is any voluntariness in this behavior, it consists in the fact that the initial acts have been voluntary, and that we are not coerced when we perform subsequent acts. Second, our willing has become so habitual that though we would prefer not to, we continue to do the act. Mill cited habits of "excess" and "indulgence" which may be harmful. These too, we might say, have doubtful credentials as voluntary acts, for it seems as plausible to claim they are done "against" our will, or that our will is too weak to resist. The picture is that of a person who cannot control his behavior through the process of deliberation, or that he does, perhaps, deliberate, but has become habituated to weigh considerations in the wrong way. Finally, there are cases in which habitual willing is in fulfillment of one's general intention. A person may desire to treat children with warmth and kindness, and through practice at it find himself or herself behaving that way as a matter of course.

CHARACTER

This last sort of case is of importance for us, because Mill labeled this state of mind as having a "purpose." Some actions, he claimed, flow from purposes; not all actions are caused by "likings and aversions." Having purposes which are not at the mercy of our momentary likes and dislikes is a matter of having a "confirmed character." Further, he maintained that it is extremely important that people develop certain kinds of character and suppress others. As we shall see, he held that character development is the most important part of morality. We need to understand better, however, what Mill meant by having "a confirmed character."

Unfortunately, Mill did not present an extended analysis of this concept. There are hints, however, of how he might have explicated the notion. In the first place, acting from "fixed purposes" is not a matter of mere mechanical repetition. This is *one* sort of habituated behavior, but not what Mill indicated as bound up with the development of character. In the second place, Mill wrote of character development as something which is a matter of "self-education" and "training, by the human being himself, of his affections and will."[22] Having a character, then, is a matter of having trained dispositions of feeling, desire, and action, which we ourselves have inculcated, and it is important that the actor himself has had a role in producing that state. In *On Liberty*, Mill went so far as to claim that a person whose desires and impulses are not "his own" does not *have* a character.[23]

Having a character, then, seems to involve having inculcated in oneself certain dispositions of both feeling and action associated with being a certain kind of person, for example, a virtuous person. Such training at first requires some effort, and perhaps conscious focusing of attention; but gradually, with time and practice, both become "matter of course" responses to appropriate conditions. The person of confirmed virtue just does desire to do the right thing in difficult moral situations, and performs morally required acts without any thought of pleasure to be obtained. He or she is "naturally" pained at the very idea of evil actions. Habit is involved only in a loose sense. Mill's habitual willings which evidence a confirmed character are like what Aristotle termed a "hexis." Indeed, the development of appropriate character in Aristotle parallels Mill's view almost exactly.[24] It is of interest to compare one commentator's description of the state of virtue in Aristotle with our depiction of it in Mill:

> Let us begin with the generic definition of Moral Excellence or Virtue in the narrower sense. The term cannot denote a mere natural feeling or susceptibility to feeling, such as anger, fear, pity—as these, considered merely as such, are not objects of praise or blame: it denotes a settled habit, formed by a course of actions under rule and discipline in which vicious excess and defect have been avoided, of experiencing the natural emotions just mentioned in a duly limited and regulated manner; so that the virtuous man, without internal conflict, wills actions that hit the happy mean in their effects. So far Virtue is like technical skill, which also is the result of practice, and is manifested in the successful avoidance of the contrasted errors of "too much" and "too little"; but Virtue differs from skill in involving a deliberate choice of virtuous acts for the sake of their intrinsic moral beauty, and not for any end external to the act.[25]

In a later chapter dealing with rules, we shall discuss why Mill thought it so important that character development receive attention from moralists. The concern here has been to show how Mill accounted for actions done with no prospective pleasure being sought, but rather as manifestations of a state of character. In particular, a virtuous state of character, in which one desires or does right acts for their own sake without anticipating pleasure to be obtained, is possible on this account. Finally, we must recall a point previously made: we all have natural, unique predispositions to feel and respond in certain ways, and to be pleased by certain things or activities. Character development also involves trying out and developing that which is unique in us. Without the chance to work out what is individual in us, we cannot achieve that sense of self-fulfillment which is requisite for our well-being. This point has obvious implications for Mill's concept of happiness, and for his arguments for freedom.

We shall return to this subject in discussing Mill's concept of happiness. In *Utilitarianism*, he seems to have been arguing that utility can make a claim as the principle of morality (in part) because people desire only happiness. He must, then, explain how he can also (consistently) claim that people can and should seek to do virtuous acts for their own sakes.

SYMPATHY AND SOCIAL FEELINGS

I want to turn now to the second major misconception of Mill's views that commentators have sometimes held, namely, their attribution to him of a version of psychological egoism. This is the doctrine that people always seek their own pleasure or good in their voluntary acts. Of course, we have already seen that Mill rejected such a view, since he held that people can come to desire the doing of certain acts without thought of any pleasure or other good for themselves which might result. This may not be entirely convincing, however, since we seem originally to be motivated by desires for pleasures. It may be thought, then, that nothing can be desired by us which has not been a source of pleasure to us. If we originally desire only our own pleasure, it may be thought to follow that the "ultimate" end of our voluntary acts is our own pleasure.

Of course, this reasoning is not valid; even if all the premises attributed to Mill really were held by him, he would not be logically committed to the conclusion. Once we have achieved a confirmed state of character, for example, virtue, we can continue to desire doing virtuous acts even if we know *we* will not derive pleasure from them. There is nothing in the theory which requires Mill to hold that the new source of motivation is *weaker* than the old source and really a form of achieving *its* object. Indeed, he pointed out that sometimes habitual willings can motivate behavior (e.g., excessive indulgence in tobacco or drink), even against our preferences.

The argument is mistaken, however, in another respect. Mill held that it is a part of human nature that we sympathize with others—take pleasure in their pleasure and feel pain at the thought of their pain. Moreover, there are other social feelings which form a part of human nature. To have a full picture of the psychological views which underly

Mill's theories in morals and politics, we must explore the social nature of persons which he accepted.

Let us look at the main source of difficulty for Mill in (consistently) accepting a motive of sympathy as a part of human nature, namely, his view that pleasure and pain determine human acts. Of course, it is always one's own pleasure or pain which one experiences; hence, it could (mistakenly) be inferred that we always act from the idea of our own pleasure (or pain). We saw earlier that Mill rejected the view that we always act from the desire of (idea of) a pleasure to be gained from an action. Some ideas are themselves pleasurable, and the pleasantness of the idea causes us to act. The motive is produced by a pleasure we experience in the contemplation of the act (and, perhaps, its consequences). This, however, does not imply that the *object* of our action need be a pleasure of ours. As Mill argued, there need be *no* pleasure contemplated at all. Moreover, in cases where there *are* pleasures contemplated as the upshot of our acts, it need not be our *own* pleasures which are contemplated. The idea of others experiencing pleasure through acts of our own can itself be pleasurable and a cause of our acts. Mill made clear that he recognized the distinction between the *source* or *cause* of our desire—a pleasure of our own—and the "reference" or object of the desire, which may be the pleasure of someone else. In a note he added to his father's work, *Analysis of the Phenomena of the Human Mind*, he warned of just this confusion into which his father's writings might lead his readers:

> That the pleasures or pains of another person can only be pleasurable or painful to us through the association of our own pleasures or pains with them, is true in one sense, which is probably that intended by the author, but not true in another, against which he has not sufficiently guarded his mode of expression. It is evident, that the only pleasures or pains of which we have direct experience being those felt by ourselves, it is from them that our very notions of pleasure and pain are derived. It is also obvious that the pleasure or pain with which we contemplate the pleasure or pain felt by somebody else, is itself a pleasure or pain of our own. But if it be meant that in such cases the pleasure or pain is consciously referred to self, I take this to be a mistake. By the acts or other signs exhibited by another person, the idea of a pleasure (which is a pleasurable idea) or the idea of a pain (which is a painful idea) are recalled, sometimes with considerable intensity, but in association with the other person as feeling them, not with one's self as feeling them.[26]

Similarly, in commenting on Bentham, he warned of the possibility of a like misreading of Bentham's views:

> In laying down as a philosophical axiom, that men's actions are always obedient to their interests, Mr. Bentham did no more than dress up the very trivial proposition that all persons do what they feel themselves most disposed to do, in terms which appeared to him more precise, and better suited to the purposes of philosophy, than those more familiar expressions. He by no means intended by this assertion to impute universal selfishness to mankind, for he reckoned the motive of sympathy as an *interest*, and would have included conscience under the same appellation, if that motive had found any place in his philosophy, as a distinct principle from benevolence. He distinguished two kinds of interests, the self-regarding and the social: in vulgar discourse, the name is restricted to the former kind alone.[27]

Now, there is some question as to the extent to which sympathy can be said to be "natural" for Mill. Though he wrote that it is "as much an ultimate fact of our nature, as care for ourselves,"[28] he qualified this by saying it is true "in an admissible sense." Similarly, in "Sedgwick's Discourse," he wrote that "the idea of the pain of another is naturally painful; the idea of the pleasure of another is naturally pleasurable,"[29] and he held that "in this, the unselfish part of our nature, lies a foundation, even independently of inculcation from without, for the generation of moral feelings."[30] However, he seems to have been trying to show that we need not be *trained* and *taught* to have such feelings; they may still arise only through a process of association. Indeed, in his essay on Whewell, he wrote that the good of others is a pleasure to us only because we have "learnt to find pleasure in it."[31] His idea seems to have been that sympathy arises out of a process of association in which we experience pleasure in the pleasure of others, and pains in their pains. While society in fact seeks to provide these associations, we are disposed to experience them without conscious inculcation (perhaps only as a result of perceiving that our own happiness is ultimately bound up with that of others). As human life is lived with others, we "naturally" come to take pleasure in the pleasures of others and to be pained by their pains. *Training* is not necessary; social experience suffices.

Sympathy was not, for Mill, a moral feeling, though it is the foundation of moral feelings (we shall discuss this in connection with his theory of the moral sentiments). Moreover, it is "weak" in human beings, and must be nurtured and developed. Hence, Mill held that a large part of the responsibility of education is to develop concern with others. Sympathy was not, however, the sole basis in Mill's view for the development of social concern and social life in man. There is a further "powerful natural sentiment" which is operative in men: " . . . the desire to be in unity with our fellow creatures, which is already a powerful principle in human nature, and happily one of those which tend to become stronger, even without express inculcation, from the influences of advancing civilization."[32]

This desire takes many complex forms, according to Mill. In his essay "Utility of Religion," he discussed the great hold over us that public opinion enjoys precisely because of this desire to be in accord with others. It is manifested in such forms as "the love of glory; the love of praise; the love of admiration; the love of respect and deference." It is also shown in "the fear of shame, the dread of ill repute, or of being disliked or hated." Even the esteem we have of ourselves, he pointed out, is in large measure a function of our assessment of how others perceive us. So strong is this orientation to be in accord with others and to have their approbation that Mill regarded it as bound up in virtually all we do: "Through all departments of human affairs, regard for the sentiments of our fellow-creatures is in one shape or other, in nearly all characters, the pervading motive. And we ought to note that this motive is naturally strongest in the most sensitive natures, which are the most promising material for the formation of great virtues."[33]

Given such strong natural motivation, and the development in people of sympathy, there are very forceful propensities in people's nature toward a social state. Moreover, the realities of life impress on one the mutual interdependence of persons, so that the very process of growing up into adulthood carries with it the "natural" result that we do have a concern for the interests and feelings of others; we do perceive our own well-being as bound up with that of others; we do make the interests of others our own interests. The social state is a natural offshoot of elements in human nature; people are, in fact, virtually inconceivable outside it: "The social state is at once so natural, so necessary, and so habitual to man, that, except in some unusual circumstances or by an effort of voluntary abstraction, he never conceives himself otherwise than as a member of a body; and this association is riveted more and more, as mankind are further removed from the state of savage independence. Any condition, therefore, which is essential to a state of society, becomes more and more an inseparable part of every person's conception of the state of things which he is born into, and which is the destiny of a human being."[34]

Indeed, Mill recognized no limit to the extent to which people could come to take on the well-being of others as their own, through the influences of education, political authority, religion, and public opinion. This provided the basis of the very possibility of the utilitarian ethic—which requires a concern for the well-being of all persons. It also is part of the basis of his fear that authority might stamp out individual self-development by exploiting the natural, strong need to conform to social values and standards.

THE MORAL SENTIMENTS

Despite Mill's insistence that people are by nature social, he did not hold that *moral* feelings or sentiments are an "original" part of a person's constitution. They are built up from the constituents in human nature, and are acquired through the process of association. "Young children have affections, but not moral feelings," he held against Professor Sedgwick.[35] Fellow-feeling, affection for others, sympathy—these are the elements on which the moral feelings are grafted, but which, unalloyed, do not themselves constitute moral sentiments.

There are, indeed, a variety of kinds of moral sentiments: approbation, disapprobation, indignation, and so on. These feelings, when *moral* feelings, are to be distinguished from mere likings and dislikings. It is one thing to express moral disapproval of someone's behavior, and quite another thing to show merely that *we* dislike it. Mill recognized this, and pointed out that an adequate theory must be able to account for differences among the moral sentiments themselves, as well as for differences between the moral sentiments and other feelings.[36]

To have given such an account would have been very useful to later commentators, as it would facilitate discussion of the different kinds of moral judgment, and the different areas of morality. Unfortunately, Mill gave an extended treatment (in several places) only of judgments that an act *ought* to be done, or is our *duty* to perform. Of these, his general position was that acts which it is our duty to do not only arouse sentiments of approval but also give rise to the idea of punishment as appropriate for failure to perform the act. Mill described this idea as arising from an animal desire for retaliation at a hurt to ourselves or those we care for. However, "this impulse to self-defence by the retaliatory infliction of pain, only becomes a moral sentiment, when it is united with a conviction that the infliction of punishment in such a case is conformable to the general good, and when the impulse is not allowed to carry us beyond the point at which that conviction ends."[37]

It must be added, however, that the punishment which is appropriate need not be legal punishment. The general good may not be served by legal sanctions being applied to the particular case, or to that class of cases. The punishment which is appropriate to an offender may be the "displeasure and ill offices of his fellow creatures."[38] In *Utilitarianism*, he added that if the sanctions of others are not in order, then the punishment is to consist in "the reproaches of his own conscience."[39] Moreover, in a letter to Dr. W. G. Ward, in which he outlined aspects of his theory of the moral sentiments, he described "a true moral feeling," when expressed in an "ought" judgment, as "a feeling of pain in the fact of violating a certain rule." In the case of someone who asserts an act ought to be done, and who thereby expresses a moral sentiment, "the word *ought* means, that if they act otherwise, they shall be punished by this internal, and perfectly disinterested feeling."[40] The gist is that when we say someone ought to do something, and we have a moral feeling which we are expressing, we mean that he deserves punishment (at least in the form of self-reproach), and that we have a feeling of disapprobation (e.g., in the form of indignation, resentment, disgust) at the idea of his nonperformance. When we say *we* have a duty to do something, or that we ought to do something, we assert the appropriateness of punishment for nonperformance, and express our negative sentiments at such an idea.

There is something else of interest in the letter to Ward concerning the moral sentiments. Mill held that "ought" is not univocal. Not all who assert that acts ought (or ought not) to be done have a moral feeling when making the assertion. In such a case, they do not thereby express *their* "recoil" at such acts. All they can mean, Mill held, is that others expect it, "with perhaps the addition that they have a strong motive for themselves requiring the same from other people." Such a use of "ought," of course, makes the ought-statement equivalent to a statement about other people's expectations and behavior. Moreover, Mill indicated that "ought" then "seems to me to lose its proper meaning." This suggests that the judgment is not truly a *moral* judgment. In his *Logic*, he distinguished judgments which assert that something *ought to be* or *should be* from ones which state that something *is* or *will be*. The former, he held, enjoin or recommend something; in addition, they assert "that the conduct recommended excites in the speaker's mind the feeling of approbation."[41] The suggestion that we may draw from this is that one expresses a bona fide moral judgment only if he expresses a state of feeling concerning an act or acts.

If this view is correctly attributed to Mill—that having a feeling of a certain sort is a necessary condition for asserting a moral judgment—then it is of further interest to know something of the details of the relation between moral feelings and moral judgments. Contemporary theorists (e.g., A. J. Ayer and C. L. Stevenson) have made much of the distinction between *asserting* that one has a feeling and *expressing* that feeling. A statement which does the former asserts a fact about the speaker; the latter sort of judgment need assert nothing, just as an expletive may express feelings without asserting that one has those feelings.[42]

The passages we have cited seem to align Mill with the subjectivist view that moral judgments state something about the speaker. Even in the passage in the *Logic*, however, he describes normative judgments as "enjoining or recommending" conduct, which may place him in the camp of those noncognitivists who regard such functions of ethical language as an irreducible part of the meanings of ethical terms. More importantly, in criticizing his father's theory of the moral sentiments, he held that his father mistakenly described expressions of praise and blame as being made *in order to* promote useful conduct. While this *may* be done, it is not the usual circumstance. He held that "when there is a moral feeling in our minds, our praise or blame is usually the simple expression of that feeling, rather than an instrument purposely employed for an end."[43]

Of course, there would be no inconsistency for Mill to have held that moral judgments both assert that we have certain feelings *and* are expressions of those feelings. Moreover, the contemporary metaethical distinction had not been drawn in Mill's day. It is of interest, however, to see that he did have views which anticipated more modern theories.

It is important to stress that, in Mill's view, while desiring retaliation for hurtful acts is part of having a *moral* sentiment, it is not enough. As he described the etiology of moral sentiments,[44] moral feelings arise out of our capacity to sympathize with others with whom we recognize common bonds of dependency. Our sympathy, combined with our intelligence, which enables us to perceive the mutual needs of the members of society, causes us to desire retaliation for harms to ourselves and others, even society at large. This feeling, however, is not a moral sentiment unless it is combined with a concern for the general welfare, that is, the feeling is aroused only if, and to the extent that, it is believed the act is beneficial to the interests of society (in the case of a dutiful act) or harmful to common interests (in the case of a transgression of duty).[45] One need not assert that one has this belief, of course, and the feeling may be combined with this belief only in the sense that it arises out of a concern with the general well-being; it need not be articulated in the speaker's own mind. In commenting on the sentiment of justice in particular, Mill wrote: "but a person whose resentment is really a moral feeling, that is, who considers whether an act is blamable before he allows himself to resent it—such a person, though he may not say expressly to himself that he is standing up for the interest of society, certainly does feel that he is asserting a rule which is for the benefit of others as well as for his own. If he is not feeling this—if he is regarding the act solely as it affects him individually—he is not consciously just; he is not concerning himself about the justice of his actions."[46]

It was Mill's view, then, that feelings become moral only when they arise from, and are in conformity with, a regard for the general welfare. We have seen how he applied this analysis to ought-judgments, and the feeling which is associated with them—the desire for the infliction of punishment. I want to discuss next a difficulty of interpretation to which that analysis points. In his comments on his father's views, and in *Utilitarianism*, he seems to be saying that what distinguishes mere dislike of an act from moral disapproval is that, in the latter case, we also desire that punishment be suffered. But what of acts of which we morally *approve*? Are they always and only acts the not-doing of which would arouse moral sentiments of disapproval? If not, how is moral approval to be distinguished from mere liking? The issue has some importance, as it appears that among the moral categories into which acts may fall are those which are (a) permissible, (b) obligatory, and (c) supererogatory, that is, praiseworthy if performed, but not morally required. This last category has special importance, as we think of people who go beyond duty as morally admirable and highly virtuous; but the supererogatory cannot be a *moral* category if all moral judgments concern acts the not-doing of which are blameworthy.

There are certain grounds for thinking that Mill had a narrow conception of the concerns of morality. He often seems to have regarded practical morality as a system of rules which define duties (and, in some cases, correlative rights), and that all other criteria of evaluation lie outside morality. The "Art of Life," he seems to have held, includes morality as only one subdivision, and it is limited to a concern with what dictates it is beneficial to society to enforce as duties. We shall explore this interpretation in a later chapter, as it involves a serious problem regarding the role of Mill's principle of utility in morality. In this section, I want to try to show that there is strong evidence that Mill did not restrict his conception of morality to the view that moral judgments concern only the question of what duties one has. In particular, I shall try to show that he recognized the category of supererogatory acts, and that he regarded such acts to be fit subjects of moral evaluation.

The most extended discussion of supererogatory acts is found in his critique of Comte. Comte, he complained, would make everything which is beneficial to society a duty. Such a view, he objected, "does not perceive that between the region of duty and that of sin there is an intermediate space, the region of positive worthiness. It is not good that persons should be bound, by other people's opinion, to do everything that they would deserve praise for doing. There is a standard of altruism to which all should be required to come up, and a degree beyond it which is not obligatory, but meritorious."[47]

People must, of course, respect the "essential interests" of others, and punishment and "moral blame" are the appropriate instruments of insuring this. To go beyond this, while not required, is praiseworthy: "If in addition to fulfilling this obligation, persons make the good of others a direct object of disinterested exertions, postponing or sacrificing to it even innocent personal indulgences, they deserve gratitude and honour, and are fit objects of moral praise."[48] Two paragraphs later, he explained that beyond what is required for the general welfare is "an unlimited range of moral worth."[49] Moreover, in his notes to his father's ethical views, he sought to explain why feelings of moral approbation are aroused by supererogatory acts.[50] It must be said that Mill's discussions leave it somewhat unclear what it is that is approved—the act, the agent, or both. Also, it is left somewhat unclear how to distinguish *these* feelings from mere liking of the agent or his act. Fortunately, we have not been left without clues. Desires for retaliation and sympathy are "moralized," we saw, when they arise from a concern or belief that the act in question is injurious to the general welfare. Taking that hint, we may say that moral approbation is involved with regard to supererogatory acts when approval is conjoined with the belief that such acts, or the dispositions they reflect, are beneficial to the common interests of persons. This interpretation is lent support by Mill's discussion in *Comte* in which he indicated that in a progressing society supererogatory acts will become more common, thus arousing greater expectation of them. As it is wrong to disappoint expectations, more and more of what is now supererogatory will come to be required; the not-doing of these acts will be a violation of a duty. However, these acts could not become duties were it not that they conduce to the general well-being.

It would seem, in conclusion, that the class of moral judgments—those judgments which express moral sentiments—embraces not only judgments of duty, but also judgments of moral worth. In both cases, the sentiments expressed are "moralized" by virtue of their connection with a regard for the general welfare.

PROGRESS AND HUMAN NATURE

Before leaving Mill's treatment of human psychology, we must mention a feature of his views which has some importance for his moral and political theories. I am referring to his belief that society and the individuals who comprise it are developing progressively better institutions and individual moral natures. He believed that human nature, together with the requisites of social life, naturally result in forces which tend toward improvement.

We have already seen that Mill believed people are by nature social; people have social feelings which form an important source of motivation, and which lead them to conceive themselves only as members of a society of persons. In *Utilitarianism*, Mill went on to claim that an essential condition of society is that people consider the interests of others, and that, insofar as the essentials of society become conceived as bound up with one's own interests, people come to view their own welfare as requiring a concern with others. There are both natural and artificial forces which strengthen the feelings of union with others, and the development of civilization itself has the effect of fostering their development.[51] In his essay entitled "Civilization," he emphasized that a necessary condition of civilization is the capacity to cooperate, to subordinate immediate personal advantage to the common interest, and that, with the expansion of civilization, persons become more and more dependent on one another.[52]

Moral progress is not, however, an inevitable development from civilization's tendencies. All that can be definitively stated is that the social development of persons results in certain tendencies toward moral progress, which are an outgrowth of natural sentiments in human nature. The full flowering of people's moral nature (which Mill described as never desiring for oneself what cannot be shared with others)[53] may never be achieved for two reasons. First, any element of man's nature can be suppressed, or even eliminated.[54] It matters greatly what sort of education and training one receives, and the general climate of sentiment within which one grows up. Second, the advance of civilization also carries with it tendencies which can lead to the weakening of character, for example, by channeling individual energies into areas of self-interested monetary success. Of course, Mill also feared the pressures to conformity to mass culture which modern civilization spawns.[55]

The upshot is that Mill believed there are forces at work tending to the betterment of persons. These, however, require artificial means of support, through human institutions, in education, literature, and art—all means of moral teaching and influence. Only through the application of intelligence can people control the social forces at work in human social development, so that the tendencies to an increase in social feeling and concern do not result in the suppression of individual initiative, spontaneity, and autonomy.

2

MILL'S CONCEPT OF HAPPINESS AND THE PROOF OF ITS DESIRABILITY

HAPPINESS

According to Mill, morality requires a first principle of conduct.[1] The principle that he endorsed he referred to most often as "the Greatest Happiness Principle." Mill's most detailed explanation and defense of the principle is to be found in his famous essay *Utilitarianism*. Initially published in three issues of *Fraser's Magazine*, the essays were later published as a unit in book form. Though there are reasons to think Mill himself did not regard it as a definitive statement of utilitarianism,[2] the essay has, in fact, been the primary source of most philosophers' views of Mill's version of utilitarianism. I believe the essay has, in the process, engendered serious confusion concerning Mill's aims and doctrines. In particular, I believe that Mill's concept of happiness has been misinterpreted by commentators, leading many to assign to Mill inconsistencies of a serious order.

For a very long time, the commonly accepted version of Mill's theory (based almost exclusively on *Utilitarianism*) was that he accepted the Benthamite doctrine that men are motivated to act always and only by desires for pleasure; that all actions are undertaken with the prospect of obtaining some pleasure as a result. Moreover, pleasure is the only thing which has value. Happiness, then, is conceived as a sum of pleasures, and is obtained when pleasures predominate over pains in one's life. Now, it is true (the account admits) that in *Utilitarianism*, Mill distinguished higher and lower pleasures, but such a qualitative distinction among pleasures presupposes that something *other* than pleasure has value. Also (it is further admitted), Mill *did* claim that people desire things such as power, money, and virtue as parts of happiness, but in claiming this, he either mistakenly confused the desire for, say, money, with a desire for pleasure, or he contradicted his original claim that people always and solely desire pleasure. Moreover, in applying his theories to political philosophy, especially in the defense of freedom, he had to use *non*utilitarian arguments, since he could not show that respecting freedom always has as a further consequence the maximization of pleasure. He had to recognize freedom as having intrinsic value; it is held, though, that he did so inconsistently.[3]

Virtually no part of this interpretation is any longer universally accepted, and certain parts of it are quite widely rejected. Recent Mill scholarship has, indeed, made most of it suspect.[4] Nonetheless, the orthodox interpretation continues to be widely promulgated, and it cannot be said with confidence that an alternative view has supplanted the old. It is important, then, to seek to clarify Mill on happiness, and to try to elucidate the theory given in *Utilitarianism* in light of his other writings.

The difficulties for an alternative reading of Mill begin early in *Utilitarianism*, in his initial description of the theory he is to defend:

> The creed which accepts as the foundation of morals, Utility, or the Greatest Happiness Principle, holds that actions are right in proportion as they tend to promote happiness, wrong as they tend to produce the reverse of happiness. By happiness is intended pleasure, and the absence of pain; by unhappiness, pain, and the privation of pleasure. To give a clear view of the moral standard set up by the theory, much more requires to be said; in particular, what things it includes in the ideas of pain and pleasure; and to what extent this is left an open question. But these supplementary explanations do not affect the theory of life on which this theory of morality is grounded—namely, that pleasure and freedom from pain, are the only things desirable as ends; and that all desirable things (which are as numerous in the utilitarian as in any other scheme) are desirable either for the pleasure inherent in themselves, or as means to the promotion of pleasure and the prevention of pain.[5]

Later, Mill attempted his famous "proof" of the Principle of Utility, in which he asserted that each man desires his own happiness. He then seems to try to show that nothing else is desired for its own sake;

everything else desired is desired either as a means to happiness or as a part of happiness. With regard to the desire for virtue, Mill held:

> It results from the preceding considerations, that there is in reality nothing desired except happiness. Whatever is desired otherwise than as a means to some end beyond itself, and ultimately to happiness, is desired as itself a part of happiness, and is not desired for itself until it has become so. Those who desire virtue for its own sake, desire it either because the consciousness of it is a pleasure, or because the consciousness of being without it is a pain, or for both reasons united; as in truth the pleasure and pain seldom exist separately, but almost always together, the same person feeling pleasure in the degree of virtue attained, and pain in not having attained more. If one of these gave him no pleasure, and the other no pain, he would not love or desire virtue, or would desire it only for the other benefits which it might produce to himself or to persons whom he cared for.[6]

To the reader unfamiliar with Mill's other work, or who has insufficiently attended to his arguments, it might appear from these passages (and several others in the essay) that Mill maintained the following:

1. People desire and seek only happiness.
2. Happiness is pleasure and the absence of pain, thus, people desire and seek only pleasure and the avoidance of pain.
3. All other things are desired and sought *for* the pleasure in them, that is, it is the *pleasure* to be had *from* them which is desired, not the things themselves.

In chapter 1, I tried to show that Mill, in fact, explicitly rejected the claim that people always and solely are motivated to act by desires for pleasure. One of his chief criticisms of Bentham was that the latter mistakenly appeared to hold that people act from anticipation of pleasure as a result of action. Mill's view was that actions are *caused* by pleasures or pains, but not necessarily anticipated pleasures or pains. We sometimes act, or recoil from acting, from the pleasantness or unpleasantness of the idea of that act, with no further pleasure or pain being sought or avoided. Moreover, we saw that he also explained how, through the operation of the laws of association, actions not themselves originally pleasurable come to be desired for their own sakes, and how, through the operation of habit, can come to be done even in the absence of pleasure altogether. In fact, I want to show that Mill held these same views in *Utilitarianism*. To those who hold the old interpretation of the essay, the following passage must seem to be a mere inconsistency:

> But does the utilitarian doctrine deny that people desire virtue, or maintain that virtue is not a thing to be desired? The very reverse. It maintains not only that virtue is to be desired, but that it is to be desired disinterestedly, for itself. Whatever may be the opinion of utilitarian moralists as to the original conditions by which virtue is made virtue; however they may believe (as they do) that actions and dispositions are only virtuous because they promote another end than virtue; yet this being granted, and it having been decided, from considerations of this description, what *is* virtuous, they not only place virtue at the very head of things which are good as means to the ultimate end, but they also recognize as a psychological fact the possibility of its being, to the individual, a good in itself, without looking to any end beyond it; and hold, that the mind is not in a right state, not in a state conformable to Utility, not in the state most conducive to the general happiness, unless it does love virtue in this manner—as a thing desirable in itself, even although, in the individual instance, it should not produce those other desirable consequences which it tends to produce, and on account of which it is held to be virtue. This opinion is not, in the smallest degree, a departure from the Happiness principle.[7]

Mill cannot hold, as he does in this passage, that virtue, or anything else not itself pleasure, is capable of being sought for its own sake, if it is the pleasure to be had *from* it which is sought. In *Utilitarianism*, however, Mill nowhere says it is the pleasure to be gotten from virtue which is sought. Though virtue would not be sought if, at some stage, it was not associated with pleasure, it does not follow that pleasure is the object of the desire for virtue. Indeed, he explained the development of desires for things in themselves in the same associationist manner he employed elsewhere. The desire for money, he pointed out, is one of the strongest motives. Indeed, in the case of neurotic misers, it has been so associated with pleasure that its mere possession is desired; but in such a case, that which is desired, though not sought for the sake of an end to be attained with it, has now become part of the end—the person thinks he or she would be unhappy without it:

> The desire of it is not a different thing from the desire of happiness, any more than the love of music or the desire of health. They are included in happiness. They are some of the elements of which the desire of happiness is made up. Happiness is not an abstract idea, but a concrete whole; and these are some of its parts.[8]

In a later paragraph, he wrote:

> So obvious does this appear to me, that I expect it will hardly be
> disputed: and the objection made will be, not that desire can possibly be
> directed to anything ultimately except pleasure and exemption from pain,
> but that the will is a different thing from desire; that a person of confirmed
> virtue, or any other person whose purposes are fixed, carries out his
> purposes without any thought of the pleasure he has in contemplating
> them, or expects to derive from their fulfillment; and persists in acting on
> them, even though these pleasures are much diminished, by changes in his
> character or decay of his passive sensibilities, or are outweighed by the
> pains which the pursuit of the purposes may bring upon him. All this I
> fully admit, and have stated it elsewhere [the reference is to the *Logic*,
> quoted in chapter 1 of this book], as positively and as emphatically as any
> one. Will, the active phenomenon, is a different thing from desire, the
> state of passive sensibility, and though originally an offshoot from it, may
> in time take root and detach itself from the parent stock; so much so, that
> in the case of an habitual purpose, instead of willing the thing because we
> desire it, we often desire it only because we will it.[9]

These passages are entirely in keeping with the views we explored
in chapter 1, which Mill expressed in other writings, throughout his
life. Moreover, they go some way toward helping us to understand the
passages in *Utilitarianism* in which Mill seemed to be expressing the
view that people desire only pleasure.

In the passage above, Mill pointed to the process of association to
explain desires for things in themselves. That process, we have seen,
results in the idea of certain actions being pleasant. Now, finding the
thought pleasant, and being caused by that to desire doing the action, is
not the same thing as desiring the pleasure of the action or of the idea of
it. It is a desire to do that act which desire is caused by the pleasantness
of the idea of the act. Thus, when Mill wrote that virtue is desired
because the idea of it is pleasurable, and that one would not desire it if it
gave no pleasure, he was remarking about the psychological formation
and causation of the desire, not about the object of the desire. Now, the
will is normally the resultant of desires. However, habitual acts of will
can become dissociated from pleasure, and performed even when no
pleasure, either immediate or anticipated, is involved. This latter case
does compromise somewhat the claim that all desires are caused by
pleasure, but even here Mill was quick to point out that the desire owes
its origin to pleasure.

With the exception of these cases of habitual willings which are dissociated from pleasure, and cases of desiring something as a means to an end, it will be the case that something is desired if, and only if, it is thought pleasant. Moreover, things with which we have come to associate pleasure, and thus the thought of which is pleasant, may come to take great hold on us, so that we think we would be happy with it, unhappy without it. It is in this sense that one desires it as a part of happiness. What *causes* the desire for it now is the pain of the thought of being without it or the pleasantness of the thought of obtaining it (or doing it in the case of an action). Moreover (though there are serious problems with this claim), our desire for these things is part of what is involved in desiring our happiness, that is, we desire happiness if, and only if, we desire everything we believe it to be composed of. Happiness is not some *further* object to be had as a result or product of obtaining these. These *are* pleasures to us, and happiness consists in their attainment.

There is in this theory of Mill's an important unclarity that has misled even sympathetic commentators. Mill's language was somewhat unguarded, and he did not give an adequate account of what it means to say that someone desires something as part of his happiness. Moreover, he may have been somewhat confused. Still, he has been needlessly saddled with one mistake that has been the subject of widespread criticism. The "mistake" is outlined by D. P. Dryer as follows:

> What appears to trouble Mill is how to acknowledge the disinterestedness of virtue without acknowledging that it is something other than happiness desired for its own sake, and therefore desirable for its own sake. The solution Mill adopts is that when a man desires virtue for its own sake, he desires it only as a part of happiness, that is, in the belief that it will enhance his happiness. This solution will not do. If a man desires to be virtuous because it will enhance his happiness, he falls short of being genuinely virtuous just as when he desires to be virtuous as a means to happiness. When a man desires to be virtuous he also hopes for happiness, but he does not desire to be virtuous out of the hope that it will yield him happiness.[10]

Mill did not really say that desiring something as part of happiness means desiring it "out of the hope" that it will make one happy. In fact, he said there is no ulterior end in view. He *did* say, of course, that the person "is made, or thinks he would be made" happy by it, and "is made unhappy by failure to obtain it." The phrase "thinks he would be made" carries the suggestion that the desire is preceded by the *thought* of one's happiness and thus that happiness is the object of the desire. However, Mill's disclaimer that there is no ulterior end should direct us to seek an alternate reading—and, indeed, there is one. One can be said to "think" something will make one happy even if no such thought is occurring at the time, just as one can believe all sorts of propositions which one is not considering at the time. There is not only an "occurrent" sense of "thinks that" or "believes that" (or even "hopes that"), but also a "dispositional" sense. Someone can be said to think something if the person *would* assent to it *if* asked or if the person considered it explicitly, or if it *had* been assented to when considered. Just such an interpretation is suggested by Mill's assertion that the person *is* made happy by it, and *is* made unhappy by the failure to obtain it. It is not that the person seeks it with the occurrent thought that it will make him or her happy, but, rather, that the person cannot *be* happy without it. That the individual's happiness is constituted in that way is what *causes* him or her to be pleased at the thought of obtaining it, hence, resulting in desiring it. When it is said the person desires it as part of his or her happiness, this means the person desires it for itself, and would be unhappy without it. It may also mean that he or she *thinks* it will make him or her happy in a dispositional sense, but it need not mean that the person desires it with the thought occurring that it will make him or her happy.

Indeed, the etiology described by Mill of desires for things for their own sakes involves a process whereby one *does* perceive them as associated with pleasure, but comes to habitually pursue them as part of a confirmed character. The person of virtuous character, on Mill's description, eventually will straightaway do the right thing without giving any further thought to his or her happiness. Such a person will be pained by the very idea of acting unvirtuously, and that will motivate the actor's action. Still, there *is* a sense in which desiring to do virtuous acts is not different from desiring happiness. A person can be said to desire happiness if he or she desires those elements the person conceives happiness to consist in. Insofar as one conceives (in the dispositional sense) his or her happiness to require the doing of virtuous acts, desiring to perform virtuous acts is part of the person's desiring happiness. Indeed, the fact of the person's desiring happiness (in the dispositional sense) is part of the causal explanation of his or her desiring to do virtuous acts.

Do these explanations suffice, however, to account for the passage in which Mill described the "Greatest Happiness Principle"? He stated there that "pleasure and freedom from pain, are the only things desirable as ends," and that "by happiness is intended pleasure, and the absence of pain." Not only do our explanations seem inadequate to handle this passage, but the passage seems also to support another key element of the traditional interpretation, namely, that Mill defined happiness as an accumulation of pleasures which outweigh experienced pains. Following this passage is Mill's attempt to distinguish higher and lower pleasures, and he thereby appears to run into further trouble. Having asserted that pleasure is the only thing desirable as an end, it is held by his critics to be inconsistent for him to regard some pleasures as more valuable than others, since whatever property or properties serve as the basis for the qualitative distinction cannot also be pleasures.

I shall leave the question of whether this line, commonly attributed to Mill, is really inconsistent. I wish, instead, to offer an interpretation that avoids that issue entirely, one which will also bring the passage in question in line with my argument that Mill did not hold that we seek only pleasure as the object of our actions.[11]

It is instructive to begin with the very paragraph in which Mill states that "by happiness is intended pleasure, and the absence of pain." The sentence which follows it is almost universally ignored in the literature. It reads: "To give a clear view of the moral standard set up by the theory, much more requires to be said; in particular, what things it includes in the ideas of pain and pleasure; and to what extent this is left an open question." Now, if Mill meant to define happiness *merely* by saying it is pleasure, it is not clear that anything more needs to be said at all. For the most part, we have little doubt in our minds what pleasures and pains are. We recognize them easily. In what follows, Mill makes no attempt to provide a *philosophical* analysis of the notions of pain and pleasure; those notions are taken as perfectly clear.[12] It is not in that respect that he goes on to attempt to clarify what is included in the idea of pleasure or of pain. If one looks closely at Mill's discussion, it seems more accurate to say that, rather than analyzing the concepts of pleasure and pain, Mill presented an analysis of the notion of *happiness* with which he was working, thereby indicating what, in the way of pleasures, was included in that idea. Happiness, he indicated, is *composed* of pleasures, but not *every* composite of pleasures which outweigh accompanying pains constitutes happiness. Mill may have thought that all pleasures have intrinsic value, and all pains disvalue; he almost certainly held that not all pleasures are equally valuable *when considered in relation to their possessor's happiness*.[13]

Thus, the paragraph in question, in which Mill described his Greatest Happiness Principle, was *not* his final definition of "happiness." It was only a preliminary outline of the conception, in need of fleshing out before it could be ultimately accepted.

If, indeed, this account accurately captures the logic of Mill's discussion, it is true—but seriously misleading—to say that he held that pleasure is the only thing of value. It would be more accurate to say that happiness is what has value, or that it is pleasure *in so far as it is a constituent of a person's happiness which has value*. (It should be remembered that it is entirely open to a utilitarian to ascribe value to whatever he thinks is valuable. In order to be consistently a utilitarian, his theory of what acts are *right* must take a certain form, but anything at all may be taken as having value.)

The conception of value I have outlined puts Mill's discussion of higher and lower pleasures in a very different light. If I am right, then Mill would have been arguing that some pleasures are more crucial to happiness than others, and *thus* more valuable. Indeed, it seems to me that this is precisely the form Mill's argument took. In answer to the charge that Epicureans and others who hold that pleasure is man's ultimate goal maintain a doctrine fit only for swine, Mill replied:

> When thus attacked, the Epicureans have always answered, that it is not they, but their accusers, who represent human nature in a degrading light; since the accusation supposes human beings to be capable of no pleasures except those of which swine are capable. If this supposition were true, the charge could not be gainsaid, but would then no longer be an imputation; for if the sources of pleasure were precisely the same to human beings and to swine, the rule of life which is good enough for the one would be good enough for the other. The comparison of the Epicurean life to that of beasts is felt as degrading, precisely because a beast's pleasures do not satisfy a human being's conceptions of happiness. Human beings have faculties more elevated than the animal appetites, and when once made conscious of them, do not regard anything as happiness which does not include their gratification.[14]

Mill went on to hold that some pleasures are inherently more valuable than others, and he offered his famous test for the superiority of pleasures. The test consists in consulting those who have experienced competing pleasures, who have the capacity to enjoy and appreciate them; and if such persons prefer one over others, even if it is also "attended with a greater amount of discontent," then it is superior in quality. In the following paragraph, Mill claimed that there *are* such pleasures—those which are involved in the fulfillment of a person's higher faculties. For the most part, people are *not* happy without the fulfillment of those capacities; they will not give up those needs in exchange for maximum fulfillment of more animal-like desires.[15]

It is usually considered generous to Mill to ignore the paragraphs cited, or to downgrade their significance in one way or another. He cannot, it is thought, literally *define* higher pleasures as those which would be chosen in the way indicated. Of course, that much is true; at best, he has given a rough *test*, not the very *meaning* of the expression "higher pleasures." These passages are important, however, because they indicate an important feature of the choice process, namely, the basis on which a competent judge would select some pleasures over others, or the significance of his choice. The ground is, of course, his sense that some pleasures are requisite for his happiness, while others are not; indeed, who would be a better judge as to which of two pleasures is requisite for the happiness of creatures with certain capacities than someone with those capacities who has experienced those pleasures? Mill is clearly asserting in these passages that not just any accumulation of pleasures will make a person happy, and, thus, happiness cannot consist merely in the accumulation of pleasure and the avoidance of pain. Indeed, it is only at *this* point that Mill indicates his *ultimate* definition of happiness, or of the Greatest Happiness Principle, in which it is clear that the ultimate end sought is happiness, conceived as made up of pleasures, but *not* indiscriminately compounded. The later definition reads:

> According to the Greatest Happiness Principle, as above explained, the ultimate end, with reference to and for the sake of which all other things are desirable . . . is an existence exempt as far as possible from pain, and as rich as possible in enjoyments, both in point of quantity and quality; the test of quality, and the rule for measuring it against quantity, being the preference felt by those who, in their opportunities of experience, to which must be added their habits of self-consciousness and self-observation, are best furnished with the means of comparison. This, being, according to the utilitarian opinion, the end of human action, is necessarily also the standard of morality.[16]

There is an extremely important consequence of this conception: human happiness is not an open concept in the sense that it consists of pleasures completely unspecified. Mill's concept of happiness is partly determinate in the sense that there are *particular* elements requisite to it. It is partially open in the sense that an indeterminate number of things *can come to be* seen as elements in a person's happiness. *Human* well-being—given human capacities—requires some particular elements, and may come to require many others which cannot be specified ahead of time. (Recall that in the paragraph in which Mill first described the Greatest Happiness Principle, he indicated that to some extent what is included "in the ideas of pain and pleasure," is left "an open question.")

If this is a correct view of Mill, we should be able to indicate the permanent aspects of happiness. Moreover, doing so will bring out the fullness of Mill's conception of happiness. In the last passages cited above, Mill asserted:

> A being of higher faculties requires more to make him happy, is capable probably of more acute suffering, and is certainly accessible to it at more points, than one of an inferior type; but in spite of these liabilities, he can never really wish to sink into what he feels to be a lower grade of existence. We may give what explanation we please of this unwillingness; we may attribute it to pride, a name which is given indiscriminately to some of the most and to some of the least estimable feelings of which mankind are capable; we may refer it to the love of liberty and personal independence, an appeal to which was with the Stoics one of the most effective means for the inculcation of it; to the love of power, or to the love of excitement, both of which do really enter into and contribute to it: but its most appropriate appellation is a sense of dignity, which all human beings possess in one form or other, and in some, though by no means in exact, proportion to their higher faculties, and which is so essential a part of the happiness of those in whom it is strong, that nothing which conflicts with it could be otherwise than momentarily, an object of desire to them.[17]

Here, Mill was asserting that the requisites of happiness include a sense of one's independence and self-determination, a sense of power, of freedom, a measure of excitement, and, described generally, whatever is necessary to maintain human dignity.

There are other parts of the essay in which Mill elaborated his conception of happiness. For example, in his discussion of rights and justice, he wrote:

> To have a right, then, is, I conceive, to have something which society ought to defend me in the possession of. If the objector goes on to ask why it ought, I can give no other reason than general utility. . . . The interest involved is that of security, to everyone's feelings the most vital of all interests. Nearly all other earthly benefits are needed by one person, not needed by another; and many of them can, if necessary, be cheerfully foregone, or replaced by something else; but security no human being can

possibly do without; on it we depend for all our immunity from evil, and for the whole value of all and every good, beyond the passing moment; since nothing but the gratification of the instant could be of any worth to us, if we could be deprived of everything the next instant by whoever was momentarily stronger than ourselves. Now this most indispensable of all necessaries, after physical nutriment, cannot be had, unless the machinery for providing it is kept unintermittedly in active play.[18]

Whatever else he claimed in this passage, Mill was asserting that security (and perhaps the sense of it) is crucial to happiness, and that rights are a device which ensure security; thus, respect for rights occupies a high place on the list of duties. This is the mode of Mill's defense of the importance of the rules of justice:

Justice is a name for certain classes of moral rules, which concern the essentials of human well-being more nearly, and are therefore of more absolute obligation, than any other rules for the guidance of life; and the notion which we have found to be of the essence of the idea of justice, that of a right residing in an individual, implies and testifies to this more binding obligation.[19]

Particular rules of justice were defended by Mill on grounds of their connection with maintaining what, loosely speaking, may be termed one's sense of security:

The important rank, among human evils and wrongs, of the disappointment of expectation, is shown in the fact that it constitutes the principal criminality of two such highly immoral acts as a breach of friendship and a breach of promise. Few hurts which human beings can sustain are greater, and none wound more, than when that on which they habitually and with full assurance relied, fails them in the hour of need; and few wrongs are greater than this mere withholding of good; none excite more resentment either in the person suffering, or in a sympathizing spectator.[20]

From these passages (and others in the essay *On Liberty*), we can describe Mill's conception of the essential elements of human happiness. Roughly they divide into two related categories. First, are the constituents and requirements for an individual's sense of being his or her own person, of developing one's life as one chooses—a sense of freedom, power, excitement, and so on. Second, are those things requisite for a sense of security, the prime ones being the fulfillment by others of the rules of justice, and their respect for our rights. These are related, and overlapping, of course, because foremost among the rules of justice are those that prescribe respect for freedom. To this description must be added Mill's endorsement of Von Humboldt's conception of happiness in chapter 3 of *On Liberty*. The additional element brought in here is the notion of a harmonious ordering and arrangement of the elements of a personality, fully developed in its capabilities and powers.

It is important to bear in mind that Mill described a way in which other elements come to be regarded as requisites of one's happiness. We have already seen that Mill recognized that virtually anything, or any mode of behavior, can come to be desired in such a way that failure to obtain it is viewed as a diminution of one's happiness. This will mean that happiness (or one's conception of it) consists of two kinds of required aspects or elements: (a) those requisites associated with being *human*, with certain human capabilities, needs, and requirements, and (b) those elements which are *acquired* requisites for one's happiness. Into the latter category would go the fulfillment of the desire for virtue *when* virtue has come to be sought for its own sake.

Now, both kinds of goods—the "natural" requisites of happiness, and those which are acquired—can be desired for their own sakes; but for Mill this did *not* entail that they are equally *worthy* of pursuit. At least, this does not follow if it is taken to mean that both kinds of goods are *intrinsically* valuable. I wish to show that Mill thought it to be the first group of goods which controls, in that other ends, including ones which have come to be parts of one's conception of happiness, ought to be sought only if they do not conflict with the basic elements of happiness, that is, only if they do promote it.

As we have seen, Mill considered it possible to desire a number of kinds of things for their own sakes, such as virtue, money, power, by the process of association with pleasure. He adds, however, that there is an important difference between virtue and the others, namely, that the desires for the others may be injurious to happiness by making the person obnoxious, while this is not possible with respect to virtue. Thus:

> the utilitarian standard, while it tolerates and approves those other acquired desires, up to the point beyond which they would be more injurious to the general happiness than promotive of it, enjoins and requires the cultivation of the love of virtue up to the greatest strength possible, as being above all things important to the general happiness.[21]

Even with respect to virtue, however, what justifies making it an end in itself is the contribution of a virtuous state of character to the general welfare. Mill urged the inculcation of the desire to be virtuous for its own sake, and urged the formation of character in which being virtuous is among one's "fixed purposes," and virtuous action has become a matter of confirmed character. Ultimately, the actions come under the control of habit, and do not spring from an experience of a pleasurable thought, or from the anticipation of a pleasure. The only thing which could justify the continuance of such habitual desiring, and its general inculcation, would be its contribution to happiness, but happiness defined independently of any reference to virtuous action. Indeed, Mill held:

That which is the result of habit affords no presumption of being intrinsically good; and there would be no reason for wishing that the purpose of virtue should become independent of pleasure and pain, were it not that the influence of the pleasurable and painful associations which prompt to virtue is not sufficiently to be depended on for unerring constancy of action until it has acquired the support of habit. Both in feeling and in conduct, habit is the only thing which imparts certainty; and it is because of the importance to others of being able to rely absolutely on one's feelings and conduct, and to oneself of being able to rely on one's own, that the will to do right ought to be cultivated into this habitual independence. In other words, this state of the will is a means to good, not intrinsically a good; and does not contradict the doctrine that nothing is a good to human beings but in so far as it is either itself pleasurable, or a means of attaining pleasure or averting pain.[22]

What follows from this analysis is that not everything desir*ed* for its own sake is intrinsically desir*able*; also, we should seek to inculcate desires for some things for their own sakes, because the existence of such desires contributes to the general welfare. Thus, I conclude, the ultimate criterion of the value of all actions, and also of all desires for doing actions, is what is requisite for the happiness of man *as a creature of elevated faculties*. In the second, and subsequent, editions of the *Logic*, Mill included a paragraph explaining that ends other than happiness should be sought; that, in particular, the desire to perform virtuous acts without further consideration of happiness should be inculcated in people. He added:

The character itself should be, to the individual, a paramount end, simply because the existence of this ideal nobleness of character, or of the near approach to it, in any abundance, would go further than all things else towards making human life happy, both in the comparatively humble sense of pleasure and freedom from pain, and in the higher meaning of

rendering life, not what it now is almost universally, puerile and insignificant, but such as human beings with highly developed faculties can care to
have.[23]

Moreover, the essay *On Liberty* will be misunderstood if this point is
not grasped. Mill explained quite early in that work: "I regard utility as
the ultimate appeal on all ethical questions; but it must be utility in the
largest sense, grounded on the permanent interests of man as a progressive being."[24] And the first part of chapter 3, entitled, "Of Individuality
as One of the Elements of Well-Being," is a quite explicit attempt to
outline some of the basic components of such a conception of happiness,
including Mill's endorsement of Von Humboldt's statement of the
"end" of humankind as consisting in the full and harmonious development of people's powers and capabilities.

There is a final point I wish to make, which will be taken up more
fully in the section that follows. Mill is sometimes criticized as having an
"atomistic" conception of society, in which society is seen as a composite of self-concerned individual "atoms" each striving to fulfill its own
needs, and in which social interests are just a mathematical function of
the individual interests. In large measure, Mill rejected this picture, in
Utilitarianism and elsewhere. In the much neglected chapter 3 of *Utilitarianism*, Mill referred to a "powerful natural sentiment" in persons:
"the desire to be in unity with our fellow creatures." Not only is this a
natural desire, it is reinforced by the influences of social progress and
civilization itself, so much so that people never conceive themselves as
other than members of a social body. Moreover, as we saw in chapter 1,
he held that sympathy is a natural part of our constitution. Thus,
through natural and artificial influences, people living in society do or
come to regard the interests of others as among *their* interests, culminat-
ing in an ideal utilitarian society in which people do not desire benefits
for themselves which cannot be had by the others.[25]

Mill did recognize that the extent of social feeling varies from person
to person, and is dependent on the state of moral and cultural advance,
and on the primary social institutions including education. At whatever
level of intensity, however, it is clear that human well-being requires
the fulfillment of people's social needs; the well-being of others is not
merely an instrument of the well-being of the individual. There are
many important aspects of Mill's moral and political philosophy which
are illuminated by stressing the role of the "social feelings" in people.

In the section that follows, we shall look at some of the implications
of the present interpretation of Mill on happiness, especially with

regard to his infamous attempt to give a "proof" of the Greatest Happiness Principle.

SOME DIFFICULTIES: THE "PROOF" OF THE GREATEST HAPPINESS PRINCIPLE

The points that have been made concerning the interpretation of Mill's views on happiness will naturally prompt the question of how this interpretation fits in with his proof of his first principle of morality. I believe that my account does help in some ways to understand Mill's proof. On the other hand, it raises special problems of its own. In the remainder of this chapter, I will proceed as follows: I will first cite the passages in Mill's proof that have created the greatest furor, then discuss the special problems my interpretation poses; finally, I will take up the most important traditional criticisms.

My Interpretation and the Proof

Mill very nearly destroyed his reputation as a philosopher (at least for twentieth-century readers) by one paragraph in *Utilitarianism*. The fourth chapter of the book discusses the proof of the principle of utility, and the first half of the proof is given in this paragraph:

> The only proof capable of being given that an object is visible, is that people actually see it. The only proof that a sound is audible, is that people hear it: and so of the other sources of our experience. In like manner, I apprehend, the sole evidence it is possible to produce that anything is desirable, is that people do actually desire it. If the end which the utilitarian doctrine proposes to itself were not, in theory and in practice, acknowledged to be an end, nothing could ever convince any person that it was so. No reason can be given why the general happiness is desirable, except that each person, so far as he believes it to be attainable, desires his own happiness. This, however, being a fact we have not only all the proof which the case admits of, but all which it is possible to require, that happiness is a good: that each person's happiness is a good to that person, and the general happiness, therefore, a good to the aggregate of all persons. Happiness has made out its title as *one* of the ends of conduct, and consequently one of the criteria of morality.[26]

It would be of interest to speculate what would have been the reaction to *Utilitarianism* had this argument, or the entire chapter, not occurred. I rather suspect that Mill's stature as a philosopher would have been much greater, and that of several critics not nearly so great.

In any case, the second half of the proof is Mill's attempt to show that *only* happiness is sought (or is capable of being sought) without regard for an end beyond itself. Now, I believe I have shown that Mill maintained that people do not always give thought to happiness or pleasure as the object of all their voluntary acts. In *Utilitarianism*, he held that people can and should desire the doing of virtuous acts without giving thought to further consequences. Acts done without any regard to happiness—those made part of our confirmed character through the development of habitual willing—seem to be counter-examples to the claim in the proof that only happiness is an ultimate end.

I believe it will not solve the problem to interpret Mill as having held that these acts are not done from desire, but from the will, which is different. In the first place, Mill wrote in *Utilitarianism* that we desire it *because* we will it, and in the *Logic* he said "we still continue to desire the action, and consequently to do it";[27] so it is *not* clear that desires for the acts are no longer involved. More importantly, the interpretation will not remove the difficulty. If we can and do voluntarily *seek* things other than happiness, it will not suffice to show that all we can *desire* is happiness. If what we seek without regard to a further end is not happiness, then our actions *can* aim at something other than happiness.

It may be that Mill thought that in these cases the desire to do these acts really is part of the desire for happiness, even though no thought is actually given to happiness. At the least, he thought this is *sometimes* the case, that is, when we have reached the point where the not doing of such acts (or the *idea* of not doing them) is sufficiently painful that we cannot be satisfied without doing them. Following the suggestion made in the previous section, we could say that though the agent gives no thought to his or her happiness, nonetheless, he or she would be unhappy without performing these acts, and this causes him or her to do the acts. Happiness might, in some sense, be regarded as the *ultimate* object of the desires to do these acts.

The penultimate paragraph of chapter 4, and the one preceding it, suggest a different interpretation, however (at least for those habitual willings that have become entirely independent of pleasant or painful feelings or thoughts). What is suggested is this: Mill *did* regard the class of acts done from habit as containing counterexamples to the claim that only happiness is desired or sought. He did not, however, think this admission undercut the claim of happiness as the end fit to be the test of morality. As he argued in that paragraph, *these* are cases of ends sought *out of habit alone*, which fact disqualifies them as candidates for that which is intrinsically good. Though these are not ends sought for the sake of something else, they are not sought *for the value in or of them*. The admitted exception to the claim in the proof, then, does not undercut the conclusion. (This is, of course, speculation on my part; Mill is not sufficiently clear on the matter.)

The second difficulty provoked by my interpretation of Mill arises from an ambiguity in the phrase "desires happiness." He suggested that desiring happiness consists in desiring the elements which comprise one's happiness, but he seems to have left it open that people do not desire happiness as he (Mill) conceived it, that is, with the particular elements and weightings among them which he gives. Unreflective people may not view intellectual development, or self-determination, as requisite beyond a minimal degree for their happiness, and therefore may have no great desire for these. Similarly, someone may desire something such as wealth, *thinking* it requisite for his or her happiness, when it is not. In either case, desiring happiness does not seem to be the same as desiring the elements of happiness, at least not as Mill depicted happiness—as the end and test of morality. Either people do not always desire happiness, or they do not desire happiness as Mill conceived it, or both. Thus, even if we except acts done by virtue of being habitual, it is not clear that Mill *did* show that happiness, *as he conceived it*, is fit to be the test of morality, because it is the only thing people pursue ultimately for its own sake.

This is a difficulty Mill did not address, so there is no question of coming up with the "right" interpretation. Nonetheless, there is a line of defense open to him which, if acceptable, would be an important addition to Mill's defense of utilitarianism.

In the first place, it is quite clear that he recognized that not all people have the same conception of their happiness. He recognized that there are marked differences in the extent to which the higher capacities are and can be developed in people. He also recognized that social arrangements can lead to alteration of what people regard as necessary for their well-being, and can even lead to the extirpation of desires for freedom, dignity, and self-sufficiency.[28] This is one of his complaints against grinding poverty, the inferior status of women, and slavery.

Now, it is true that in defending his view that desires for virtue, health, and money are parts of our desire for happiness, he had said that happiness "is not an abstract idea, but a concrete whole," meaning that in desiring happiness, we desire its elements, not an abstraction. Still, this does not entail that there is not an abstract description of happiness in terms of which what each person desires in particular *counts* as part of his or her desire for happiness. Indeed, some such abstract conception seems to underly Mill's argument that the higher pleasures are requisite for the happiness of human beings. It may be variously described, but seems to be captured in the following: happiness is a product of whatever fulfills one's capacities, is satisfying, is desirable for its own sake, and which leaves one's life lacking in nothing important.[29] Though various parts of the description may be questionable, something like it must have been accepted by Mill, in terms of which he could say that the preferences of experienced persons for freedom, and so on, concern their happiness. He argued that beings with higher faculties not only prefer more than do lower beings, but require more to make them happy. What is required for happiness is a function of a creature's capacities, provides pleasure in its mere possession, and is something the agent does not wish to be without.

The significance of this point must now be sketched. "Desires" is one of the verbs of propositional attitude. Someone could desire X; it could be true that X is identical with Y; yet, it need not be true that the person desires Y. This would be the case if the person does not know that in fact X is Y. Whether someone can be truly said to desire something will depend on the way the thing is described. I may desire a piece of candy before me, not knowing it is poisoned. It does not follow that I desire poisoned candy. Where the object of desire is described in abstract terms, people could be said to agree in desiring it, though disagree as to what meets the abstract definition, and hence disagree as to what particular things they desire. People may agree, then, in desiring happiness, *abstractly* described, but disagree in their conceptions of what is requisite for happiness.

If one looks at Mill's argument to show that only happiness is desired, it is clear that he did not attempt to show that all things are desired as parts of freedom and dignity, or as requisites to the exercise of intelligence. Rather, what he showed is that whatever is desired for its own sake is desired in such a way that the person does not want to be without it. These things are desired *as* the particular elements in which the person conceives his or her happiness to consist.

This explanation still leaves a problem. If Mill's conception of happiness is to have great importance for his moral and political philosophy, it is because he took *it* to be the proper end and test of morality. It is clear in the places in which he outlined it that he intended it as such.[30] For that purpose it would not be enough to show that all persons desire their well-being, abstractly described. Some further ground would be needed to show that a particular conception of well-being is the one fit to be the end and test of morality.

Mill did not defend this last point in his proof because it is not part of the proof. He was merely trying to show that happiness is the end of human endeavor. In chapter 2, he had indicated that one need *not* accept his conception of happiness to accept the utilitarian principle. Moreover, he held that on any legitimate conception of happiness, the encouragement of characters of the sort he described would follow, if only for the reason that people who are happy in the way he described make everyone else happier.[31]

Still, there are places in which Mill's own moral reasoning makes explicit reference to what may be termed his "enlarged" conception of human happiness,[32] and there can be little question that his own brand of utilitarianism incorporated this enlarged theory of value. We may well ask, then, what would justify this, insofar as the proof does not show that happiness as Mill viewed it is the end of conduct.

As I pointed out, Mill did not discuss the issue, posed in this manner. On the other hand, he *did* outline a decision-procedure for adjudicating conflicting claims in value theory, and *did* give an argument in support of his value theory. If we must decide which of two pleasures is of a greater value, the only appeal is to the judgment and preference of those who can appreciate both. Mill thought that, in fact, the preference of people over the course of human history has been decidedly in favor of the active, self-determining mode of life in which the faculties of choice and deliberation are developed, and the intellectual capacities encouraged. Thus, insofar as *this* conception of happiness is superior, *it* is fit to be the end or test of morality. Moreover, this is not mere elitism, as all persons possess some measure of the special human faculties, and any conception of happiness which will serve large numbers of people must allow the development of Mill's favored elements to some extent.

Whatever difficulties there may be in accepting Mill's decision-procedure, or his conclusions when applying it, I think we must take it seriously as an interpretive tool, because it provides a way out of other difficulties in Mill's theory as well. (I shall examine some of the problems with Mill's decision-procedure in my final chapter.) There are two final problems which are posed for the conception of happiness I have attributed to Mill for which his proposed decision-procedure can help provide a solution.

There is a serious incompleteness in Mill's theory. The happiness which he favors requires such things as security, freedom, a sense of dignity, and so on. It is possible, however, that provision of one, say security, can detract from another, for example, freedom. This is true whether we are considering the happiness of an individual, or that of a society. Unless we have a standard way to resolve such conflicts, we cannot ultimately decide what ought to be done in such situations of conflict in an objective, rational way. Part of Mill's insistence on the need for a first principle was his fear that, without one, people decide what to do merely by asking themselves how they feel about the contemplated act.

There is one important feature of this difficulty which we must note. The problem for Mill is not *merely* one of efficiency, that is, how to maximize the achievement of the various separate elements of happiness. The problem is also one which his theory of *value* must face: what combinations and weightings are intrinsically good, or constitutive of human happiness? This places limits on the problem of efficiency. If happiness required freedom as an essential ingredient, then *no* amount of security that destroys freedom can produce happiness. Similarly, if dignity is an essential ingredient of happiness, then increases in the power of people who can then dominate others, or discriminatory treatment which degrades individuals will necessarily decrease human well-being in one dimension. Such features of Mill's value theory can help to avoid some of the worst difficulties the conflict problem seems to pose.

There are two further points to be made. In *On Liberty*, Mill did adopt Von Humboldt's view that happiness requires a harmonious ordering and combination of the elements of a personality which has been fully developed. Moreover, the point of a major portion of the essay is to show that this is possible only through the provision of liberty, circumscribed only by duties to others. *On Liberty*, then, *is* an attempt to argue for the importance of a particular component of happiness because of its special relation to all others.

Ultimately, however, in decisions concerning intrinsic goods, the final evidence is what is preferred by persons who are experienced and knowledgeable. There can, then, be no complete resolution of conflicts on an a priori basis. In the end, it is a matter for persons of intelligence and experience to decide, on the basis of that experience, as well as a knowledge of history, what weightings of the elements of happiness are satisfying to creatures with the nature and capacity of humans. Even *On Liberty*, then, could only be an attempt to describe an abstract principle which can guide decision-making, but which, by itself, cannot ultimately prescribe the details of duty and the limits of freedom.

Finally, Mill's decision-procedure can help resolve another unclarity. I have argued that he took the "natural" needs of people as central in determining their happiness. However, he also held that people can come to desire other things as part of their happiness. What ground could there be for preferring the natural faculties and natural sources of pleasure? This is especially problematic in light of his claims in the essay, "Nature," that all good has come from controlling and limiting nature, and his view that "there is not one natural inclination which it [education] is not strong enough to coerce, and, if needful, to destroy by disuse."[33]

In the first place, we must recall that acquired goods become goods through the mechanism of habit, and Mill held that habit alone provides no ground for the intrinsic value of something. Of course, the mere fact that something is naturally desired provides no such ground either. What is crucial to Mill's view is that certain needs—generated by the distinctively human capacities—must be provided for in order for people to be happy. Even "natural" desires are subject to alteration, direction, limitation, as the ultimate end—happiness—requires. The requisites of security, freedom, dignity, intellectual activity, and so on, are central, not so much because they are natural, as that people who are sufficiently experienced and wise find them required for their happiness. Nonetheless, the "natural" has a special role to play as such, insofar as Mill believed that the "bindingness" of moral duty must be ultimately constituted by internal motivations toward the performance of the dutiful acts. Given his theory of human motivation, then, nothing can become a duty with "binding" force that cannot be generated from basic human nature.

TRADITIONAL DIFFICULTIES WITH THE PROOF

Although I have discussed some of the traditional objections to Mill's proof (especially the last part in which he tries to show that all things sought for their own sakes are sought as part of happiness), I have said little or nothing about objections to the first part of the proof embodied in the Mill paragraph quoted above. This paragraph has been widely criticized, and numerous defenders have attempted to fend off the charges.[34] It probably is not possible to give a definitive defense or interpretation (for that matter), since the entire first part of the proof is given in that one paragraph, and Mill did not sufficiently discuss elsewhere the elements of the proof that have caused concern. I shall not, therefore, attempt to do what I now think to be impossible. I shall, instead, indicate what I regard as the two most important objections,[35] and then I shall make some explanatory points which are intended to illuminate what Mill may have been about—what *he* thought he had to show, and how various aspects of his psychological and moral theories contribute to that showing. Among other things, I will defend the notion that Mill did not intend the argument in question to be a deductively valid one.

It has been widely objected against Mill that one cannot show something to be desirable merely by showing it is desired. The analogy between the visible, the audible, and the desirable breaks down at precisely this point. From the fact something *is* seen, it follows that it *is* visible. From the fact that something is desired, it does not follow that it is desirable.

Moreover, the attempt to show that the general happiness is desirable as an end fails, it is alleged, since from the fact that each person desires his or her own good, one cannot conclude that each person desires the general good. Alternatively, from the fact that each person's happiness is a good to that person, it does not follow that the general happiness is a good, either without qualification, or "to the aggregate of all persons."

Most defenses of Mill begin with the important reminder that he had indicated that "ultimate ends do not admit of proof, in the ordinary acceptation of the term." In the introduction to *Utilitarianism*, Mill had written that we can appeal to more than merely our intuitions in deciding, as "considerations may be presented capable of determining the intellect either to give or withhold its assent."

It is important to keep these warnings in mind, since they suggest that at crucial places the inference of a conclusion from premises need not be taken as based on a deductive connection. Still, this is not enough to defend Mill, since the (alleged) fact that ultimate ends cannot be established by proof does not entail that bad arguments *will* establish them (and Mill's arguments have seemed not merely unsound deductively, but totally unconvincing).

I do not believe, however, that we can know how to evaluate the effectiveness of Mill's proof independently of an assessment of what he thought he had to show, and to whom the proof is addressed. It is clear he was trying to force agreement, by confronting opponents with "considerations" that would lead them to the general happiness as the ultimate end of conduct. Mill indicated that in order to do this, he had to convince objectors that happiness is *one* of the ends of conduct, and it is the *only* end of conduct. The proof, on this characterization, has two main parts. It is very striking, however, that the first part is compressed into one small paragraph, while the second part goes on, at times in extravagant detail, to approximately ten times that length. It is possible, of course, that he thought he had definitive arguments for the first part, and that the psychological theory employed to demonstrate the second part needed greater elaboration. What I want to suggest, to the contrary, is that he had in mind specific opponents who agreed with him on the points which would be needed to make the first part convincing, but who would disagree strongly with the second claim for which he tried to argue. If this suggestion were correct, it would explain why he divided his attention in the chapter so unequally between the main parts; it would also explain why he responded in a nonchalant, unsatisfactory manner to objections which had been pointed out to the first part of the proof.[36]

If the proof is to be explained with reference to presuppositions about his opponents, it is fairly clear that Mill had in mind the intuitionists who believed that people have a moral sense of right and wrong which is a basic part of human nature, and that our moral sentiments are the appropriate guides to conduct.

In his essay, "Bentham," Mill had held it to be essential to a rational morality "that it be referred to an *end* of some sort," and not be merely left to "vague feeling or inexplicable internal conviction."[37] Apparently, he thought that *only* if a moral theory is so structured that it derives its conceptions of right and wrong from its conception of the good, conceived as something to be aimed at, will it be possible for there to be rational discussion and argument about right and wrong. Moreover, if the only alternative is a theory on the basis of which ethical questions are decided by appeal to feelings, then Mill's position may indeed be reasonable. (In my final, critical chapter, I shall question Mill's assumption that there is no other alternative.) Having made that assumption, however, it would appear sufficient to defend his principle of morality by showing that it enjoins pursuit of the only end people find desirable.

Moreover, in his "Remarks on Bentham's Philosophy," he more or less outlined the nature of the argument that would be needed to defeat the intuitionists. He berated Bentham for not having treated the opposition fairly, and for not having come to grips with the obvious defense they would make of their view:

> The answer of such persons to Mr. Bentham would be, that by an inductive and analytical examination of the human mind, they had satisfied themselves, that what we call our moral sentiments, (that is, the feelings of complacency and aversion we experience when we compare actions of our own or of other people with our standard of right and wrong,) are as much part of the original constitution of man's nature as the desire of happiness and the fear of suffering: That those sentiments do not indeed attach themselves to the same actions under all circumstances, but neither do they, in attaching themselves to actions, follow the law of utility, but certain other general laws, which are the same in all mankind naturally; though education or external circumstances may counteract them, by creating artificial associations stronger than they. No proof indeed can be given that we ought to abide by these laws; but neither can any proof be given, that we ought to regulate our conduct by utility. All that can be said is, that the pursuit of happiness is natural to us; and so, it is contended, is the reverence for, and the inclination to square our actions by, certain general laws of morality. . . . They set up as a standard what are assumed (on grounds which are considered sufficient) to be the instincts of the species, or principles of our common nature as universal and inexplicable as instincts.[38]

Here, again, is the recognition that one cannot prove first principles, one can only show that they express a natural and universal aspect of human nature. To overcome the intuitionist position, then, the utilitarian would have to show that the pursuit of happiness is an aspect of human nature and that there are no other such ends which are distinguishable from happiness. In *Utilitarianism*, in the chapter preceding the proof, Mill characterized the intuitionists as holding that "the feeling of duty" is innate. However, he pointed out that among the "intuitive moral obligations" they recognize is that of consulting the general welfare:

> Even as it is, the intuitive moralists, though they believe that there are other intuitive moral obligations, do already believe this to be one; for they unanimously hold that a large *portion* of morality turns upon the consideration due to the interests of our fellow creatures.[39]

Thus characterized, the intuitionists would agree that the general well-being is an appropriate end of conduct; they would not agree that it is the sole end of conduct, subsuming all others. To convince the intuitionists of the primary status of the general welfare, he must, then, above all else, show it to be the only end of human endeavor which can be regarded as ultimate. The great bulk of his proof is directed at precisely that problem.

This is, of course, conjecture. There are reasons for doubting it as an account of Mill's perception of what had to be demonstrated. *Prior* to the chapter containing the proof, he had denied that the moral feelings are innate, and he returned to this theme in the chapter on justice which follows the proof to show that the sentiment of justice can be explained as an outgrowth of more basic natural feelings. This should not have been necessary if he had already shown that the moral sentiments are not more basic than the desire for happiness. Moreover, his argument in the second part of the proof is based on the associationist psychology which had been around for a long time and was already known to the intuitionists.

In response, it should be noted that while it is true that Mill held in the previous chapter that the moral sentiments are not innate, he presented no *arguments* to show this, nor was he concerned with that issue. His concern there was only to show that people *can* come to accept the utilitarian principle as binding on them, and that this operates through a natural sentiment so that the "bindingness" will not disappear on analysis. Rather than undercutting the view of Mill's concern which I have outlined, the previous chapter supports it. He there contended that no end could be lastingly "binding" on a person which was not either itself a natural end or strongly connected with one. However, that chapter leaves it open to be shown that happiness is the only end with reference to which the moral feeling of duty is to be explained. Moreover, chapter 3 depicts the intuitionist as willing to accept the utilitarian end as one of his, also.

The chapter on justice hardly militates against my view. It was written originally as a separate essay.[40] Moreover, the reduction of the sentiment of justice to utility would be superfluous (logically speaking) to *any* interpretation of the proof. Had the proof been successful, then all moral obligations must be referred ultimately to the general welfare. Of course, it would still be useful to show this possible with respect to the most important and powerful moral sentiment which opponents propose as a counterexample. Still, it makes as much sense for Mill to have taken this route on my view of his objectives as on any other.

Finally, with respect to the associationist psychology which underlies the most important part of the proof, it must be pointed out that

Mill had important clarifications to make of the theories Bentham and his father had propounded. Both, he thought, had misled readers to attribute to them a narrow, egoistic theory of human motivation; Bentham in particular had led others to the view that people do *not* seek virtue, dignity, the well-being of others, and so on, as ends in themselves. It *was*, then, important to provide recognition of the complexities of human motivation, while showing that all these ends can be encompassed within happiness. While Mill had addressed these issues elsewhere (e.g., the essays on Bentham, and in the *Logic*), it had not been done with the thoroughness and detail that is exhibited in *Utilitarianism*.

Suppose we were to accept that the proof was directed at intuitionist opponents for whom the second part of the proof would be more crucial. What could be said of the first part of the proof? What sorts of argument would explain that portion of the proof?

Let us look first at the connection between the (alleged) fact that everyone desires his or her happiness and the ultimate desirability of happiness. Mill was seeking to get his reader to agree that happiness is desirable as an end. To agree to that entails *judging* that happiness is desirable as an end. To make such a judgment is to make a judgment of intrinsic value; but, in Mill's view (as we saw in chap. 1 of this book), to make a favorable value judgment entails approving that which is judged. To approve of something requires at least that the idea of it is pleasant.[41] If we are pleased at the idea of something which we can seek, we shall desire it. Hence, one cannot get someone to judge something desirable without getting him or her to desire it. Mill explained in the penultimate paragraph of the chapter that one could go about getting someone not already virtuous to be so,

> only by making the person *desire* virtue—by making him think of it in a pleasurable light, or of its absence in a painful one.[42]

In commenting on an abstract he published of Plato's *Gorgias*, he had written:

> All valid arguments in favour of virtue, presuppose that we already desire virtue, or desire some of its ends and objects. You may prove to us that virtue tends to the happiness of mankind or of our country; but that supposes that we already care for mankind or for our country. . . . The love of virtue, and every other noble feeling, is not communicated by reasoning, but caught by inspiration or sympathy from those who already have it.[43]

Convincing someone that something is desirable as an end is a psychological process only partly amenable to rational discussion, in particular, to showing it to be connected with, or to be one of, the things we desire as ends as part of our nature. The audible and visible are precisely analogous to the desirable in that the ultimate source of conviction is internal sensation.

Mill's metaethical views were hardly idiosyncratic, and he had published them before. They were held in one form or another by most writers in his tradition. Moreover, the intuitionists would certainly agree that a moral judgment expresses a moral sentiment, and that convincing someone of a moral conclusion entails evoking a sentiment of approval or disapproval. They did not reject happiness as *an* end of conduct (indeed, some were willing to adopt the promotion of happiness as the sole *test* of morality), and would certainly take common desires for an ultimate object as evidence of a common moral intuition.

Thus far, then, Mill seems vindicated (at least if we are willing to accept his metaethical assumptions). His conclusion, however, raises further problems:

> No reason can be given why the general happiness is desirable, except that each person, so far as he believes it to be attainable, desires his own happiness. This, however, being a fact, we have not only all the proof which the case admits of, but all which it is possible to require, that happiness is a good: that each person's happiness is a good to that person, and the general happiness, therefore, a good to the aggregate of all persons.[44]

It requires explanation as to how the fact that each person desires his or her own happiness gives a reason for concluding that the general happiness is desirable. If the last sentence quoted above is meant to be that explanation, it falls far short. The reasoning seems straightforwardly fallacious. Again, I shall not propose a definitive solution, but shall explore several possibilities.

The simplest explanation of this remarkable argument is suggested in a letter Mill wrote to a correspondent, Henry Jones, to clarify the passage:

> As to the sentence you quote from my "Utilitarianism"; when I said that the general happiness is a good to the aggregate of all persons I did not mean that every human being's happiness is a good to every other human being; though I think, in a good state of society and education it would be so. I merely meant in this particular sentence to argue that since A's

happiness is a good, B's a good, C's a good, &c., the sum of all these goods must be a good.[45]

To many, this explanation is insufficient as it appears quite clearly to commit the fallacy of composition. Just because A, B, and C possess property X, it does not follow that a whole, composed solely of A, B, and C, possesses property X. If I have a headache, an aspirin in my (full) aspirin bottle is good for me, and any one will do. But it is not true that the whole bottle will be good for me. So, if Mill meant to be presenting a deductively valid argument at this stage, then, unless he can be supplied with further unstated premises, the argument fails.

He may not, however, have intended the conclusion to follow deductively (despite the use of "must be" in the letter to Jones). While a collective whole need not have the properties of its components, it sometimes *does*. If each person in a crowd makes a loud sound, the crowd will sound loud; if each flower in a field is red, the field will be red. So, Mill may simply have supposed that one who agreed that each person's happiness is a good would agree that the sum—the general happiness—is a good. After all, he depicted the intuitionists as already recognizing the general welfare as a good.

The problem Mill left open is sometimes depicted as that of having to show how we can get from egoistic eudaemonism to altruistic eudaemonism, how to convince the egoist or skeptic that the general welfare is desirable. The proposed explanation hardly attacks that difficulty. This is almost certainly a misdescription of the situation, however. When Mill says that it is a fact each person desires his or her own happiness, he ought not be taken to have meant that each person desires *only* the person's own happiness (in a narrow sense [i.e., desires only his or her own pleasures]). He had argued in the previous chapter that social feelings, including sympathy, are present in all people, and can be cultivated. The *extent* of altruism present in people differs, but it is natural for us to have it. In some people, the welfare of others becomes indissolubly linked with their own happiness; they cannot be happy without the happiness of the others. He had already dispensed with egoism as a viable psychological theory.

Still, the paragraph containing the first part of the proof does seem to require a strong connection between people's desiring something and its being desirable. The utilitarian end cannot be acknowledged by anyone unless it is so both in theory and in practice. The end which he has to show is so acknowledged is the general happiness; the reason he gives for thinking it is so acknowledged is that each person desires his or her own happiness. It is tempting at this stage to say that there is a missing premise or assumption here, namely, that Mill believed there *is* a strong connection between an individual's welfare and the general welfare. Each individual's welfare is *included in* the general welfare, so, if a person desires that person's own welfare, and it is therefore a good to them, the general welfare is also a good to them. Of course, it does not follow that they *desire* the general welfare, because *they* may not see the connection; yet, because of their desires for their own happiness, it will be true that the general welfare is good for them. Moreover, they can come to desire the general welfare when made aware of the connection, especially if social life is requisite for their happiness, and a requisite of social life is a regard for the general welfare (as Mill had argued in chap. 3).

There are many problems with this line of argument, both interpretive—as a representation of Mill's views—and critical—as an argument in its own right. A few of these are worth looking at here. In the first place, it would seem that Mill *should* have shown that everyone *desires* the general happiness as an end, not merely that they can or would desire it. Nothing can be an end which is not acknowledged to be so, he had held. But this is misleading. He had argued in chapter 3 that the utilitarian standard can be "binding" on a person because it *can* become acknowledged as an outgrowth of natural sentiments and desires—the social feelings. It should suffice, then, to show that something can be acknowledged as an end, if one can show that it can become sought as an end, and that the desire for it is strongly connected with basic aspects of human nature.

In fact, looking back at chapter 3 provides further insight into the proof. In that chapter, he had argued for the social feelings as experienced by almost everyone to some extent or other. To whatever extent a person has social feelings, and is capable of sympathizing with others, that person will require the well-being of the others for his or her own happiness. Thus, to *some* extent, the general happiness *is* an end to virtually everyone. The reason it is so is that they desire their own happiness (broadly conceived as including fulfillment of the desire for the well-being of others). Of course, Mill recognized these feelings to be weak in most individuals, and in need of cultivation. Accordingly he could hardly have held that the general welfare is *in fact* desired by everyone as an end *and* as an overriding end. He was as aware as anyone else that in cases of conflict between the selfish and unselfish desires, most people will, more often than not, sacrifice the fulfillment of the unselfish ones.

The very possibility of such a sacrifice, however, entails the possibility of there being more than one end; and, therefore, the possibility of conflict between the general good and the self-conceived good of the individual. This would introduce another gap in the argument that the general happiness is *alone* desirable as an end.

Moreover, I think there is ample evidence that Mill did not embrace the simplistic Pollyanna view that one's own interests always (really) coincide with the general interest. In the *Logic*, he had written:

> That nothing which is a cause of evil on the whole to other people, can be really good for the agent himself, is indeed a possible tenet, and always a favourite one with moralists, although in the present age the question has rather been, not whether the proposition is true, but how society and education can be so ordered as to make it true. At all events, it is not proved merely by the fact that a thing beneficial to the world, and a thing beneficial to a person himself, are both in common parlance called *good*. That is no valid argument, but a fallacy of ambiguity.[46]

In his "Remarks on Bentham's Philosophy," Mill had written:

> No man's individual share of any public good which he can hope to realize by his efforts, is an equivalent for the sacrifice of his ease, and of the personal objects which he might attain by another course of conduct. The balance can be turned in favour of virtuous exertion, only by the interest of *feeling* or by that of *conscience*—those "social interests," the necessary subordination of which to "self-regarding" is so lightly assumed.[47]

Finally, in *Utilitarianism*, he had recognized the possibility of voluntarily doing without happiness, to the extent even of martyrdom, involving the complete sacrifice of one's happiness. He thought this only justified for the general good, but *did* think it is sometimes justified.[48] He also seems to have thought that human affairs can be so ordered that such sacrifices need never occur; nonetheless, they are not so ordered.

At this stage, it is very hard to see that the fact each person desires his or her own happiness provides any ground for the conclusion that the general happiness is desirable. There is, however, one further possibility worth taking up. An excerpt from "Remarks on Bentham's Philosophy," given earlier, attributed to Mill the view that a share of the public good often is not equivalent to the sacrifices required to produce it, and, thus, in the particular case, there may be a conflict between the general and individual interest. This quotation was, however, taken out of context. The entire passage from which this excerpt was taken makes a different point, namely, that many people act primarily from a confirmed state of moral virtue, which overrides concern for personal interest. Moreover, Mill held that nothing in human nature forbids this being true of all people, and "until it is so, the race will never enjoy one-tenth part of the happiness which our nature is susceptible of."[49] Mill went on to describe such a state of mind in a person as one "without which his own enjoyment of life can be but poor and scanty."

This view parallels claims made in *Utilitarianism* for the higher pleasures and "noble character" in general. This state of character, Mill held, makes everybody happier, and everyone gains by it. Moreover, the higher nature is intrinsically superior; it involves the fulfillment of human capacities, and no one who has such capacities can be truly happy without their development. Mill depicted the social sentiments as natural, and, in the comments on Bentham, seems to have been saying that the person in whom these are fully developed is capable of greater happiness. In addition, in "Utility of Religion," he maintained that people have strong desires for "grandeur of aspiration" and a passion for "ideal excellence," and concluded that because of this people can come to identify with all mankind.[50]

What this line of argument strongly suggests is that the greatest happiness of persons *does* lie in the greatest happiness of all, insofar as there is a superior kind of happiness which involves identifying the interests of all as one's own. Persons capable of the highest happiness *do* desire the general happiness; it *is* desirable in the eyes of those whose judgment is determinative of intrinsic value. And, as Mill claimed, they desire the general happiness *because* they desire their own.

This explanation has certain advantages. It provides a way of explaining the claim that desiring one's own happiness provides a reason for the general happiness being desirable. While Mill may have stretched the notion of "happiness" here, the claims involved have some plausibility. Moreover, Mill could consistently hold—as he did in numerous places—that most people have not yet attained that level of character development wherein their own greatest happiness can be achieved; and he could admit, with no inconsistency, that the social feelings are "much inferior in strength to their selfish feelings."[51] As most persons conceive their happiness, then, there are apparent conflicts between the general good and their own. Ultimately, he could claim, they would be happier still if they could be gotten to pursue and identify as their own interest that of mankind in general. There is, here, a serious problem concerning *conflicts* between the happiness possible given one's *actual* character and desires, and the happiness which is possible given an *ideal*, not realized, state of character. I shall return to this problem in my final chapter. The point to be made here is that the admission of the possibility of such conflicts is not inconsistent with the structure of Mill's proof. Insofar as people do desire their own greatest happiness, they would have reason to pursue the general welfare.

In addition, this explanation need not go so far as to claim a *necessary* connection in all instances between what is good for the individual and what is good for society. Mill's discussion of martyrdom makes it clear that he thought the martyr must *sacrifice* his or her own happiness, and that it is possible to do this. The martyr's sacrifice is for "something which he prizes more than his individual happiness."[52] This *is* possible because the social feelings can be developed by education, social influence, and the inculcation of habitual modes of desiring and acting, which result in a confirmed state of virtuous moral character. But, one may wonder, how can the desire for one's own happiness possibly provide ground for developing a state of character which could allow one to forego one's own happiness for the general welfare? Even if we grant the psychological possibility of developing that state of character *from* the desire for one's own happiness, how could that desire provide a *reason* to develop it? A complete answer to the question cannot be given until we explore further the importance for Mill of habit in character development. Enough has been said to outline the answer. The best hope an individual has of sufficient self-development and the fulfillment of the person's capacities, needs, and desires, *is* just to pursue the general welfare, and to identify the social good with his or her own. Moreover, given the requirements of social life, all social influences, education, and self-training should be brought to bear on developing that identification—at least to the point that it does not conflict with the human good of freedom. This will mean the development of a state of character in which one is willing to sacrifice one's own good for others, at least where the latter will truly be realized. In an imperfect state of social arrangements, the sacrifice may sometimes have to be made. But, Mill implied, as more and more persons take the general welfare as bound up with their own, the chances of having to make such sacrifices are lessened. To put the point in terms of rational choice considerations: one's best chance of attaining the highest happiness lies in inculcating in oneself and others the ideal state of character described, in which one conceives one's own happiness as bound up with that of others. It would *not* suffice to seek only to develop that in others (thus minimizing the chances of one's own sacrifice while allowing oneself to exploit the sacrifices of others). The point is that we *are* creatures whose *own* highest happiness lies in identifying with others. We would cut off from ourselves the achievement of our social selves, wherein lies our full flowering. Thus, while it poses some risk to ourselves, the development of this identification, to this extent, provides our best chance for happiness. There are problems posed by the fact that we know the majority of persons have not yet sufficiently made this identification. Accordingly, an intelligent "strategy" may call for inculcating recognition of "loophole" situations. In fact, Mill did not hold that extreme sacrifice of self is obligatory (except in the case of special duties), and he resisted doctrines that require utter subordination of self-interest to the general interest.

I do not know to what extent this reasoning reconstructs Mill's ideas in the "proof." It does draw on points he made in a number of places, and would, I think, provide a stronger underpinning for Mill's argument in the proof. It is also entirely in keeping with his later explanation of how the desire to be virtuous itself arises out of the desire for happiness.

There is *no* direct evidence, however, that my hypothetical line of argument was one that Mill employed. *If* it was, one would surely expect considerably more explanation. Indeed, the entire argument is merely suggested by the quote in the "Remarks on Bentham's Philosophy"; I know of no place where it was fully developed by Mill. I can only conjecture further that the "higher" happiness had become so second nature to his thinking that it simply did not occur to him to elaborate on it in the proof, especially as aspects of that view had been developed in the two prior chapters.

Several parts of the exposition, however, are close paraphrases of things Mill *did* say; and I note that his father argued explicitly from rational choice considerations for the reasonableness of accepting the general happiness as the ultimate end.[53] There are, then, good reasons to think that this account captures Mill's views.

3

THE GREATEST HAPPINESS
PRINCIPLE AND MORAL RULES

During the past several decades, an enormous literature has developed concerning the role of rules in a utilitarian moral theory. It has become common to distinguish two versions of utilitarianism—act-utilitarianism and rule-utilitarianism. Act-utilitarians hold that an act is right if, and only if, it would produce the best consequences among all the acts the agent can perform. (Presumably, an act which is not right is wrong.) Rule-utilitarians hold that acts are right if, and only if, they are prescribed by rules which are in turn justified by the consequences of their being adopted or conformed to. Several varieties of rule-utilitarianism can be distinguished according to the nature of the rules stressed (e.g., actual vs. ideal rules), or the nature of the consequences to be considered.[1]

That utilitarians should want to be able to use rules in moral calculation is evident. If we literally had to calculate the full consequences of every act we voluntarily perform, it is doubtful we could get out of bed in the morning. The act-utilitarian would want to hold at the least that rules can guide our daily conduct, insofar as they have been arrived at on the basis of past experience and are sufficiently reliable to justify using them for ordinary matters. Such rules, in an act-utilitarian theory, are often regarded as "rules of thumb," to indicate that the rules are *only* guides, and may be dropped in favor of calculation when time and circumstance permit, or where a situation is quite unusual.

To many critics, such a view of moral rules fails to do justice to their rule in moral reasoning. This attitude seems to sanction, for example, breaking the rule of promise-keeping whenever greater utility is produced by doing so. Moreover, it seems to sanction going through the calculations of the utility of keeping a promise whenever one has time to do so. Rights and duties appear to occupy an unstable position in such a moral world.

It is primarily in response to criticisms of this sort that rule-utilitarian theories have arisen. Such theories prohibit appeal to the consequences of the particular act, and, on one hand, thus appear to avoid the problems of special (seemingly unjustified) exceptions. On the other hand, the rule-utilitarian view accepts utility as the end which adherence to the rules must achieve.

The distinction, in the form of explicitly articulated and contrasted doctrines, is of recent origin. The classical utilitarians have traditionally been regarded as act-utilitarians who adopted rules as guides in practical affairs. Interestingly, however, Mill has been brought into the contemporary debate, and a body of literature has arisen over the side issue of whether Mill is to be properly interpreted as an act- or rule-utilitarian. Indeed, it would not be unfair to say that much of the current attention to the more general controversy stems from an article published in 1953 by J. O. Urmson, arguing for a kind of rule-utilitarian interpretation of Mill.[2]

I do not wish to enter into this controversy. Mill's theory was neither an act- nor a rule-utilitarian theory as those terms are strictly defined. He took an approach to rules throughout his work that gives rules a strong role in determining what we are to do in practical life that is consistent even with an act-utilitarian theory, but he introduced into his account of right and wrong certain elements that take his view out of the act-utilitarian category. In particular, he emphasized that acts which are wrong are ones for which we may properly be punished, and no act is wrong for which we are not liable for punishment. Furthermore, he held that there are some acts that are praiseworthy if done, but for which punishment is not appropriate if we fail to perform them. Finally, he held that some acts—self-regarding ones—concern only the agent and that these raise no questions of moral right and wrong.

Virtually all commentators agree that Mill held that self-regarding acts are not liable to punishment, hence, it would follow that they cannot be moral wrongs even when they fail to maximize utility. On this ground alone, Mill was not, strictly speaking, an act- or a rule-utilitarian, since, on the strict definitions, *every* act is either right or wrong.

To say this, of course, is not to say anything much about the role of rules in Mill's moral theory. Hence, the terms "act-utilitarianism" and "rule-utilitarianism" cannot serve our purposes very well. The crucial question we need to ask is: within the class of morally assessible acts, what role, if any, do moral rules play in determining rightness and wrongness, and what role, if any, do the consequences of acts play in determining their rightness and wrongness?

I want to show that there is no easy answer to this question in Mill's writings. There is an approach to the use of rules that runs throughout his work, and which he inherited from his mentors—Jeremy Bentham, John Austin, and his father, James Mill—that is consistent with what I call an "act-consequence" interpretation. I shall explore this approach (which I shall label the "strategy conception of rules") in the writings of these figures who helped form Mill's views. I shall then show how it appears throughout John Mill's work. Considerable strain is placed on aspects of this interpretation, however, by the essay *Utilitarianism*. On the one hand, he indicated that acts are right "in proportion as they tend to promote happiness" and are wrong "as they tend to produce the reverse of happiness." This statement is most plausibly interpreted as an *act-consequence* theory—one that makes the consequences of the act itself determinative of (or importantly relevant to) the rightness or wrongness of the act. On the other hand, in addition to the "proportionality" criterion, he introduced the "punishability" thesis indicated earlier, and several commentators have argued that this commits him to a *rule-consequence* theory—a view that makes useful rules determinative of (or importantly relevant to) the rightness or wrongness of an act.

I shall consider some of the alternative interpretations that have been offered. I shall try to show that none has unequivocal support in Mill's texts. Part of the reason for this is that Mill's introduction of the punishability criterion is unclear, permitting at least two interpretations. Furthermore, he gave no indication as to how the proportionality and punishability criteria are to be reconciled. This part of his theory was never sufficiently clarified or developed.

Nonetheless, I shall hold that the evidence supports a view on moral rules that *could* be justified on *either* strict act-consequence or rule-consequence interpretations. The view that I claim to have been Mill's holds that in *practical* deliberations, we should follow useful rules in determining our moral duties, except in extreme or special circumstances where a great deal is at stake, or the rules conflict, in which case we determine what morality requires by appeal to the consequences of the act. This result is important for the chapters on justice and freedom that follow, since, I shall contend, Mill's emphasis on the importance of rules helps explain and make more defensible his theories of justice and freedom. The act-consequence/rule-consequence controversy, that is, the argument as to whether the rules literally *define* our duties, or, on the other hand, are useful indirect devices to be strongly relied on for producing right acts, is significant, then, only at the *theoretical* level. At that level, a wide range of views is possible. An act-consequence view could make the production of the best consequences a necessary condition of rightness, or a sufficient condition, or both. Furthermore, it could take consequences of the act to be always a relevant factor, to be considered with others. Since another factor (or necessary or sufficient condition) could be accord with rules, the act-consequence/rule-consequence distinction, as I defined these terms above, is not mutually exclusive. This was done purposely, as some interpreters of Mill seek to combine act-consequence and rule-consequence considerations in the definition of right conduct.

I shall begin by outlining the "strategy" conception of rules and show it to be consistent even with an act-utilitarian theory. I will then discuss the role of rules in the moral theories of Mill's predecessors and teachers, with the intent of showing how the strategy conception elucidates their work, and will turn to Mill's work to show evidence of that conception. Finally, I shall discuss the essay *Utilitarianism* to show that the strategy use of rules is also compatible with that work. It is here that the "punishability" criterion of wrongness plays a major role, however, and I shall discuss the interpretations of others that would require a rule-consequence criterion of rightness and wrongness.

THE TENDENCIES OF ACTS, UTILITARIANISM, AND RULES

The conception of the role of rules in a utilitarian theory that I wish to develop can be elucidated by considering an argument that has been used by J. O. Urmson in his attempt to show Mill to have held a rule-consequence theory of right and wrong. Urmson's argument draws attention to Mill's initial statement of the "proportionality" criterion of right and wrong: "The Creed which accepts as the foundation of morals, Utility, or the Greatest Happiness Principle, holds that actions are right in proportion as they tend to promote happiness, wrong as they tend to promote the reverse of happiness."[3]

For the most part, this statement has not provoked interpretive debates until quite recently. It has been taken by most readers as a clear statement of an act-utilitarian position. Urmson, however, claims that it makes sense only to speak of the tendency of a *class* of acts, not of an individual act, and that this would commit Mill to a rule-consequence position.

Urmson's claim is of great interest, since virtually all of the classical utilitarians used the language of "tendencies," and this was especially true of Mill's circle—his father, Bentham, and John Austin. If Urmson's argument were right, all should be committed to rule-utilitarianism or rule-consequentialism, though, as Urmson points out, the language *may* be taken as a loose way of stating an essentially act-utilitarian position. Urmson's argument is as follows:

> But note that strictly one can say that a certain action tends to produce a certain result only if one is speaking of type- rather than token-actions. Drinking alcohol may tend to promote exhilaration, but my drinking this particular glass either does or does not produce it. It seems, then, that Mill can well be interpreted here as regarding moral rules as forbidding or enjoining types of action, in fact as making the point that the right moral rules are the ones which promote the ultimate end. . . . And this, or something like it, is the interpretation which consistency requires.[4]

Though Urmson is partly right, his main argument seems to me mistaken. It is true that one can use the word "tends" with reference to types or classes of acts. Moreover, there are indeed places where Mill used the term in this way. When so used, as, for example, when one says that drinking alcohol tends to produce exhilaration (or, what seems nearer the truth—depression), one does seem to be asserting that it is *usual* for actions of that *type* to produce the indicated results. Moreover, it is not clear *with respect to exhilaration*, what it would mean to attribute such a tendency to a particular act of drinking alcohol. This does not show, however, that it makes no sense to speak of the tendency of particular acts to produce *happiness* or its reverse. There are other uses of "tends to" which make it sensible to attribute to a particular act a tendency to produce happiness.

The important fact to focus on is that a particular act can have numerous and manifold consequences. Moreover, an act can have consequences for many persons over a range of time. Some of these consequences may be good for some people and bad for others, thus making some people happy and others unhappy. Furthermore, it may have both good and bad consequences for the *same* person. In such cases, it makes perfectly good sense to say that the act *tends* to promote happiness if, on balance, it produces more happiness than unhappiness, that is, if it acts predominantly in the direction of happiness. The greater the difference is between the total of bad consequences, the greater is its tendency to produce good. We might add that it also makes sense to say that an act has *some* tendency to good if it has *any* good consequences, though, of course, that need not be its predominant tendency.

I shall show later that Bentham and Austin explicitly adopted such a meaning for "tendency" in explicating their versions of utilitarianism. J. S. Mill defined the tendency of an event as a power to produce a certain result, such that the result will obtain unless counteracted. I will show that Mill's use of this concept in regard to the rules governing conduct turns out to be equivalent to that of Bentham and Austin.

My purpose at this stage, however, is to point to the possibility of such a rendering of the terminology, and to sketch a kind of utilitarian theory consistent with it, but which gives a significant role to rules in moral reasoning. Later, I will show that the essential elements of the theory were held by the classical thinkers, and that this theory is thus a reasonable "rational reconstruction" of their views.

The theory I wish to sketch rests on a distinction (explicitly adopted by Austin and James Mill) between the *meaning* of a term and a *test* or *criterion* for its application. In the case at hand, there is a distinction to be made between the meaning of the expression "tendency of an act" and a test for determining the probable tendency of an act. While I am skeptical that a philosophical account of this distinction can be given which is adequate for all the purposes for which it has been used, a rough characterization can be presented by way of examples which, for present purposes, may provide some clarity. (As this kind of distinction was widely employed by English moral philosophers in Mill's tradition, and by those in his circle, it may serve to illuminate the utilitarians' theories, whether it is ultimately defensible or not.)[5]

1. A familiar test for the presence of oxygen is to light a match to see if it will burn. Premature extinction, or a dim burning, indicate little or no oxygen. No one would be inclined to suggest that this, or the sentence reporting the test result, is part of the meaning of oxygen.

2. In the sentential calculus, a tautology is a sentence which is true under any assignment of truth-values to its atomic constituents. A test for tautologousness is the construction of a truth-table. (We tend to forget that the truth-table test was a *discovery* and did not come hand-in-hand with our conception of logical truth. Indeed, an alternate test—deducibility from certain axioms—predated truth-tables.)[6]

3. A good typist is one who types rapidly with good accuracy; this is what it *means* to be a good typist. An employer might, however, set specific standards of performance to be used as criteria for acceptable typists in his or her firm.[7]

The distinction could be employed in a utilitarian theory as follows: what it *means* to say that the tendency of an act is good is that its effects are predominantly good, that is, that it produces more happiness than unhappiness. In practice, it is difficult to assess all the consequences of acts; time is often short; information limited; the long-range effects are difficult to foresee. Moreover, acts do not occur in utter isolation. They may be enjoined or forbidden by widely recognized rules, so that cases of rule observance or violation can have effects on an established practice. Further, acts spring from and foster general habits and states of character in the actor, and have effects on such states of others. These sorts of consequences are very difficult to assess, looking at the act by itself. What is wanted for practical situations is a guide (or guides) to conduct that have some degree of reliability in predicting all of these consequences, and which can be applied with sufficient convenience that it is fit to serve as a practical test of our actions.

In cases where the act in question is governed by well-accepted general rules, these can serve as guides to conduct, for, to a certain extent, they represent the judgment of one's predecessors as to what acts are useful. Moreover, if a general rule is useful and widely respected, there is further reason to think it is likely that acts in accord with the rule are right. One's own adherence or violation can have effects (e.g., by way of example) on the adherence of others to the rule, and in one's own case in future situations. One sees the rule-related utilities of the particular act better by asking what it would be like if this sort of act were *not* generally done, and by considering that doing it is the rule.

Where there is not a general rule, or when the rules seem inadequate or otherwise defective, it is usually helpful to consider what would be the result if this sort of act *were* made the rule and *were* generally done, that is, what would be the *ideal* rule to adopt. Whatever rule-making tendencies the act may have will be more clearly visible, along with their consequences.

The appeal to rules, either actual or ideal, may be a useful guide, and even the sole basis of our acts where time is short, and so on. But such considerations, though practical *tests* of the tendencies of acts, do not suffice as the ultimate canons of rightness and wrongness. No set of rules which people establish could possibly *always* enjoin only acts with good tendencies and forbid only acts with bad tendencies. Knowledge of the consequences of acts in the innumerable circumstances in which they occur can never be complete; and accepted rules must not be too complex to be useful in practical situations. Moreover, while the accepted rules of a society embody its wisdom, they also embody its foolishness and stupidity. People are wont to blindly follow what is generally done, so the mere survival of a rule is no guarantee of its having been found useful through careful examination. There is, then, always room for moral reform, and where time and knowledge permit calculation, it is in order to look at the consequences of the act at hand, and apply the Principle of Utility itself, rather than some subordinate moral rule, to the act.

Three further explanatory points need to be made. The first is that the view outlined trades on the fact (often urged by Mill) that if one wants to achieve a certain goal, it is sometimes best not to aim directly at it, but to seek some other goal, the achievement of which carries along with it the achievement of the ultimate goal. This is not an unfamiliar phenomenon. Sailors going against the wind tack in a criss-cross pattern in order to end up at a point opposite the start. Bowling lanes are marked with arrows a dozen feet or so in front of the bowlers; many bowlers do best by aiming at the lane markings, rather than at the pins, and are more likely to score well this way than they would be were they to aim at the pins. In such cases, the doing or not doing of what one aimed at is not taken as the ultimate criterion of success. Similarly, in trying to act morally, one will usually try to act according to useful secondary principles. That one has done so, however, is not a final determination that one has done what is right. A person has done what is right only if what the person has done has predominantly useful consequences. Of course, in judging this, we will often run into the same difficulties of judgment as one contemplating an act. Thus, in

making practical judgments, we shall normally find ourselves employing the same criteria—the secondary principles which apply. Moreover, the fact that the agent acted on secondary principles on which it
was reasonable to base one's behavior, may excuse the person from
blame in the case where it is shown that the act was ultimately wrong.
For the most part, then, we will act on, and judge conduct by secondary
rules, and thus the moral quality of our lives will be largely determined
by our secondary principles. Such principles are, however, always
subject to correction and improvement.

The second point I want to make is extremely important: the theory
is not committed to regarding the secondary principles it urges we
adopt in practice, or which are commonly adopted, as mere "summaries" of what has been found useful. It may be thought that it is
because the rules have been found useful that they have been adopted
and have survived; or the agent may perceive that in most cases the rules
will prove useful. When adopted, however, the rules serve as principles
or standards for directing and assessing conduct. The rules are appealed
to in deciding what to do and in making everyday judgments; they are
not shorthand ways of stating facts about past or prospective experience. The adoption of such rules to govern one's everyday moral life is
part of a strategy or policy designed to guarantee the maximum achievement of the ultimate end of conduct. The rule is adopted as a direct
standard of conduct because it is useful; but the reason justifying adoption of the rule is not itself *part* of the rule. It is, of course, consistent to
make it one's rule to do a certain sort of thing, but also recognize that in
unusual circumstances one may appeal to a criterion that takes precedence over the rule.

Finally, it must be pointed out that the "strategy" conception of
moral rules does not commit the utilitarian to regard moral rules as mere
"rules of thumb," if that is meant to imply that the rules are subject to
constant scrutiny and assessment, and may be readily foregone if the
agent judges them not useful in the particular case. The "strategy"
conception leaves open the possibility that circumstances dictate strict
adherence to rules, and forsaking of private judgment. It may be, for
example, that certain rules are extremely important—providing crucial
benefits—and that the sorts of considerations that are relevant are
difficult to have accurate knowledge about in particular cases on the
basis of private judgment. Moreover, the risks may be great if one
miscalculates. In such a situation, the best policy may be to adopt the
applicable rule as a strict standard. From a theoretical point of view, of

course, it is conceivable that one will occasionally do what is wrong, but this may be a risk worth taking, given the difficulties of knowledge and the stakes involved in miscalculation. If, in addition, stability of conduct is important in this sort of case for others to be able to rely on, and a firm state of character difficult to maintain, it would be prudent to avoid contrary temptation by a strict policy. Thus, it is not inconsistent for even an act-utilitarian to urge the adoption of a secondary principle as an inflexible standard of one's conduct. This might be urged, not because the utilitarian thinks such conduct is right in itself, but because by so acting one is most likely to do most often what is right (as would be determined by an act-utilitarian calculator with perfect knowledge, and so on). Rules which are part of a strategy may be as weak or as strong as circumstances dictate, and such an act-utilitarian need not give up a basically act-utilitarian criterion of right action by insisting on the relatively inflexible adoption of rules. Of course, should there be rare cases where one *can* be fairly certain of good consequences, or where the rules adopted conflict, the act-utilitarian must then sanction resorting to the Principle of Utility itself, judging the act directly by its consequences.[8]

I have elaborated on these last points, because they are not often recognized in comtemporary discussions, and because John Stuart Mill seems to have had such a view of the rules of justice.

MILL'S MENTORS: BENTHAM, AUSTIN, AND JAMES MILL

In this section, I shall take a brief look at the views of Mill's teachers in moral theory. All used the terminology of tendencies, and (with the possible exception of Bentham) placed stress on rule-related considerations in moral deliberation. This investigation has its own historical interest, but I wish to pursue it primarily because I think it sheds light on J. S. Mill's theory.

The best known source of Bentham's moral theory is his *An Introduction to the Principles of Morals and Legislation*. In that work, he explained the Principle of Utility as follows:

> By the principle of utility is meant that principle which approves or disapproves of every action whatsoever, according to the tendency which it appears to have to augment or diminish the happiness of the party whose interest is in question: or, what is the same thing in other words, to promote or to oppose that happiness. I say of every action whatsoever; and

therefore not only of every action of a private individual, but of every measure of government.[9]

He went on to explain his use of "utility":

> By utility is meant that property in any object, whereby it tends to produce benefit, advantage, pleasure, good, or happiness, (all this in the present case comes to the same thing) to prevent the happening of mischief, pain, evil, or unhappiness to the party whose interest is considered: if that party be the community in general, then the happiness of the community: if a particular individual, then the happiness of that individual.[10]

He added that something is *for* the interest of an individual "when it tends to add to the sum total of his pleasures: or, what comes to the same thing, to diminish the sum total of his pains."[11]

Moreover, he explained the conditions for an act to conform to the Principle of Utility:

> An action then may be said to be conformable to the principle of utility, or, for shortness sake, to utility, (meaning with respect to the community at large) when the tendency it has to augment the happiness of the community is greater than any it has to diminish it.[12]

None of this bears Urmson's interpretation of "tendency." Tendencies are attributed to individual acts, and it is supposed that it makes sense to say of an act that it has contrary tendencies. This could hardly mean that the act is of a class which *usually* has certain consequences.

Finally, we must note that in a later section of his book, Bentham explicitly accepted the interpretation of "tendency" I outlined earlier:

> The general tendency of an act is more or less pernicious, according to the sum total of its consequences: that is, according to the difference between the sum of such as are good, and the sum of such as are evil.[13]

Bentham is probably best known for his detailed instructions for determining the general tendency of an act. This is done by means of calculations employing what is referred to as the "hedonic calculus." Though I shall not explore the calculus in detail, there are certain features of it which are of interest.

The calculus is intended to provide a guide for measuring the value of pleasures and pains produced by acts. Where there are numbers of persons affected by the act, the calculus calls on one to judge pleasures and pains by the following criteria: the intensity, the duration, its certainty or uncertainty, its propinquity or remoteness, fecundity (i.e., propensity to produce *further* similar sensations), its purity, and extent (i.e., the number of people affected by it).[14]

While there is much to be said of Bentham's method, I wish to remark on a general feature of it. As Bentham recognized with respect to the criteria of fecundity and purity, not all of these measure the *value* of a pleasure or pain. A pleasure already experienced is certain, and is not remote. It may, however, be relatively valueless. Its value is a function of features other than the probability of its occurrence or the distance in time at which it is likely to occur. An entirely improbable pleasure may be highly valuable should it occur.

The addition of the criteria Bentham adopted makes sense, of course, if one views the calculus as a device for *planning* future actions. If one is trying to maximize the production of pleasure by one's actions, then it is reasonable to take account of all these criteria. Adopting the calculus, then, amounts to adopting a strategy for producing a greater balance of good over bad consequences by our acts. Thus understood, certainty or uncertainty, propinquity or remoteness, *are* relevant in determining the value *to be given* a prospective pleasure or pain *in one's calculations*. Prospective acts, then, will be assessed according to (a) their likelihood of producing certain effects, and (b) the value to the community of those effects *if* they take place.

Aside from bringing into focus Bentham's use of the expression "tendency of an act," and the fact that he accepted the calculus as a device of strategy, there is little that is surprising in the above account. No one had supposed anything other than that Bentham is correctly interpreted as an act-utilitarian, assessing every act by *its* consequences. Indeed, Ernest Albee, in his *A History of English Utilitarianism*, commenting on the use of rules in Herbert Spencer's theory, remarked: "this insistence upon the necessity of general rules, as the direct guides of action, is by no means a novelty in English Utilitarianism. Nobody but Bentham, in fact, seems to have failed to recognise the need of depending upon such general rules."[15]

I believe it can be shown, however, that Bentham was willing to take account of considerations which would make appeal to useful rules a reasonable way of pursuing the general happiness. Indeed, there are certain passages in the *Principles* which are virtually unintelligible on any other reading.

A point of embarrassment for act-consequentialists has been the problem of contributions to joint or cooperative ventures. So long as enough others cooperate, an individual, it would seem, could produce greater good on occasion by not doing his or her part. Tax schemes appear to be such a case. The individual's contribution to public benefits may be slight, whereas his or her well-being can be augmented by nonpayment. Interestingly, Bentham considered just such a case in the *Principles*. He considered the question of whether nonpayment would be a mischievous act, and answered "Yes, certainly." To be successful, the tax scheme presupposes a chain of events: the receipt of monies by public officials, the application of the monies to public projects, the carrying out of the projects, and finally the production of public benefits. The prospective benefits are "contingent," then. Nonetheless, in a normally operating government, they are nearly certain. Of course, an individual's contribution may still be so small as not to appreciably affect the level of benefits. Bentham's response to this is enlightening:

> If, then, speaking of any small limited sum, such as the greatest which any one person is called upon to pay at a time, a man were to say, that the non-payment of it would be attended with mischievous consequences; this would be far from certain: but what comes to the same thing as if it were, it is perfectly certain when applied to the whole. It is certain, that if all of a sudden the payment of all taxes was to cease, there would no longer be any thing effectual done, either for the maintenance of justice, or for the defence of the community against its foreign adversaries. . . . The mischief, in point of *intensity* and *duration*, is indeed unknown: it is *uncertain*: it is *remote*. But in point of *extent* it is immense; and in point of *fecundity*, pregnant to a degree that baffles calculation.[16]

The passage shows that Bentham interpreted the calculus as committing one to overriding the fact that the production of bad consequences is very unlikely when, *if* they occur, they are disastrous. It represents a strategy which opts for taking certain losses when not to do so runs some risk, perhaps a very small one, of utter disaster. This may or may not be good strategy (could one get out of bed in the morning if one took it seriously?), but it clearly *is* a strategy to apply to prospective acts. It is a strategy which tells one to give great weight to possible bad consequences which are extensive in effect, even if not likely.[17]

If this line of reasoning were systematically employed, it would provide strong ground for conformity to useful social rules in general; for whenever acts of a kind are generally practiced in accord with accepted rules, and social benefits are thereby produced, failure on the part of an individual to conform creates some, perhaps minute, risk that the benefits will be interrupted or reduced. Though the likelihood is very small, the *extent* of any such danger is great (or *can* be great), so that there would be a presumption in favor of compliance. Of course, not all social rules will fare equally well, and the particulars of the case may give reason for scoring the case differently. As an instance, with a *non*useful rule, noncompliance may be called for. Still, it would seem that the consistent appeal to such considerations would give a strong role to such facts as that a given act is required by an accepted social rule, or that an act that one is contemplating is one which, if adopted by everyone, would result in very bad consequences. At the very least, Bentham's argument provides grounds for taking accepted rules as guides for conduct in practical affairs.

I shall next examine certain features of John Austin's moral theory. In his *Autobiography*, Mill cited Austin as the one figure among those who had influenced his early thinking with whom he most agreed after his break from narrowly conceived utilitarianism;[18] in a letter to John Pringle Nichol, he wrote that "Of all the views I have yet seen taken of the utilitarian scheme, I like Austin's best, in his book on *The Province of Jurisprudence Determined.*"[19]

Austin was led into his discussion of utilitarian moral theory by consideration of the Divine Law. His purpose was to distinguish civil or positive law and its duties from those of a religious nature. Of God's laws, some are *revealed* (known through Scripture, etc.) while others are *unrevealed* and known by the "light of nature." Our guides to the unrevealed law are God's goodness, together with the principle of utility. Knowing that God is good, we know his purpose is that his creatures be happy:

> Some human actions forward that benevolent purpose, or their tendencies are beneficent or useful. Other human actions are adverse to that purpose, or their tendencies are mischievous or pernicious. The former, as promoting his purpose, God has enjoined. The latter, as opposed to his purpose, God has forbidden. He has given us the faculty of observing; of remembering; of reasoning: and, by duly applying those faculties, we may collect the tendencies of our actions. Knowing the tendencies of our actions, and knowing his benevolent purpose, we know his tacit commands.[20]

Of great interest is Austin's definition of the *tendency* of an act. He explicitly defined the notion, and proposed a *test* for determining the tendency of an act:

> Now the *tendency* of a human action (as its tendency is thus understood) is the whole of its tendency: the sum of its probable consequences, in so far as they are important or material: the sum of its remote and collateral, as

well as of its direct consequences, in so far as any of its consequences may influence the general happiness.

Trying to collect its tendency (as its tendency is thus understood), we must not consider the action as if it were *single* and *insulated*, but must look at the *class* of actions to which it belongs. The probable *specific* consequences of doing that single act, of forbearing from that single act, or of omitting that single act, are not the objects of the inquiry. The question to be solved is this:—If acts of the *class* were *generally* done, or *generally* forborne or omitted, what would be the probable effect on the general happiness or good?[21]

The definition is clearly act-consequentialist; the test calls for rule-consequentialist-type considerations. The definition is almost exactly the conception of "tendency" for which I have argued. I want now to show that the reason for taking such considerations into account as the test of tendencies fits (at least roughly) the "strategy" conception of the role of rules.

There are at least two places in which Austin explained the reasons for considering an act as part of a class, and the explanations augment one another. First, he offered an explanation of why "most" of God's commands "are general or universal." The main reason given is that unless there is a motive to forbear from wrong acts, they will be frequently committed. Acts which, considered separately, have consequences different from most members of their class, will, then, be performed if there is some immediate gain to be gotten. Thus:

If the act were permitted or tolerated in the rare and anomalous case, the motives to forbear in the others would be weakened or destroyed. In the hurry and tumult of action, it is hard to distinguish justly.[22]

It is important to note that this sort of argument in fact appeals to a (somewhat hidden) tendency of the particular act itself, namely, its tendency to weaken one's resolve in important cases. The argument also appeals to the fact that it is difficult in practice to make the relevant distinctions. Rules are adopted to keep such tendencies from being realized by virtue of our faulty judgment. Austin argued that because God is good he desires the general happiness, and because he knows of human weakness and the tendencies of acts, he enjoins or forbids acts "by a *rule* which probably is inflexible."[23]

Austin used this point that God mostly commands classes of acts to deal with the objection to utilitarianism that it is impossible to accurately calculate the consequences of acts. Austin's response was that it is not necessary to calculate in every case. In virtue of the fact that testing the tendency of an act calls for consideration of the effects of acts of that class, we are led to conclude that acts are enjoined or forbidden by general rules. We need only appeal, then, to rules which we regularly employ in daily practice. Austin's gloss on this is important:

> To preface each act or forbearance by a conjecture and comparison of consequences, were clearly superfluous and mischievous. It were clearly superfluous, inasmuch as the result of that process would be embodied in a known *rule*. It were clearly mischievous, inasmuch as the *true* result would be expressed by that rule, whilst the process would probably be faulty, if it were done on the spur of the occasion. . . . To review on the spur of the occasion a host of particulars, and to obtain from those particulars a conclusion applicable to the case, were a process too slow and uncertain to meet the exigencies of our lives.[24]

Here, it is made clear that we cannot judge accurately in particular cases, and, therefore, the appeal to rules *will*, in fact, more often give us the true result. The rules that we come to adopt were described by Austin as having been arrived at by past observation and calculation "of which they are handy abridgments." The use of such rules, then, even as "inflexible" standards, represents the choice of a strategy for maximizing the performance of acts which themselves have predominantly good tendencies.

It must be added that with all of Austin's talk of "inflexible" rules, and of God commanding classes of acts "without exception," he did not believe that appeal to rules can resolve all moral difficulties. Early in his discussion of the "test" for the tendency of an act, he said that it is "true generally (for the proposition admits of exceptions)" that the true tendency of an act is determined by asking what would happen if it were generally done or not done.[25] In a later discussion, he wrote:

> There certainly are cases (of comparatively rare occurrence) wherein the specific considerations balance or outweigh the general: cases which (in the language of Bacon) are "immersed in matter": cases perplexed with peculiarities from which it were dangerous to abstract them; and to which our attention would be directed, if we were true to our presiding principle. It were mischievous to depart from a rule which regarded any of these cases; since every departure from a rule tends to weaken its authority. But so important were the *specific* consequences which would follow our resolves, that the evil of observing the rule might surpass the evil of breaking it. Looking at the reasons from which we had inferred the rule, it were absurd to think it inflexible. We should, therefore, dismiss the *rule*; resort directly to the *principle* upon which our rules were fashioned; and calculate *specific* consequences to the best of our knowledge and ability.[26]

To round out this historical survey and prelude, I shall examine the views of James Mill. A better understanding of John Mill's theory can be obtained by the comparison, especially as John Mill reprinted parts of his father's views in the footnotes to his edition of the *Analysis of the Phenomenon of the Human Mind*, and commented on them. In addition, Mill wrote in his *Autobiography* that on rereading his father's work "I found little in the opinions it contains but what I think just."[27]

For the most part, James Mill's ethical theory has come down to us in his *A Fragment on Mackintosh*. Much of the ethical theory presented consists of a defense of Bentham's views, which had been criticized by Mackintosh. James Mill agreed with Bentham that the morality of an act does not depend on the motive or desire from which it is done. Good acts may be done from bad motives, and bad acts are sometimes performed with excellent motives. On the other hand, the morality of an act *is* dependent on the intention with which it is done, that is, on the consequences which the agent foresees it will produce. The question of the rightness or wrongness of the act is, then, a question of the consequences, and judging the morality of an act is a matter of calculating the consequences:

> If a man intends by any act a greater amount of evil than of good, his intention is bad; his conduct criminal. Morality, or immorality, therefore, depends, by the very nature of the case, upon calculation. A man cannot act without intention, without looking at the consequences of his act. . . . An intention therefore is good or bad, according as the good or evil consequences of the act predominate.[28]

This account is clearly in the act-consequentialist tradition. It corresponds almost exactly to Bentham's view. Mill's discussion of these points was part of his consideration of the orthodox objection to utilitarianism that it requires constant (and impossible) calculation. To this, Mill replied that often it is so obvious what the consequences of an act are likely to be that "no man can be at a loss about it." Moreover, most cases fall under general rules which are universally accepted "so that a man acts upon them, as pre-established decisions, which he may trust." In these cases, it is not necessary to calculate "because the calculation has already been made."[29]

This view is not explicitly a version of the strategy conception of moral rules, but it is not inconsistent with it. Where there is little question about the specific consequences of the act, we go by those alone; otherwise, moral rules can be the basis of action insofar as they represent the results of previous calculation. Moral rules are introduced (partly) to deal with situations of uncertainty. James Mill's theory, then, shares some of the most important features of the strategy conception. Other important aspects of his theory were brought out in later discussion by Mill of exceptions to moral rules.

Mackintosh had complained that utilitarians make unwarranted exceptions to moral rules, rather than insisting on rigid rule-observance. Mill responded that one of the most important moral rules is the rule of making exceptions. The necessity arises when moral rules conflict, and such cases "are so numerous as to cover a large portion of the field of human action."[30] Mill's discussion then turned to an account of the origin and development of moral rules and their exceptions. Moral rules, he held, arose from the fact that people have discovered that some of the acts of others are agreeable and others disagreeable. There arose an interest in repetition of the agreeable acts, and prevention of the others. Thus, moral rules, which prescribe "what is to be done . . . in a class of instances," presuppose a classification of acts into those in which people have an interest in the repetition, and those in which there is an interest in preventing. Of those society has an interest in, there are some in which the actor has an identical interest. In this sort of case, "they were pretty sure to take place, without any stimulus from without."[31] Such acts (which may be termed "self-regarding"), are neither moral nor immoral. Thus, not every act falls within the injunctions of morality.

On the other hand, with respect to acts which society has an interest in, but in which the agent has none, or a contrary interest, there is need of a motive "artificially created," to secure them. The devices society has to create such motives are moral approbation and disapprobation, which are employed for the purpose of getting people to perform the useful acts and to abstain from the harmful ones. This leads to the first moral rule: "Moral acts are to be performed; immoral acts are to be abstained from."[32] The rule, of course, is predicated on the classification: moral acts versus immoral acts. Further classifications are required, however. For example, there are acts it is useful for the community to control through law, and those which should be subject to individual control by the moral sentiments. Moreover, within the class of moral acts can be distinguished further subclasses—just acts, beneficent acts, brave acts, prudent acts, temperate acts.[33]

Exceptions to moral rules arise because of the possibility of conflicts. In some cases, entire classes are excepted in favor of others. Thus, in cases of conflict, rules of justice take precedence over duties of benevolence. The reason given is that much more of "what is good for mankind depends upon the performance of just, than of generous actions."[34] Rules of exception, then, are an important part of morality. Mackintosh had held that if exceptions are allowed, soon the benefits of the rule will be lost. Mill's response was a classic piece of satire:

> Let us try his proposition by a case or two. The habit of walking is impaired by occasional sitting, or standing. The habit of talking is impaired by occasional silence. The habit of speaking English is impaired by learning to speak French. Is he not a strange companion, who could make a general proposition, involving these particular ones? Did Sir James really imagine that a man could not have in perfection the habit of performing generous acts, and yet make all the exceptions which the superior calls of justice required?[35]

James Mill's final conclusion was that in many cases we can merely appeal to rules. We readily perceive the act as one "of such ordinary and frequent occurrence" as to fall into a class governed by a rule. In the other cases, "a direct estimate of the good of the particular act is inevitable; and the man acts immorally who acts without making it."[36]

John Stuart Mill reproduced portions of his father's earlier book in the footnotes to his edition of James Mill's *Analysis of the Phenomena of the Human Mind*. His commentary on the quoted passages is of some interest, and we shall return to it later in this chapter. I shall next consider the role of rules in J. S. Mill's own moral theory.

JOHN STUART MILL ON MORAL RULES

DIFFERENCES WITH EARLIER "BENTHAMISM"

In his *Autobiography*, Mill chronicled his near mental breakdown at the end of 1826.[37] As a result of this crisis, his opinions underwent change. He came to see the views of Bentham and his father on human nature as too narrow, and he saw that their conception of what is required for human happiness was inadequate. Two significant points of difference emerged. First, he came to see that pursuing secondary ends, rather than directly seeking happiness itself, is often the best way of achieving happiness:

> I never, indeed, wavered in the conviction that happiness is the test of all rules of conduct, and the end of life. But I now thought that this end was only to be attained by not making it the direct end. Those only are happy (I thought) who have their minds fixed on some object other than their own happiness; on the happiness of others, on the improvement of man-

kind, even on some art or pursuit, followed not as a means, but as itself an ideal end. Aiming thus at something else, they find happiness by the way. The enjoyments of life (such was now my theory) are sufficient to make it a pleasant thing, when they are taken *en passant*, without being made a principal object. . . . This theory now became the basis of my philosophy of life. And I still hold to it as the best theory for all those who have but a moderate degree of sensibility and of capacity for enjoyment, that is, for the great majority of mankind.[38]

In the last chapter, we saw how Mill explained the psychological mechanisms whereby people can desire things for their own sakes, and how these contribute to happiness though the agent does not explicitly *aim* at happiness directly. Now, Mill clearly did *not* think there is anything necessary about this relationship between secondary ends and happiness. He described it as a fact about most people most of the time, especially those with "moderate" sensibilities and capacities of enjoyment.

The second point of importance was Mill's recognition of the need for the "internal culture" of the individual. Happiness, he came to see, requires the balancing of a person's faculties, including one's emotional sensibilities. Thus, music and poetry, which had been dismissed by the utilitarians, were now seen as important "instruments of human culture."

Similar themes were echoed in his essays on Bentham. The first point was expressed in the form of a criticism of Bentham's mode of applying the Principle of Utility:

> While . . . we entirely agree with Bentham in his principle, we do not hold with him that all right thinking on the details of morals depends on its express assertion. We think utility, or happiness, much too complex and indefinite an end to be sought except through the medium of various secondary ends, concerning which there may be, and often is, agreement among persons who differ in their ultimate standard; and about which there does in fact prevail a much greater unanimity among thinking persons, than might be supposed from their diametrical divergence on the great questions of moral metaphysics. As mankind are much more nearly of one nature, than of one opinion about their own nature, they are more easily brought to agree in their intermediate principles, *vera illa et media axiomata*, as Bacon says, than in their first principles: and the attempt to make the bearings of actions upon the ultimate end more evident than they can be made by referring them to the intermediate ends, and to estimate their value by a direct reference to human happiness, generally terminates in attaching most importance, not to those effects which are really the

greatest, but to those which can most easily be pointed to and individually identified. Those who adopt utility as a standard can seldom apply it truly except through the secondary principles; those who reject it, generally do no more than erect those secondary principles into first principles. It is when two or more of the secondary principles conflict, that a direct appeal to some first principle becomes necessary; and then commences the practical importance of the utilitarian controversy; which is, in other respects, a question of arrangement and logical subordination rather than of practice; important principally in a purely scientific point of view, for the sake of the systematic unity and coherency of ethical philosophy.[39]

This passage reiterates the theme of the need for appeal to secondary ends, and thus the need to utilize secondary principles in seeking human happiness. But, it is important to see that this passage does not commit Mill to rule-consequentialism. First, Mill urged the adoption of secondary principles because judging acts directly by their consequences is usually mistaken; we usually focus attention "not to those effects which really are the greatest." It is our *judgment*, though, which is mistaken; the attempt to *apply* the Principle of Utility directly is usually wrong because it will give the wrong result. However, the right result would seem to be what the Principle of Utility would tell us to do, applied directly, but *correctly*. It is because use of secondary principles will yield *that* result that their adoption is urged. This is consistent with holding that the true test of the rightness or wrongness of the act *is* the Principle of Utility.

Second, some commentators have supposed that Mill, in this and other passages, took the view that *only* if secondary principles conflict is an appeal to the first principle justified. The passage does not say this (nor does any other passage I can find in Mill). The present passage asserts, first, that direct applications of the principle of utility are *seldom* correct, and, second, that it is *necessary* to apply the principle directly when secondary principles conflict. From these points, it certainly does not follow that it is *wrong* to apply the first principle directly in other circumstances. Indeed, the grounds given which justify appeal to secondary principles would seem to imply that if we *are* able to calculate correctly, direct appeal to the principle of utility is *right*.

Finally, we should note that the passage explicitly recognizes the distinction between the test of morality from a theoretical point of view, and the test which must be employed in practice. All of these points are consistent with the "strategy" conception of moral rules; all are in fact integral to it.

In his earlier essay, "Remarks on Bentham's Philosophy," Mill had a further criticism of Bentham's mode of applying the Principle of Utility which has some importance. He pointed out that Bentham had given greater attention to matters of law rather than to morals, and he thought this "fortunate":

> . . . for the mode in which he understood and applied the principle of Utility, appears to me far more conducive to the attainment of true and valuable results in the former, than in the latter of these two branches of inquiry. The recognition of happiness as the only thing desirable in itself, and of the production of the state of things most favourable to happiness as the only rational end both of morals and policy, by no means necessarily leads to the doctrine of expediency as professed by Paley; the ethical canon which judges of the morality of an act or a class of actions, solely by the probable *consequences* of that particular kind of act, supposing it to be generally practised. This is a very small part indeed of what a more enlarged understanding of the "greatest-happiness principle" would require us to take into the account. A certain kind of action, as for example, theft, or lying, would, if commonly practised, occasion certain evil consequences to society: but those evil consequences are far from constituting the entire moral bearings of the vices of theft or lying. We shall have a very imperfect view of the relation of those practices to the general happiness, if we suppose them to exist singly, and insulated.[40]

The account of why Bentham's view was too narrow is drawn from Mill's conception of the relationship of action with states of character:

> All acts suppose certain dispositions, and habits of mind and heart, which may be in themselves states of enjoyment or of wretchedness, and which must be fruitful in *other* consequences, besides those particular acts. No person can be a thief or a liar without being much else: and if our moral judgments and feelings with respect to a person convicted of either vice, were grounded solely upon the pernicious tendency of thieving and of lying, they would be partial and incomplete; many considerations would be omitted, which are at least equally "germane to the matter;" many which, by leaving them out of our general views, we may indeed teach ourselves a habit of overlooking, but which it is impossible for any of us not to be influenced by, in particular cases, in proportion as they are forced upon our attention.[41]

He went on to accuse Bentham of confusing the Principle of Utility with "the principle of specific consequences," which judges every act solely by "the consequences to which that very action, if practised generally, would itself lead."[42] Mill's complaint here is not that Bentham failed to consider that an act generally done has consequences which must be considered. Indeed, he attributes to Bentham (as well as Paley, who explicitly adopted this formulation) the view that an act is to be judged by its consequences "supposing it to be generally practised." Mill's objection was that Bentham did not sufficiently consider the relation of the act to a general state of character which may be manifested in a *variety* of specific behavioral forms. In other words, Bentham was solely concerned with outward behavior, without considering the general states of mind of which actions are evidence, and from which they spring. It was in this context that Mill went on to criticize Bentham's view of human nature, and his account of human motivation. Insofar as states of character involve development of certain emotional sensibilities rather than others, and stimulation of certain desires rather than others, Mill's complaint in his "Remarks" echoes his point in the *Autobiography* that the development of emotional sensibilities is important for happiness.

In chapter 1, we saw that Mill thought of character development as a matter of coming to have relatively fixed dispositions of belief, feeling, and action. Moreover, coming to have relatively fixed dispositions is, to a great extent, a matter of inculcating habits. Insofar as such development is furthered by rule-observance, the desirability of fostering certain states of character will provide reason for urging the following of rules. Consequently, there *is* a connection between Mill's insistence on considering the relation of an act to character, and his view of moral rules. I shall discuss this relationship in greater detail later. In criticizing his teachers, however, Mill was *not* accusing them of overlooking moral rules or considerations based on the general practice of an act; rather, it was their overlooking of an important property a particular act can have—its relation to other acts by virtue of its connection with states of character.

THE SCIENCE OF ETHOLOGY AND MORAL RULES

The argument for a rule-consequence interpretation of Mill is largely based on passages in *Utilitarianism*. In fact, however, Mill's most extensive outline of his views on rules in morality is to be found in his *Logic*, and in the earlier work "On the Definition of Political Economy."[43] In the *Logic*, he explained his conception of a science of human behavior, based on the laws of human character. This science he termed "ethology." He then discussed the relationship between such a science and the practical concerns of people—the Art of Life, in general, and the art of morality, in particular. Though there is much of intrinsic interest in Mill's discussion, what is of importance for present purposes is the role which he gave to moral rules.[44]

According to Mill, the most general branch of social science is psychology, which seeks to establish the general laws of the mind, that is, the laws "according to which one mental state succeeds another—is caused by, or at least is caused to follow another."[45] Principally, these are the laws of association, and they are ascertained by observation and experience. Ideally, social science would have further laws sufficient to explain and predict what anyone will do (or think or feel) under any given circumstances; but human actions are the resultant not merely of the particular circumstances, which are extremely variable, but also spring from the person's character and dispositions. Character and dispositions are themselves the effects of the person's entire past history and experience, which are, in various respects, unique. Since the causal factors involved in an action are never precisely like others, exact laws are not possible.

Nonetheless, to some extent, actions are the result of "circumstances and qualities which are common to all mankind," thus it is possible to arrive at approximate generalizations. Ethology is a science which seeks to discover the laws of the formation of character, and which seeks to trace the operations of the mind in complex combinations of circumstances. Mill described ethology as bearing a deductive relationship to psychology; its laws are obtained by "deducing" them from the laws of psychology by considering what kinds of character will result from various circumstances. Observation and experience can yield only empirical connections which can be used to verify the laws of ethology, or to suggest them, but the laws of ethology cannot be obtained by observation and experience alone. What is observed must be explainable in terms of the operation of the laws of the mind. The laws of ethology are therefore the "middle principles, the *axiomata media*" of psychology.

Though ethology cannot predict anyone's character at a given future time with complete accuracy, for practical purposes it is usually not necessary to have perfect accuracy:

> There may be great power of influencing phenomena, with a very imperfect knowledge of the causes by which they are in any given instance determined. It is enough that we know that certain means have a *tendency* to produce a given effect, and that others have a tendency to frustrate it.

When the circumstances of an individual or of a nation are in any considerable degree under our control, we may, by our knowledge of tendencies, be enabled to shape those circumstances in a manner much more favourable to the ends we desire, than the shape which they would of themselves assume. This is the limit of our power; but within this limit the power is a most important one.[46]

The laws of ethology, to *be* genuine scientific laws, must be framed as attributing tendencies to events or things. For his notion of tendencies, Mill relied heavily on the science of mechanics. A body subjected to a force moves in the direction of the force. At least this is the case if that force is not impeded or counteracted by another. Since this latter event is always possible, we cannot say it is a law of mechanics that a body subjected to a force moves in the direction of the force. Mill's resolution of the difficulty is important for our purposes:

> To accommodate the expression of the law to the real phenomena, we must say, not that the object moves, but that it *tends* to move, in the direction and with the velocity specified. We might, indeed, guard our expression in a different mode, by saying that the body moves in that manner unless prevented, or except in so far as prevented, by some counteracting cause.[47]

Mill goes on to explain that even if the movement of the body *is* counteracted, it still *tends* to move in the direction predicted. Supposing the forces to be equal and opposite, the body will remain in the same place. Its position, however, is a resultant of two forces really operating. The language of "tendencies" is used to express these facts, according to Mill: "All laws of causation, in consequence of their liability to be counteracted, require to be stated in words affirmative of tendencies only, and not of actual results."[48]

It is important to note that though the laws which report tendencies apply to classes of cases, the laws ascribe tendencies to each member of the class. The statement that a body subjected to a force tends to move in the direction of the force ascribes such a tendency to each and every body subjected to a force. It asserts that each such body will move in such a direction unless the force applied is counteracted. Mill's use of "tendency," then, is such that individual things, events, actions, can be said to have tendencies. As we may suppose that whatever tendencies an act has can be expressed as a result of other properties the act has, we can say that for Mill, to say an act A has a tendency to produce an effect X means that A possesses some property y such that, in virtue of y, A

will produce *x* unless some event takes place to counteract that result.[49] Thus, every kind act has some tendency to produce good, since each has a property—being pleasing to recipients of the kindness and to observers—in virtue of which it will produce good unless a further event takes place which overcomes that effect. This use of "tendency" is not at all in accord with Urmson's claim that only classes of acts can exhibit a tendency. Moreover, Mill used this conception in a systematic way; for example, it is also to be found in his discussion of the nature of social science in his essay "On the Definition of Political Economy"[50] to which we shall turn later.

What must next be examined is the relationship of social science to morality. According to Mill, morality is expressed in the imperative mood—the characteristic of an "art," rather than a science. Every art declares some end as desirable, and affirms the attainment of the end as desirable. It then turns to science to discover the means by which the end is attained:

> The only one of the premises, therefore, which Art supplies, is the original major premise, which asserts that the attainment of the given end is desirable. Science then lends to Art the proposition (obtained by a series of inductions or of deductions) that the performance of certain actions will attain the end. From these premises Art concludes that the performance of these actions is desirable, and finding it also practicable, converts the theorem into a rule or precept.[51]

All things considered, science can only provide an imperfect guide to art. As we seldom know all relevant future circumstances, and rarely possess complete knowledge of the causes which can counteract tendencies, we cannot predict with perfect accuracy the effects of acts. Still, perfect knowledge is not necessary "for the wise conduct of the affairs of society." Thus, "we must seek our objects by means which may perhaps be defeated, and take precautions against dangers which possibly may never be realized."[52] This is the language of the "strategy" conception of rules. It suggests that social science can give us information on the basis of which we can frame rules for maximizing in our action the achievement of the ultimate end. Measured against the criterion of the attainment of the end, the rules of an act must always be imperfect. Not only is social science imperfect in its results, but if *all* counteracting causes are included in our practical rules, "the rules would be too cumbrous to be apprehended and remembered by ordinary capacities, on the common occasions of life."[53] Thus, Mill is led to his ultimate judgment as to the role of rules in a practical art:

By a wise practitioner, therefore, rules of conduct will only be considered as provisional. Being made for the most numerous cases, or for those of most ordinary occurrence, they point out the manner in which it will be least perilous to act, where time or means do not exist for analysing the actual circumstances of the case, or where we cannot trust our judgment in estimating them. But they do not at all supersede the propriety of going through (when circumstances permit) the scientific process requisite for framing a rule from the data of the particular case before us. At the same time, the common rule may very properly serve as an admonition that a certain mode of action has been found by ourselves and others to be well adapted to the cases of most common occurrence; so that if it be unsuitable to the case in hand, the reason of its being so will be likely to arise from some unusual circumstance.[54]

As I shall attempt to show, this was basically Mill's position in *Utilitarianism* also. But he expressed this view in other places as well. In his review of Carlyle's *History of the French Revolution*, he wrote:

It should be understood that general principles are not intended to dispense with thinking and examining, but to help us to think and examine. When the object itself is out of our reach, and we cannot examine into it, we must follow general principles, because, by doing so, we are not so likely to go wrong, and almost certain not to go so far wrong, as if we floated on the boundless ocean of mere conjecture; but when we are not driven to guess, when we have means and appliances for observing, general principles are nothing more or other than helps towards a better use of those means and appliances.[55]

It would appear so far that Mill's theory was an act-consequentialist theory that places great stress on the use of rules as a device for maximizing the achievement of good. Mill's view, it would seem, consists in, or implies, each of the following propositions: (a) if it were always possible for us to calculate perfectly the consequences of acts, the principle of utility would always itself be the direct test of our actions; thus (b) the rightness or wrongness of acts from the standpoint of the *theory* is a direct function of the consequences of acts; (c) whenever we *can* calculate fully, and can have no reason to distrust our judgment, it is proper to do so; (d) in *practice*, we may have to appeal to moral rules in trying to maximize happiness; (e) when we resort to moral rules, these are not the *ultimate* tests of the rightness of conduct, since any judgment based solely on the applicability of the rules is always revisable when further knowledge is present concerning the consequences of acts.

That the above constitutes an essentially act-consequence theory can hardly be doubted. There are, however, grounds to doubt that Mill was committed to proposition (b). It is here relevant to cite the ending paragraph of his "Definition of Political Economy," as well as his letter to John Venn. In the "Political Economy," he wrote:

It is only in art, as distinguished from science, that we can with propriety speak of exceptions. Art, the immediate end of which is practice, has nothing to do with causes, except as the means of bringing about effects. However heterogeneous the causes, it carries the effects of them all into one single reckoning, and according as the sum-total is *plus* or *minus*, according as it falls above or below a certain line, Art says, Do this, or Abstain from doing it. The exception does not run by insensible degrees into the rule, like what are called exceptions in science. In a question of practice it frequently happens that a certain thing is either fit to be done, or fit to be altogether abstained from, there being no medium. If, in the majority of cases, it is fit to be done, that is made the rule. When a case subsequently occurs in which the thing ought not to be done, an entirely new leaf is turned over; the rule is now done with, and dismissed: a new train of ideas is introduced, between which and those involved in the rule there is a broad line of demarcation; as broad and *tranchant* as the difference between Ay and No. Very possibly, between the last case which comes within the rule and the first of the exception, there is only the difference of a shade: but that shade probably makes the whole interval between acting in one way and in a totally different one. We may, therefore, in talking of art, unobjectionably speak of the *rule* and the *exception*; meaning by the rule, the cases in which there exists a preponderance, however slight, of inducements for acting in a particular way: and by the exception, the cases in which the preponderance is on the contrary side.[56]

In a letter Mill wrote to the English logician John Venn in 1872, he said:

I agree with you that the right way of testing actions by their consequences, is to test them by the natural consequences of the particular action, and not by those which would follow if every one did the same. But, for the most part, the consideration of what would happen if every one did the same, is the only means we have of discovering the tendency of the act in the particular case. In your example from Austria, it is only by considering what would happen if everybody evaded his share of taxation, that we perceive the mischievous tendency of anybody's doing so. And that this mischievous tendency overbalances (unless in very extreme cases) the private good obtained by the breach of a moral rule, is obvious if we take into consideration the importance, to the general good, of the feeling of security, or certainty; which is impaired, not only by every known actual violation of good rules, but by the belief that such violations ever occur.[57]

This is, of course, far from settling the matter. Though I believe I have shown that there is ample evidence in Mill's explicit statements supporting an act-consequence interpretation, there remain difficulties which must be addressed. Indeed, the letter to Venn suggests one of these: why *should* consideration of what would happen if everyone evaded taxes reveal anything concerning the consequences of individual cases? It is important to address this issue since it will permit exploring a very important aspect of Mill's theory, and because it will make somewhat easier the handling of one of the most recalcitrant passages in *Utilitarianism*.

In his critical article, "Whewell on Moral Philosophy," Mill made a point which is essential to understanding the role of appeal to rules. The contemporary philosopher Whewell had raised the familiar criticism against utilitarianism that it is not possible to calculate accurately the consequences of acts. In a case of telling a lie, for example, it is impossible to assess the bad consequences of shaking human confidence in people's statements; likewise it is difficult to tell the effect of this "solitary act upon the whole scheme of human action and habit," when compared to the immediate pleasure it will bring.

Mill retorted that not only is the bad effect small in relation to the happiness of all mankind, so is the pleasure to be obtained. To weigh these consequences, he argued, we must not only look at the individual case:

> We must look at them multiplied, and in large masses. The portion of the tendencies of an action which belong to it not individually, but as a violation of a general rule, are as certain and as calculable as any other consequences; only they must be examined not in the individual case, but in classes of cases.[58]

Apparently, Whewell had anticipated this response; Mill quotes him to the effect that the utilitarian cannot guarantee that the evil of violating the rule overbalances the pleasure of the violation. The violator need not deny the general usefulness of the rule; he merely says "I do not intend that this one act should be drawn into consequence." Mill's response is crucial:

> But it does not depend on him whether or not it shall be drawn into consequence. If one person may break through the rule on his own

judgment, the same liberty cannot be refused to others; and since no one could rely on the rule's being observed, the rule would cease to exist. If a hundred infringements would produce all the mischief implied in the abrogation of the rule, a hundredth part of that mischief must be debited to each one of the infringements, though we may not be able to trace it home individually. And this hundredth part will generally far outweigh any good expected to arise from the individual act. We say generally, not universally; for the admission of exceptions to rules is a necessity equally felt in all systems of morality. . . . That the moralities arising from the special circumstances of the action may be so important as to overrule those arising from the class of acts to which it belongs, perhaps to take it out of the category of virtues into that of crimes, or *vice versa*, is a liability common to all ethical systems.[59]

What is confusing, of course, is Whewell's reference to the actor's intention, a point of complete irrelevance in this context. (What *would* be relevant are facts which show the unlikelihood of that bad consequence in the actual, particular case.) Nonetheless, three points emerge from Mill's response: (1) it is intended to deal with "establishing moral rules," or else with established rules, otherwise the mention of what would happen if one person could break the rule on his own judgment would make no sense; (2) the evil resulting from the breakdown of a rule is a causal consequence of *all* of its instances, and causal responsibility is to be distributed over all instances; and (3) sometimes, circumstances do, in fact, warrant violation of the rule.

These points are all compatible with the form of utilitarianism I have been attributing to Mill. Moreover, Mill's analysis of the causal process that would be involved if nonobservance were often enough practiced is also applicable to the causal consequences of acts of rule observance; that is, the good consequences resulting from classes of such acts must be distributed over all the acts in assessing causal responsibility.[60] Thus, all cases of observance of a useful rule have *some* definite utility; each such act has *some* tendency to produce good. This tendency is revealed in considering its relation to other similar acts and the consequences of the performance of the class.

This treatment also sheds light on a passage in *Utilitarianism* which has seemed to some commentators to be absolutely inconsistent with an act-consequence interpretation. Mill wrote:

In the case of abstinences indeed—of things which people forbear to do, from moral considerations, though the consequences in the particular case might be beneficial—it would be unworthy of an intelligent agent not to be consciously aware that the action is of a class which, if practised generally, would be generally injurious, and that this is the ground of the obligation to abstain from it.[61]

At first glance, the passage appears to make the rightness or wrongness of certain kinds of acts dependent solely on the fact that a general practice is useful, while the act itself may not be. The passage must be placed in context, however. Mill was responding to the objection that utilitarianism requires too much of people, in that it is too difficult to always act from a desire to promote the general welfare. Mill responded by pointing out: (1) utilitarianism does not require always acting from the desire to promote the general welfare; it provides a standard of action, not an injunction to act from any given motive; (2) most of the time our actions affect only a few people and, for the most part, we need only be concerned with those limited interests; and (3) people *are* capable of showing a concern for the general welfare as is evidenced by the sorts of abstinences spoken of. The concluding lines of the passage, which follow immediately the passage quoted above, read: "The amount of regard for the public interest implied in this recognition, is no greater than is demanded by every system of morals; for they all enjoin to abstain from whatever is manifestly pernicious to society."[62] Mill's claim, then, was that such acts *are* harmful, that this is the ground of their wrongness, and that people are capable of recognizing this and acting from such considerations. These acts bear a relation to other, similar acts; as this is the case, they have tendencies toward evil (if not abstained from) which are most clearly seen by considering the consequences of general nonperformance. The very point of the discussion in the "Whewell" article is that consideration of the effects of the general practice is a means of calculating the rule-related tendencies *of the particular act*. The same view is stated in the letter to Venn quoted earlier. (Consideration of the general practice "is the only means we have of discovering the tendency of the act in the particular case.") Thus, reference to the consequences of the general practice *was*, in Mill's view, a way of assessing the consequences of the particular act. When he said that this consideration was the ground of the obligation, he did not suppose himself to be referring to something independent of the consequences of the particular act.

There is one final point to be made about such cases, but which must await the next chapter for full development. The sorts of cases Mill has in mind are ones in which some good is produced by a general practice. While the good may be produced with less than complete compliance, lacking agreed procedures for exceptions, those who comply will normally expect the others to do likewise. Moreover, it would be useful to society (or the group) to enforce general compliance, as each beneficiary of the practice would have an interest in the performances of the others. To fail to comply would thus endanger the interests of the others. Further, I shall try to show in the next chapter that the participants could all claim a right to the compliance of the others. To the extent that violations of rights endanger security and justice, each such case will have a set of bad consequences. Assuming this argument can be worked out, and plausibly attributed to Mill, it would provide further ground for thinking that *each* case of compliance *does* contribute to the general welfare, and that this is the ground of its obligation. This is perfectly compatible with holding that the ground is revealed only by viewing the act *as* part of (or, as a violation of) a general practice.

MORAL "JUDGES," HABITS, AND CHARACTER FORMATION

It is of some importance to stress that the version of act-consequentialism I have, to this point, found in Mill is consistent with further claims, yet to be explored. First, there is the view that the assessment of *persons* or personal *character* is to be made on some basis other than the consequences of the acts they perform (e.g., on the basis of the motives from which they are disposed to act). Second, the theory can also consistently hold that right action need not be motivated in particular cases by an immediate, occurrent concern for (or thought of) the general happiness. Thus, as we have seen in Mill's case, a utilitarian theorist can hold that right action may be motivated by concern for ends other than the general welfare, and may even assert that education and popular morality should encourage a concern for a variety of ends. Of course, an act-consequence theorist can consistently make such claims *only if* he or she believes that by the cultivation of a multiplicity of concerns, human beings being what they are, the likelihood of achieving the ultimate end is thereby increased.

In this section, I wish to explore the consequences these views have (all were maintained by Mill) for his conception of the role of moral rules. This is of some importance, since there are passages that must be understood in light of his emphasis on character development.

Several of these passages occur in the *Logic* itself. At the beginning of his discussion of the Art of Morality, he wrote:

In all branches of practical business, there are cases in which individuals are bound to conform their practice to a pre-established rule, while there are others in which it is part of their task to find or construct the rule by which they are to govern their conduct. The first, for example, is the case of a judge, under a definite written code. The judge is not called upon to determine what course would be intrinsically the most advisable in the particular case in hand, but only within what rule of law it falls; what the legislature has ordained to be done in the kind of case, and must therefore be presumed to have intended in the individual case. . . . The legislator is bound to take into consideration the reasons or grounds of the maxim; the judge has nothing to do with those of the law, except so far as a consideration of them may throw light upon the intention of the law-maker, where his words have left it doubtful. To the judge, the rule, once positively ascertained, is final.[63]

At the end of the first and second editions of the *Logic*, he concluded:

Without entering into the disputed questions respecting the foundation of morality, we may consider as a conclusion following alike from all systems of ethics, that, in a certain description of cases at least, morality consists in the simple observance of a rule.[64]

Though these passages do not support a general position of rule-utilitarianism, they do suggest that in many situations our duties are strictly determined by moral rules. In those kinds of cases, it would seem, we are reduced to moral "judges," having to follow rules inflexibly.

It will not suffice to explain these as anomalous passages which Mill disowned. Though it is true the last passage was replaced in the third and subsequent editions, the initial distinction between legislator and judge was not withdrawn.[65] Rather, there are three points I want to stress: (a) Mill did *not* think judges do, or ought to, merely apply rules without a concern for consequences; (b) the point he was making is entirely consistent with the "strategy" conception of rules; and (c) Mill seems to have had in mind primarily the rules of justice, which, he argued, advance utility partly by relatively strict observance, though even these may be violated in specific cases.

In his essay, "Bentham," Mill discussed the work of English judges, and Bentham's role in undoing the worst consequences of their influence on English law. Bentham's great achievement had been to point out the various absurdities in the existing state of legal theory, and to provide needed clarification. The confused state of theory, Mill held, was due largely to the work of judges. He described their role as follows:

> In the English law, as in the Roman before it, the adaptations of barbarous laws to the growth of civilized society were made chiefly by stealth. They were generally made by the courts of justice, who could not help reading the new wants of mankind in the cases between man and man which came before them; but who, having no authority to make new laws for those new wants, were obliged to do the work covertly, and evade the jealousy and opposition of an ignorant, prejudiced, and for the most part brutal and tyrannical legislature. Some of the most necessary of these improvements, such as the giving force of law to trusts, and the breaking up of entails, were effected in actual opposition to the strongly-declared will of Parliament, whose clumsy hands, no match for the astuteness of judges, could not, after repeated trials, manage to make any law which the judges could not find a trick for rendering inoperative.[66]

According to Mill, this process left the law a "thing of shreds and patches," upon which English lawyers constructed their philosophy of law. The result was the confused state of legal theory. It is clear from this discussion, however, that Mill was well aware that judges do not merely apply existing rules to actual cases without considering human welfare. Moreover, there can be little question that Mill thought the work of the judges to be justified and an important contribution to happiness. Could there be any doubt that Mill regarded "the adaptation of barbarous laws to the growth of civilized society" as anything but beneficial? To be sure, he was in the midst of citing an important bad consequence—the absurd state of legal theory—but there is no suggestion that society would have been better off if they had left that work undone. Thus, it is not plausible that Mill was proposing that a model of the judge as never going beyond existing, recognized rules be *the* model for moral "judges."

On the strategy conception of rules, he could consistently do so, however, for, if one seeks to maximize the doing of good acts, it is at least logically possible that the risks of misjudgment in particular cases are so great that the rules ought to be rigidly followed. Indeed, the final passage from the earlier editions makes a point very like this:

> The cases in question are those in which, although any rule which can be formed is probably (as we remarked on maxims of policy) more or less imperfectly adapted to a portion of the cases which it comprises, there is still a necessity that some rule, of a nature simple enough to be easily

understood and remembered, should not only be laid down for guidance, but universally observed, in order that the various persons concerned may know what they have to expect: the inconvenience of uncertainty on their part being a greater evil than that which may possibly arise, in a minority of cases from the imperfect adaptation of the rule to those cases.

Such, for example, is the rule of veracity; that of not infringing the legal rights of others; and so forth: concerning which it is obvious that although many cases exist in which a deviation from the rule would in the particular case produce more good than evil, it is necessary for general security, either that the rules should be inflexibly observed, or that the license of deviating from them, if such be ever permitted, should be confined to definite classes of cases, and of a very peculiar and extreme nature.[67]

This is, of course, the language of the strategy conception, and it does recognize that an appropriate strategy would permit exceptions in extreme cases. Finally, I would point out that Mill's examples refer to principles requiring truth-telling, and, in general, observance of the rules of justice. I shall discuss the latter in the chapter which follows; however, he did assert in *Utilitarianism* that even with rules of justice particular cases can occur in which they may properly be violated.[68] The same point is made there concerning the duty to tell the truth. Indeed, his attitude is rather graphically shown in a piece he wrote with George Grote:

> Philosophy commands that in dealing with any particular case, the whole of the circumstances, without exception, should be taken into view, essential as well as accidental: and if a man wilfully overlooks the latter, when they are pregnant with mischievous consequences, he cannot discharge himself from moral responsibility by pleading that he had the general rule in his favour. What should we say to a physician, who communicated an agonising piece of family intelligence, in reply to the inquiry of our sick friend, at a moment when the slightest aggravation of malady threatened to place him beyond all hope of recovery? In a case like this, surely there is no man of common sense or virtue, who would think for a moment of sheltering himself under the inexorable law of veracity, and refusing to entertain any thought of the irreparable specific mischief on the other side.[69]

It is of further interest to examine the passage which takes the place of the paragraph about judges and legislators in later editions of the *Logic*.

> I do not mean to assert that the promotion of happiness should be itself the end of all actions, or even of all rules of action. It is the justification,

and ought to be the controller, of all ends, but is not itself the sole end. There are many virtuous actions, and even virtuous modes of action (though the cases are, I think, less frequent than is often supposed) by which happiness in the particular instance is sacrificed, more pain being produced than pleasure. But conduct of which this can be truly asserted, admits of justification only because it can be shown that on the whole more happiness will exist in the world, if feelings are cultivated which will make people, in certain cases, regardless of happiness. I fully admit that this is true: that the cultivation of an ideal nobleness of will and conduct, should be to individual human beings an end, to which the specific pursuit either of their own happiness or of that of others (except so far as included in that idea) should, in any case of conflict, give way. But I hold that the very question, what constitutes this elevation of character, is itself to be decided by a reference to happiness as the standard. The character itself should be, to the individual, a paramount end, simply because the existence of this ideal nobleness of character, or of a near approach to it, in any abundance, would go further than all things else towards making human life happy; both in the comparatively humble sense, of pleasure and freedom from pain, and in the higher meaning, of rendering life, not what it now is almost universally, puerile and insignificant—but such as human beings with highly developed faculties can care to have.[70]

In this paragraph, Mill endorsed the position we have mentioned earlier, that character development must not be ignored in moral reasoning. Moreover, he makes the point that a concern for happiness need not be the motive of every action. Indeed, he held that states of character ought to be cultivated in which people do *not* act from a concern with happiness, and in which considerations of happiness can be overridden. Combined with his earlier remarks about moral "judges," one might be led to conclude that certain rules of morality should be inculcated in people in so inflexible a way that appeal to the rule is sufficient to override the utilities of particular cases. Of course, we have seen that Mill did *not* intend so inflexible a treatment of rules. Also, such a treatment could be consistently maintained even by an act-utilitarian as part of a strategy for maximizing the doing of right acts. Indeed, the quotation bears the strategy interpretation. A state of character that leaves people without a regard for happiness is desirable *only* if its inculcation would promote happiness more than alternatives.

Now, there *is* a connection between character and its maintenance and rules. A state of character consists in general dispositions to feel and act in certain ways, which are evidenced in matter-of-course performances which are more or less habitual, rather than the result of careful calculation. A person is of a truly generous character only if he or she spontaneously helps others, rather than doing so after lengthy deliberation. As we have seen in chapters 2 and 3, such states are inculcated through the association of the appropriate acts or displays of feelings with pleasure. Thus, if a particular act which evinces a given character has bad consequences, but is of a class which usually has good consequences, the association of the idea of acts of that kind with pleasure is weakened. Therefore, where it is important to have acts of that kind generally performed, and thus to maintain the general readiness to perform them, it will be useful to encourage relatively inflexible adherence to rules.

According to Mill's associationist psychology, when we have become "habituated" in certain ways so as to have fixed dispositions, we come to desire many and various things for their own sakes. His point here, then, is that such states of desiring should be encouraged if they will be useful. Of course, this means that there will be cases in which we will lose some utility. The risk in such a strategy must be balanced, however, by considering that systematically trying to get those values itself involves a risk, namely, that of weakening useful character patterns. As Mill put it in his discussion of the formation of policy judgments: "We must seek our objects by means which may perhaps be defeated, and take precautions against dangers which possibly may never be realized."[71]

We have seen, of course, that Mill did *not* hold rules or the requirements of character to be absolutely inflexible. It is one thing to hold the following proposition:

1. We know that in acting generally from a given state of character we shall sometimes lose utilities.

It is quite another to hold that:

2. In performing the present act (by acting from our habitual, predisposed stance), we shall knowingly produce more harm than good.

Mill sanctioned encouraging states of character of which (1) will be true. But he did *not* sanction acting in a certain way when (2) can be confidently asserted. His treatments of truth-telling and of the rules of justice show this. I know of no passage in the Mill corpus in which he asserted that we must stick to a rule even when we know for sure that, all things considered (including effects on character, on general practices, etc.), more utility would be produced by violating the rule.

Moral Rules in *Utilitarianism*

We can now turn to Mill's best known work in moral philosophy, upon which so much in the traditional interpretations of his theories has been based—the series of essays collected under the title *Utilitarianism*. Though it is not the case that Mill's discussion is a careful, closely argued statement of his position (it is more polemical and aimed at a general audience), there is no reason to reject it as Mill's most complete statement of his moral theory.[72] Moreover, the chapter on justice is indispensable to an understanding of Mill's moral and political theories, and is referred to in a number of other writings by Mill as definitive of his views on several points.

I shall begin by discussing passages prior to Mill's introduction of the "punishability" criterion of wrongness that some commentators have thought require a rule-consequence interpretation. I will argue that, taken alone, these passages are consistent with the act-consequence theory of right and wrong and that the "proportionality" criterion presents.

It has been held by D. P. Dryer that Mill committed himself to a rule-consequence view of morality early in the essay, since, in the introductory section, Mill wrote that "the morality of an individual action is not a question of direct perception, but of the application of a law to an individual case." (Urmson also cites this passage as showing Mill's theory to be rule-consequentialist.)[73] The quotation has, however, been taken out of context. Somewhat more fully, it reads:

> The intuitive, no less than what may be termed the inductive, school of ethics, insists on the necessity of general laws. They both agree that the morality of an individual action is not a question of direct perception, but of the application of a law to an individual case. They recognise also, to a great extent, the same moral laws; . . .[74]

In this passage Mill is only making the point that his main opponents—the intuitionists—are in agreement with him that moral judgments necessarily involve appeal to some moral principle or principles. The intuitionists did not think we can intuit in each particular case, without reference to rules, the rightness or wrongness of an act. Intuition was not held to be a capacity like the capacity to discriminate the color red; one does not "see" in an action its rightness without a standard, in the way one does just "see" the redness of a chair without a further test of redness. The entire passage from which the quotation is taken makes the point that some one ultimate principle is needed for resolving conflicts among rules, but nowhere in this section does Mill commit himself to the role of the various secondary principles.[75] Thus, taken by itself it provides no evidence whatever for a rule-consequence interpretation.

Urmson also cites a passage in which Mill responded to the familiar criticism of utilitarianism that it is not possible to take time to predict accurately the consequences of acts. Mill held that the past experience of people has provided knowledge of the consequences of acts, which have come down as practical maxims on which we can usually rely. He added that "philosophers" can certainly improve on these. Then follows a statement which Urmson quotes:

> But to consider the rules of morality as improvable, is one thing; to pass over the intermediate generalizations entirely, and endeavour to test each individual action directly by the first principle, is another. It is a strange notion that the acknowledgement of a first principle is inconsistent with the admission of secondary ones. . . . Men really ought to leave off talking a kind of nonsense on this subject, which they would neither talk nor listen to on other matters of practical concernment.[76]

Given all that has already been said, there is no difficulty in reconciling this quotation with even an act-utilitarian interpretation. Moreover, in citing these sentences, Urmson has passed over analogies Mill employed which are extremely injurious to his interpretation, as has been pointed out by J. D. Mabbot.[77] The first analogy is that of telling a traveler his destination. This does not, he wrote, "forbid the use of landmarks and direction-posts on the way." Clearly, these are devices or tools for achieving a goal; but it is surely irrational to stick to the tool in circumstances where one has reason to think one will not be able to achieve the goal by using it in a particular circumstance, or when one has a better tool available.

The second analogy is that of sailors using the Nautical Almanac, a navigational aid. When they go to sea, they will tend to rely on its ready-made calculations, and make no attempt to calculate at sea. Calculation is foregone because one has reason to think that the Almanac is more trustworthy than one's own calculations are likely to be. If, however, one had reason to distrust them, and calculation at the time were feasible, it would be foolish to go blindly by the Almanac. Today, of course, we have computers to do this work in a highly reliable way. In the early days of the Almanac, however, the calculations were done by hand and the Almanac had numerous errors. Sailors who stuck by it rigidly sometimes, in fact, were shipwrecked.[78] The example shows quite clearly that goal-oriented behavior cannot justify the knowing pursuit of intermediate goals which frustrate the achievement of the ultimate goal.

Urmson also cites the conclusion of Mill's discussion of the use of rules:

> We must remember that only in these cases of conflict between secondary principles is it requisite that first principles should be appealed to. There is no case of moral obligation in which some secondary principle is not involved; and if only one, there can seldom be any real doubt which one it is, in the mind of any person by whom the principle itself is recognised.[79]

Urmson concludes from this quote that it shows that moral rules were not for Mill merely rules of thumb, "but an essential part of moral reasoning." With that conclusion I do not wish to quarrel. Indeed, I have attempted to show that even an act-utilitarian can consistently assign such a role to moral rules in practical life. I do not think, however, that the passage Urmson cites supports a rule-consequence interpretation.

First, the passage says that an appeal to the Principle of Utility is *requisite* only in cases of conflict of rules; it does not say such an appeal is *inappropriate* in other cases. Second, it is one thing to hold that, for practical purposes, one must rely on convenient rules, and quite another thing to hold that what justifies an act is that it is in accord with a rule. The passage does not make the latter claim; moreover, it would seem inconsistent with Mill's statement earlier in the very same paragraph:

> It is not the fault of any creed, but of the complicated nature of human affairs, that rules of conduct cannot be so framed as to require no exceptions, and that hardly any kind of action can safely be laid down as either always obligatory or always condemnable. There is no ethical creed which does not temper the rigidity of its laws, by giving a certain latitude, under the moral responsibility of the agent, for accommodation to peculiarities of circumstances.[80]

It is true that Mill wrote that there is no case of moral obligation in which there is not a secondary principle which applies. Furthermore, after a discussion of the meaning of the Greatest Happiness Principle, he indicated that morality may be "defined" as "the rules and precepts for human conduct, by the observance of which an existence such as has been described might be, to the greatest extent possible, secured to all mankind," and, he added, to all sentient creatures.[81] I do not think these were slips on Mill's part. There is reason to think he believed that wherever there is a moral obligation, some secondary principle can be cited which applies, and that every moral system requires such rules. There is also reason to think that this is due to the fact that he believed that in cases where issues of morality arise, the possibility of good consequences presents *some* reason for doing the act, while the possibility of bad consequences presents some reason against, and that those reasons can be expressed in the form of some secondary principle. Consider the following passage in the review written with George Grote:

> To admit the balance of consequences as a test of right and wrong, necessarily implies the possibility of exceptions to any derivative rule of morality which may be deduced from that test. If evil will arise in any specific case from our telling truth, we are forbidden by a law of morality from doing that evil: we are forbidden by another law of morality from telling falsehood. Here then are two laws of morality in conflict, and we cannot satisfy both of them. What is to be done but to resort to the primary test of all right and wrong, and to make a specific calculation of the good or evil consequences, as fully and impartially as we can? The evil of departing from a well-known and salutary rule is indeed one momentous item on that side of the account; but to treat it as equal to infinity, and as necessarily superseding the measurement of any finite quantities of evil on the opposite side, appears to us to be most fatal of all mistakes in ethical theory.[82]

Apparently, the secondary rule here is something like "avoid producing evil" (where "evil" is defined as "bad consequences"); but *this* rule will apply whenever an act is likely to have consequences detrimental to the general welfare. No doubt, he thought that in practice one would invoke so general a rule only in special cases; or, perhaps, he thought that morality contains something like his father's "rule of exceptions," to be invoked in special circumstances. The important point to stress here is that the admitted necessity of conceiving one's practical morality as constituted by moral rules does not establish that those principles are definitive of rightness and wrongness at the theoretical level.

By far, the most significant passage in *Utilitarianism*, with respect to his ultimate criterion of right and wrong, is the passage in which Mill introduced the "punishability" criterion. This passage, together with points he made about the "art of life" and its relation to morality, have generated a number of interpretations that attribute a rule-consequence moral theory to Mill. I think that all of these are open to objection, either on philosophical or textual grounds. I have no better account to offer, however, as I am convinced that Mill did not adequately develop this aspect of his views. I do not believe that the discussion undercuts my claim that Mill's view on moral rules was essentially that of the strategy conception, and that he held that *in practice*, we should stick to useful rules except in exceptional circumstances or where the rules conflict, when we must decide what is morally required by appeal to the consequences of the act.

THE "ART OF LIFE," WRONGNESS AND PUNISHMENT, AND MORALITY

It is useful to start with Mill's statement of the "proportionality" criterion of rightness and wrongness:

> The creed which accepts as the foundation of morals, Utility, or the Greatest Happiness Principle, holds that actions are right in proportion as they tend to promote happiness, wrong as they tend to produce the reverse of happiness. By happiness is intended pleasure, and the absence of pain; by unhappiness, pain, and the privation of pleasure. To give a clear view of the moral standard set up by the theory, much more requires to be said; in particular, what things it includes in the ideas of pain and pleasure; and to what extent this is left an open question. But these supplementary explanations do not affect the theory of life on which this theory of morality is grounded—namely, that pleasure, and freedom from pain, are the only things desirable as ends; and that all desirable things (which are as numerous in the utilitarian as in any other scheme) are desirable either for the pleasure inherent in themselves, or as means to the promotion of pleasure and the prevention of pain.[83]

This passage has usually been taken as Mill's statement of an act-utilitarian theory. We should note, however, that there is sufficient imprecision in Mill's formulation of the criterion of right and wrong to question this attribution. For example, the criterion *could* be read as a *noncomparative* principle, certifying an act as right so long as the consequences of the act are predominantly good, independent of consideration of alternative acts. Moreover, it could be read as asserting only that the rightness or wrongness of an act is fully determined by the act's contribution to happiness (or the reverse). That formulation leaves it open that there could be some acts (e.g., self-regarding ones) that are neither right nor wrong, since it says only that *if* an act is right or *if* it is wrong, this is due solely to its relation to the production of happiness.

Professor D. G. Brown has proposed an interpretation of Mill's theory of morality that has far-reaching implications for the interpretation of the passage.[84] It has been adopted by other commentators, and used in conjunction with the "punishability" criterion to develop rule-consequence versions of Mill's theory.

Brown's concern was with Mill's understanding of the Principle of Utility. After surveying Mill's various formulations of the principle, he points out that most commonly it was described as setting out the "ultimate end of action," or what is "desirable as an end," or what is "good in itself." Brown concludes that the Principle of Utility, as Mill understood it, is best formulated as: Happiness is the only thing desirable as an end. Put this way, it is solely a principle of the good; it says nothing about right or wrong, and asserts nothing about moral duties. Thus, it need not be taken as prescribing any conduct as *morally* incumbent on anyone.

The most obvious difficulty Brown's claim faces is the passage in which Mill set out the "proportionality" criterion of right and wrong. Brown concedes that the passage *does* set out a criterion of right and wrong; but the passage could be read as saying that those who hold this moral doctrine also hold the Principle of Utility, which is the foundation of morality, as well as of prudence and aesthetics. Thus, the principle is not to be identified with the moral criterion which it supports:

> Once we grasp this possibility, we can see what to do with the rest of the passage. In what sense is Utility the foundation of morals? In the sense which is at once explained, namely that the theory of morality is grounded on a theory of life; and the Principle of Utility is the theory of life. But that theory is actually stated. So we learn from this passage after all what the Principle of Utility is. It is the principle that pleasure and freedom from pain are the only things desirable as ends.[85]

David Lyons, who accepts Brown's view, notes that in concluding the "proof" of the principle, Mill wrote: "If so, happiness is the sole end of human action, and the promotion of it the test by which to judge of all human conduct; from whence it necessarily follows that it must be the criterion of morality, since a part is included in the whole."

By itself, this analysis does not entail that Mill was committed to a rule-consequence theory. The "proportionality" criterion *does* state a principle of conduct, and Brown regards it as a moral principle, and he holds further that Mill is properly to be interpreted as an act-utilitarian.[86] Accordingly, even if we think of the Principle of Utility as simply a statement about the good, this would not resolve the question of the role of act-consequence/rule-consequence considerations in the determination of morally right conduct. Brown's interpretation has, however, been used in conjunction with the passage that introduces the punishability criterion to develop a complex, rule-consequence theory that, in several variations, has been attributed to Mill. As the most extensive development of this view is given in a series of important papers by David Lyons, I will summarize the chief elements of his approach.

Lyons's interpretation relies heavily on the following passage:

> The above is, I think, a true account, as far as it goes, of the origin and progressive growth of the idea of justice. But we must observe, that it contains, as yet, nothing to distinguish that obligation from moral obligation in general. For the truth is, that the idea of penal sanction, which is the essence of law, enters not only into the conception of injustice, but into that of any kind of wrong. We do not call anything wrong, unless we mean to imply that a person ought to be punished in some way or other for doing it; if not by law, by the opinion of his fellow creatures; if not by opinion, by the reproaches of his own conscience. This seems the real turning point of the distinction between morality and simple expediency. It is a part of the notion of Duty in every one of its forms, that a person may rightfully be compelled to fulfill it. Duty is a thing which may be *exacted* from a person, as one exacts a debt. Unless we think that it might be exacted from him, we do not call it his duty. Reasons of prudence, or the interest of other people, may militate against actually exacting it; but the person himself, it is clearly understood, would not be entitled to complain. There are other things, on the contrary, which we wish that people should do, which we like or admire them for doing, perhaps dislike or despise them for not doing, but yet admit that they are not bound to do; it is not a case of moral obligation; we do not blame them, that is, we do not think that they are proper objects of punishment. How we come by these ideas of deserving and not deserving punishment, will appear, perhaps, in the sequel; but I think there is no doubt that this distinction lies at the bottom of the notions of right and wrong; that we call any conduct wrong, or employ, instead, some other term of dislike or disparagement, according as we think that the person ought, or ought not, to be punished for it; and we say that it would be right to do so and so, or merely that it would be desirable and laudable, according as we would wish to see the person whom it concerns, compelled, or only persuaded and exhorted, to act in that manner.[87]

Some commentators have thought it to be obvious that the passage requires a rule-consequence interpretation. However, the passage makes no reference to moral rules; its point is simply that the idea of punishment is involved in the ideas of right and wrong. Perhaps the reference to law has misled the commentators. Still, there is no stress in the passage on an analogy between kinds of *rules*; the stress is on the connection between duty and punishment.

Lyons's treatment of the passage is elaborate.[88] First, he holds that the passage gives as Mill's analysis of the *meaning* of "ought" statements that they entail liability to punishment. In Lyons's view, Mill was making a *conceptual* connection between moral obligation and punishment. Mill did not limit the notion of punishment to legal sanctions, but included informal social sanctions such as verbal reprovals of conduct, as well as personal pangs of conscience. In addition, Lyons points out, Mill connected retrospective sanctions of these types with the notion of "coercion" or "compulsion," which operate prospectively, as discouragements to conduct. "But," according to Lyons, "the latter can be rational only if attached to clear guidelines laid down for future behavior."[89] In another place, he holds that such a conception "presupposes that sanctions are attached to general rules."[90]

Informal social rules, according to Lyons, can be conceived as coercive commands, which are matters of common knowledge, widely diffused in the community. Personal values require a more subtle treatment, as these need not be the same as those shared community-wide, though, of course, whatever values are community values must be held widely as personal values. For there to *be* social rules, the corresponding values must be internalized by members of the group. Thus, anything which was a reason for a social rule would be a reason for instilling internal sanctions (of guilt, conscience, etc.) in people. Lyons summarizes the theory as follows:

> These considerations suggest that Mill had a view like this. To call an act wrong is to imply that guilt feelings, and perhaps other sanctions, would be warranted against it. But sanctions assume coercive rules. *To show an act wrong, therefore, is to show that a coercive rule against it would be justified.* The justification of a coercive social rule establishes a moral obligation, breach of which is wrong.[91]

According to Lyons's reconstruction, when Mill distinguished morality from mere expediency, he was implying that not every act which fails to maximize utility is wrong. If an act is not liable to punishment, it is not wrong. Furthermore, this view makes the Principle of Utility the most general principle of the "Art of Life," and the test of all departments of that art including prudence and morality. Though every act may be judged by its standard, and ranked accordingly, it sets down no *moral* duties; it is not a moral principle. The Principle of Utility on this view is a test of moral rules; when applied directly to acts, it can give a basis for an ordering in terms of values, or preference, without thereby implying anything about the rightness or wrongness of the acts. The rightness or wrongness of acts depends on the obligations we have, as defined by those moral rules that meet the test of utility. Put somewhat differently: though every act may indeed be subjected to the test of utility, the resulting judgment will not be a *moral* judgment; moral judgments involve a reference to secondary rules.

Lyons does not appear to argue that Mill's statements *require* his interpretation at all crucial points. He appears to be presenting a rational reconstruction of a position which is compatible with much that Mill had to say, and which avoids important problems with which Mill otherwise may be saddled. A fair assessment cannot, therefore, be given merely by looking at Mill's texts. Nonetheless, it is not beside the point to inquire as to how well it holds up with the texts, as well as to what philosophical problems it may pose.

Central to Lyons's interpretation is his connecting moral obligation with liability to punishment, and that, in turn, to moral rules. The argument seems to me sound, but may not yield as strong a conclusion as Lyons draws. Since punishment is meant to operate in part prospectively, that is, to discourage unwanted conduct, it must be attached to guidelines that make it clear that behavior like the behavior being punished will also be punished. So far, this argument is unexceptional. Unless *classes* of acts are aimed at by punishment or coercion, there can be no future utility from either. We are not guided in any way if sanctions are not tied to a property of an act which it shares with others, and which would make the others undesirable also; but the "proportionality" criterion of right and wrong can be understood as setting out a rule in *this* sense, hence, the argument does not establish that reference to the secondary rules is part of the very notion of moral right and wrong. There are, of course, Mill's references to morality as consisting of rules, and so on, that have been explored earlier. These do lend considerable weight to Lyons's account as an accurate reconstruction of Mill's theory. On the other hand, the earlier discussion also showed that such an interpretation is not *required*.

Indeed, a number of commentators who have been influenced by the sorts of considerations Lyons urges for his account of Mill's moral theory have taken divergent positions with respect to the role of rule-consequence considerations in the theoretical determination of right and wrong. David Copp, for example, seeks to accommodate *both* the proportionality criterion and the punishability criterion in his account, without making essential reference to rules.[92] On his account, that the act produce the best consequences among alternatives is a necessary condition for its rightness, while a further necessary condition is that the good would be best served if the failure to do the act were accompanied by (at least) the internal sanction of regret. If both conditions hold, the act is right. If at least one condition does not hold, the act is wrong.

D. P. Dryer also seeks to combine the proportionality criterion and the punishability criterion, *along with* essential reference to moral rules.[93] Dryer accepts the bifurcation between expediency and morality, and holds that, for Mill, a statement that something ought to be done does not entail that it would be wrong not to do it. "Wrongness"-statements do entail "ought not"-statements, however. Thus, to say an act is wrong entails (for Mill, on this view) that it ought not to be done, and this entails that it would not be most productive of happiness if done. The full account of wrongness says that it is wrong not to do an act if, and only if, the act would be most productive of happiness, and it falls under a rule that would be most productive of happiness if generally observed, and if the act is of a kind that it would be most productive of happiness to punish someone for not doing.

John Gray also accepts the separation of expediency and morality, as well as the claim that the Principle of Utility is not a moral principle, and determines no moral duties. On the one hand, his view, as is the case with Lyons's, gives no role to the proportionality criterion of right and wrong, and, hence, no role to the consequences of the act itself in determining rightness and wrongness. On the other hand, he gives no essential role to rule-consequence considerations. On his view, the necessary and sufficient conditions for an act to be wrong is that punishing it has the best consequences.[94]

Finally, L. W. Sumner, in a searching analysis of the problem, has concluded that Lyons's interpretation, though not definitive, makes the best reading of Mill's work, which, he believes, is unlikely to yield some one authoritative interpretation.[95] Even he, however, believes that Lyons's account requires amendment. He takes it that the coercive rules to which Lyons refers must only be expedient, that is, produce more good than bad. In his view, this requirement should be that a rule be maximally expedient, that is, that it be the best alternative.

All of the proposed renditions of Mill's theory are open to textual or philosophical objections. I shall indicate some of these. I want only to maintain that the use of rules in practical decision-making that I have traced in Mill's work, and that of his teachers, survives any plausible rendering of his moral theory.

Both Copp and Dryer require of an act that it be "maximally expedient" for it to be right, but, as Sumner correctly points out, acceptance of the distinction between dutiful acts and supererogatory ones is inconsistent with this requirement.[96] The act which has the best consequences may be supererogatory, while something short of that may be required as a duty. One can rightly be castigated for not doing *something* to help a drowning person (say, throw a rope, or hold out a stick, and so on), but it is not a duty that one risk one's own life by jumping into the rushing river in a rescue attempt.[97] This does seem to be something Mill would agree to, and it does call into question the condition that a right act be the one alternative most productive of good. (Sumner has two other arguments—that Mill nowhere actually gives the condition as part of the criterion of rightness, and that Mill allows that *violating* one's duty may be more productive of good consequences. However, Mill's statement of the proportionality criterion of rightness and wrongness seems to belie the first claim; and, I shall contend, there is reason to think the second is false.)

Similarly, the interpretations that make reference to rules definitive of rightness and wrongness are problematic. Some of these problems stem from Mill's never having clarified the sorts of rules he had in mind when referring to "moral rules." It cannot be the case, for example, that what is right or wrong was thought by Mill to be strictly determined by any proposed set of rules. (It is clear enough that he did not identify moral obligation with any *actual* set, as Urmson comes close to suggesting.) We have already given reason to think Mill would regard any proposed set as imperfect, subject to improvement, and as requiring discretion "under the moral responsibility of the agent, for accomodation to peculiarities of circumstances."[98] Lyons suggests Mill had an "ideal" set of rules in mind (the rules that "would be justified"), but given the various passages in Mill's work cited earlier, it is not clear that Mill would not insist that the ideal set should include a rule such as "avoid doing evil," or "calculate consequences when time and circumstances make accurate calculation possible." Nothing in Mill's discussions of the role of moral rules forbids regarding such a second-order rule as the latter as part of one's "morality," and the arguments he gives for *having* rules would make it rational to include such. Since (as we saw earlier) Mill seemed to believe that, in ordinary cases, moral rules give the same results about a particular case as would perfectly correct

calculation, and a "rule of exceptions" would permit or require calculation in the exceptional cases, the rule-consequence interpretation would
collapse into an act-consequence interpretation (at least in the sense of
being extensionally equivalent to it).

There are further problems. Lyons's account has the rightness or
wrongness of acts determined by rules which *would* be productive of
utility *if* generally adopted. But this would entail that we could have
duties based on rules that have *not* been adopted or recognized. In *all* the
cases where Mill discussed appeal to hypothetical consequences, it was
always a case of supposing a *recognized* rule (e.g., that of truth-telling) to
be generally *dis*regarded. I know of no case where he supposed that
appeal to hypothetical consequences of hypothetical rules is appropriate. Moreover, that position has unpalatable results, for, in cases
where an ideal rule is *not* practiced, adherence to it can prove disastrous.
Disarmament would be an ideal rule for nations, but so long as some
powerful nations do not adopt the rule, it is not obvious that any others
have a duty to abide by it. Furthermore, this is a difficulty with the
theory that Lyons acknowledges.[99]

Both Gray and Sumner hold that justificatory appeal is to an entire
moral code which includes social rules, customs, and socialization
practices that involve the development of appropriate dispositions,
attitudes, and sentiments that will produce desirable behavior. Gray
holds that the more elaborate conception debars reference to rules as
essential to the conception of rightness, whereas Sumner holds that his
view continues to take reference to rules as essential, though their utility
must be measured in terms of their relation to the utility of the general
moral code.[100] I shall not discuss these futher views in detail; in each
case, I find much that is unclear in the conception, and I believe they
prove open to objections similar to the ones made of Lyons's account.
Moreover, the view of Sumner and Gray (and Dryer, as well) share
features with Lyons's interpretation that seem to me not fully support-
able by Mill's texts.

The features that these interpretations have in common that seem to
me problematic are threefold. First, they all accept D. G. Brown's
argument that the Principle of Utility was conceived by Mill as *solely* a
statement about what is ultimately desirable, and, hence, as not a moral
principle about what should be done. Direct appeal to the Principle of
Utility, then, will always be an appeal to the good, not to what it is
morally right or wrong to do. Second, these accounts all identify

morality with duty-required acts and thus accept the punishability criterion as Mill's definitive criterion of moral right and wrong. Third, the interpretations of these commentators do concede that Mill's theory permits violations of moral rules (or character requirements, etc.) in exceptional circumstances, and that appeal may be made directly to the Principle of Utility. In these cases, action is determined by appeal to the consequences of the act itself.[101] However, since the Principle of Utility is not a moral principle, it does not yield *moral* judgments. Therefore, these are cases of overriding moral duties by appeal to what is best or expedient. In one place, Sumner describes these as cases where the moral rules conflict, hence, where there is a conflict of duties:

> It is in such cases that he permits direct appeal to the principle of utility, i.e. to what is best. Mill certainly appears to assume that in such cases each of the items in conflict is a genuine obligation or duty; in resorting to the principle of utility we do not descover which alternative is *really* our duty, but rather which duty it would be better to perform in the case in question.[102]

A bit later, he writes:

> Where following a rule will lead to catastrophe our course as utilitarians is clear: we should prefer what is best to what is right. Long-range social utility is maximized not by establishing a set of absolute rules, nor by allowing unlimited utilitarian exceptions, but rather by enforcing rules which are the best we can devise and making exceptions only in extreme circumstances. An ideal utilitarian arrangement consists of a society with a well-designed set of conventional moral rules whose members feel guilty about breaking those rules even when they know they are justified in doing so.[103]

Perhaps some such set of views is the most defensible version of utilitarianism. There is, however, evidence that Mill did not clearly embrace these last three positions.

In the first place, there are reasons to think that Mill did not systematically distinguish statements about what ends are desirable from assertions as to what one should do. He seems, in fact, to have believed that fixing on the ultimate end just *is* determining what should be done. In discussing first principles of conduct, he wrote indifferently of them as fulfilling *both* functions. In the *Logic* (where much of the argument must rest), he described a first principle of conduct as enunciating "the object aimed at" and affirming it desirable, but in the same paragraph, he characterized such principles as "enjoining" or "recommending" that something "should be." He also said of first principles that they are expressed with the language of "ought" or "should be."[104] In *Utilitarianism*, he wrote of happiness as "the directive rule of human conduct,"[105] and in the "Remarks on Bentham's Philosophy," he discussed the Principle of Utility in a way that seems to treat it as both stating an end as desirable, and as entailing a criterion of right and wrong action.[106] Furthermore, there are elements of his psychological views that would help explain his willingness to deduce statements about what should be done from ones about what is desirable. We should recall that in discussing his father's conception of desire, Mill held that desire is not a merely passive state, but is the "initiatory stage of volition" (see chapter 1, "Will"). Desire involves the incipient stirrings toward action. Moreover, Mill appears to have regarded value judgments as expressive of the speaker's sentiments (see chapter 1, "The Moral Sentiments," and chapter 2, "The Traditional Difficulties"). To judge an end as desirable, then, will involve having a desire for it, which will include having a tendency or urge toward achieving it. Thus, a favorable judgment concerning an ultimate end will also be expressive of an inclination toward achieving it, hence, will express what is expressed by a "should" judgment. In at least simple sorts of cases—when a person judges an end desirable for himself or herself— the judgment will carry with it the judgment that the end should be pursued. Supposing such an analysis applies to the judgment that the general happiness is the only thing desirable as an end, then anyone who accepts it as enunciating the ultimate end will also accept a practical directive to the effect that one should seek to promote it. The value judgment and the principle of conduct would be two aspects of one principle. This still does not make the Principle of Utility a moral principle; one could still hold that appeal to it does not ever imply that any act is morally right or wrong. Still, the correctness of this analysis would call into question the bifurcation of judgments of goodness and of practice.

The various interpreters of Mill that we have considered (with the exception of John Gray), recognize that Mill did explicitly say that there are special occasions when appeal must be made directly to the Principle of Utility. These are cases, in their analyses, of appealing to the good as overriding morality. The above considerations are grounds for thinking this to be an oversimplification at best; but what is the evidence that in these cases, the direct appeal to utility is not an appeal to morality? Recall Sumner's claim that in the special cases (e.g., where moral rules conflict), each of the duties is a "genuine" duty and remains so whatever is decided, and that, in referring to the Principle of Utility "we do not discover which alternative is *really* our duty." But I know of no textual support for these claims, and there is textual evidence to show that it was Mill's view that in the exceptional cases (sometimes described as involving conflicts of rules, sometimes as created by peculiarities of the circumstances), the direct appeal to utility determines *what it is right or wrong to do.* Indeed, I have cited some of the relevant passages earlier. In the essay on *Whewell* he had said that the special circumstances of the case may take an act out of the class "of virtues into that of crimes."[107] In *Utilitarianism*, he had written that every moral theory gives "a certain latitude, *under the moral responsibility* of the agent, for accommodation to peculiarities of circumstances."[108] In the essay on "Taylor's Statesman," written with Grote, it is said that the "whole of the circumstances" of the particular case must be considered, and if a person ignores some of the circumstances "when they are pregnant with mischievous consequences, *he cannot discharge himself from moral responsibility* by pleading that he had the general rule in his favor."[109] These statements surely are meant to imply that the direct appeal to the Principle of Utility in these cases determines what it is right or wrong to do. In "Thornton on Labour and its Claims" (where he continued to accept the punishability criterion as picking out duties), he described the "maxims of right and wrong" as "*prima facie* presumptions" that what they will require will be productive of good.[110] Thus, I do not think it can be sustained that Mill viewed the exceptional cases as ones where expediency overrides morality.

This survey of competing interpretations of Mill's theory of right and wrong does, I believe, warrant two conclusions. The first is the chief point of this chapter: that Mill maintained that in practical moral reasoning, the determination of what should be done should be made by relatively strict adherence to moral rules, except in exceptional cases, where the right action must be determined by appeal to the consequences of the act (including any rule-related tendencies *it* may have). This position could be held on *either* an act-consequence or rule-consequence conception of right action (or on a view that combines them). On the one hand, so long as an act-consequence theory can pick out the relevant class of duty-assessable acts, it could hold that within that class, right acts are made such by their consequences. On the other hand, so long as a rule-consequence account of right action allows for there to be a moral "rule of exceptions," it can yield the same result. Either sort of theory could be argued for with the "strategy" considerations to which Mill consistently appealed.

The second conclusion our survey yields is that Mill did not sufficiently resolve the conflict between the "proportionality" criterion of right action and the "punishability" criterion. This is not, I should add, because he came in later life to reject the first, which was a vestige of the Benthamism that he altered in a number of ways. It may well be that the punishability conception came to dominate his thinking. But, the part of *Utilitarianism* in which the punishability account was given—the chapter on justice—was written *before* the part of the book in which the proportionality standard was set out. Moreover, the essay on *Hamilton* shows *both* criteria at work, though written well after *Utilitarianism*,[111] and a similar duality is displayed in "Thornton on Labour," also written after *Utilitarianism*.[112]

I shall close this chapter by showing that the interpretive problem is aggravated by features of Mill's account of the punishability criterion of right and wrong that commentators have tended to overlook. First, Mill's statements explaining it do not always coincide. Second, his chief explanation—consistently referred to by him as his most complete account—is unclear in important ways, and does not yield an unequivocal reading.

One of Mill's earliest statements of the criterion was in a letter to William George Ward. He had indicated (as I argued in chapter 1) that a moral judgment expresses a moral sentiment, and he held that a "true moral feeling" is "a feeling of pain in the fact of violating a certain rule." He went on to say that to those who have this feeling "the word *ought* means, that if they act otherwise, they shall be punished by this internal, and perfectly disinterested feeling."[113] As we shall see, this differs from the account given in *Utilitarianism*. Furthermore, it explicates the meaning of "ought" in terms of sanctions that one can expect *will* befall one, yet he criticized his father for seeming to confuse the *expectation* of punishment with *deserving* punishment. Blameworthiness, he held, involves the latter notion.[114] In the letter, as well as in other places, he indicated that *Utilitarianism* contains his most complete account. Strangely, that account has not been sufficiently explored.

Lyons holds that Mill's statement of the punishability account of the meaning of "wrong" is neutral with respect to moral theories; it only connects "X is wrong" with "a coercive rule against X would be justified." Sumner's version says: "a coercive rule against X would be maximally efficient." John Gray interprets the criterion as asserting that an act is wrong if, and only if, it would promote the most utility to punish it. Both Copp and Dryer employ act-consequence criteria, but neither seeks to find them in Mill's statement of the punishability criterion of right and wrong. Let us take a closer look at Mill's own statements.

Mill had indicated in the essay that duty is connected with deserv- ingness of punishment, and he attempted to account for this idea. He held that it involves a "desire to punish a person who has done harm to some individual." A desire for retaliation or revenge is a "natural" reaction to harm to ourselves or those for whom we care. But this natural feeling is not a moral feeling. It must be "moralized" by "the exclusive subordination of it to the social sympathies," that is, it must be conformable to the general good, "just persons resenting a hurt to society, though not otherwise a hurt to themselves, and not resenting a hurt to themselves, however painful, unless it be of the kind which society has a common interest with them in the repression of."[115]

Two paragraphs later, he summarized his account of the "sentiment of justice" by writing:

> And the sentiment of justice appears to me to be, the animal desire to repel or retaliate a hurt or damage to oneself, or to those with whom one sympathizes, widened so as to include all persons, by the human capacity of enlarged sympathy, and the human conception of intelligent self- interest. From the the latter elements, the feeling derives its morality; from the former, its peculiar impressiveness, and energy of self- assertion.[116]

These passages admit of at least two interpretations. One could read them as asserting that what "moralizes" the sentiment or desire is that it has been subjected to consideration of the general well-being (and *not* that it is subjected to the consideration that punishment is useful). This was the approach I took in Chapter 1. Let us review some of the grounds for favoring this interpretation. Elsewhere, before summariz- ing his account of the notion of duty, he indicated that "the class of feelings called moral embraces several varieties, materially different in their character."[117] And, in another place, he said that supererogatory acts "are fit objects of moral praise."[118] However, these further senti- ments expressed in moral judgments can hardly be "moralized" by reference to the utility of punishment. Many acts that do not deserve punishment also do not deserve moral praise. Furthermore, in the paragraph in *Utilitarianism* that intervenes between the passages I have quoted, he contrasted feelings of resentment that arise from self-concern alone with a moral sentiment. "A person whose resentment is really a moral feeling," he wrote, "certainly does feel that he is asserting a rule which is for the benefit of others as well as for his own." He added: "if he is regarding the act solely as it affects him individually— he is not consciously just; he is not concerning himself about the justice of his actions."[119] This interpretation would have the further advantage of making the punishability criterion somewhat more amenable to reconciliation with the proportionality criterion, and would align Mill's theory of the moral sentiments with that of Hume, who held that a feeling of approval of an act (or character trait) is not a moral feeling unless the act (or character) has been "considered in general, without reference to our particular interest."[120]

On the other hand, the passages could be read as holding that the desire for retaliation is "moralized" by arising from, and being limited by, the consideration that punishment of that kind of act would be in the general interest. The passages already quoted strongly suggest this interpretation, and it fits nicely the overall interpretation of morality as defined by the class of punishable acts. Furthermore, it is given support by Mill's summary of the theory in the notes to his father's *Analysis of the Phenomena of the Human Mind*:

> This impulse to self-defence by the retaliatory infliction of pain, only becomes a moral sentiment, when it is united with a conviction that the infliction of punishment in such a case is conformable to the general good, and when the impulse is not allowed to carry us beyond the point at which that conviction ends.[121]

The last quotation is not utterly conclusive, however. What is peculiar to the sentiment associated with *duty* is the connection with punishability. This is the larger point made in that discussion, where he had earlier said the moral feelings are various. So (it could be held), what makes the connection with punishability morally relevant is that *that* judgment concern itself with the general well-being.

There are several further points that these passages suggest that have not been sufficiently observed in the literature. In the first place, the punishability criterion, as analyzed in the passages to which I have been attending, has an unmistakable act-consequence feature. Every judgment of wrongness involves the belief that someone has been harmed, that is, that the act that is condemned has produced harmful consequences to someone. As we shall see in the next chapters, this view of Mill's raises hard problems for cases of wrongful behavior that involve omissions. Though this problem must be faced, no interpretation of Mill's theory of right and wrong can simply ignore this act-consequence feature of his analysis. Several of the accounts we have examined do overlook this feature.

However, it must be noted that these are unclarities that are involved in its statement. Is the claim that an act has harmed someone *noncomparative*, that is, does it assert that the bad consequences of that act for a person or persons predominate over the good consequences, or does it claim that the act produced worse consequences than any alternatives? Those who have attributed an act-consequence feature to Mill's theory (e.g., Copp, Dryer, Brown) take it to be the latter, that is, that a right act must be "maximally expedient." Mill's treatment, while undeniably having an act-consequence feature, is inconclusive, making it difficult to interpret that feature.

The second point I want to make is that Mill's discussion makes it look quite probable that his criterion of right and wrong also had a rule-consequence feature. In *Utilitarianism*, he indicated that the interest harmed in a wrongful act must "be of the kind which society has a common interest with them in the repression of." This seems to imply that a wrongful act is one that it is useful, *as a matter of rule*, to punish. I shall argue in the next chapter that Mill *did* seem to tie duties of *justice* to certain moral rules; the sentence quoted above is, in fact, an excerpt from his discussion of the duties of justice. Moreover, this would explain how an act could be wrong, and *deserve* punishment even though, *all things considered*, punishment should not be given in the particular case. Still, the summary quotation from his notes in his father's work, which deals with the general conception of duty (and is not limited to duties of justice), is not so clear-cut. Though we are told there that the infliction of punishment in "such a case" must be conformable to the general good, we are also told that the impulse must not "carry us beyond the point at which that conviction ends." If, however, in the case at hand, we are convinced that punishment will *not* be for the general good (though in most such cases it would be), would not the desire for retaliation lose its moral basis?

Perhaps it has been unfair to test the interpretations of the various commentators so rigorously against Mill's texts. Lyons is clearly engaged in reconstruction of a theory, not, essentially, textual elucidation. Sumner states explicitly that he believes it to be a "waste of

scholarly energy" to seek to determine the unique, "authoritative interpretation."[122] That is a judgment with which I heartily concur. Nonetheless, showing in detail the grounds for *that* judgment, via a close
examination of the texts, has not, I believe, been a fruitless exercise.
What has survived the discussion has been the conception of the role of
rules in *practical* morality that I have traced through Mill's forebears,
and throughout his own writing. I shall turn in the next chapter to his
theory of justice, in which rules play a central role. Furthermore, I shall
try to show that the theory of justice played a central role, in turn, in his
practical thinking on moral and political questions.

Part II
MILL'S POLITICAL THEORY

4

THE THEORY OF JUSTICE

The chief difficulty that utilitarians have faced is the problem of reconciling the dictates of utility with what seem clearly to be moral duties, but based on considerations of justice. The requirements of justice appear in some cases to outweigh (or make irrelevant) the consequences of acts. Mill addressed this problem in *Utilitarianism*, but the result has not served to silence the critics of utilitarianism on this score. In part, this is due to the fact that Mill's position in the chapter on justice is not entirely clear, nor is it entirely convincing where it is clear. Still, I do not think Mill's views on justice have been given their due.[1] One of the aims of this chapter, then, is to give an account of Mill's theory of justice and to show how it provides a more powerful treatment of issues of justice than the critics of utilitarianism have supposed. I do not believe Mill's theory is fully adequate, however, and I shall suggest some ways in which it might be supplemented, while in my concluding chapter I shall argue that there are unresolved difficulties that any utilitarian theory must still face.

A second objective of this chapter is to show that Mill's theory of justice was a central part of his moral theory. His views on the nature of practical reasoning will be seriously misunderstood without a full grasp of his conception of the role of considerations of justice. (By "practical reasoning" here, I mean reasoning about "real-life" moral decisions, *not* the philosophical theory of justification.)

Finally, I shall try to show how his theory of justice is crucial for understanding his substantive positions with respect to social, political, and economic issues. The most important application of his theory of justice, I shall argue, is his theory of liberty. That theory, I believe, is equally crucial to an understanding of his substantive claims in social, political, and economic theory. For these reasons, I shall devote the chapter that follows to his theory of freedom.

THE PROBLEM OF UTILITARIANISM AND JUSTICE

A brief survey of the problems of justice that have been posed for utilitarians is in order, for it is in this area that many believe that definitive objections to utilitarian theories are to be found. The objections all stem from the fact that utilitarian theories are "consequentialist," that is, they judge the rightness or wrongness of acts by their consequences. Duties of justice, however, appear to have bases in considerations other than consequences, or in considerations other than that good consequences have been maximized or not.

Consequentialist theories are said to be "aggregative" theories; they require amassing goods through action. The chief duty (it is alleged) for a consequentialist is to produce the greatest amount of happiness, or pleasure, or whatever else is taken as good in the theory of value. (In my concluding chapter, I shall suggest that the "greatest good" need *not* be considered this way.) Since it is the *amount* of good that is produced, and that alone, the consequentialist must be indifferent toward distributions of utilities except insofar as distributions affect the total produced. In a great many cases, then, the utilitarian seems to be required to act in ways that are unjust because they ignore principles that require certain distributions of good.

The most glaring of these problems concern rights. To assert that someone has a right does not entail that his acting in the way protected by the right will produce the best consequences, nor does the statement that the person's right should be respected entail anything about the consequences of doing so. If you agree to pay me for a service I perform, it would be wrong of you to sit down to calculate the consequences of paying me or not when payment time arrives (except in very unusual circumstances). Here, the duty is based on a "backward-looking" consideration—the fact that you made an agreement with me to pay for the service. The existence of the duty does not depend on the calculation of probable future consequences. I have a *right* to your payment which should constrain how you *distribute* goods in the future through your action.

Moreover, if maximizing good is one's overall duty, considerations of fairness seem to go by the boards. A distribution of the economic pie, for example, that concentrated it in the hands of a privileged few would be preferred to a more fair distribution if, by so concentrating it, a larger "pie" was thereby produced. At the extreme, it has been claimed that utilitarianism permits sacrificing the liberty of some for the greater good of others.[2] In addition, duties of fairness in cooperative ventures seem to be inexplicable in utilitarian terms. If a group of people are engaged in a mutually beneficial scheme that requires following rules or otherwise restricting behavior, it is held by some to be a violation of "fair play" not to do one's part when it comes one's turn.[3] The basis of such a duty seems to reside in the fact that one has received benefits from the sacrifices of others, *not* on the basis of a calculation of future utility to be produced by cooperation in the particular case. The person who takes benefits but fails to do his or her part is said to be a "freeloader" on the scheme—an epithet of disapprobation.

These problems of distribution appear to present especial embarrassment for hedonistic and eudaemonistic utilitarians since enormous increases in certain frivolous or even degraded pleasures would warrant deprivations of important rights of others. Thus, if a great many persons derive great enjoyment from seeing a person humiliated on stage,[4] doing so seems not only right, but a duty on the part of those who have it within their power to bring this about. If pushpin is as good as poetry, then suppress poetry if that will vastly increase the total amount of enjoyment obtained from pushpin and few get any pleasure from poetry. It is easy to see that a wide range of injustices in daily life might be generated in this way. A teacher assigning grades would distribute them, not according to the merits of performance, but according to the contribution to happiness that different grades would make; a judge dealing with litigants in court would no longer determine statuses and treatment in accord with the legal rights and duties applicable to the case, but in accord with what decision will be most productive of pleasure, happiness, and so on.

Finally, the utilitarian conception of morality has been thought to treat persons as mere receptacles of pleasure and pain, or "units" of happiness and unhappiness. Two defects are thought to spring from this. In the first place, the view ignores the "separateness" of persons; it results in overlooking respect for persons as such and their "inviolability" as persons.[5] Thus, persons are treated as means to be used for the ends of others, not as ends in themselves. The second alleged defect in the utilitarian conceptions of persons and morality is that since it is concerned with producing a maximum of pleasure or happiness, it can give no role to *desert* in allocating the good. But the notion of desert is crucial to retributive justice—only the guilty deserve punishment. A utilitarian scheme, however, could, in theory at least, permit punishing innocent people if that would thereby maximize the general well-being.

If these charges can be sustained, I think few philosophers would be willing to hold to utilitarianism as an acceptable theory. Except for certain of the details, all of these criticisms were made against utilitarianism in Mill's day, or were conceived of by him. He believed these either not to be consequences of his theory, or not defects if they did, indeed, follow. I shall attempt to reconstruct his account of justice and outline some of the chief defenses he could or did make to the objections. This chapter is not intended as a definitive defense of utilitarianism or Mill's theory of justice. Rather, it is intended as a program for such a defense. I believe the criticisms in some cases reflect serious misconceptions of utilitarianism and I want to show this. Moreover, there are elements in Mill's theory for responses to some of the chief criticisms. In my concluding chapter, however, I shall indicate grounds for doubting that even a revised utilitarianism can resolve all the problems of justice the critics have proposed.

RIGHTS AND JUSTICE

As I have earlier shown (chapter 1, "The Moral Sentiments"), Mill held that moral judgments express moral sentiments. The problem he set himself, then, in dealing with issues of justice, was to show how the sentiment of justice can be fitted into a utilitarian framework. He remarks that the "feeling of justice" might be a natural, powerful instinct, but it does not follow that it points to "an inherent quality in things" or that the judgments it leads to should be infallible. But it was Mill's belief that the "reality to which the feeling of justice corresponds" is not something in actions over and above the utilities they have "presented under a peculiar aspect."[6] The chief purpose of his discussion of justice in *Utilitarianism* was to show that appeal to utilitarian considerations can adequately account for our judgments of justice in this sense. Moreover, he acknowledged that the sentiment of justice is different from that of "General Expediency," and that it is accompanied by a greater intensity and sense of imperativeness. He was obliged, then, to also show how the sentiment of justice, accounted for in terms of the utilities of acts, can be felt with such peculiar incumbency, and how such judgments differ from those of mere expediency.

The task, as Mill saw it, was to find the sorts of actions that are called "just" and "unjust" to discover what the acts in each category have in common which "excite the sentiments associated with those names."[7] He then reviewed various accounts of the sorts of considerations that prompt judgments of justice or injustice. This survey serves as an introduction to his own theory of justice. The main upshot of the review is his conclusion that one thing our various judgments of justice and injustice have in common is the idea of punishment: "When we think that a person is bound in justice to do a thing, it is an ordinary form of language to say, that he ought to be compelled to do it."[8] He quickly added that there may be utilitarian grounds for *not* applying the punishment, but that this does not exhaust the analysis of justice, since the idea of punishment enters into the idea of duty in general, not just the idea of a duty of justice:

> The above is, I think, a true account, as far as it goes, of the origin and progressive growth of the idea of justice. But we must observe, that it contains, as yet, nothing to distinguish that obligation from moral obligation in general. For the truth is, that the idea of penal sanction, which is the essence of law, enters not only into the conception of injustice, but into that of any kind of wrong. We do not call anything wrong, unless we mean to imply that a person ought to be punished in some way or other for doing it; if not by law, by the opinion of his fellow creatures; if not by opinion, by the reproaches of his own conscience. This seems the real turning point of the distinction between morality and simple expediency. It is a part of the notion of Duty in every one of its forms, that a person may rightfully be compelled to fulfill it. Duty is a thing which may be *exacted* from a person, as one exacts a debt. Unless we think that it might be exacted from him, we do not call it his duty. Reasons of prudence, or the interest of other people, may militate against actually exacting it; but the person himself, it is clearly understood, would not be entitled to complain. There are other things, on the contrary, which we wish that people should do, which we like or admire them for doing, perhaps dislike or despise them for not doing, but yet admit that they are not bound to do; it is not a case of moral obligation; we do not blame them, that is, we do not think that they are proper objects of punishment. How we come by these ideas of deserving and not deserving punishment, will appear, perhaps, in the sequel; but I think there is no doubt that this distinction lies at the bottom of the notions of right and wrong; that we call any conduct wrong, or

employ, instead, some other term of dislike or disparagement, according as we think that the person ought, or ought not, to be punished for it; and we say that it would be right to do so and so, or merely that it would be desirable or laudable, according as we would wish to see the person whom it concerns, compelled, or only persuaded and exhorted, to act in that manner.[9]

The further element that is involved in the idea of justice is the idea of a *right* held by a particular ("assignable") person or persons who is or are wronged by a violation of the duty. There are other duties—duties of "imperfect obligation"—that do not carry correlative rights; he mentioned the duty to be generous, which no particular persons can claim from us. Duties of "perfect obligation"—the duties of justice— entail a correlativity of duties and rights. "Justice," he wrote, "implies something which it is not only right to do, and wrong not to do, but which some individual person can claim from us as his moral right."[10]

Now that the elements of the idea of justice had been picked out, Mill turned to the question of how the sentiments expressed by judg- ments of justice and injustice could develop around these ideas, and whether it is possible to explain the association by means of people's concern for the general welfare. If this could be shown, then the moral sentiment of justice would not be a sign that something other than utility is basic to morality. Mill's conclusion on the matter was that the sentiment of justice does not develop "from anything which would commonly, or correctly, be termed an idea of expediency," however, "whatever is moral in it does."[11]

The *sentiment* of justice, according to Mill, consists of a desire to punish someone who has done harm, together with the knowledge or belief that a particular person has been harmed. The desire to punish, he maintained, derives from two "natural" (perhaps instinctual or "ani- mal") sentiments: the impulse of self-defense, and sympathy. We natu- rally seek to repel harms to ourselves and to those with whom we sympathize. Our sympathy, together with our intelligence, which reveals a community of interest with others, causes us to "resent," "repel," or "retaliate" against "any conduct which threatens the secu- rity of society generally."[12]

The desire to retaliate or exact vengeance is not itself a moral sentiment, it must be "moralized" by our social feelings so that "it only acts in the directions conformable to the general good: just persons resenting a hurt to society, though not otherwise a hurt to themselves, and not resenting a hurt to themselves, however painful, unless it be of the kind which society has a common interest with them in the repression of."[13]

Mill argued further that for one whose resentment results merely from considering how the act affects himself or herself, the sentiment is not "really" a moral feeling. The person who has a genuine *moral* sentiment "certainly does feel that he is asserting a rule which is for the benefit of others as well as for his own."[14]

Now this is the first place in his discussion of justice where Mill mentioned the notion of a rule. No explanation was given of how that idea got in, but it reappears in his summary of his analysis of justice:

> To recapitulate: the idea of justice supposes two things; a rule of conduct, and a sentiment which sanctions the rule. The first must be supposed common to all mankind, and intended for their good. The other (the sentiment) is a desire that punishment may be suffered by those who infringe the rule. There is involved, in addition, the conception of some definite person who suffers by the infringement; whose rights (to use the expression appropriated to the case) are violated by it. And the sentiment of justice appears to me to be, the animal desire to repel or retaliate a hurt or damage to oneself, or to those with whom one sympathizes, widened so as to include all persons, by the human capacity of enlarged sympathy, and the human conception of intelligent self-interest. From the latter elements, the feeling derives its morality; from the former, its peculiar impressiveness, and energy of self-assertion.[15]

In the next section of this chapter, I shall discuss the significance of Mill's references to rules in these passages. For now, we must return to the idea of a right in the idea of justice. In the text, Mill explained the "elements" of the idea of a right which is violated as: a hurt to an assignable person or persons, and the "demand" for punishment. He then continued:

> When we call anything a person's right, we mean that he has a valid claim on society to protect him in the possession of it, either by the force of law, or by that of education and opinion. If he has what we consider a sufficient claim, on whatever account, to have something guaranteed to him by society, we say that he has a right to it. If we desire to prove that anything does not belong to him by right, we think this done as soon as it is admitted that society ought not to take measures for securing it to him, but should leave it to chance, or to his own exertions.[16]

Now there was no argument given by Mill to connect his analysis of the idea of right with the claim that having a right implies something society should protect. On the one hand, he seems at times to view the claim as following from the analysis of the idea of justice; on the other hand, he seems to have drawn the claim (as in the above quotation) as a conclusion of an appeal to an ordinary language-type argument about the necessary and sufficient conditions for asserting that someone has a right ("when we call . . ."; "a person is said . . .").

From the text, and other writings of Mill, his reasoning seems to have been somewhat as follows: Duties of justice involve interests that are common. A harm to such interests of a person thus calls forth reactions on the part of social beings. The natural reactions to harms are feelings of resentment, indignation, and a desire for revenge and retaliation. In a footnote commentary that he added when editing his father's *Analysis of the Phenomena of the Human Mind*, Mill wrote that "our earliest experience gives us the feeling . . . that the most direct and efficacious protection is retaliation,"[17] and we seek to have our social institutions provide this for us. This feeling is not, by itself, a moral feeling, of course. As previously explained, the feeling is "moralized" by its connection with the social feelings—the concern with the general wellbeing. Since everyone has an interest in reacting to and suppressing such conduct, the desire for retaliation in these cases is a moral sentiment. The consequent judgment that society should punish such conduct would be a true moral judgment if common social interests would indeed be furthered. Otherwise, the desire for social punishment, and the corresponding moral judgment, would not be justified. It would follow that someone has a right if, and only if, society should provide him protection from certain conduct by means of punishment.

It remained for Mill to explain how the duties of justice come to have such great weight and be regarded as so stringent. He explained this by pointing out that the sentiment of justice is not entirely rational; there is "also an animal element, the thirst for retaliation." The intensity of the feeling, as well as its "moral justification," derive from the fact that the interest protected by justice is "the most vital of all interests"—security. Beneficial conduct by others can often be foregone, or at any rate, we are not so dependent on it as we are on others abstaining from harming us:

> . . . security no human being can possibly do without; on it we depend for all our immunity from evil, and for the whole value of all and every good, beyond the passing moment; . . . Now this most indispensable of all necessaries, after physical nutriment, cannot be had, unless the machinery for providing it is kept unintermittedly in active play. Our notion, therefore, of the claim we have on our fellow-creatures to join in making

safe for us the very groundwork of our existence, gathers feelings round it so much more intense than those concerned in any of the more common cases of utility, that the difference in degree (as is often the case in psychology) becomes a real difference in kind.[18]

The rest of his chapter on justice is devoted to consideration of a wide range of principles of justice that are appealed to in practical argument on subjects ranging from punishment to taxation. Mill continually points to plausible counterprinciples in each case—an equally plausible principle that is inconsistent in some cases with the one cited. The only further appeal possible, he contended, is to expediency or utility to resolve the conflicts. Moreover, he held, in practice, the courts and others *do* appeal to utility in deciding among conflicting claims.

Mill's discussion of justice in *Utilitarianism* has left many important questions unanswered, nor is it clear that he set a foundation for dealing with the criticisms of utilitarian justice outlined earlier. Before I can turn to these issues, however, I must bring out more clearly a point that is indicated in *Utilitarianism*, but not fully discussed there—the role of rules in the concept of justice.

RULES AND JUSTICE

In the last section, we saw that Mill thought of duties of justice as given by rules, and that at a certain point in his analysis he introduced reference to rules as part of the very idea of justice. That he should have been led to think in terms of rules at this stage of his discussion is easy enough to explain in light of two points already discussed: (1) we saw in chapter 3 that he placed great stress on the need for rules in practical morality; (2) he maintained that justice protects our interest in security, hence, conformity to rule would further promote it.

In another place, however, Mill made a stronger point about the relation of rules and justice that not only capitalizes on the points just mentioned, but which also explains his reference to rules as part of the idea of justice. In a letter to George Grote, he said:

> human happiness, even one's own, is in general more successfully pursued by acting on general rules, than by measuring the consequences of each act; and this is still more the case with the general happiness, since any other plan would not only leave everybody uncertain what to expect, but would involve perpetual quarrelling: and hence general rules must be laid down for people's conduct to one another, or in other words rights and obligations must, as you say, be recognised; and people must, on the one

hand, not be required to sacrifice even their own less good to another's greater, where no general rule has given the other a right to the sacrifice; while when a right *has* been recognised, they must, in most cases, yield to that right even at the sacrifice, in the particular case, of their own greater good to another's less. These rights and obligations are (it is of course implied) reciprocal. And thus what each person is held to do for the sake of others is more or less definite, corresponding to the less perfect knowledge he can have of their interests, taken individually; and he is free to employ the indefinite residue of his exertions in benefitting the one person of whom he has the principal charge, and whose wants he has the means of learning the most completely.[19]

Several points of importance are made in the letter. General rules are needed in order to achieve most successfully the end of happiness, and this is due, in part, to difficulties of knowledge and the need for regularity of conduct. The rules of justice, then, are a device for achieving the end of happiness. But the rules of justice are of a special kind—they specify rights and reciprocal obligations. Thus, for the most part, in determining what one should do, one would base action on the rights that bear on the case. Rights, then, should play an important role in ordinary reasoning about morality.

It is extremely important to stress the conceptual connection between rights and rules. For many of the objections to a utilitarian theory of justice can be met by stressing this point, together with other points made by Mill in the letter to Grote. For example, act-utilitarian theories seem to make the existence of a right depend on the consequences of acts in the particular case. But this is not how right claims are supported. Also, the act-utilitarian appears committed to overriding a right whenever it is perceived that greater utility will thereby be produced, even if the gain is quite small. Rights, however, cannot be overridden in this way if they are to be taken seriously. Mill's theory, even on the act-consequence interpretation I have attributed to him, has neither of these untoward consequences. The possession of a right (either recognized or claimed) is a matter of the rules of justice that are applicable, not a matter of the utilities of the particular case. Although rights in a particular case can be overridden, only very unusual circumstances could justify this, since the device of rights is meant to forestall calculation in each case, and the security they protect would be endangered if the belief that small gains would be obtained by violation were taken as ground for ignoring a right. (As we shall see below, further serious disutilities would result, almost surely cancelling out any small gains anticipated.)

It is useful at this stage to give a summary statement of the necessary and sufficient conditions for someone to have a right according to Mill's theory of justice. I believe the following captures Mill's conception of a right: A person has a right to X (i.e., perform some act, be treated by others in a certain way, to have some thing, and so on), if, and only if, there is, or ought to be, a recognized moral rule that requires society not to interfere with, and to protect, the person's exercise of, enjoyment of, possession of X. Society's "protection," for Mill, consists in providing some means of punishment, legal or social (e.g., in the form of public opinion), for violations. It follows from this conception of a right, together with the Principle of Utility, that someone can (truly) claim a moral right to some mode of behavior or treatment if, and only if, it is something that it is in the general social interest to protect as a matter of recognized rule. If, on the other hand, it is *not* something the systematic, general protection of which would be useful, then it is not something the person can claim as a right.

In all of his discussions of justice, Mill referred to the "rules of justice," and he discussed a number of these rules in various places.[20] For the most part, however, he was concerned with arguing in these places that there are a number of such rules, all of which in some circumstances appear sacred and inviolable, but that contrary rules can be cited which appear equally compelling, and, hence, that utility must be consulted to resolve the conflicts. A consequence of Mill's special concern with justice is that we are not left with a very clearly articulated substantive theory of justice—an account of which principles Mill would hold, under what conditions, for what reasons, or *how* utility is to decide among them. Fortunately, Mill wrote on substantive moral issues, and from these writings it is possible to ferret out a somewhat systematic set of principles and values that constitute the elements of Mill's substantive theory of justice.

In the section that follows, I shall attempt to outline Mill's substantive theory of justice in several central areas of concern—punishment and desert, fairness and cooperation, equality and economic-political justice. I believe this is worth doing for four reasons. In the first place, it has never, to my knowledge, been done before. Though *some* of Mill's substantive theories have been discussed by others,[21] there has never been an attempt to track down Mill's basic principles and tie them together in an interconnected theory of justice.[22] Thus, the history of philosophy can be served by the study.

Second, the survey will reveal important aspects of Mill's moral theory. We shall see better how the complex conception of happiness plays a crucial role in his substantive ethical thought, and how various practical positions he took are to be justified within his ethical theory.

Third, we shall be better able to generate replies to the various criticisms of utilitarianism cited earlier in this chapter.

Finally, I shall argue that the understanding of Mill's theory of justice—both his general conception and the substantive theory—shed considerable light on his very important theory of freedom, which is the subject of the chapter that follows. I shall contend that Mill's theory of justice is central to his theory of freedom, while elements of the latter play essential roles in his substantive theory of justice.

FURTHER DEVELOPMENTS—THE SUBSTANTIVE THEORY

My discussions of aspects of Mill's substantive theory are not intended to be comprehensive in several respects. I shall not, for example, give a complete description of his theory of responsibility. It is well known that as a metaphysical determinist he faced severe problems in accounting for the concept of responsibility. Other commentators have detailed these problems, and I have nothing to add to their accounts.[23] More importantly, that particular issue does not shed light on Mill's moral theory. Nor shall I attempt to answer all of the chief criticisms of utilitarian justice. By dealing with some, I shall have indicated the sorts of steps a Millean utilitarian might take. A full defense, however, would take me too far afield, and, as shall be clear here and in my concluding chapter, I do not think such a defense can be ultimately successful. I am convinced, however, that many criticisms are based either on misunderstandings, or inadequate conceptions of utilitarianism.

PUNISHMENT AND DESERT

Since punishing someone requires the performance of an act or series of acts that cause pain, suffering, or deprivation, inflicting punishment requires justification. However, if acts are justified by their consequences, then punishment in any case would seem to depend on the consequences of inflicting it. Considerations of guilt, desert, responsibility, conscience, and so on, appear irrelevant, or, alternatively, if given a utilitarian analysis and meaning, will fail to accord with our moral senses of these terms. For example, Alan Ryan (as have others) has claimed that Mill's analysis of what is meant when we say a person is responsible for acting wrongly is that he is likely to change his mind about acting in that way in the future if he is punished.[24] Of course, to *hold* someone responsible on such grounds—to actually *punish* the person—would not necessarily be just because it need not be tied to guilt or desert, as we understand those notions. Moreover, Ryan has contended that Mill's attempt to explain the concept of desert in *Utilitarianism* failed: "Nothing in Mill's account of the importance of security explains the notion of merit or desert."[25] I want to show that these claims are mistaken; they confuse Mill's *analysis* of the ideas of responsibility and desert with the ultimate justifications for conditioning punishment on desert.

On the one hand, Mill rejected outright the extreme retributivist doctrine on punishment:

> If anyone thinks that there is justice in the infliction of purposeless suffering; that there is a natural affinity between the two ideas of guilt and punishment, which makes it intrinsically fitting that wherever there has been guilt, pain should be inflicted by way of retribution; I acknowledge that I can find no argument to justify punishment on this principle.[26]

On the other hand, he held that our concept of justified punishment is tied to conceptions of responsibility, desert, guilt, and the like. "Responsibility," he wrote, "means punishment,"[27] in the sense that to *feel* morally responsible is to feel liable to, or deserving of, punishment. In his discussion of Sir William Hamilton's philosophy, he gave an account of the genesis of the feeling of accountability or responsibility in associationist terms. A person who acts wrongly becomes "a natural object" of the dislike of others, and they, "through the normal action of their natural sentiments," will seek to protect themselves, probably through punishment. Thus, wrongdoing comes regularly to be associated with pain, to the point that the thought of a wrongful act will "cause the mind to shrink from it even when, in the particular case, no painful consequences are apprehended." The feeling of pain at the very idea of doing wrong becomes so immediate and strong that it appears as natural and instinctual.[28] Mill's account of the feeling of responsibility parallels his discussions of the notion of "conscience" elsewhere.[29]

In the case of one who does wrong, of course, the force of the motive
to act rightly—the sense of pain at the idea of acting wrongly—has
been insufficient to prevent the wrongful act. Thus, punishment can be
justified for the dual objectives of reforming the actor and to protect
society by strengthening the motive to abstain from repetitions by the
actor and others. The first objective Mill described as for "the benefit of
the offender himself," and he held that "to benefit a person cannot be to
do him an injury"; thus, punishing him for his own good "is no more
unjust than to administer medicine."[30] Punishment for the self-defense
of society is justified because it protects "just rights."

There are aspects of Mill's account that require further clarification,
and some obvious objections suggest themselves which require discussion. Some of this work was done by Mill in later editions of *Sir William
Hamilton's Philosophy*. (A particular place in which Mill addressed his
critics is especially enlightening, as I will point out later.)

One objection to Mill's view is that it seems to be inconsistent with
that of *On Liberty*, in which he appears to have held that punishment is
not justified for a person's own good. Mill responded that he had not
asserted this as an absolute principle in the first place, having excluded
children and adults in backward barbarian communities. Nor had he
asserted that, "when for the protection of society" we punish wrong-
doers, reform "is not one of the ends to be aimed at, in the kind and
mode, at least, of the punishment."[31] In the usual case, then, a necessary condition for justified punishment is that some wrongful act has
been performed. Mill's explanation of the concept of "deserved punishment" is not upset by his discussion in *On Liberty*. There are, of course,
further problems that Mill has missed here, and these failures do
seriously undermine his defense. No part of his analysis of the idea of
desert entails any connection between the nature of the crime and "the
kind and mode" of punishment, nor, I might add, does it connect to the
issue of degree. In addition, Mill seems not to have seen that the two
ends of punishment might be served by *different* punishments, or punishments of differing degree. A principle would be needed to resolve
such conflicts. Moreover, Mill's justification for punishment for the
good of the offender is too strong. If to benefit someone is to do one no
injury that requires *any* further justification, then there can no longer be
an objection to punishing persons who have committed no crimes, in
order to make them better (at least so long as the punishment is likely to
accomplish that end). Perhaps this is one of those places where Mill
overstated his case. He *did* say that we can seek to reform when acting
for "the protection of society," and that the reform is to direct the

person again toward a state of mind where "love of right" is again a dominant motive. Reform of the individual, then, may be seen as an aspect of society's attempt at self-protection—the objective being protection from future recurrences by this individual. Reform is undertaken *to protect society.*

Generous as the last bit of interpretation may be to Mill's text, it still may not be strong enough. If it is societal protection that justifies punishment, why condition desert on having committed a crime, and why restrict reformative-preventive tools to punishment? If reward could produce the desired reforms and prevention, the justification of punishment would disappear entirely for the utilitarian, especially one concerned with maximizing human happiness.

The appropriate response to the claim that it might be more protective of society to reform persons who have done no wrong by punishing them is to be found in Mill's account of the importance of autonomy and individuality. That discussion must await the next chapter. His response to the other claim that reward might be more efficacious than punishment is extremely instructive.

Mill's response had four parts. First, he claimed that rewarding the offender would *not* deter *others.* Second, he claimed that in fact punishment is "vastly more efficacious than reward." Punishment alone, he thought, can make the idea of wrongful behavior truly repugnant, and thus provide a strong motive against doing acts injurious to society. (Recall his associationist theory of the development of the idea of deserving punishment.) By producing such aversion, our social ties are strengthened. Third, he held that even if reward *were* as efficacious, it would not satisfy the "natural," "animal" desire for retaliation which is at the root of the "feeling of justice." Though not a moral sentiment, it is "moralized by being allied with, and limited by, regard for the general welfare," and it then becomes "our moral sentiment of justice."[32] Since in the real world as we know it, punishment *is* necessary, this sentiment is "entitled to consideration." Fourth, if rewarding offenders really *were* more useful (all things considered) than punishment, then "there would be no need of this particular moral sentiment, and, like other sentiments the use of which is superseded by changes in the circumstances of mankind, it might, and probably would, die away."[33] Mill went on to point out that he had discussed the concept of desert in *Utilitarianism*, and chided his critics for not paying heed to that discussion.

Indeed, the treatments of responsibility in *Sir William Hamilton's Philosophy*, and of the sentiment of justice in *Utilitarianism*, tie together—they are aspects of his account of the concept of desert. Desert and responsibility originate in our "natural," "instinctual," "animal" desire for retaliation to harms to ourselves and those with whom we sympathize, and eventually, everyone with whom we share society. As society does express this desire through punishment, we associate pain with doing wrongful acts, and come, eventually, to be pained at the idea of doing acts that are wrongful. This is *why* punishment is efficacious. The desire for revenge is made a moral sentiment by its conformity with utility. Similarly, the aversion we feel at doing a wrongful act is not yet conscience; it becomes so "when disinterested, and connecting itself with the pure idea of duty."[34]

This last point is important, for Mill's doctrine on conscience is easily misunderstood, since he did not always add the qualifier when discussing conscience. A mere feeling of pain at the idea of our doing an act is not conscience. As Alan Ryan has expressed the criticism:

> The obvious objection is that an agent who feels pain at the thought of an action may ask himself whether he is right to feel this, and it is no answer to this question merely to tell him that he feels it because of a complicated process of internalization. It is, moreover, not much help toward answering the problems of remorse, i.e., of guilt feelings about some past action. A man may very well feel pain at the thought of an action he has performed, and yet not agree that he was either wholly or partially responsible; merely feeling pain does not draw a line between regret that something should have happened, where we do not assume responsibility for it, and remorse at having done whatever it was, where we do. In other words, guilt requires both that we should think that what was done was in some sense deplorable—not merely something we had come to feel averse to—and that we should think we had some choice about what happened.[35]

As we have seen, Mill was not open to this objection, since he held that the feeling of pain must be conjoined with the sense that a *duty* has been violated. (I have not taken up Mill's views on "choice." He is well known as a "compatibilist," hence, he would not disagree with Ryan's incorporation of that notion in that of responsibility. It is another matter as to whether or not he can make adequate sense of that concept.)

Mill emphasized that the sentiment of justice is connected with the powerful, natural desire for retaliation, and is itself impressed upon us from early childhood on, reinforcing the connection between harm to others and liability for punishment, so that the moralized sentiment comes itself to have great force, and to appear itself as a natural, "original" part of our very nature. As stressed in *Utilitarianism*, further reinforcement results from the fact that the duties enforced by justice protect an urgent need of all people—security.

The upshot is that a statement that someone deserves punishment entails that the actor harmed someone and it expresses a (moralized) desire that retaliation be suffered by the actor. This is Mill's *analysis* of the concept of desert. The analysis does *not* connect assertions of desert with the consequences of inflicting punishment. In *this* respect only, it would not be improper (though it is possibly misleading) to say that his analysis of the concept is nonutilitarian. Furthermore, it *is* a consequence of his analysis that only the guilty deserve punishment.

Nonetheless, Mill did not give up his utilitarianism. To say that someone deserves punishment is *not* to say that the person ought, all things considered, to be punished. Though there are places where Mill seems to have interchanged "deserves punishment" and "ought to be punished," it is clear from his analysis that no simple identification of meaning can be made. If punishment does not serve good ends, it ought to be abandoned: "As a legitimate satisfaction to feelings of indignation and resentment which are on the whole salutary and worthy of cultivation, I can in certain cases admit it; but here it is still a means to an end."[36] Of course, since it is properly used to defend "just rights," themselves protective of essential elements or conditions of happiness, utility *is* served in our world by punishing violators. The violator has no basis for complaint; he or she will deserve punishment, "and is responsible for the evil which falls upon him by his voluntary breach of a just law."[37] Not only, then, does society have a right to punish, but it is also justified in actually inflicting it so that the threat of it will not be "idle mockery," to other possible offenders.[38] To the challenge that his theory permits punishment of the innocent, Mill's response is the traditional utilitarian one that punishing the innocent adds nothing to the deterring effect, hence, is the infliction of gratuitous, unjustified suffering.[39]

I have argued that rights for Mill are a device for maximizing utility. They are defined by rules, and they protect crucial aspects or conditions for happiness. Our ordinary moral reasoning, then, will appeal to rights. The discussion of punishment and desert, however, brings out another important aspect of Mill's moral theory. Desert is an idea that has roots in our natural reactions and feelings. The idea of desert involves those feelings as socialized. The notion of desert, then, is part of what may be termed our sense of "natural justice." We do have a somewhat natural sense of the fittingness of punishment for wrongdoing. Natural justice, however, is not (for Mill) self-certifying. We still require good reasons (based in utility) for allowing these feelings to play a significant role in our moral lives.

I shall turn, in the next section of this chapter, to other aspects of Mill's moral theory. I shall argue that there were other principles of justice to which Mill appealed that are also aspects of "natural justice," and which played important roles in his economic and political thought. Before I do that, however, I want to stress aspects of Mill's theory of punishment and desert that bear important similarities to significant contemporary views. These points may appear to be tangential to my exposition, but I believe the digression is useful as it shows Mill to have anticipated current thought on the subject. Moreover, the discussion demonstrates how a utilitarian can take account of aspects of punishment and desert that are often thought to lie outside the explanatory power of utilitarianism.

As we have seen, Mill emphasized that punishment is tied to natural attitudes of resentment, vindictiveness,[40] and the desire for retaliation. He also emphasized that moral praise or blame is usually not an instrument "purposely employed for an end," but "the simple expression of that feeling."[41] Punishment, then, is (in part) an expression of our natural reactive attitudes toward harmful conduct by others. Such a point of view has been defended by influential contemporary philosophers.

Professor Joel Feinberg, for example, has maintained that an expressive feature is definitive of punishment: "I think it is fair to say of our community . . . that punishment generally expresses more than judgments of disapproval; it is also a symbolic way of getting back at the criminal, of expressing a kind of vindictive resentment."[42] He goes on to argue that aspects of our punitive institutions can best be explained by reference to this feature of punishment, for example, in determining when a privation or hardship is merely "regulative" or fully "punitive," or in distinguishing punishments from mere taxes on conduct.

In a later discussion, Feinberg cites Mill as possibly the first important philosopher to draw attention to the sorts of distinctive sentiments associated with justice. However, Feinberg interprets Mill as having held that the sentiment of justice is the desire to retaliate for injury, widened by our sympathy to apply to wrongdoing against others. This, Feinberg argues, is inadequate:

> Perhaps such elements *are* commonly part of the sentiment of injustice, but they would also be present, I should think, when we apprehend

wrongdoing of other kinds, or even when we perceive harm caused to persons in an innocent or accidental way. Those elements peculiar to the sentiment of injustice that endow it with its uniquely righteous flavor have not been mentioned in Mill's account.[43]

I am not sure what Feinberg intends by his notion of a "uniquely righteous flavor" in the sentiment of justice. His own account of the sentiment of justice is as follows:

> It is natural enough to respond to hurt with anger, but when the hurt seems to have been arbitrarily inflicted in the manner characteristic of unjust discrimination, anger is transmuted into moral indignation. Because the treatment is offensive to reason as well as hurtful, responsive anger borrows some of the authority of reason; it becomes righteous and impersonal, free of self-doubt, and yet disinterested and free of mere self-preference.[44]

He adds that it is this sentiment that distinguishes our awareness of injustice from our awareness of other kinds of wrong or harmful conduct.

Mill's account of the sentiment of justice probably does differ from Feinberg's in important ways. When Feinberg aligns the sentiment with "reason," he seems to have in mind our reactions to "arbitrary" or discriminatory treatment—there is the sense that such behavior offends reason itself since, being arbitrary, there can be no reason for it. This is *not* part of Mill's treatment because he did not restrict injustices to discriminatory "unfair" behavior.[45] There are problems with this which I shall discuss later. The element of disinterestedness and impersonal concern *was*, however, a part of Mill's analysis. Feinberg has here confused Mill's account of the genesis of the moralized sentiment with his final account of the content of the moralized sentiment, or, alternatively, he has confused the "animal" impulse conjoined with sympathy with the moral sentiment of justice; the former emotion is not a moral sentiment for Mill without being "moralized."

Another influential contemporary philosopher whose views on punishment contain elements emphasized by Mill is Professor H. L. A. Hart. In defending the requirement of responsibility before the law can justly subject one to punishmentlike treatment, he makes the point that the "principle of responsibility" reflects a deep-seated aspect of human nature:

> If you strike me, the judgment that the blow was deliberate will elicit fear, indignation, anger, resentment: these are not voluntary responses; but the

same judgment will enter into deliberations about my future voluntary conduct towards you and will colour all my social relations with you. Shall I be your friend or enemy? Offer soothing words? Or return the blow? All this will be different if the blow is not voluntary. This is how human nature in human society actually is and as yet we have no power to alter it. The bearing of this fundamental fact on the law is this. If as our legal moralists maintain it is important for the law to reflect common judgments of morality, it is surely even more important that it should in general reflect in its judgments on human conduct distinctions which not only underly morality, but pervade the whole of our social life. This it would fail to do if it treated men merely as alterable, predictable, curable or manipulable things.[46]

Thus, Hart maintains that the requirement of responsibility will have a place "even when retributive and denunciatory ideas of punishment are dead."[47] He goes on to contend that it ought not be applied as an absolute principle; there *can* be justified exceptions, and these appear to be justified for him by a calculation of the gains obtained by the exceptional cases against the sacrifice of principle involved.

There is one further sort of contemporary view on punishment I want to consider. It has sometimes been proposed as inconsistent with utilitarianism, but, I shall argue, some of its most distinctive and important features are perfectly compatible with Mill's theory. The sort of theory I want to address maintains that punishment, and the attendant feelings or attitudes of indignation and resentment, are ways in which we treat others as persons, rather than as animals or inanimate objects. To treat crime as calling for remedial therapy, for example, amounts to treating the criminal as an object to be manipulated and changed for the social good.

One advocate of this type of view is Professor Herbert Morris. In a provocative and penetrating essay, he argues that the criminal has a *right* to his punishment.[48] Morris gives several intertwined arguments for this claim, one being that punishment is justified as required for there to be a just distribution of benefits and burdens in a community, but I shall here be concerned with another strand of his argument. Morris holds that (at least in an ideal system) punishment is conditioned on the agent's voluntary, free, choice. This is in contrast with therapy, for example, in that *this* sort of treatment regards the agent as not in control, or not fully so. Alternatively, we can say that to treat someone as *not* a person, or not fully so, is to "consider the person as incapable of rational choice." Thus, the appropriate attitude when therapy is administered is compassion rather than resentment. However, according to Morris, we have a right to be treated as persons, hence, we have a right to have our choices respected. Punishment, then, respects this basic right, since it treats the actor as a choosing person. Moreover, the person may be regarded as the cause of the results of the act (at least in an ideal model where participation in formulating the rules and penalties is maintained), and so, may be thought of as having chosen the punishment. In both respects, the criminal is treated as a rationally choosing person.

A similar sort of theory is given by Professor P. F. Strawson in an extremely important essay entitled "Freedom and Resentment."[49] Strawson calls attention to certain kinds of attitudes that play important roles in our lives, such as gratitude, resentment, and forgiveness. He refers to these (and others) as "participant reactive attitudes" because they are called up as reactions to the behavior of others with whom we share a common moral life. These attitudes are of great importance to us when displayed because they show our regard for one another as appropriate objects of good will and concern. Basic to these attitudes is an expectation and demand for display of good will. Doing injury to another violates that demand unless it can be claimed the agent was "deranged," or "couldn't help it," or something like these. But among the sorts of excuses that can be offered are ones that invite what Strawson labels "objective" attitudes. For example, if we say that a person was "deranged" or "insane," we judge the agent as not a full participant in our human interpersonal world; we judge that the actor is or was not a responsible moral agent. As such, he or she may be an appropriate object of treatment for social ends. But such treatment involves taking the "objective" point of view toward the person.

Now Strawson is not maintaining that questions of social utility are irrelevant to punishment (nor does Morris make such a claim). His point is that condemnation and punishment are not mere instruments of social policy; they are "correlates" of the moral demands we make of morally responsible agents.

Neither Morris nor Strawson contend that this line of argument provides a complete justification for actually inflicting punishment, especially as we know it. Morris, for example, concedes the possibility that some other reactions might be consistent with respecting a person's choices. And Strawson is willing to admit that there is surely no contradiction in supposing *all* of the participant reactive attitudes to disappear. He claims, however, that this is "practically" inconceivable, and we really do not have any choice in the matter. Indeed, toward the end of his essay he writes: "Our practices do not merely exploit our natures, they express them."[50]

It is obvious that portions of this sort of theory are to be found in Mill's theory, especially the emphasis on punishment as an expression of deep-seated attitudes of resentment and indignation. There is more, however. According to the sort of theory being considered, our feelings and attitudes are not bare sensations caused by the actions of others; they have a sort of "structure" or "logic." A display of gratitude, for example, reflects the belief that another has acted in a way beneficial to the agent *in order to* provide benefits, shows that the action is appreciated, and that the recipient regards the other as a person of good will, not as a mere instrument of benefits, and it reinforces the bonds of moral community. It is a recognition of a *particular* sort of act, and it displays *particular* sorts of attitudes. Because it displays how we are regarded, it has value *as* an expression of those attitudes, without regard for any further consequences.[51]

Mill did not explicitly analyze the moral emotions or sentiments in these terms. But important portions of his moral theory will be misunderstood if it is not made clear that he recognized important differences in what I have termed the "structure" or "logic" of our attitudes. For example, in *On Liberty*, Mill admitted to the propriety of lessened opinions when a person sinks low through "self-regarding" faults, and he held it appropriate to avoid such persons, or to express one's distaste, and so on. At least this is appropriate where the reactions are "the spontaneous consequences of the faults themselves," and not "purposely inflicted on him for the sake of punishment." Mill conceded that the privations one can suffer when we react naturally or in furtherance of our own desired life-style, can be as great as those suffered through punishment. Nevertheless, he contended:

> The distinction between the loss of consideration which a person may rightly incur by defect of prudence or of personal dignity, and the reprobation which is due to him for an offence against the rights of others, is not a merely nominal distinction. It makes a vast difference both in our feelings and in our conduct towards him, whether he displeases us in things in which we think we have a right to control him, or in things in which we know that we have not. If he displeases us, we may express our distaste, and we may stand aloof from a person as well as from a thing that displeases us; but we shall not therefore feel called on to make his life uncomfortable. We shall reflect that he already bears, or will bear, the

whole penalty of his error; if he spoils his life by mismanagement, we shall not, for that reason, desire to spoil it still further: instead of wishing to punish him, we shall rather endeavour to alleviate his punishment, by showing him how he may avoid or cure the evils his conduct tends to bring upon him. He may be to us an object of pity, perhaps of dislike, but not of anger or resentment; we shall not treat him like an enemy of society: the worst we shall think ourselves justified in doing is leaving him to himself, if we do not interfere benevolently by showing interest or concern for him.[52]

Still, these points fail to recognze the main thrust of the Morris-Strawson position, namely, that punishment reflects our regard for the violator as a person, by treating him or her as a choosing, morally responsible agent. I do not know if Mill *would* have found this acceptable. He *could* have accepted it, however. As pointed out earlier, in his little known essay "On Punishment," he had presaged Morris's views that the violator "is responsible for the evil which falls upon him by his voluntary breach of a just law."[53] Furthermore, it would tie in with an important part of his moral theory—his theory of freedom and autonomy. *If* conditioning the expression of our resentment on the agent's having acted voluntarily shows respect for the agent as an autonomous person, it will, *to that extent*, further a crucial element in Mill's theory of value. Similarly, if human dignity is furthered by treating persons as "morally responsible" agents, and this is manifested in a system of punishment that employs a maximum of regard for the free choices of individuals, then there are utilitarian reasons for an adherent of Mill's philosophy to adopt such a system.

I shall return to aspects of Mill's discussion of punishment at various points in the remainder of this chapter. There are two final points I want to make in this section. First, I want to emphasize that Mill need not, and probably would not, take the last points made—based on the considerations raised by Morris and Strawson—as a definitive basis for actually inflicting the pain of punishment. In the first place, he appears to have been more sanguine about the possibilities for reforming human nature than Strawson. In addition, there is no necessity to suppose that the denunciatory function of punishment, implying the moral responsibility of the violator, can only be accomplished through the infliction of pain and suffering. It has been pointed out, for example, that white collar workers in our own society are effectively deterred from crime by measures falling far short of the loss of liberty involved in imprisonment that other persons in our society face when they commit crimes.[54] It is not implausible to suggest that disgrace alone is, in many cases, an effective deterrent. It may be, of course, that the pain of being denounced or disgraced is itself a kind of punishment. There would still be a distinction to be made between being punished *through* being denounced, and being denounced *by* being punished. The former, Mill could regard as a "natural" consequence of the violator's retaining *his or her* sense of moral responsibility. The pain would be consequent upon the violator's *caring* about his or her moral status in the eyes of others. It would *not* be a *further* privation inflicted *by society*. There are very strong utilitarian reasons for retaining the feelings of regret, remorse, shame, and so on, that are part of the lives of moral persons, along with the pains that are part of the "structure" of these reactive states. Failing an appeal to deterrent efficacy, I do not think Mill would have thought there are sufficient utilitarian grounds for punishment *per se*.

The final point I want to make has to do with the claim that certain actions, for example, condemning or punishing a wrong-doer, manifest certain attitudes toward that person. The point I want to stress is clearly seen in cases of gratitude, when we respond to beneficent acts of others. When we show our gratitude, we show our benefactor that we regard him or her as having displayed good will toward us. We would *not* display gratitude (it would be inappropriate) if the benefit had been produced accidentally, or against the person's will. Since we care about our moral status in the eyes of others, the display of gratitude by another has value to us *as such*, apart from any further consequences. This means that certain actions *incorporate* or *manifest* things we value, hence, are valued *for their own sakes*.[55] Perhaps this point can be shown to be ultimately consistent with the classical utilitarian formula: "Actions are means to an end,"[56] but the formula is at least misleading. There is no reason, in principle, however, why a utilitarian cannot ascribe value to actions themselves, in the way I have indicated. If certain acts incorporate elements we desire as part of our well-being (e.g., displays of goodwill or love of others for us), then these acts *contribute* to well-being. It does not matter whether we regard the contribution as a separable *consequence* of the act or as bound up with features inherently part of the act. As we shall see later, the notion that some acts have value as the acts they are can play an important role in responding to critics of utilitarianism.

I want to turn next to some issues of justice that some critics have thought resistant to utilitarian treatment—those that arise with respect to fairness in cooperative ventures.

FAIRNESS AND COOPERATION

Mill's views on cooperation, especially as they bear on his attitude toward socialism, have been explored by other commentators at some length.[57] These views can be summarized in a single paragraph. He believed that increasing civilization itself produces an increase in cooperation. People are more interdependent as a result of the increasing division of labor, and greater compromise is necessary. Individuals must be more willing to sacrifice "individual will, for a common purpose."[58] Savages, for example, are incapable of such self-control, which helps keep them in their barbarian status. In addition, while Mill was ever insistent on the virtues of competition, for example, as an impetus to industry and self-exertion,[59] he was quite open to the claims of moral superiority of cooperative relationships.[60] He endorsed workers' cooperative partnerships, which he believed would help to remake society, with a greater stress on cooperative principles. He was, in fact, willing to call himself a socialist.[61] Nonetheless, he believed a thoroughgoing socialistic, cooperative society requires very high moral qualities in persons, so that while, perhaps, one day, the "selfish principle" in people could be overcome, in his own day, a fully cooperative society would be possible only for the "elite."[62] Moreover, he expressed great fears for freedom and individuality in a socialist society. Thus, although approving of many of the values and claims of socialists (especially their criticisms of the inequities in the existing distribution of goods), he felt that the socialist ideal remained to be proven, and should be undertaken in the form of piecemeal experiments.

I shall not be especially concerned with these issues. There is, however, a matter involving a moral issue that arises within cooperative arrangements that has been the subject of considerable philosophical interest recently. Some philosophers believe that cooperation (under certain conditions) generates duties of fairness on the part of the participants who benefit from the cooperation. Once having enjoyed the benefits of the efforts of the others, it is unfair not to do one's part when it comes one's turn. To take the benefits and not perform is to "freeload" on the scheme. This sort of duty of fairness or "fair play," it has been held, cannot be accounted for in utilitarian theories, since the performance may *not* maximize utility. In any event, that one *has* the duty is based on past receipt of benefits as a participant in a cooperative enterprise.

With the exception of an essay of my own, there has been very little recognition in the literature that Mill acknowledged and defended such duties.[63] The account he gave of these duties fits in neatly with his general theory of justice. By stressing certain features of Mill's treatment of these duties, we shall also be able to illuminate further puzzling features of his moral theory, and shall find a new utilitarian argument for placing great stress on rights in ordinary moral reasoning. I shall present Mill's position by first outlining a kind of utilitarian approach, and then show that points he made fit the account.

Central to Mill's account of justice was his claim that the rules of justice protect security. There are two ways in which this is true, which should be brought out more clearly. First, the rules of justice forbid us to harm one another, and they engage societal protection from harm through social enforcement. Second, by producing regularity of behavior, by virtue of the rule-governed nature of justice, the behavior of persons forms part of a *system* of social justice. There are recognized rights and duties which regulate the behavior of persons; the congruence of the acts of people is not a happenstance event. We can plan our lives more readily without fear of harm to ourselves, and with greater assurance of the security of our belongings, arrangements, and undertakings. Mutual trust and reliance are facilitated. Thus, a system of rights, "kept unintermittedly in active play," provides the "machinery" whereby security is maintained.[64]

This second point shows that the recognition of rights creates a new range of interests, deriving from the existence of the system itself. Everyone who shares in the system has an interest in maintaining it. We can call these "systemic" interests. One consequence of the creation of a system of rights is that almost all violations of rights have some disutility. By reintroducing the uncertainties associated with departure from the rules, a violation of a right is a form of harm in and of itself merely *as* a violation of a right. This strengthens the utilitarian ground for taking rights seriously.

A bit of reflection will show that there are also what may be called "antecedent" or "underlying" systemic interests. Given the uncertainties of constant calculation, we all have an interest in the establishment of enforced rules. Acting on calculation in a particular case always has the disutility of not being system-related. Prior to the establishment of the "rule of the road," for example, driving on the left is no more (nor less) dangerous than driving on the right. But *both* pose dangers to others by virtue of not being system-related. Once a "rule of the road" is established, then one mode of driving becomes generally safer than the other, and safer than both were before.[65]

The sorts of interests I have labeled "systemic" are important for a utilitarian treatment of cooperation. Cooperation is engaged in because there is some state of affairs which is wanted but which it is perceived can only be achieved (or can be achieved best) if most persons involved engage in coordinated effort. Either they do the same kind of thing, or undertake interrelated roles with corresponding duties. Cooperation, then, serves an "underlying" interest. It also furthers the interest in the goods produced. Failure to comply, by upsetting trust, disappointing expectations, giving evidence of an uncooperative character, or, even, by raising the mere possibility of doing these, poses a threat to both sorts of interests.[66]

Mill was aware of such interests, and he recognized that cooperation is needed to serve those interests. Moreover, he was aware that cooperation is "unstable" to the extent that some in the group fail to comply. Indeed, he held that the law may properly be used to guarantee sufficient compliance in certain cases. In an important section of his *Principles of Political Economy*, he called attention to cases in which law is needed "not to overrule the judgment of individuals respecting their own interest, but to give effect to that judgment."[67] As an example, he suggested that workers in a factory, cutting back to nine hours a day from ten, could receive wages as high, or nearly as high, for the shorter workday. If an individual cut back alone, he or she would either lose his or her job or would sacrifice a day's portion of wages. (I presume here that Mill had assumed the employer would respond in one of these ways.) The individual cannot safely set the example unless convinced the others will follow suit. Nor is it likely that a voluntary agreement among them which is not enforced in a rigorous way will bring about the desired cooperation. "For however beneficial the observance of the regulation might be to the class collectively, the immediate interest of every individual would lie in violating it."[68] Ideally, of course, it would be desirable if the nine-hour day were the general rule, while those who wished to work extra time would be free to do so. It is not likely this could be maintained, however. The workers might, then, be better off with an enforced law that guarantees that each may safely work the shorter hours.

Mill also held that the government may rightfully regulate the acquisition of land. He argued that even if it is in the general and individual interest for persons not to occupy more than they can culti-vate, "it can never be the interest of an individual to exercise this forebearance, unless he is assured that others will do so too."[69] He went so far as to hold that the criminal law as a whole is based primarily on the consideration that each complying citizen is given some guarantee that his or her restriction of behavior will not be a sacrifice to those who do not comply. As we saw earlier, just such a claim was made by Professor Herbert Morris as one of the justifications of punishment. A similar analysis is found in Professor H. L. A. Hart's classic work, *The Concept of Law*.[70]

Thus, the need for systematizing behavior generates a need for cooperation, and that, in turn, creates a need for an enforceable rule that sets out a duty of compliance. A similar discussion is found in *On Liberty*, in the section in which Mill discussed "Sabbatarian legislation." He there recognized that where there is a cooperative practice enforced by law, it is "grounded in the direct interest which others have in each individual's observance of the practice."[71] The interest referred to here is clearly what I have called a systemic interest.

If we combine this analysis of cooperation with Mill's theory of rights, we get the beginnings of a theory of fairness. As we have seen, cooperation springs from and generates systemic interests of the partici-pants. There are times when those interests ought to be protected by means of a socially enforced rule. These are precisely the conditions under which Mill's analysis of rights commits him to holding that each cooperator has a right to the performances of the others. The interest which is systematically protected is the interest each has in the others' performances (as well as their interests in the goods produced). The correlative duty, then, has important features of a duty of fairness.

The relation of Mill's view to the contemporary debate can be seen by comparing Mill's position with statements by two leading present-day proponents of such a duty—Professors H. L. A. Hart, and John Rawls. Hart's formulation of such a duty was given in his well-known article, "Are There Any Natural Rights?" Hart wrote:

> when a number of persons conduct any joint enterprise according to rules and thus restrict their liberty, those who have submitted to these restric-tions when required have a right to a similar submission from those who have benefited by their submission . . . the moral obligation to obey the rules in such circumstances is *due* to the cooperating members of the society, and they have the correlative moral right to obedience.[72]

Rawls's statement of the principle (influenced by Hart's) reads:

> The main idea is that when a number of persons engage in a mutually advantageous cooperative venture according to rules, and thus restrict their liberty in ways necessary to yield advantages for all, those who have submitted to these restrictions have a right to a similar acquiescence on the part of those who have benefited from their submission. We are not to gain from the cooperative labors of others without doing our fair share.[73]

Now there is little in any of the accounts I have so far quoted that quite captures the notion of the "unfairness" involved in freeloading on a cooperative scheme. In an earlier paper, Rawls had given an explanation that can be accepted in terms of Mill's theory on rights. Cases of freeloading involve someone's taking the benefits of a scheme and the additional benefit of not sacrificing the time or effort or expenditure involved in following the rules. The benefits of cooperation, however, are a social product. Rawls put the objection against taking the "free benefit" as follows: "The reason one must abstain from this attempt is that the existence of the benefit is the result of everyone's effort, and prior to some understanding as to how it is to be shared, if it can be shared at all, it belongs in fairness to no one."[74]

While this statement takes us a bit further, there is still an unanalyzed sense of "fairness" in the last part of the statement. Perhaps this is unanalyzable and represents a primitive moral concept. Indeed, I shall argue later that Mill accepted certain "natural" principles of justice for which no further *analysis* can be given. (Of course, a *justification* must be given for *employing* them in our moral considerations.) Among these was a principle of distributive entitlement that apportions reward to voluntary effort and exertion. If this is regarded as a primary principle of distributive fairness, then freeloading would be a violation (at least under certain conditions). However, Mill need not appeal solely to a primitive "natural" sense of unfairness here. There are good utilitarian reasons for giving such a principle sway in many cases of freeloading, which have an independent ground.

It is clear that Mill would agree with Rawls that in clear-cut cases, the freeloader has no *right* to the "free benefit." This is to say, for Mill, that it would not be in the general interest to systematically protect persons who seek to grab off these benefits. In the first place, there are all the disutilities connected with the threat to security such behavior raises. Further, to *protect* freeloading would encourage attitudes of a selfish nature, whereas strict adherence to the grounds of cooperation strengthens the sense of interdependence and trust. It displays those attitudes of mutual regard and concern for the maintenance of cooperative relations that help social efforts to succeed, and which promote further cooperation. In addition, it is plausible that as cooperative social life thrives, the willingness to defer immediate gain for maintenance of social cooperation comes to be seen as a sign of respect for the participants as equals in the process. The cooperator does not take a benefit the others cannot also claim unless a process of entitlement has been decided on that *can* establish claims to the extra benefits.

There are, to be sure, all sorts of circumstances in which we would want to relax these claims, and some in which we would not want them to apply at all. The usual examples in the literature of lawn-crossings are precisely to the point. The issues involved are normally of such little concern to anyone that ordinary people do not tend to think issues of fairness are involved at all. There are good utilitarian reasons *not* to hold to any strict duty of fairness in these cases. My point is that there are almost always *some* disutilities entailed by freeloading, and, where the benefits and exertions or sacrifices really matter, the disutilities can be quite marked, especially if one throws in the matter of disrespect for the others that is taken as signalled by one who seizes advantages produced by the efforts of others. There is the further advantage to the person who does conform his or her behavior of retaining the respect of the others, which Mill thought an important need of persons. Thus, we may conclude, there could not be a general entitlement to those benefits, on a utilitarian theory of rights such as Mill's.

There is much more that needs to be said about duties of fairness. Robert Nozick, for one, has given convincing examples to show that it is not always wrong to take free benefits made available by others.[75] Mill would have no difficulty dealing with these examples, as it is clear that there are strong utilitarian reasons *against* a general obligation of such a sort. We could hardly lead autonomous lives if we could become obligated to others merely by their doing things that happen to benefit us. For anyone who accepts some principle of fairness, then, there is a serious problem of delimiting the conditions of its application.[76] As I shall show later, Mill seems to have placed at least one limit on such a duty, namely, that those obligated have been voluntary participants in the scheme. There are, however, certain ambiguities in Mill's statement on the matter. What I hope I have shown is that some such principle *can* be accepted within Mill's theory of justice, and that it is plausible to suppose that utilitarian considerations are available for setting out the content of such a principle (e.g., how insecure *is* the scheme, how important *are* the benefits, how onerous *are* the burdens, to what extent do participants have a choice with respect to participation and determination of the duties, to what extent *is* nearly universal cooperation required, and so on). Whether utilitarian arguments will support principles that accord with our intuitions in these matters cannot be answered without further study, however.

Before leaving this subject, there is one point I have made with respect to the rights of cooperators that I want to expand on; it can provide further reason for utilitarians to take rights seriously. I have pointed out that rights protect important interests, and that a good bit of their utility consists in their regular observance as part of a *system* of justice. Violators of the rights of cooperators, I argued, display an affront to the sense of dignity of the others by exempting themselves from the forebearances the others must abide by and which help define them as equals. However, in any advanced society that incorporates at least a rudimentary system of rights, those rights are strongly connected to one's sense of worth and adherence to those rights is a means of respecting the dignity of others. One maintains dignity *by* "standing on" rights. Unfortunately, Mill did not give an extended treatment of the requirements of human dignity. He seems most often to have thought of it as consisting in the sense of being an autonomous, free person. As we shall see, he held that being deprived of a voice in managing social affairs is an affront to human dignity; but he also said (in connection with a particular right) that people have a sense of "collective degradation" such that they will feel the withholding of an advantage from a person "because of a circumstance which they all have in common with him, an affront to all."[77] Insofar as respect for one another and dignity are central requisites of human well-being, rights will be integrally bound up with the general happiness, and we shall have another reason for holding that a violation of rights *as such* is wrong.

Desert and Distribution—Economic and Political Justice

In order to present Mill's substantive positions on issues of distributive justice, it will be necessary to extend his theory of desert. So far, we have discussed only the notion of desert in connection with punishment. But desert is a basis for reward also, and this must be brought in when economic and political justice are concerned. I shall summarize the general features of Mill's account of desert and reward and then I shall turn to specific issues of importance within economic and political justice.

Desert and Reward

Mill conceived justice in large part as enjoining that we refrain from harming others. Beneficence we may possibly not need from others, but one "always needs that they should not do him hurt." It is for this reason that the coercive apparatus of justice is maintained. Among the most serious cases of injustice, according to Mill, "are acts of wrongful aggression, or wrongful exercise of power over someone," to which he adds (though it is of lesser importance) the withholding of a good from someone "which is his due."[78]

We saw in the last section that Mill's theory of rights can give ground for a duty to perform positive acts, hence, duties of justice were not limited to forebearances from harming others. Similarly, in the passage just cited, Mill held that we sometimes have a duty to produce a positive good for a person when it is due the person. He proceeded to elaborate on this point in order to show that positive duties to do good are also connected to avoiding hurt or injury, even though the connection is not obvious.

> He who accepts benefits, and denies a return of them when needed, inflicts a real hurt, by disappointing one of the most natural and reasonable of expectations, and one which he must at least tacitly have encouraged, otherwise the benefits would seldom have been conferred. The important rank, among human evils and wrongs, of the disappointment of expectation, is shown in the fact that it constitutes the principal criminality of two such highly immoral acts as a breach of friendship and a breach of promise. Few hurts which human beings can sustain are greater, and none wound more, than when that on which they habitually and with full assurance relied, fails them in the hour of need; and few wrongs are greater than this mere withholding of good; none excite more resentment, either in the person suffering, or in a sympathizing spectator.[79]

He thus concluded that the principle of desert can be summarized as "good for good as well as evil for evil." It should be pointed out, however, that Mill did *not* think the connection with hurt explained above is the *only* ground for duties of positive good. He had explained that "its social utility is evident," and also that there is a "natural human feeling" associated with it. In other words, just as it is natural for us to desire retaliation for harms, it is natural to desire good for those who do good. Reward for good is a part of our natural response to the behavior of others, just as retaliation is a natural response to harms. The positive aspect of our sense of desert also has a natural basis.

Mill did not hold, however, that we have a duty to do all the good we can (in his sense of an enforceable duty). Were others to be said to have our unlimited benevolence *due* them, we would have a duty of justice and justice would swallow up all of morality. Similarly, he argued that if it were said that such concern for others is owed for what society does for the individual, then benevolence is assimilated to a duty of gratitude—another case of justice.[80] There are, to be sure, good utilitarian reasons for not enforcing a *general* requirement to do all the good we can. As Mill argued, we *require* that others not harm us, whereas we can often get along without their help. In addition, he held in several places—including the letter to George Grote cited earlier— that we can most often *do* our best for society by caring for ourselves, since we can know our own interests better,[81] and we only rarely have it in our power to significantly aid more than ourselves.[82] Furthermore, continual concern for others would involve our meddling in their affairs while neglecting our own. Such a general duty, then, would be anti-thetical to the principle of autonomy.

In another work, "August Comte and Positivism," Mill gave an explanation of how we acquire duties to perform beneficial acts to others that parallels his account in *Utilitarianism*:

> And inasmuch as every one, who avails himself of the advantages of society, leads others to expect from him all such positive good offices and disinterested services as the moral improvement attained by mankind has rendered customary, he deserves moral blame if, without just cause, he disappoints that expectation. Through this principle the domain of moral duty, in an improving society, is always widening. When what once was uncommon virtue becomes common virtue, it comes to be numbered among obligations, while a degree exceeding what has grown common, remains simply meritorious.[83]

This account by Mill raises a serious question of the status of duties of *imperfect* obligation. If the wrong done when we fail to promote customary goods is that of disappointment of expectation, it would appear that all duties to do good would become duties of justice, since particular persons would be denied a good that they can claim should be provided. They could claim a right, but if *this* is the way promoting positive good becomes a *duty*, then there seems no way to bring in beneficence in general, or charity in particular, *as* duties. I shall return to this subject later. For now, it is enough to see one way in which there can be duties to provide positive goods.

As the quotation from the "Comte" essay makes clear, Mill thought that accepting "the advantages of society" is a basis for duties to provide goods to others. In *On Liberty*, he indicated that "everyone who receives the protection of society owes a return for the benefit."[84] In the "Comte" essay, the return was made to consist of those goods customarily expected. In *On Liberty*, he appears to have thought of the return as extending to any "joint work necessary to the society of which he enjoys the protection."[85] Unfortunately, I know of no place where Mill explained how acceptance or receipt of the benefits of society obligate one, or how one is to determine what obligations are engendered. It may simply be that he thought this *also* to be a part of "natural justice." As social beings who also naturally desire and expect good for good, we desire and expect positive services as a return for the goods enjoyed from society. Such sentiments of desert could clearly be "moralized" in the way the desire for retaliation is in the "sentiment of justice."

It will be useful to focus on important features of Mill's full account of desert and reward. Judgments concerning desert, according to Mill, express certain "natural" sentiments that are "moralized." We *have* a nature as human beings that causes us to react in certain ways to harms to ourselves and others, and to beneficent behavior by others. There are good utilitarian reasons for allowing desert, so conceived, to be a basis for determining our treatment of one another. The most general principle of desert that emerges requires "good for good, evil for evil."

It must be emphasized that "doing good" and "doing bad" are matters of voluntary behavior. The sentiments of resentment or approval, for example, are not engaged by involuntary acts. If a person hurts us accidentally, or as the result of a physical impairment rendering the person not in control, we may regret the behavior, but do not *resent* it. Similarly, one who benefits us *only* as an unanticipated result of that person's *self*-interested act is not praised or rewarded for the benefit. Responsibility, choice, effort, sacrifice, and so on, are the notions which play a role in the concept of desert. Put generally: penalties and rewards are merited by voluntary efforts. As will be clear, some such principle was central to Mill's theory of distributive justice. A further principle falls out from this first one: natural ability or disability alone are *not* bases for reward or penalty.

A further point that must be emphasized is the role of the notions of freedom and autonomy in Mill's thought on distributive justice. There are two ways those notions enter in. On the negative side, we must stress that autonomy helps to define the "primary moralities." Unjustified interference with freedom and wrongful exercise of power over others are among the "most marked cases of injustice."[86] Thus, impeding the autonomous life of others is an important basis for desert, justifying consequent penalties. On the positive side, reward is deserved for goods produced by voluntary, autonomous behavior.

I shall turn in the following sections to an examination of how Mill's primary principle of desert enters into his substantive views on distributive justice. It will be useful, however, to begin by examining his views on the subject of equality.

Equality

There are few subjects that so inflame the passions and numb the intellect as that of equality. Quite a lot of nonsense has been written on this topic; as we shall see, Mill made his own contributions to this state of affairs. Commentators on Mill have thus been led to make highly qualified judgments of his opinions on equality.

Pedro Schwartz, for example, takes Mill to have been an egalitarian, but holds that "he was no leveller."[87] According to Schwartz, Mill favored a *kind* of equality, but not the "mechanical 'soak the rich' brand."[88] Schwartz explains Mill's goal as that of a cooperative society of equals, unencumbered by class strife and division, and not centered on large numbers filling a dependent role within wage relationships. The goal was to be achieved through the development and proliferation of worker cooperatives, not by a forced redistribution of wealth to effect a general levelling.

Professor R. J. Halliday, in a recent commentary on Mill, correctly points out that Mill had endorsed equality as an end in itself. Still, he cites a passage wherein Mill states that while equality is one of the ends of government, it is not the sole end, so that while all should be done to further equality, such efforts must stop short of "impairing the security of the property which is the product and reward of personal exertion."[89] Halliday remarks that priorities are indicated in the quotation, and that "those priorities seem to favour the institution of private property above the end of equality."[90] In discussing Mill's views in *Considerations on Representative Government*, he notes that "very little remains of Mill's stated commitment to equality."[91] Still, this is no inconsistency, as "his commitment to equality was always vague and insubstantial."[92]

Finally, Professor John Gray, in an excellent paper outlining Mill's theory of property, remarks on the same passage cited by Halliday about the security of property. Gray correctly notices that Mill was not endorsing *property* as good in itself, but as a device for "guaranteeing deserved rewards."[93] Nonetheless, the quotation shows, according to Gray, that Mill's acceptance of the labor theory of value "entailed no overriding commitment to equality."[94]

I shall not contend that these depictions of Mill on equality are wrong. They are, however, seriously misleading, in that they attribute to him a somewhat "weak-kneed" acceptance of the end of equality. I shall contend that Mill, in fact, had a strong commitment to a substantive conception of equality, and that he favored significant changes in the economic and political structure of his day to further that equality.

Unfortunately, the one place where Mill explicitly addressed the issue of equality in an extended treatment is a disaster. In *Utilitarianism*, he discussed those "maxims of equality and impartiality" that are among the rules of justice:

> In one point of view, they may be considered as corollaries from the principles already laid down. If it is a duty to do to each according to his deserts, returning good for good as well as repressing evil by evil, it necessarily follows that we should treat all equally well (when no higher duty forbids) who have deserved equally well of us, and that society should treat all equally well who have deserved equally well of it, that is, who have deserved equally well absolutely. This is the highest abstract standard of social and distributive justice; towards which all institutions, and the efforts of all virtuous citizens, should be made in the utmost possible degree to converge. But this great moral duty rests upon a still deeper foundation, being a direct emanation from the first principle of morals, and not a mere logical corollary from secondary or derivative doctrines. It is involved in the very meaning of Utility, or the Greatest-Happiness Principle. That principle is a mere form of words without rational signification, unless one person's happiness, supposed equal in degree (with the proper allowance made for kind), is counted for exactly as much as another's. Those conditions being supplied, Bentham's dictum, "everybody to count for one, nobody for more than one," might be written under the principle of utility as an explanatory commentary. The equal claim of everybody to happiness in the estimation of the moralist and the legislator, involves an equal claim to all the means of happiness, except in so far as the inevitable conditions of human life, and the general interest, in which that of every individual is included, set limits to the maxim; and those limits ought to be strictly construed. As every other

maxim of justice, so this, is by no means applied or held applicable universally; on the contrary, as I have already remarked, it bends to every person's ideas of social expediency. But in whatever case it is deemed applicable at all, it is held to be the dictate of justice. All persons are deemed to have a *right* to equality of treatment, except when some recognised social expediency requires the reverse.[95]

None of this supports a substantive view of equality, and much of it reflects extraordinarily confused thinking. If reward is to be strictly conditioned to desert, then unequal treatment will be favored whenever there has been differential desert. Further, counting each person for one permits the complete sacrifice of the happiness of some. That everyone counts only guarantees that each person's happiness be *considered*; but if, after weighing that person's happiness too, it is discovered that "the inevitable conditions of human life, and the general interest" favor ignoring that person's happiness, no further appeal to equality seems necessary. Also, if we took seriously Mill's parenthetical reference to "the proper allowance made for kind" in assessing people's claims to happiness, we would have to conclude that the claims of some are stronger than the claims of others. Finally, the reference to a "claim" to happiness can hardly be a reference to an equal right, unless that right be construed in the weak sense of a right to consideration discussed above. There is nothing in the abstract statement of the "Greatest-Happiness Principle" that entails that the general welfare is best achieved by having a rule of justice that guarantees against sacrificing some for the greater good. There may be good utilitarian reasons, given the nature of persons and facts of life, to *have* such a rule. Indeed, Mill's theory of value and his theory of justice provide strong ground for such a rule (as I shall argue), but no such principle, guaranteeing an equal right to minimal happiness, seems to follow as a matter of "rational signification" alone from the Principle of Utility.

I want to show that Mill held what I shall term a "baseline" conception of equality. This conception can be summarized in four propositions:

1. Substantive inequalities of wealth, education, and power are *prima facie* wrong, and require justification.
2. Substantive inequalities must not permit any to "go to the wall"; redistribution to provide subsistence must be guaranteed.
3. Inequalities must not undermine the status of persons *as equals*. In concrete terms, this means that inequalities must not result in

some gaining complete power over the lives of others, or in some
persons being degraded.
4. Only *certain* kinds of grounds serve to justify inequality—that
the inequality will make no one worse off, or that it is the result
of rewarding according to desert. Advantages must be *earned*
through voluntary effort.

These propositions imply that inequalities must not be permitted to
push anyone below a certain "baseline": minimum means to happiness
must be guaranteed as a right to all; status as a full-fledged participant in
the common social life must be guaranteed as a right. Furthermore, as I
shall try to show below, Mill did not have an "overriding" commitment
to property, or even to the principle of desert; he was willing to interfere
with both in order to preserve "baseline" equality. Though no "wel-
fare-statist," he certainly had no absolutist objections to income trans-
fers or redistributive taxation in order to preserve the equality I have
described.

The four propositions define a conception of equality in the sense
that they specify minimal conditions for distributions that would guarantee status as equals. Adherence to these propositions would secure for
everyone a share in the goods needed to preserve dignity and independence. Power and wealth would be restricted so that one not be subjected to the arbitrary will of others. On the other hand, the conception
specifies grounds for departures from strict equality that do not necessarily undercut equal status. Inequalities that do not violate the other
conditions can be justified if they have been earned. Thus, these
propositions provide a conception of what it is to have the moral status
of an equal of others in a complex society.

I shall support my claims concerning Mill on equality in the following way. In the remainder of this section, I shall summarize some of the
arguments Mill gave for equality or against inequality; in this way,
some of the arguments for the four propositions above will be brought
out. In the following sections, I shall discuss Mill's views on economic
and political justice. It will be made clearer how Mill's conception of
equality applies in those areas, while, at the same time, further grounds
will be presented to support my claim that Mill *had* the position on
equality I have attributed to him.

The first important argument for equality involves Mill's claim that
modern life, and civilization itself, increasingly require equality. Mill
maintained that a definitive feature of civilization is the extent to which

cooperation takes place. Joint efforts for common goals are spurred by increasing civilization. Cooperation spurs greater productivity, and one result is an increase in capital accumulation and its spread to the masses.[96] An increase in cooperation, and the concomitant division of labor, create a greater interdependence among persons. Indeed, he held that in modern life, the most crucial elements of, or conditions for, happiness are secured by society:

> As civilization advances, every person becomes dependent, for more and more of what most nearly concerns him, not upon his own exertions, but upon the general arrangements of society. In a rude state, each man's personal security, the protection of his family, his property, his liberty itself, depend greatly upon his bodily strength and his mental energy or cunning: in a civilized state, all this is secured to him by causes extrinsic to himself.[97]

Historically speaking, increased literacy has resulted, along with a corresponding increase in the powers of communication among the masses. As property, intelligence, and the "power of combination" are all sources of power, the lower classes have, and will continue to, gain power as against that of the higher classes.[98] These levelling tendencies inherent in civilization will result in a feeling among the working classes against all inequalities, and, he held, "the only way of mitigating that feeling is to remove all inequalities that can be removed without preponderant disadvantages."[99] Mill also maintained that there are certain prerequisites for societal cohesion and permanence. Among these is that there be a source of allegiance or loyalty for members of the society, and, for the reasons given, the only such sources likely to be successful in the future are "the principles of individual freedom and political and social equality, as realized in institutions which as yet exist nowhere, or exist only in a rudimentary state."[100]

A second reason to be found in Mill's writing in favor of equality is that inequality has harmful effects on those at the lower end of the scale. He wrote that great inequalities of "wealth and social rank" have a "demoralizing effect" on the disadvantaged.[101] He also maintained that the state has a duty to compensate for natural inequalities, for "in the race of life all do not start fair," so that if the state fails to act "the unfairness becomes utterly crushing and dispiriting."[102] While we may question on what basis it should be judged at the outset that the failure of the state to act is "unfair," at the very least it is indeed plausible to argue that those left behind at the starting line will be "crushed and dispirited" if not assisted. In addition, Mill maintained that everyone is stimulated to greater exertion when "all start fair," thus citing a further consequential ground for compensating natural disadvantage.[103]

Other bad effects were cited by Mill as resulting from those inequalities that leave some in "abject poverty." A laboring class kept in such status is likely to be kept in a state of subjection, unable to have an autonomous role in the common social and political life.[104] One of the chief elements in a happy life is utterly defeated.

Even the wage relationship was condemned by Mill for its inherent inequalities and the bad consequences for laborers. The wage relationship creates a social arrangement in which the parties have hostile interests, and one party—the laborer—is left in a position of dependency on the capitalist. Again, the central value of autonomy is defeated, and Mill insisted that the aim of improvement should be to enable people to work with or for one another "in relations not involving dependence."[105]

A third reason Mill gave for promoting equality was that inequality has bad effects on those who are *favored*. In a social situation marked by large inequalities of means and power, those who rule have a tendency to underestimate the interests of those less well off, and to give greater emphasis to the interests of those with whom they identify. In his own society, he believed that a result of inequality was that the sense of obligation was "lamentably unequal." Consequently:

> The comfort and suffering of one man, on the foreknowledge of which all rational sense of obligation towards him is based, counts in general estimation for something infinitely more than that of another man in a different rank or position. The great mass of our labouring population have no representatives in Parliament, and cannot be said to have any political station whatever; while the distribution of what may be called social dignity is more unequal in England than in any other civilized country of Europe, and the feeling of communion and brotherhood between man and man more artificially graduated according to the niceties of the scale of wealth. Assuming perfect rectitude of intentions on the part of a statesman, it is hardly possible that his moral calculations should not be more or less vitiated by the impurities of such an atmosphere.[106]

At times, Mill put his point more strongly, by emphasizing that the exercise of power over others, especially when the power has not been earned, morally corrupts those who are so favored. Large-scale inequalities of wealth and social status were both implicated on these grounds. It is not the *amount* of wealth that corrupts, but inequality itself, especially when it is not merited and has been obtained without personal exertion.[107] The relation of superiors to inferiors, he wrote, "is the nursery of these [selfish] vices of character, which, wherever else they exist, are an overflowing from that source."[108] Among these vices are pride, wilfulness, overbearingness, arrogance, self-indulgence; if left unrestrained, unearned indulgence of power can lead to actual physical cruelty.[109] Though some of these last points were made in connection with the marriage relationship, it is clear that Mill thought the points can be generalized. He described the marriage relationship as one example of "the corrupting influence of power," and wrote that it is true of servitude "except when it actually brutalizes," that it is corrupting to both but "less so to the slaves than to the slave-masters."[110]

Unearned luxury has the further effect, according to Mill, of deadening and enervating the mind. Contrary to those who claim pleasure has this effect, he insisted that the impetus to exercise one's intellect and talents is lessened when one's fortunes are secure and unquestioned without personal effort.[111]

Mill indicted inequality as a source of power over others, and held that this corrupts those favored by the inequalities. Yet he often emphasized, quite strongly, the evils of power itself, and this can be seen to connect with his most important arguments in favor of equality.

Mill, in various places, distinguished the desire for liberty from the desire to control others. In a passage in the essay "Centralisation," he made this point graphically:

> We look upon this confounding of the love of liberty with the love of power, the desire not to be improperly controlled with the ambition of exercising control, to be both a psychological error, and the worst possible moral lesson. If there be an ethical doctrine which more than all others requires to be taught, and has been taught with deepest conviction by the great moral teachers, it is, that the love of power is the most evil passion of human nature; that power over others, power of coercion and compulsion, any power other than that of moral and intellectual influence, even in the cases where it is indispensable, is a snare, and in all others a curse, both to the possessor and to those over whom it is possessed; a burthen which no rightly constituted moral nature consents to take upon itself, but by one of the greatest sacrifices which inclination ever makes to duty. With the love of liberty it is wholly the reverse. The love of liberty, in the only proper sense of that word, is unselfish; it places no one in a position of hostility to the good of his fellow-creatures; all alike may be free, and the freedom of one has no solid security but in the equal freedom of the rest. The appetite for power is, on the contrary, essentially selfish; for all cannot have power;

the power of one is power over others, who not only do not share in his elevation, but whose depression is the foundation on which it is raised.[112]

Similarly, in his essay on Comte, Mill had described what he regarded as the ideal state of human desiring, and wrote that the one passion which is "permanently" incompatible with it is "the love of domination, or superiority, for its own sake; which implies, and is grounded on, the equivalent depression of other people."[113]

Part of the significance of the emphasis on the evil of illegitimate exercise of power is that Mill could claim that equality (or inequality) does not have merely instrumental value (or disvalue). To be sure, it has bad effects on both the inferior and superior parties, and it may be that we are most secure in our rights when others share in them; but if relations of domination are inherently bad, if they necessarily incorporate a negation of basic aspects of human well-being, then inequalities that manifest those power relations are *in themselves* evil. As was pointed out at the outset of my discussion of equality, Mill had written that equality is one of the *ends* of "good social arrangements," and should be promoted so long as that property that is the "product and reward of personal exertion" is not impaired.[114] And, in *Considerations on Representative Government*, he argued for proportional representation of minorities in the ruling power, for otherwise they would be ruled by the majority, and equality, which is "the very root and foundation" of democracy, would be subverted.[115] In a letter to Arthur Helps, he wrote:

> As I look upon inequality as *in itself* always an evil, I do not agree with anyone who would use the machinery of society for the purpose of promoting it. As much inequality as necessarily arises from protecting all persons in the free use of their faculties of body and mind and in the enjoyment of what these can obtain for them, must be submitted to for the sake of a greater good: but I certainly see no necessity for artificially adding to it, while I see much for tempering it, impressing both on the laws and on the usages of mankind as far as possible the contrary tendency.[116]

In this same letter, Mill had written that the art of living with others "consists first and chiefly in treating and being treated by them as equals." This was a theme he often emphasized. I showed earlier that he thought modern society is tending in this direction. This may be a weak ground for promoting equality insofar as there appear to be overwhelming countertendencies that have arisen in our own day, when the multinational corporation imposes a manner of existence on everyone, and traditional centers of wealth in oil, banking, and so on, continue to dominate the political life of the community. Mill was aware that even in his own day there were contrary tendencies evident. Today, it would seem the evidence is strong that future life need not be that of genuine social and political equality.

If, on the other hand, inequalities are part of social relations that involve inherently evil power relations, then the objection to such inequalities is stronger in that it does not depend on the contingency of what tendencies in society are likely to be realized. Indeed, if corporate democracy fosters or preserves or requires *de facto* inequalities that permit domination of some by others, then Mill's theory of equality provides a ground for condemning it. Furthermore, Mill's theory will not accept a justification that appeals to greater efficiency, or increased material prosperity, because an essential element of happiness for the great mass of people is undercut by the relationships inherent in the structure of economic and social life of corporate power.

The letter to Arthur Helps also hints at a positive aspect of the value of equality. It is not merely that *in*equality entails objectionable power relations. Living with others involves treatment as equals; an ideal state of human character essentially involves regarding others as one's equal. In "Utility of Religion," Mill held that in superior persons sympathy and benevolence, together with "the passion for ideal excellence," leads to a morality based on the good of the whole, "neither sacrificing the individual to the aggregate nor the aggregate to the individual." These same feelings, together with the "force of shame," tend in the same direction among inferior natures.[117] In *The Subjection of Women*, he maintained that:

> the true virtue of human beings is fitness to live together as equals; claiming nothing for themselves but what they as freely concede to every one else; regarding command of any kind as an exceptional necessity, and in all cases a temporary one; and preferring, whenever possible, the society of those with whom leading and following can be alternate and reciprocal.[118]

In the essay on Comte, Mill condemned the desire for power, and described the ideal state of desiring as one in which persons habitually wish to share their pleasures with others, and scorn "to desire anything for oneself which is incapable of being so shared."[119] In *Utilitarianism*, Mill emphasized that the social feelings—sympathy, "the desire to be in unity with our fellow creatures"—together with the influences of "advancing civilization," promote a society of equals.[120] His point is not merely that there is such a contingent consequence to be expected. Rather, his point is that our social natures cannot be fully satisfied, we cannot be fully happy, without those relations of sympathetic unity. In *The Subjection of Women*, he wrote of a justice grounded on "sympathetic association; having its root no longer in the instinct of equals for self-protection, but in cultivated sympathy between them; and no one being left out, but an equal measure being extended to all."[121] A person's feeling of unity with others, he reiterated in *Utilitarianism*, "if perfect, would make him never think of, or desire, any beneficial condition for himself, in the benefits of which they are not included."[122]

Mill did add that emphasis on the social feelings could be too great, resulting in excessive interference with freedom and individual development. Happiness *is*, after all, complex. Adjustments have to be made among its elements. But status as equals is inherently good *as* an aspect of a happy life.

I believe my discussion of Mill's views on equality has gone a long way toward establishing that he held to the four propositions, outlined above, giving the essence of the "baseline" conception of equality. I shall turn to a discussion of his conceptions of economic and political justice. It will be clearer *how* he employed his views on equality, and the discussion will bring forth further evidence that he adhered to the view of equality I have advanced.

Economic Justice

I shall not attempt a general survey of Mill's economic and political theories. Other commentators have done this far better than I could.[123] My objective shall be to bring out the basic principles of economic justice to which Mill adhered; and I shall pick out certain important economic issues to show how those principles were applied by Mill. I shall begin by listing Mill's basic principles, along with some of the textual support for my claim that he held the principles. I shall then discuss his positions on property, taxation, the wage relation, and the Poor Laws. In some cases, I will try to show how Mill's positions can be extended and applied to matters of contemporary importance and debate.

Basic Principles. The most basic principle of economic justice in Mill's work is the principle that economic rewards should be proportioned to one's labor, or exertions. In several places, he criticized the economic arrangements of his day for permitting some to "be born to the enjoyment of all the external advantages which life can give, without earning them by any merit or acquiring them by any exertion of their own."[124] Throughout his work, we see some economic arrangement or other condemned or supported by appeal to its inconsistency or congruence with this principle.

I know of no argument by Mill to support this principle. He did refer to it as an "acknowledged" principle of justice,[125] and there is no question that he believed the principle to be accepted by the socialists and capitalists of his day. He depicted the former group as *standing* on this principle as a basis for criticizing contemporary social arrangements, and, he described the injustice of a scheme that violates the principle as "obvious."[126] The principle does not quite fall within the dictum of "good for good, evil for evil," because useful, productive exertion or effort is not necessarily a case of "doing good," which he seems to have regarded as requiring an intention to help others. He may have thought that in a modern economy, labor can be viewed as falling within those cooperative arrangements that generate duties of reciprocity as discussed earlier, so that the principle may, via that route, fall within the scope of the most general principle of distributive justice. At times, he also *seems* to have equated this principle with a basic principle of private property—that a laborer has a right to the product of his or her labor. The principles are *not* equivalent, however. As Mill understood this principle, the right to the produce of labor includes the right to what the product itself can be exchanged for, as well as the right to what one can get for one's labor itself. Understood in this way, the principle of private property is *not* equivalent to the principle of reward proportionate to exertion. The right to *a* reward or payment is not the same as a right to the very product of labor; and what the product or one's labor can be exchanged for need not reflect exertion. Exchange value in the market can involve such arbitrary elements as market conditions (e.g., the demand for *that* product or *those* skills), and luck (e.g., weather conditions or other natural events that have made that product scarce). As we shall see, Mill appealed to just such facts in differentiating the tax treatment of skilled and unskilled labor, and of income from labor and income from rents. Moreover, Mill held out as an ideal state of society one in which the *product* of labor would be commonly owned, "when it will no longer either be, or be thought to be, impossible for human beings to exert themselves strenuously in procuring benefits which are not to be exclusively their own, but to be shared with the society they belong to."[127] Moreover, he described the private property principle as one necessitated by the existing failures of society to do perfect justice. Since society does *not* guarantee reward for exertion, it is just that laborers have a right to the produce of labor. However, he clearly favored *shared* property within a system that makes reward more closely related to effort. That there are problems reconciling the two aspects of this ideal is not germane to my point here, which is that the private property principle was most often thought of by Mill as a separate principle from that which holds that economic rewards should be proportioned to labor. This principle, then, cannot be justified by reference to his acceptance of the labor theory of private property.

What seems most likely to me is that Mill thought the basic principle of economic reward to be a part of "natural justice," that is, it is one of those natural reactions to the efforts of ourselves and others within an economic framework to desire that those efforts be met with reward. He described the principle of private property as a "natural impression of justice," and he most likely thought of the more general principle in the same way. Indeed, he described the "socialist" principle that all should be born to equal advantages as also a "natural impression." The "natural impressions" of justice must be adjudicated by appeal to utility—"the tendency of things to promote or impede human happiness."[128] If I am right, then the general account of desert as being based on natural feelings produced by conduct fits Mill's account of economic justice as well.

A second important principle of economic (and political) justice that Mill employed requires that the distribution of economic goods must not permit some to gain unrestrained power or control over the lives of others. It should be recalled that part of Mill's argument for what I termed "baseline equality" involved this principle. I pointed out that he condemned the wage relationship partly because it involves objectionable relations of dependence. Further, he consistently argued that the state has the right to regulate the accumulation and use of land (which he contrasted with "movable property"), partly on the ground that control of land in excess of that needed for personal subsistence results in some having power over others, and in ways that affect "their most vital interests."[129]

Given the great value attributed to individual autonomy in Mill's theory of value, it is almost axiomatic that there should be a right to autonomy, at least in the sense of imposing a duty on society not to interfere with autonomous behavior except for self-protection. As I shall argue in the next chapter, Mill's theory of liberty was, in fact, a branch of his theory of justice, and is best understood as an extended argument for a right to act as an autonomous agent. It would follow that if society permits economic accumulation that results in the destruction of autonomy, it fails to protect a basic right (and a basic element of happiness), and thus is unjust.

In addition, Mill believed that governmental power in a community tends to mirror the real power in a society.[130] Economic power can be crucial, especially if inequalities reach a state where some are kept in abject poverty. Such a state results in being kept under subjection by the privileged classes, and autonomy is impossible.[131] We should expect, then, that Mill would endorse a corollary to the principle opposing economic distribution that permits domination. The corollary would, at the least, require redistributive efforts to guarantee at least a minimal level of subsistence. I argued earlier that such a principle played a role in Mill's conception of "baseline" equality, and I shall show that he did favor redistribution—in the form of taxation exemptions and the Poor Laws—that would maintain minimal support levels.

Mill did not stop short at favoring redistribution to rectify unjust socially induced inequality. As we saw earlier, he used the analogy of "the race of life," in arguing that the state must act so that some are not left behind at the starting point, and he described the failure to redress natural inequalities as "unfair."[132] He condemned greater taxation of the poor and weak because they derive protection from the state they otherwise could not provide themselves as "the reverse of the true idea of distributive justice, which consists not in imitating but in redressing the inequalities and wrongs of nature."[133]

To be sure, the analogy of "the race of life" is misleading. As Robert Nozick correctly points out: "life is not a race in which we all compete for a prize which someone has established; there is no unified race, with some person judging swiftness"; but then, neither is "life" as Nozick has described it:

> there are different persons separately giving other persons different things. Those who do the giving (each of us, at times) usually do not care about desert or about the handicaps labored under; they care simply about what they actually get. No centralized process judges people's use of the opportunities they had; that is not what the processes of social cooperation and exchange are *for*.[134]

Indeed, life is not a race in the literal sense Nozick describes. Still, some people, *as things exist*, are permitted to accumulate goods, or the means to goods, that others, *due largely to matters of birth*, cannot obtain because the existing "processes of social cooperation and exchange" permit distribution to ignore need and desert. While Mill wrote of inequalities of "nature," a natural feature of a person, *in a social setting*, is a handicap or inequality only to the extent that that natural feature is a basis for disadvantage, or makes it more difficult to achieve a basis for reward. The "processes of social cooperation and exchange" are not *for* any purpose outside of the social ends to which they are put. Thus, life *is* somewhat racelike in that there is a measure of competition for things, and the terms of social and economic interchange can impose penalties on some by virtue of natural features of persons. Whether any natural feature is a "handicap" in getting one's needs met depends on how society *chooses* to require or permit distributions of things,[135] as well as on the things valued in that society.[136]

Finally, there is a negative corollary to the principles already picked out, to which Mill systematically appealed. This principle states that it is wrong to *penalize* industry and thrift, or unnecessarily interfere with liberty. The previously stated principles directly entail this principle, of course, but Mill sometimes appealed to it directly, citing the utilitarian grounds which support it, and the more general principles from which it follows. For example, in *Considerations on Representative Government*, he argued that a taxation scheme that "does not impede the industry, or unnecessarily interfere with the liberty, of the citizen" both preserves and promotes the increase of community wealth, while encouraging "a more active use of the individual faculties."[137]

Before I embark on showing how these basic principles of economic justice were employed by Mill, it is important that I clarify their status. These principles are extremely general and have been formulated in abstract, even vague terms. For example, I have stated the first principle as basing reward on "merit or exertion." Mill used these terms himself. But he used others as well, such as "industry," "sacrifice," "contribution," and "effort." Not all of these are equivalent, and where they do not coincide in meaning, there can arise conflicts that raise serious problems of justice. As an instance, in a cooperative venture, there can be conflicting demands on the benefits produced based on the actual contribution as opposed to the actual sacrifice on the part of workers. While there are good utilitarian reasons to reward those with greater skill when they actually employ it in production, the skills themselves may involve "natural" advantages to which the workers are born, and which they have not earned or merited. Mill was aware of such subtleties, and he did not suppose that abstract principles of the sorts I have enunciated can alone resolve such conflicts.[138]

There is a further problem in formulating the rights that can be claimed are correlated with these "principles" of justice. What, specifically, is entailed by the principle that natural inequalities are to be redressed? Do people have a right that their physical appearance will play no role in determining their life prospects? In what *areas* of life could such a right be asserted: job hiring? choice of marriage partners? Of course, some of the rights that would be needed to realize some of the principles given could require taking things or income, or demanding labor from others. What limits must be observed here, and what would justify doing *any* of these things at all? While I do not think these are insuperable problems that show there cannot *be* rights that correlate with principles such as those I have attributed to Mill, these difficulties show at least that I have not adequately formulated definitive principles.

In these respects, it may be claiming too much to call the formulations I have given "principles." It may be better to regard them as stating important, relevant, considerations in determining the justice of economic arrangements. This attitude is, perhaps, underscored, when one considers that Mill thought all such principles require utilitarian justification in their application.

I want to turn now to specific topics of economic concern.

Property. We saw earlier that Mill endorsed a principle of private property—that individuals have a right to the fruits of their labor. I showed that he considered this principle to be correlated with a "natural impression" of justice. He also thought, however, that, given the way in which society is organized, and the limited cooperativeness of human nature as it has so far developed, demands of security justify the principle of private property. Mill made this point forcefully:

> Insecurity of person and property, is as much as to say, uncertainty of the connexion between all human exertions or sacrifice, and the attainment of the ends for the sake of which they are undergone. It means, uncertainty whether they who sow shall reap, whether they who produce shall consume, and they who spare to-day shall enjoy to-morrow. It means, not only that labour and frugality are not the road to acquisition, but that violence is. When person and property are to a certain degree insecure, all

the possessions of the weak are at the mercy of the strong. No one can keep what he has produced, unless he is more capable of defending it, than others who give no part of their time and exertions to useful industry are of taking it from him.[139]

He also claimed that it contributes to the general welfare by promoting greater productivity;[140] but this means that private property is a means to an end, not a part of the end itself, and Mill stated this in just those terms.[141] Furthermore, it will follow that distributive mechanisms involving property are unjustified to the extent that they fail to accord with the principle of private property—that property "belongs" to the person or persons who produced it. Though he made proper allowance for the role of capital and past labor in the production of present capital, he consistently and vehemently condemned the practice of property in his day as inconsistent with the basic principle of private property:

> The principle of private property has never yet had a fair trial in any country; and less so, perhaps, in this country than in some others. The social arrangements of modern Europe commenced from a distribution of property which was the result, not of just partition, or acquisition by industry, but of conquest and violence. . . . The laws of property have never yet conformed to the principles on which the justification of private property rests. They have made property of things which never ought to be property, and absolute property where only a qualified property ought to exist. They have not held the balance fairly between human beings, but have heaped impediments on some, to give advantage to others; they have purposely fostered inequalities, and prevented all from starting fair in the race.[142]

Because private property is a means to an end, and because existing property institutions failed to conform to the principle that justifies property, he held that society has the right both to limit the accumulation of private property and to control its use. Subject to the principle that compensation must be made for dispossession, "society is fully entitled to abrogate or alter any particular right of property which on sufficient consideration it judges to stand in the way of the public good."[143] Mill did distinguish between "movable property" and property in land. Of the former, he thought it in the interest of society to limit acquisition, rather than to control the use of it.[144] While acknowledging the abstract right, he believed it best that it not be exercised in practice.

He did believe unlimited accumulation of wealth to be an evil, though he emphasized that it was the *distribution* more than the amount that is objectionable.[145] I have reviewed Mill's reasons for this claim when discussing his position on equality. The two basic considerations to which he seems to have appealed, with respect to accumulation, were that personal effort or exertion (and perhaps thrift or "abstinence" from use) justify reward, while accumulation that impedes the "base equality" of others may be interfered with (at least in the form of redistributive taxation). These considerations were reflected in his insistence that rights of inheritance and bequeathal may be strictly limited, with no one person entitled to receive more than "the means of comfortable independence."[146] The considerations mentioned were reflected in his view that the law should guarantee a subsistence to the poor.[147] The considerations *permit* accumulation that results from personal effort, and he seems to have acknowledged the propriety of accumulation (apparently, whether "earned" or not) that "Makes none of the others worse off than they otherwise would be."[148] Of course, large-scale economic benefits always carry the potential of making others worse off (even if only via increased economic power), and no one can claim a *right* to unearned benefits; hence, such accumulation can be tapped, for example, through taxation, for the benefit of society.

It is important to emphasize two aspects of Mill's views on inheritance and bequeathal. The right of bequeathal, he thought, *is* a part of the idea of property, but the right of inheritance is not. Moreover, there are good utilitarian grounds for recognizing rights of bequeathal. No one person should be permitted, however, to receive an excessive inheritance; this is wrong on the dual grounds that it provides unearned reward, and impedes fair competition in society:

> It is not the fortunes which are earned, but those which are unearned, that it is for the public good to place under limitation. A just and wise legislation would abstain from holding out motives for dissipating rather than saving the earnings of honest exertion. Its impartiality between competitors would consist in endeavouring that they should all start fair, and not in hanging a weight upon the swift to diminish the distance between them and the slow. Many, indeed, fail with greater efforts than those with which others succeed, not from difference of merits, but difference of opportunities; but if all were done which it would be in the power of a good government to do, by instruction and by legislation, to diminish this inequality of opportunities, the differences of fortune aris-

ing from people's own earnings could not justly give umbrage. With respect to the large fortunes acquired by gift or inheritance, the power of bequeathing is one of those privileges of property which are fit subjects for regulation on grounds of general expediency; and I have already suggested, as a possible mode of restraining the accumulation of large fortunes in the hands of those who have not earned them by exertion, a limitation of the amount which any one person should be permitted to acquire by gift, bequest, or inheritance.[149]

Thus, the first point I want to emphasize is that among the objectives of the limitation on inheritance is a redistributive one—that of making people's life opportunities more equal.

The second point I want to emphasize is that Mill apparently thought his proposals on this subject were *radically* redistributive. In his biography of Mill, Alexander Bain remarked that Mill thought that adoption of his proposals "would pull down all large fortunes in two generations."[150]

As I pointed out earlier, Mill distinguished "movable" property from land. Both may be controlled for the social good, but he was unwilling in practice to limit or control *earned* movable property. Land was a different matter, however: "all the land might be declared the property of the State, without interfering with the right of property in anything which is the product of human labour and abstinence."[151]

Raw land, Mill said, is not the product of labor, and, as such, belongs to no one. But most of the value of land does result from labor, and tenure in land is necessary for industry to bear its fruits. So, expediency will justify some property rights in land. And expediency should determine which ones:

> To me it seems almost an axiom that property in land should be interpreted strictly, and that the balance in all cases of doubt should incline against the proprietor. The reverse is the case with property in moveables, and in all things the product of labour: over these, the owner's power both of use and of inclusion should be absolute, except where positive evil to others would result from it: but in the case of land, no exclusive right should be permitted in any individual, which cannot be shown to be productive of positive good. To be allowed any exclusive right at all, over a portion of the common inheritance, while there are others who have no portion, is already a privilege. No quantity of moveable goods which a person can acquire by his labour, prevents others from acquiring the like by the same means; but from the very nature of the case, whoever owns land, keeps others out of the enjoyment of it. The privilege, or monopoly, is only defensible as a necessary evil; it becomes an injustice when carried

to any point to which the compensating good does not follow it. . . . The species at large still retains, of its original claim to the soil of the planet which it inhabits, as much as is compatible with the purposes for which it has parted with the remainder.[152]

Thus, he held that property in land need not imply exclusive right to access to the land (say to enjoy its scenery), nor does it imply a right to more than one intends to cultivate; if anyone is permitted to cultivate large quantities of land, the use of it may be regulated.

Mill's position on land accumulation strikes forcefully against institutions of landed privilege, and in the essay on Coleridge, he made it clear that part of the objection to excessive landed property is that "when the State allows any one to exercise ownership over more land than suffices to raise by his own labour his subsistence and that of his family, it confers on him power over other human beings—power affecting them in their most vital interests."[153] Again, his commitment to "base equality" comes through as a ground for limitation and control of a form of property.

Taxation. There are aspects of Mill's positions on taxation that seem to run counter to themes I have thus far stressed. He opposed a graduated income tax—a premier device of redistribution—and he rejected the view that taxes should be less for those who receive less from government. Further, Alan Ryan claims that, with certain exceptions, Mill opposed taxation to equalize incomes.[154]

Mill's views on taxation are somewhat confusing, and his rejection of a graduated income tax strikes me as poorly argued and not entirely in keeping with other positions he took. I do believe, however, that a closer look will show that his essential position on taxation was strongly for its use as a social instrument, and (given the inequalities of his day) as an instrument of redistribution.

The first principle of taxation he endorsed he referred to as the principle of Equality of Taxation:

> As a government ought to make no distinction of persons or classes in the strength of their claims on it, whatever sacrifices it requires from them should be made to bear as nearly as possible with the same pressure upon all, which, it must be observed, is the mode by which least sacrifice is occasioned on the whole. If any one bears less than his fair share of the burthen, some other person must suffer more than his share, and the alleviation to the one is not, *caeteris paribus*, so great a good to him, as the increased pressure upon the other is an evil. Equality of taxation, there-

fore, as a maxim of politics, means equality of sacrifice. It means apportioning the contribution of each person towards the expenses of government, so that he shall feel neither more nor less inconvenience from his
share of the payment than every other person experiences from his.[155]

This principle, he held, should *not* be interpreted to mean that the
burden of taxation should be proportionate to the benefit received from
government. He held that the protections of government are greater for
the poor since they would suffer most if the protection of government
were withdrawn. However, to make those least able to care for themselves pay the most is "the reverse of the true idea of distributive justice,
which consists not in imitating but in redressing the inequalities and
wrongs of nature."[156] He held further that government should be
considered everyone's concern, and, as in other cooperative arrangements, people should be considered to have done their parts when they
have contributed according to means, hence, equality of sacrifice or
burden should be the rule.

There is, in this argument, a serious confusion. That the well-off
could fend better for themselves if government suddenly disappeared
hardly shows that they have benefited less from government's protection. Their privileged position may itself be the result of past governmental policies. Much of Mill's criticism of existing economic institutions was precisely to the point that government had enforced unjust
property regulations that permitted the very accumulations that would
enable the rich to survive without government and, as Mill claimed, to
enslave the poor. He himself had argued that the capitalists had benefited from the forbearances of the laboring class, as well as from their
"active support." A united laboring class, by virtue of its numerical
majority, could refuse to recognize proprietary rights "to accumulate in
large masses," and could thus extort whatever beneficial concessions it
wished, including the imposition of all taxation on the holders of
capital.[157] Hence, this particular argument against a graduated income
tax is not so strong as he claimed. The "logic" of the argument is worthy
of attention, however. Mill was opposed to the principle of graduation
proportionate to benefit because he believed that in fact it would place a
heavier burden on the poor and weak, and so could be objected to on the
basis of an acknowledged principle of justice. Given a different factual
assumption, however, it is not clear he would oppose such a principle of
graduation.

Another principle that favors graduation was rejected by Mill,
according to Ryan. This is the principle of diminishing marginal utility,

that taking a given percentage of money from a wealthy person will not be as great a burden on that person as the same percentage would be taken from a poor person. Ryan points out that acceptance of the principle would have been consistent with his utilitarianism and would justify a graduated tax to produce greater equality. "Mill did not move in this direction," he comments. He distinguished "essentials and superfluities and argued for the exemption of whatever income was needed for essentials, and a flat-rate tax on the rest."[158] No just principle of graduation could be decided upon, hence, it ought not to be a general rule of taxation.

There is not a great deal to be said in Mill's favor on this point. He *had* written of diminishing marginal utility theory that "this doctrine seems to me too disputable altogether."[159] Yet he had approved the principle of graduation for inheritance taxes. In "Civilization," he recognized a form of the general principle, writing of the wealthy that "the desire of wealth is already sufficiently satisfied, to render them averse to suffer pain or incur much voluntary labour for the sake of any further increase."[160] His father had so strongly embraced the principle that he favored dropping the phrase "of the greatest number" from the Greatest Happiness principle on the ground that diminishing marginal utility made the addition superfluous.[161]

Part of the explanation for Mill's reluctance to admit diminishing marginal utility to count in favor of a graduated income tax was that he appears to have thought it unjustifiably dictatorial to label the object of one person's preferences excessive luxuries and the objects of another person's preferences as merely comforts over and above the absolute necessities of life.[162] There is some merit in this position—but not much. Surely, the $50,000 automobiles and $500,000 yachts purchased by the wealthy are indisputably luxuries and not mere comforts; but what of the television sets bought by the middle classes and poor? Indeed, the latter may (arguably) be defended as important to anyone hoping to keep abreast of the general culture, and not as *mere* comforts.

It seems to me that there are some important defenses to be made for Mill on the subject of a graduated income tax. The first point to make is that, despite the doubt he cast on the theory of diminishing marginal utility, his position on taxation in fact *accepted* the principle. He stated that there is *some* truth in the doctrine, in that there *is* a real difference between taxing someone's *necessities*, and taxing their comforts and luxuries. The sacrifice, he said, in the former case "is not only greater than, but incommensurable with" the sacrifice in the latter case.[163]

Thus, because he *accepted* the doctrine of diminishing marginal utility, he favored an exemption from taxation of that portion of income required for providing the necessities of life.

The second point to make concerning his apparent opposition to a graduated income tax is that, when *all* his tax proposals are considered, it is clear they would result in considerable graduation, depending on how incomes are acquired. As we saw, he favored severe taxation of inherited income. More generally, he distinguished "terminable" and "perpetual" incomes, and argued for differential rates favoring the former. The former income recipient has greater *need* than the recipient of perpetual income. He or she must set aside savings to provide for old age, and for others who are his or her dependents. To the extent such savings are actually applied to these ends, he held they should be exempted from taxation.[164] Similarly, he argued that business profits should be divided according to whether they represent interest on capital or "remuneration for the skill and labour of superintendence." The latter—which can be claimed to be "earned"—should be treated as "terminable income" and taxed less.

Mill's proposals on the taxation of rent are especially revealing. He held that increments to income that involve no "exertion or sacrifice on the part of owners" of land can be at least partly appropriated. "This would not properly be taking anything from anybody; it would merely be applying an accession of wealth, created by circumstances, to the benefit of society, instead of allowing it to become an unearned appendage to the riches of a particular class," he claimed.[165] Such is the case with rent. Landlords, he said, grow richer "as it were in their sleep, without working, risking, or economizing."[166] As the rich landlords can make no *claim* to these riches "on the general principle of social justice," they would not be wronged if rent increases not justified by labor of theirs is taxed "to the highest amount required by financial exigencies." He then proposed measures that could be taken to make the process of taxation fair.

Finally, I should mention a point to which I shall return in greater detail: he was willing even to tax wages more heavily if they were paid to those in "such skilled or privileged employments, whether manual or intellectual, as are taken out of the sphere of competition by a natural or conferred monopoly."[167] Here, his idea was that persons in such positions are able to run up rewards quite out of line with anything for which *they* are responsible—their own labor or effort.

What emerges from this brief survey is that it is only *earned* income beyond that needed for subsistence that is to be taxed at equal rates. All other income can be differentially taxed, and, as we have seen, at rates that will provide large-scale income redistribution. This account, which entails considerable graduation in the overall taxation of incomes, can also explain his statements that appear to oppose taxation to equalize incomes. Actually, he did *not* write that he opposed such a principle entirely. He said that: "I am as desirous as any one, that means should be taken to diminish those inequalities, but not so as to relieve the prodigal at the expense of the prudent. To tax the larger incomes at a higher percentage than the smaller, is to lay a tax on industry and economy; to impose a penalty on people for having worked harder and saved more than their neighbours."[168]

However, this argument can be applied *only* to income it can be claimed was *earned*. He added in the next sentence that "it is not the fortunes which are earned, but those which are unearned, that it is for the public good to place under limitation."[169] I conclude, then, that the proper way to summarize Mill's views on taxation is to say that he thought it proper to tax for redistributive and other purposes conducive to the general good, that this implies that graduated taxation is *permissible* in general and *required* in particular to protect subsistence income. The one ground for (literally) equal taxation is that earned income beyond the subsistence level is to be taxed at the same rates. Of course, this position is consistent with the basic principles of economic justice that I isolated earlier, and with a strong commitment to the version of equality I outlined and attributed to Mill.

I want to turn back to Mill's willingness that wages be taxed even at graduated rates, for important contemporary analyses of economic justice involve this issue, and some extremely interesting aspects of Mill's conception of justice in this area can be brought out.

The chief philosophical opponent of taxation of income from labor is Robert Nozick. His objection is that such taxation gives persons property rights in others; it is "on a par with forced labor." Since, presumably, the person taxed must work n hours to obtain x dollars, to take from those dollars by means of compulsory taxation is to require the person to work whatever portion of n hours is needed to earn the dollars seized; of course, it is to require that labor to serve whatever purposes taxation is used for. As Nozick puts it:

> Seizing the results of someone's labor is equivalent to seizing hours from him and directing him to carry on various activities. If people force you to do certain work, or unrewarded work, for a certain period of time, they decide what you are to do and what purposes your work is to serve apart

from your decisions. This process whereby they take this decision from you makes them a *part-owner* of you; it gives them a property right in you. Just as having such partial control and power of decision, by right, over an animal or inanimate object would be to have a property right in it.[170]

There is no direct line of argument in Mill's writings of which I am aware to counter Nozick's claims. I want to put together a series of counterclaims from points Mill made in scattered places. Though I shall interpolate points of my own, I think it will be clear that Mill espoused most of the argument, and would at least be sympathetic to the rest.

To begin with, Mill did regard compulsory taxation as an interference with freedom; but he distinguished government action that is prohibitory from intervention that still leaves people free. Prohibitory regulation, he held, "partakes, either in a great or in a small degree, of the degradation of slavery."[171] Echoing the theory of *On Liberty*, he held that only for the protection of others are prohibitory regulations justified. However, there could be no theoretical limit to the positive functions of government.[172] Though he favored a principle of "*Laisser-Faire*" as a general rule in practice, he also approved a long list of significant exceptions, which would require taxation.[173] What is important about taxation is that, so long as its extent is limited, it leaves people free to chart out the course of their own lives as they see fit; it imposes a way of life or being on no one: "When a government provides means for fulfilling a certain end, leaving individuals free to avail themselves of different means if in their opinion preferable, there is no infringement of liberty, no irksome or degrading restraint."[174] To be sure, there *is* restraint in compulsory taxation, but the doctor or lawyer who is left with a sizable income after taxation can hardly complain of having been degraded or rendered nonautonomous by the levy.

Let us look a bit more closely, however, at the claim that freedom has been interfered with by taxation. Presumably, this consists in the state's having determined what is to be done with a portion of the monies one has earned, and the presumption is that the money is *one's own*, that is, that it is something to which one has a right. So far, this appears to be something with which Mill should agree, at least until that day comes when the private property principle can be safely rejected. Yet, a closer look at Mill's views does not entirely bear this out; the points on which Mill would dissent are important, and, I think, correct.

Let us turn again to the passages in which Mill discussed taxation of wages. He argued there that the appropriate degree of taxation depends on whether the wages are those of ordinary unskilled labor, or otherwise. His argument is interesting: ". . . in the present low state of popular education, all the higher grades of mental or educated labour are at a monopoly price; exceeding the wages of common workmen in a degree very far beyond that which is due to the expense, trouble, and loss of time required in qualifying for the employment."[175]

Mill's point here is important. He was claiming that skilled, trained labor is able to exact income returns that are not based in any close way on the *individual's* contribution. This point ties in with a more general one that Mill stressed: except in the most rudimentary of societies, what one labors with, and what one produces, are in large measure the result of the labors of others and conditions for labor that are provided by society. He pointed out that in a "social state," all distribution of wealth is ultimately dependent on law and custom. If society as a whole were merely passive, others would likely take what one has produced.[176] The point is that "in civilized life every human being depends for comfort, for security, often for life itself, upon things done for him by other people."[177] Indeed, he held that the security society provides is the most important of the "secondary causes which determine the productiveness of productive agents."[178] On this ground alone, the product of labor is partly a social product.

Mill's grounds for this conclusion were even stronger. In the first place, he insisted that the wealth that is produced in a country "is the joint product of present labour and of the labour of former years and generations,"[179] and he pointed to numerous ways in which the labor of others contributes to the produce of the labor of anyone.[180] In the course of this survey, he picked out the second point I want to stress—among the factors that determine what any individual produces are such things as the knowledge, skill, training, and education the individual possesses, and these, in large part, are the results of the labor of others.

Labor, he maintained, does not produce material objects; it takes matter and causes it to have certain properties. What labor produces, then, according to Mill, are utilities. Among the utilities labor produces are those "fixed and embodied in human beings." The labor of schoolteachers, professors, clergymen, physicians, trade instructors, and so on, is "productive" in the sense of producing utilities.[181] What are produced are the qualities of skill, knowledge, physical well-being, mental habits, and so on, that increase the productivity of laborers.[182] Because he thought that "in popular apprehension," the term "wealth" always refers to material products, he did not take these qualities to be part of the wealth of the community.[183] On the other hand, labor that produces such productive powers, or that helps preserve those powers, is a cost to the community. The labor of child-rearing, general education, technical and industrial training, and the labor of physicians and surgeons are all mentioned by Mill as contributing to the productive powers of others. From the standpoint of the individuals, of course, the motivation for such labor is normally the expectation of remuneration. For "most purposes of of political economy," then, this labor is not counted as part of the cost of production. However, from the community's point of view, it is necessary that such labor be done to keep up and augment the productive capacity: "when society and not the individuals are considered, this labour and outlay must be regarded as part of the advance by which society effects its productive operations, *and for which it is indemnified by the produce.*"[184]

On this view, then, the produce of the labor of anyone who lives in a "social state" (i.e., everyone) is only partly the result of that person's effort, exertion, or even natural talent. The individual's productivity is partly the result of socially produced circumstances for labor (e.g., security) and those mental and physical qualities that make possible, or augment, one's production. Thus, no one can claim that the produce of labor is solely one's own doing, and therefore, no one can claim that taxation of the income from labor is the taking of something to which the person has clear and exclusive title by virtue of its being the reward for an exclusively individual effort. While it is in my possession, of course, I might desire to use it in another way, hence, there *is* an interference with freedom if it is appropriated by society. Still, it is an illegitimate interference with freedom only if I have an overriding right to exercise my individual choice in the matter; but the basis in justice of such a claimed right—that it was *my* labor alone that produced it—is simply not true.

This line of argument, if accepted, would justify taxation of wages, at least so long as the taxation not be excessive. He excepted wages below a certain minimum entirely, believing this would exempt most manual, unskilled labor. Taxing these small incomes either "permanently degrades the habits of the labouring class," or, if the taxes are absorbed by capitalists, it is an unjustified extra tax.[185] The argument would also justify a graduated tax for highly skilled labor that is able to exact monopoly income.

This account has its problems, of course. How is it to be determined what contribution society has made, and what is the result of individual effort? Do not the returns due society depend on the nature of that society? on what opportunities it has provided the individual, or blocked? on what general social projects to which it requires taxation to contribute? Even if we had clear answers to these (and other) questions that arise, the argument hardly refutes Nozick's position. At most, it would undercut one sort of line of approach that would justify Nozick's claim that what is being seized is one's labor, and hence, that taxation of the income from labor is a form of having property in persons. There has, however, been no *argument* to show that *society* has a *right* to a return for its contribution. Utilitarian considerations could easily justify this claim, of course, but Nozick and his followers would reject that approach entirely. Since the skills, training, conditions for production, and so on, are goods obtained without force or fraud, and had not been the subject of a voluntary contract, they would hold that society can claim no right to a return. Further, the utilitarian justification of such a right violates the "separateness of persons." Nozick seems to intend this phrase in the sense given by John Rawls, which I shall discuss more fully later. The basic idea is that utilitarianism requires that all persons' desires (or wants, or satisfactions) are regarded as somehow forming a single class, and the objective of the utilitarian is to maximize the fulfillment of the desires in that class, irrespective of whose desires they are, what the desires are for, or of prior entitlements to the things desired. No part of this conception was Mill's, so he does not readily fall prey to this objection. (I shall say more on this later.)

Furthermore, Mill's argument shows at the least that there is a sense in which persons are *not* separate. We are all bound together in relations of mutual dependency, in which our capabilities, opportunities, immunities, and so on, are the result of others' labors and cooperative efforts. The values we accept, the work we think important, how we regard ourselves, are all partly influenced by society. Hence, our very identities—those features of ourselves we take as important about ourselves *as individuals*—are bound up with our social relations. One may indeed question if this nexus of relations and dependencies creates rights and duties. But one cannot base a rejection on the ground that such duties violate our "separateness" as persons except in some normative sense of that expression that incorporates the assumption that such rights and duties do not exist.

Wage-Relation and Poor Laws

I want, finally, to discuss in somewhat greater detail Mill's ideas on the wage-relation and the Poor Laws, because they display his commitment to "baseline" equality. What is wrong with the wage-relation is that it destroys the status of persons as free and equal; and what requires the passage and maintenance of the Poor Laws is the fact that poverty produces the same result.

In the first place, Mill believed that, generally speaking, the wages of ordinary, manual labor "are wretchedly insufficient to supply the physical and moral necessities of the population in any tolerable measure."[186] And, as I pointed out earlier, relations of dependence are attached to this relationship, which border on slavery: "The generality of labourers in this and most other countries, have as little choice of occupation or freedom of locomotion, are practically as dependent on fixed rules and on the will of others, as they could be on any system short of actual slavery."[187] And he thought that as society advances, the wage-relation will eventually be abandoned. At one point, he wrote:

> To work at the bidding and for the profit of another, without any interest in the work—the price of their labour being adjusted by hostile competition, one side demanding as much and the other paying as little as possible—is not, even when wages are high, a satisfactory state to human beings of educated intelligence, who have ceased to think themselves naturally inferior to those whom they serve.[188]

Mill's objections to the wage relationship are twofold. Wages tend to be too low to meet the necessities of people, and the relationship itself is destructive of the autonomous status of individuals. Both of these criticisms concern what I have termed "baseline" equality. The wage laborer can provide little in the way of comforts, education, and opportunity for self or family, and the laborer's status is that of one almost completely dependent on the will of others with respect to the most important features of life. In this description, Mill has also helped fill in his account of autonomy. What make the laborer's status border on slavery are the lack of choice and freedom with respect to crucial matters of one's life, as well as the status of dependency on the will of others concerning these matters.

If the wage laborer of his day was thought by Mill to lead a life of near slavery, his condemnation of poverty could hardly be less strong. Not only did he condemn poverty, but, I shall argue, he held that the poor have a *right* to subsistence income to be provided through governmental channels—thus his support of the Poor Laws.

We have earlier noted that Mill held that a population kept in abject poverty can also easily be kept in political subjugation.[189] In the *Chapters on Socialism*, he held that the majority of laborers are enslaved "by the force of poverty."[190] He wrote that as a consequence they are "chained" to a place, occupation, and the will of an employer, and debarred from "the mental and moral advantages" that others have by virtue of the accident of birth alone. When one's state reaches that of destitution, it becomes impossible to be self-sustaining and self-reliant. And here, Mill invoked the duty of benevolence:

> Apart from any metaphysical considerations respecting the foundation of morals or of the social union, it will be admitted to be right that human beings should help one another; and the more so, in proportion to the urgency of the need: and none needs help so urgently as one who is starving. The claim to help, therefore created by destitution, is one of the strongest which can exist; and there is *prima facie* the amplest reason for making the relief of so extreme an exigency as certain to those who require it, as by any arrangements of society it can be made.[191]

This passage is extremely important for quite a few reasons. In the first place, we find Mill appealing to a principle of "natural justice." Though I think we can take him to imply that a principle requiring helping others *would* be supported by an argument from the foundation of morals and also by an argument based on what is useful to social cooperation, he appears to have judged that the principle has strong intuitive sanction, and, hence, need not be given the more elaborate justifications.

Further, the passage shows that he was supporting a *claim* the destitute can make of society. He went on to argue that relief for the poor should not be left to private charity because there can be no guarantee that all who have need will be provided for, while excessive provision is made for others. Moreover, the state is already committed to providing subsistence to the criminal poor, so that to fail to provide for all the poor places a "premium" on crime. Finally, if relief were left to private charity, "a vast amount of mendicity is inevitable."[192] Now, these are clearly arguments to show that the poor have an interest—an interest in subsistence aid—that the state has a duty to guarantee. As we saw earlier, this is precisely the form of an argument for the existence of a *right* in Mill's theory of justice. The duty to provide subsistence is a duty of justice, with correlative rights that the destitute can claim against society. Mill went on to qualify the right in various ways. His main point was that aid should not make it more profitable not to work than to do so. Still, he insisted that "energy and self-dependence" can be impaired by the absence of help as well as by an excess of it, and "it is even more fatal to exertion to have no hope of succeeding by it, than to be assured of succeeding without it."[193] In short, poverty produces hopelessness, a deadening of the "active faculties," and a paralysis of effort. Given his theory of value, there are strong grounds for protecting the interest the destitute have in subsistence aid.

In fact, Mill went further and gave support to a right to work—the *droit au travail*. This consists of "an obligation on society to find work and wages for all persons willing and able to work, who cannot procure employment for themselves." This right, he held, could be recognized only if people abdicate any right to have children at their own discretion and without limit. Otherwise, he thought that the "common fund" would be exhausted if all were guaranteed either subsistence aid or work. Propagation is a clearly other-regarding act subject to moral obligation. Unfortunately, in his day the "superstition" persisted that individual discretion in the matter ought in no way to be interfered with. Still, he thought, a time will come when things will be otherwise, and the *droit au travail* can be safely recognized.[194]

The final point I want to make concerning Mill's argument here is that the duty being enforced by the Poor Laws is an application of a duty of benevolence. A basic premise of his argument was that it is right that people should help one another. In general, one does not have a *right* to the help of others. We are not bound to practice the virtues of generosity or beneficence toward any given individuals.[195] Nonetheless, the absence of a general right to beneficent treatment is consistent with there being *particular* assistance, in particular circumstances, that can be claimed as a right. While we *usually* can get along without the aid of others, *sometimes* our circumstances may be so reduced that our needs from them are as great as our need not to be harmed by them. In these cases, the grounds for a recognized right to positive performances are as great as they are in other cases for a recognized right to abstentions from harmful behavior. As we have seen, Mill did not back away from supporting such claims to aid. This entails that his theory of justice was *not* limited to a *negative* utilitarian conception, and, of course, it follows that his *general* theory cannot be characterized as that of a negative utilitarian. I shall return to this point later, for it bears on his conception of the role of duties of justice within his general moral theory.

I shall turn next to a brief discussion of some of Mill's views in political theory.

Political Justice

I shall not be concerned in this discussion with Mill's general political theory. There are interesting and important things to be said about the role of class divisions in his understanding of political reality, and about his views on the dynamics of social and political change. In-depth comparisons could be made between Mill's views on economic and political justice with those of other philosophers such as Hume and Marx. I shall not pursue such matters as I am concerned solely with illustrating how principles of justice played a role in his substantive theories. Moreover, some of these subjects have been treated by others.[196] Even the subjects that I shall discuss—the suffrage, representation, and the status of women—will only be lightly touched. I am concerned with *illustrating* his theory of justice in application to these subjects. I shall, however, try to stress points that other commentators have not systematically highlighted.

Basic Principles. Mill's views on politics reflected his deep immersion in the political issues of his day. He had numerous party interests and concerns, and much of his writing in this area was addressed to the political intelligentsia then active in the affairs of the day. One consequence of this was that his writings reflect the impact of generalizations about the organization and operation of political power, and assessments of the political powers of various groups in his society, more than they do any basic principles of justice. There can be little doubt, for example, that his proposals respecting the distribution of votes reflected a deep distrust of the then developed capacities of the poor and laboring class. Still, he did maintain at least one basic principle of political justice that, along with several corollaries, played an important part in his political thinking, even when dealing with issues that engaged his (apparently) elitist distrusts and fears.

The most basic principle of political justice employed by Mill was that no one has a right to exercise governing power over others. This is not to say, of course, that no one ever acquires the rights of rulers or legislators. It is to say (among other things) that persons have a right to determine their own lives that can be overridden only by stronger rights of others. I shall discuss the details of this principle in the next chapter on freedom. For present purposes, it is enough to point out that its most important corollary is that persons have a right to a voice in matters that concern them. A further important corollary is that, with respect to actions that concern the interests of others, the individual is, prima facie, responsible to others; that is, the individual does not act rightly if the person's own good alone is pursued.[197] These principles are directly involved in Mill's discussions of the suffrage. I shall turn next to that subject.

Suffrage. At first glance, Mill's positions on suffrage contradict some of the crucial claims I have made concerning his theory of justice. He argued that suffrage should *not* be viewed as a right, and he favored greater numbers of votes for the better educated. This makes it appear that he did *not* carry over his theory of justice to this substantive problem and that he here abandoned any commitment to equality. Indeed, his argument against equal votes—that people are not intellectually and morally equal—displays a nonegalitarian outlook, and his elaborations on the theme show him to have held an "elitist" attitude toward the uneducated poor.

While there is a measure of truth in these criticisms, I want to show that Mill's contentions with respect to suffrage in fact appealed to basic principles of justice; that there is a sense in which he was committed to a *right* to vote; and that his views in this area did *not* abandon his commitment to the "baseline" conception of equality.

Mill discussed the grounds for suffrage in a number of places, but virtually all of the arguments he marshalled for suffrage elsewhere are found in his "Thoughts on Parliamentary Reform." He insisted there on three grounds for granting votes to virtually all adults. First, it is a needed protection. "It can hardly be expected," he wrote, that those who have no voice in government "will not be unjustly postponed to those who have."[198] The vote is the only means of forcing the ruling classes to consult the interests of the governed. This protection is extremely important in light of certain crucial "facts" of political life which Mill emphasized elsewhere. The first such fact is that, however governmental organization purports to distribute power, it cannot differ long from the actual power distribution in society.[199] We saw earlier that he also thought unrestricted rule tends to make the best of rulers underestimate the interests of the governed, and overestimate their own.[200] Thus, the interests of the governed have no protection, and this can lead further to considerable dissatisfaction. He concluded that democracy is not ideally the best form of government unless there are guarantees that no class can prevail in pursuit of its own "exclusive class interest."[201] Where all have a vote, the interests that prevail will have been forced to appeal to reason and to "the conscience and feelings, of the governed,"[202] and will have been subjected to "discussion and agitation," so that, in the end, justice will tend to prevail.[203]

The second ground Mill presented for adult suffrage was that it is an important means of moral and political education. Participation in the political life of the community "elevates the mind to large interests and contemplations,"[204] as the individual must take account of the common interests of the political community. With no voice in the decisions of the common polity, individuals can center their concerns on self and self-related interests. It is for such reasons that the rule of a perfectly benevolent dictator is undesirable—the result will be that such a ruler will govern a "mentally passive people."[205] Since there would be no opportunity to exercise the mind on community concerns, or act as one with an influence on the general political life, such concerns and interests will atrophy and expanded sentiments will fail to take root. Knowledge about general affairs will not be sought, nor will such a populace care much for the community good. Thus, Mill held that such a situation will result in stunting the intellectual and "moral capacities" of those denied a voice in government.[206] If the bulk of the laboring class of his day be thought not prepared for the vote, there can be no better method of raising their abilities than to give them a voice and stake in the management of political affairs.[207]

The third argument in favor of suffrage that Mill gave bears most directly on the points I have stressed in this chapter. He held that power should not be exercised over others without their having a voice in its exercise. Independently of the *other* grounds for general suffrage, "it is a personal injustice to withhold from any one, unless for the prevention of greater evils, the ordinary privilege of having his voice reckoned in the disposal of affairs in which he has the same interest as other people."[208] Part of Mill's reason for accepting this proposition is important for my purposes. It is a point he made in a number of places. In *Considerations on Representative Government*, he wrote: "Every one is degraded, whether aware of it or not, when other people, without consulting him, take upon themselves unlimited power to regulate his destiny."[209] In a letter to a correspondent concerning the latter's book on representation, Mill wrote: "No one could without voluntary degradation admit that he ought to be counted for nothing."[210]

These statements show that an important part of Mill's argument for suffrage was based on an appeal to an important principle of justice—the one I cited as a basic principle of political justice, which limits persons' power over others. Moreover, that principle is crucial to the conception of "baseline" equality I have outlined. All persons are to have status as participants in the political process. We can also see how the Principle of Utility figures in arguments on justice. That principle, however it is to be formulated, picks out ends that are desirable. These, I have argued, are the things needed for persons with the faculties of human beings to be happy. Foremost among these requirements are those that comprise human dignity. The vote, then, makes an important contribution to well-being in that it preserves the sense of one's worth as a participant in the common social life. There are, in addition, other important utilities served by general suffrage, but Mill indicated that *this* ground operates independently of those—it would be a basis for the vote even if the others did not hold.

A final point I want to bring out is that if we combine Mill's argument for general suffrage with his theory of rights, it would appear that his arguments establish a right to vote. His theory of rights holds that if there are interests which ought to be protected as a matter of general rule, then one has a right; but this is precisely what Mill argued with respect to having a voice in political life—that it ought to be systematically protected via the vote.

There are two embarrassments to this account of the connection between Mill's theory of political justice and the vote. Neither can be simply brushed aside. In the first place, Mill insisted that the vote is a *trust*, and explicitly asserted that it is not a *right*. In the second place, he did not favor *equal* votes for all, and favored a scheme that gave the better educated more votes. The former embarrassment would seem to negate the claim that his theory of rights has application here, while the second point undercuts the attribution of a commitment to "baseline" equality, as differential votes do not preserve status as equal participants. I do not believe that an entirely satisfactory resolution is available of the conflicts with my interpretation. I hope to show, however, that they are not as serious as they appear.

Mill's most extended treatment of his views on suffrage as a right are to be found in *Considerations on Representative Government*, amid a discussion of the secret ballot, which he opposed.[211] His objection to regarding the vote as a right was concisely put:

> In whatever way we define or understand the idea of a right, no person can have a right (except in a purely legal sense) to power over others: every such power, which he is allowed to possess, is morally, in the fullest force of the term, a trust. But the exercise of any political function, either as an elector or as a representative, is power over others.[212]

He continued that if the suffrage were a right, "if it belongs to the voter for his own sake," then he could hardly be blamed if he sells it, or makes whatever use of it he wishes. But the vote is not an instrument of one's personal wishes; the voter is duty bound to use the vote to further the public good. This does not mean the voter's protection is not a ground for having the vote: "The suffrage is indeed due to him, among other reasons, as a means to his own protection, but only against treatment from which he is equally bound, so far as depends on his vote, to protect every one of his fellow-citizens."[213]

The problem arises from Mill's treatment of the vote as a complex political device. On the one hand, it *does* provide a protection for a significant interest each person has—the interest in having a voice in matters that concern one. Moreover, Mill's restrictions on the protection it is proper for it to provide (quoted above) must not be given a narrow interpretation, as he consistently argued that the interests of persons *themselves* may be overlooked without a vote, hence, the voter *can* look after his or her own interests (though not exclusively). On the other hand, exercise of the vote does directly affect the lives of others, does constitute an exercise of power over others.

Several points seem to follow. First, Mill's objection to regarding suffrage as a right is that it gives one power over others, and it is a basic principle of his theory of justice, I have argued, that one cannot have a right to unrestricted power over others. Interestingly, the *same* principle can be appealed to as a ground *for* suffrage, and indeed, Mill did employ it in arguing for near universal suffrage. Second, he held that the vote is *due* to the individual, and for the person's protection. However, this implies there is a *right* to a vote, given the theory of rights in *Utilitarianism*. What seems to follow is that one has a right to vote, but not a right to vote for one's own narrow interest, pleasure, or whim. One has a duty to exercise the right to vote for the public good.

There are a number of reasons to explain why Mill did not express himself this way. In the first place, he simply did not bring the special theory of rights he held in an explicit form into any of his work on political representation. Both the essay "Thoughts on Parliamentary Reform," and *Considerations on Representative Government*, were published prior to *Utilitarianism* (though the writing overlapped). Indeed, I know of no place outside of that work where Mill explicitly invoked his theory of rights. A more important reason, however, may be derived from remarks he made while introducing his argument in *Considerations on Representative Government*. He maintained that the way in which an institution works is most dependent on its *spirit*—"the impression it makes on the mind of the citizen."[214] If the vote were understood to be a *right*, he feared that people would tend to regard it as theirs, to do with as they please. It was virtually always in connection with the secret ballot that Mill discussed the issue of a right to vote. He opposed secret voting precisely because the public function of governing should be subject to review of those affected, and secrecy encouraged the use of the vote for selfish ends. One of the chief grounds that had been offered in his day for secret voting was that the vote is a right. But this "spirit," he held, "would be enough to corrupt and destroy the purest democracy conceivable."[215] Only when everyone regards himself or herself as a trustee of the others, as exercising power for the public good, is democracy possible, so to speak of suffrage as a right would suggest the wrong spirit for regarding that institution.

There may have been tactical reasons for Mill to deny that suffrage is a right, but in a day when universal suffrage had not been won, there were tactical reasons at least as strong to urge it as a right, albeit one with important duties accompanying its exercise. Furthermore, he seems to have held unrealistic views as to the operation of an open ballot and the real protections secrecy affords.[216] My point is not to defend Mill's views here (which seem to me quite wrong), but to offer an explanation of why he rejected the view to which his theory of rights (as I interpret it) committed him.

Let us turn to Mill's belief that the better educated should have greater votes. The main claim in his reasoning was the very principle of justice that has run throughout his thinking, namely, that unrestricted power over others cannot be claimed as right. The vote gives the individual power over others, but it cannot be asserted that all persons have an *equal* claim to power over others: "The claims of different people to such power differ as much, as their qualifications for exercising it beneficially."[217] People who cannot meet minimal educational standards, he held, will know too little of the world and of the great exemplars of the good and virtuous life, to exercise the power of the franchise in a beneficial manner. Indeed, at one point, he condemned the uneducated in terms that ring of a trenchant distrust and fear:

> If there ever was a political principle at once liberal and conservative, it is that of an educational qualification. None are so illiberal, none so bigoted in their hostility to improvement, none so superstitiously attached to the stupidest and worst of old forms and usages, as the uneducated. None are so unscrupulous, none so eager to clutch at whatever they have not and

others have, as the uneducated in possession of power. An uneducated mind is almost incapable of clearly conceiving the rights of others.[218]

All the arguments given before still provide reason for giving the less educated *some* vote. Still, the better educated are more "intrinsically valuable" to society, are more "capable," and "competent," and have greater knowledge; this, he held, justified a superior influence.

Superficially, Mill's argument appears to be a straightforward appeal to a principle that says that the capacity to exercise power beneficially justifies the grant and exercise of that power. By itself, of course, such a principle would undermine all the concerns for freedom and autonomy so strongly brought out in *On Liberty*. In fact, I believe that Mill's concern with plural voting sprang from some of the same fears expressed in *On Liberty*, and that his position on plural votes is of a piece with important aspects of his theory of justice. Mill's concerns in *On Liberty* involved the fear that in a modern mass culture, the initiative and individuality of superior persons will be stifled—they will be ruled by the masses. The fears expressed in his argument for plural votes were also of the dominance of the less educated. In a very revealing passage, he held that if each person in the "great majority" were given the vote without differential weighting, "under the name of equality, it would in reality count for vastly more, as long as the uneducated so greatly outnumber the educated."[219] After the catalogue of abuses he heaped on the lesser educated in the above-quoted passage, he said that "no lover of improvement can desire that the *predominant* power should be turned over to persons in the mental and moral condition of the English working classes."[220]

If this was Mill's central motivation, then his argument really took the form of a claim that without plural voting, the better educated, more able, would be governed by those less able. *Their* autonomy and well-being would be threatened by the incompetence of the others multiplied by their numbers. However, this is a *protective* argument, based as much on appeal to the demand of justice that one be self-determining, as by any appeal to the direct utility of superior qualification. As the quotation makes clear, he thought that the better people would be overwhelmed, hence, the voice of the more able would *not* count equally with that of the less educated. Putting aside the issue of the *truth* of the very questionable premises involved in his argument, the structure of it reveals it to employ some of the essential aspects of the concept of "baseline" equality.

Mill presented further claims that help relieve the tension between his commitment to equality and justice and his claims with respect to plural voting. First, he held that everyone prefers to have his or her concerns managed by one with "greater knowledge and intelligence," than by one with less, and, if both must be consulted, all would prefer to give greater weight to the voice of the better educated.[221] These seem to me to be false claims if unqualified, and Mill's theory of liberty provides excellent grounds for rejecting them in unqualified form. Again, it is to the *nature* of the argument that I draw attention. Apparently, he believed that the uneducated would *consent* to differential voting (at least insofar as they are rational!).

In addition, I have pointed out that he argued for some voice for all who meet minimal standards, partly on the ground that to have one's views counted for nothing "is revolting both to the universal conscience, and to the sense of dignity which it is desirable to encourage in every human being";[222] but there is no similar affront to weighted votes: "No one feels insulted and injured by the admission that those who are jointly interested with himself, and more capable, ought to have greater individual weight in the common deliberations."[223] Thus, no vote at all would degrade persons, hence destroy basic equality, while weighted voting would not carry a similar consequence.

Representation. A good bit has already been said concerning Mill's theory of representation. I want to bring some of these points together, and to emphasize again the role of considerations of justice in his thinking.

The same fears that led to his adoption of plural voting served as ground for his favoring representative, rather than direct democracy. In general, without regard to the disability of the working masses, he thought of governing as a special function requiring abilities not available to all. The suffrage is in part a tool of self-defense—a guarantee against *bad* government—but it is not an instrument giving license to actually govern. Those elected to office are not mere parrots of their constituencies; this, he described as "the false idea of representative democracy."[224] The representative should be elected on the basis of ability, and should act as he or she is convinced is for the general good. Of course, the people must, in the end, prevail. They cannot be well governed in opposition to their own "primary notions of right," even if they are mistaken, hence, their most fundamental convictions are entitled to an influence "in virtue of their mere existence."[225] However, though the people ought, in this sense, to be "masters," they should be "masters who must employ servants more skillful than themselves."[226]

Since it was representative institutions Mill favored, and competent, independently acting representatives he sought, it is important to emphasize that he also favored a system of voting that would guarantee representation of minorities in government. Mill's argument for this position was a straightforward appeal to justice and equality. A representative government that elects only majority representatives effectively cuts the minorities off from any further influence on government. Those in the majority, by virtue of *being* in a majority, will have representation in government; the others will have none. "There is not equal suffrage," he wrote, "where every single individual does not count for as much as any other single individual in the community."[227] The minority cannot, of course, prevail in a legislature; and if the majority has majority representation, minority rule will not occur. Still, proportional representation should be guaranteed:

> In a really equal democracy, every or any section would be represented, not disproportionately, but proportionately. A majority of the electors would always have a majority of the representatives; but a minority of the electors would always have a minority of the representatives. Man for man, they would be as fully represented as the majority. Unless they are, there is not equal government, but a government of inequality and privilege: one part of the people rule over the rest: there is a part whose fair and equal share of influence in the representation is withheld from them; contrary to all just government, but above all, contrary to the principle of democracy, which professes equality as its very root and foundation.[228]

Indeed, he pointed out that if an interest group carries a small majority in most constituencies, it will be a bare majority of the people; but legislative action is determined by a majority of the representatives, consequently, without proportional representation of minorities, actual governing could theoretically be in the hands of the representatives of a numerical minority, since the group that prevails in the legislature need not represent the interests of the numerical majority of people. What is crucial in Mill's argument for present purposes is that it bases the argument on the principle of equality. It is another application of his theory of justice.

The Status of Women. In several respects, Mill's *The Subjection of Women* was one of his most important works. With the possible exception of his attack on the institution of inheritance in *Principles of Political*

Economy, his critique of existing relations between the sexes was his most radical and far-reaching social tract. Indeed, though the former stirred up little reaction (a surprise to Mill),[229] the work on the status of women stirred more heated reaction and hostility, even among his friends, than any other work of his.[230]

The work is also an eloquent feminist tract in its own right, and contemporary feminist writers have treated it as a work with relevance to the issues of concern to feminists today.[231] In this respect, it has had as lasting an impact as his other important work (although its impact was interrupted by at least a half century of neglect).

It is also a significant work because it is a place where the most central themes in his moral philosophy are brought to bear on an issue of vital practical concern. A detailed study would show that *The Subjection of Women* both uses and elaborates his concepts of happiness, justice and freedom. As these are among the most crucial conceptions in his moral philosophy, *The Subjection of Women* is a work of central concern to the Mill scholar and to anyone concerned with understanding the version of utilitarianism that Mill maintained. It is not possible here to give this treatise the full treatment it deserves; I shall only point out the important roles played by these concepts in the work. In so doing, I hope to correct an emphasis given the work by many scholars who see Mill's arguments as stemming largely from his concern with freedom. There is no doubt that a principle of freedom was important to his argument. What I want to emphasize is that considerations of justice—an appeal to equality—also played a crucial role. Indeed, *The Subjection of Women* allows us to see that these concepts are interrelated.

In the earliest paragraphs of the essay, Mill makes it clear that he held that the existing relations of males and females violated principles of justice and freedom. The principle of subordination of one sex to the other, is "wrong in itself" and should be replaced "by a principle of perfect equality."[232] He pointed out that normally the burden of proof is on those who favor "either any limitation of the general freedom of human action, or any disqualification or disparity of privilege affecting one person or kind of persons, as compared with others."[233] The presumption is usually for "freedom and impartiality," and "it is held that there should be no restraint not required by the general good, and that the law should be no respecter of persons, but should treat all alike, save where dissimilarity of treatment is required by positive reasons, either of justice or of policy."[234] Thus, to defend the contemporary relationships, one must defeat the "double presumption" against the position.

I showed earlier that Mill had argued for equality both as something productive of further goods and as something good in itself. Using quotations from *The Subjection of Women*, among others, I pointed out that he viewed our social natures—the desire to be in unity with others, and our need of sympathetic association—as requiring a society of equals in which the desire for power over others is seen as inconsistent with the good life, and in which we would desire that whatever advantages we have be shared with others. Status as equals, then, is directly connected with human well-being. Moreover, insofar as equality is an aspect of human dignity, another essential ingredient of happiness is directly served by female equality, whereas, being treated as a child—dependent on men in all important respects—is contrary to their dignity and true interest.[235]

I also showed that Mill did not advocate a *strict* equality, that is, that there could be *no* basis for differential treatment. Reward should be apportioned according to desert, as well as punishment. Moreover, in areas where some will exercise power over others, "policy" requires that competence be a basis for higher status. This entails, then, that the system of male domination of females violates a basic principle of justice—reward and advantage are based on birth, not merit or personal exertion. This theme is found to run throughout *The Subjection of Women*. Thus, he wrote:

> The disabilities . . . to which women are subject from the mere fact of their birth, are the solitary examples of this kind in modern legislation. In no instance except this, which comprehends half the human race, are the higher social functions closed against anyone by a fatality of birth which no exertions, and no change of circumstances, can overcome.[236]

Later in the book, he wrote:

> Think what it is to be a boy, to grow up to manhood in the belief that without any merit or any exertion of his own . . . he is by right the superior of all and every one of an entire half of the human race.[237]

The effect, he believed, is to induce the worst sort of pride, and lays the foundation of domestic life "upon a relation contradictory to the first principles of social justice": "The principle of the modern movement in morals and politics, is that conduct, and conduct alone, entitles to respect . . . that, above all, merit, and not birth, is the only rightful claim to power and authority."[238]

This principle is a restatement of Mill's most basic principle of desert, which, we have seen, played a central role in all his views on economic and political justice. It is a principle that is crucial to his substantive theory of equality insofar as it provides a basis for departures from strict equality. It is important to emphasize this point, as it shows that Mill's views on the liberation of women drew on a complex of principles within his theory of justice, and were not based solely on his doctrines on freedom. Contemporary feminist commentators have correctly drawn our attention to the egalitarian elements in Mill's work. The above analysis—which picks out the important role of the principle of desert, itself a part of his substantive theory of equality— buttresses those claims, and helps to see where critics have gone wrong. One such critic, Professor Himmelfarb, contends that though Mill began by emphasizing equality, he shifted to an emphasis on liberty: "In effect, equality was the means, liberty the end."[239] The "purpose" of equality, she contends, was to foster freedom of action and individual self-development: "Equality in this sense was equality of opportunity, the freedom to compete freely and equally with men."[240]

The sole evidence presented for these claims is a passage in which Mill rejected strict equality, and argued for beneficial consequences that derive from freedom to pursue the occupations one wishes, and that no one be presumed *a priori* unfit for certain occupations.[241] This hardly demonstrates that Mill *rejected* equality as *itself* desirable, or that equality was a mere *means* to freedom for Mill. Indeed, the notion of equality of opportunity is *not* reducible to the concept of maximizing freedom, so, even if Himmelfarb were correct that it was freedom to compete freely and equally with men that Mill sought for women, it would *follow* that an appeal to equality, independent of the appeal to freedom, was involved.

However, the strongest ground for rejecting Himmelfarb's claims is that Mill explicitly employed his principle of desert in arguing for liberation, and thus he had a strand of argument based on his substantive theory of justice in his arguments for the liberation of women. There *are* important interconnections between Mill's concepts of equality and freedom, which I shall discuss shortly, but they are not reducible to one another, nor has any evidence been given to show that in his thinking on the liberation of women the concept of equality was subordinated to freedom in a "means-end" relationship.

In saying this, I do not mean to assert that Mill did not present arguments based on appeal to the principle of freedom. Indeed, there are numerous places in which he explicitly appealed to such a principle. Just prior to the passage Professor Himmelfarb cites, he wrote:

> The modern conviction, the fruit of a thousand years of experience, is, that things in which the individual is the person directly interested, never go right but as they are left to his own discretion; and that any regulation of them by authority, except to protect the rights of others, is sure to be mischievous.[242]

The closing pages of the essay are, in fact, directed primarily at emphasizing the importance of freedom. With respect to both equality and freedom, he argued that they are good for the further goods they produce, and they are good in themselves. Toward the end of the essay, he maintained that an ideal marriage involves "that best kind of equality, similarity of powers and capacities with reciprocal superiority in them—so that each can enjoy the luxury of looking up to the other, and can have alternatively the pleasure of leading and being led in the path of development."[243] Freedom, he held, "is the first and strongest want of human nature," once one is fed and clothed; and, echoing a main theme of *On Liberty*, he described "personal independence" as "an element of happiness."[244]

There are, then, two main lines of argument for freeing women—one based on equality, another based on freedom. Both arguments themselves have two lines of approach—one based on the good consequences to be obtained, the other based on Mill's conception of the elements of human well-being. The various lines of argument are not kept clearly apart; furthermore, the arguments from equality and freedom are interconnected. It is to those interconnections that I wish to turn.

In outlining what I took to be Mill's "baseline" conception of equality, I stated as an essential proposition in that conception that inequalities must not undermine the status of persons *as equals*. This, of course, is quite vague, and I tried to give it some content with the explanation that the inequalities must not result in some dominating others, or undermining their dignity as human beings. This, too, is extremely general, and it would be hard to say precisely what it entails by way of specific rights and duties. It is meant to imply that inequalities must not undermine one's status as an autonomous agent. Thus, to whatever extent Mill explicated the concept of a free person, the idea of status as equals will be given specific content. In my next chapter, I shall discuss his conception of autonomy. In *The Subjection of Women*, though, there are some indications. In an important passage, Mill argued for the good social effects of emancipating women, but he went on to argue for benefits to women themselves, and his argument elucidates his conceptions of equality and freedom:

> . . . the mere consciousness a woman would then have of being like any other, entitled to choose her pursuits, urged or invited by the same inducements as any one else to interest herself in whatever is interesting to human beings, entitled to exert the share of influence on all human concerns which belongs to an individual opinion, whether she attempted actual participation in them or not—this alone would effect an immense expansion of the faculties of women, as well as enlargement of the range of their moral sentiments.[245]

Later, he described the life of women without freedom as one without real enjoyment. Aside from sickness, "indigence, and guilt," nothing so impedes an enjoyable life as "the want of a worthy outlet for the active faculties."[246] The inability to determine the use of one's own faculties not only produces a lessened "sentiment of personal dignity," but directly thwarts the leading of a satisfying life.[247] The development and regular exercise of one's capabilities, he described as "vitally important to the happiness of human beings."[248]

What emerges from these quotations is the picture of equality as involving a sense of one's having an equal right to determine for oneself what sort of life one is to live, what sorts of pursuits to follow, according to one's own individual abilities and capacities, and having a right to a voice in those things that concern oneself. Further, an autonomous life involves the exercise of one's "active faculties," which, as I shall argue in the next chapter, involve the capacities of choice, deliberation, acquisition of knowledge. While this still is relatively abstract, it does flesh out somewhat the concepts of equality and freedom that Mill brought to bear on his discussion of women's rights.

Throughout this discussion, I have argued that there is in Mill's arguments an appeal to the justice of liberating women, and I emphasized those arguments that are based on his concepts of equality and desert. However, the appeal to freedom was *also* an argument from justice, since he held that wrongful interference with freedom *is* a form of injustice. In the next chapter, I shall seek to explain in some greater detail just how Mill's theory of freedom can be understood as an application of his theory of justice.

There is one last point I want to stress. If my arguments concerning *The Subjection of Women* are correct, then the essay is important as an application and development of the most central themes in Mill's moral and political philosophy. Consequently, it is extremely important that it not be interpreted apart from the rest of his work. I shall cite one example of the failure to do this. Julia Annas has written one of the few extensive philosophical studies of Mill's essay, and she makes some excellent critical points. However, the central themes are, I think, mistaken. She maintains that Mill pursued two different strands of argument that could not be consistently worked together. The first, which she calls a "utilitarian" justification for liberation, says that liberation is required in order to maximize the desires and needs people actually have. The alternative argument holds that a radical change in social institutions is needed in order to bring about a just society, and that some desires that derive from the unjust system must be discounted. The conflict between the "utilitarian" ground for change and the other is important:

> Mill will have trouble finding a utilitarian ground for discounting desires that can only be satisfied in an unjust system because they are engendered within it. Mill clearly thinks that these desires should *not* count, any more than women's expressed desires to remain happily dominated by men should count; they show nothing except how warped the nature of both men and women can get. But his justification for doing this cannot be a utilitarian one.[249]

A supposed illustration of the incompatibility of the two lines of argument in the essay consists in Mill's concession that women as they are have constricted natures, and, as a result, they will act poorly if they have an influence on affairs. That there is an incompatibility is argued thusly:

> If women's influence as it stands is baneful, why should we hasten to employ women in public and private jobs? What can be the utility of pressing into service all these narrow and repressed natures? . . . Mill cannot have it both ways. If women even as they are deserve employment in the same way as men, then there is no reason to think that a fundamental change of the relations between the sexes will bring great benefits. On the other hand, if a great change here *will* bring vast benefits, is it not suspicious to try to increase utility by making use of women in their present corrupted state?[250]

This line of argument (or this way of putting it) can only result from ignoring the rest of Mill's writings (and, perhaps, parts of *The Subjection of Women* also). Annas cites no place where Mill *says* that the "good" which is the end of conduct is the maximum fulfillment of people's actual desires. Indeed, in numerous places, he explicitly *rejected* such a view, the most conspicuous place being the essay *Utilitarianism*. The very point of the "higher pleasure—lower pleasure" doctrine and its accompanying test was that some pleasures (hence, the fulfillment of *certain* desires) count more heavily than others. In *The Subjection of Women* (and elsewhere),[251] he held that the desire for power over others and the desire for liberty "are in eternal antagonism," and that the former is "a depraving agency among mankind."[252] In *On Liberty*, the work in which Mill's doctrines relate most intimately to *The Subjection of Women*, he stated that while his argument appeals to utility, "it must be utility in the largest sense, grounded on the permanent interests of man as a progressive being." Among those interests, I have shown, are the interests people have in freedom and a social world in which they participate as equals.

That it was an ideal state of character and desiring that Mill stressed in deciding ethical and political questions is compatible with recognizing that people have not attained that state, and that whatever happiness they *can* achieve may depend on fulfilling their actual desires. As I shall stress in my final chapter, this creates a serious problem, and Annas is correct in noting it, but it does *not* arise because Mill had both a "utilitarian" and a nonutilitarian conception of justification.

There are two more points I want to stress. The first is that *The Subjection of Women* is seriously misunderstood if it is not regarded as recommending a wholesale changeover in fundamental institutions and concomitant alterations in people's characters and social relations. The second point is that while Mill's argument is essentially an appeal to the *justice* of female liberation, he believed that the exercise of freedom would itself help produce the sorts of long-range alterations in the basic attitudes of men and women alike that would result in the beneficial society he envisioned.

So far as Mill was concerned, the most basic social institution was based on the near total subordination of one sex to another. A system of near slavery was rigorously defined and enforced by the *law*. According to one writer, a woman had no vote, could not hold public office, if married had no legal right to property or earnings, and could enter into no contracts or sign a will. She could be jailed for refusing her husband "marital rights." She could enter none of the professions, or the universities.[253] Given the degree of legal subordination, it was not unreasonable for him to suppose that the law and institutions regulated by law were important forces in producing those qualities of mind and character that he condemned in the essay—the arrogance and unjustified pride of men, the corruption of character attendant on the exercise of unjust power, the submissiveness of women, and so on. Annas is certainly correct in pointing out that removal of legal disabilities has not proved enough to foster real equality; but this hardly shows that he was "not aware of the massive changes required in people's desires and outlooks before equality becomes a reality and its effects something that people see as beneficial."[254] It was precisely because he thought that the freedom fostered by liberation would help produce massive changes in people's attitudes and beliefs that he favored immediate abolition of the legal restrictions on women. Moreover, one of the central doctrines of *On Liberty* (as I shall show in the next chapter) was that the *exercise* of freedom helps to develop those very capacities, and strengthens those virtues of character, that are requisite for being an autonomous person who is fulfilled as a human being. Mill's argument, then, is that as a matter of *desert* and *justice*, women have a right to equality, and the freedom which is thus justified will have the further effect of improving society by abolishing those aspects of the social institutions that corrupt the natures of both men and women, and by fostering the full flowering of women as happy, autonomous beings. That women's abilities have been stunted is not a ground for denying them employment, and so, not only do they deserve freedom, but freedom will itself operate in developing their abilities. There *are* two lines of argument here, but they are complementary, not contradictory, and they share a common conception of human well-being and how it is appropriately achieved.

Annas makes two further points on which I shall comment. First, as a further conclusion to her claim that Mill failed to see the extent of social restructuring that would be needed to produce real liberation, she charges that he opposed "reverse discrimination," and, because of his individualistic views in *On Liberty*, would "presumably . . . feel quite unhappy about state-aided programmes to help women, quotas for employing women, revision of books, etc."[255]

It is indeed a weakness of Mill's theory of justice that it is incomplete, lacking in any treatment of principles of compensatory or (as I prefer to express it) remedial justice. This failure hardly justifies Annas's conclusion, however, and her reference to Mill's doctrine in *On*

Liberty represents a serious misunderstanding of it. That doctrine permits (in some cases *requires*) interferences with liberty to protect *rights* of others. There is no reason to suppose Mill would have rejected principles of remedial justice that confer such rights. On the contrary, there is reason to suppose that had he realized the intractability and pervasiveness of sexual prejudice and sexist practice, he would have *favored* some of the sorts of programs that Annas lists. After the Civil War in the United States, he expressed fears that the slaves would remain in the power of their old masters, and "they will have as little control of their own actions, as little protection for life, honor, and property, will in short be, except in a few outward incidents of slavery, almost as much slaves as before."[256] He favored setting up a "military dictatorship" of the North over the South which should be maintained for some time, as it would take several generations "before the habits and feelings engendered by slavery give place to new ones; before the stain which the position of slave master burns into the very souls of the privileged population can be expected to fade out."[257] Emancipation from slavery, by itself, he held, would leave the slaves still in the power of their old masters, thus, "it is quite indispensable to break the power of the Slaveholding oligarchy."[258] He stated that he would, if necessary, confiscate property to this end,[259] and he supported the Civil Rights bill passed in 1866, that gave lands to ex-slaves.[260]

A further point that Annas makes about the essay seems correct to me. She points out that Mill's conception of the nature of women wavered in the essay. On the one hand, he argued that we cannot know the nature of women since women have always been subjected to subordination. On the other hand, he included a number of arguments based on presuppositions about women, for example, that most women will, in fact, seek the roles of wife and mother, and will not pursue education for career purposes. Indeed, some of Mill's claims in this regard are an embarrassment, and there is a measure of inconsistency here. However, it is not an inconsistency between two different modes of argument—a utilitarian line and one based on a conception of an ideal society.

Whether my specific arguments are sound or not, I believe that this discussion shows that *The Subjection of Women* is a seminal essay in Mill's moral theory, in the sense that it brings together the most crucial themes in his moral theory, as they apply to a major practical issue. At any rate, I believe it will be best understood by bringing the whole of his theory to bear on it.

DIFFICULTIES FOR MILL'S THEORY OF JI

Mill's responses to some of the traditional criticisms that ⅃...
outset have either been given, or should be obvious from the discuss...
I shall reserve my final critical judgment of his theory of justice for my
concluding chapter. There are many further questions that can be
raised that I shall not take up.[261] I shall address three further issues,
however, because the discussion can shed further light on matters that
are important in Mill's moral theory.

RIGHTS AND JUSTICE

The first issue has to do with a point that is almost universally urged
against Mill's theory. The criticism holds that Mill's identification of
rules of justice with right-conferring rules yields consequences that are
false. I shall cite two instances of the criticism. In his commentary on
Utilitarianism in the *Collected Works*, D. P. Dryer remarks:

> When it is claimed that a man has a right to worship in accord with the
> dictates of his own conscience, it is not implied that if someone were to
> prevent him from worshipping in this manner, he would be doing some-
> thing unjust. Similarly, a man who tortures or murders another is not
> described as doing something unjust, even though it is held that he is
> doing another wrong and is doing something that others in general ought
> to prevent anyone from doing. Consequently, Mill is not correct in
> maintaining that a man is described as doing something unjust whenever
> he is regarded as doing something wrong and as violating another's
> right.[262]

The statement by Dryer makes it out as a plain fact that the
implications of the position are false. No ground or explanation is
offered. Some revealing explanation is given by Anthony Quinton,
who makes a similar point:

> Murder, assault, theft, lying and promise-breaking are ordinarily . . .
> wrong. They are, indeed, invasions or floutings of the rights of their
> victims, but they are not exactly unjust, at any rate in the current sense of
> that word, any more than incest, the favourite example of an act, which
> though morally wrong, is not unjust. What is primarily wrong with
> murder is that a man is *killed*, not that *he*, rather than somebody else, is.[263]

Quinton goes on to explain that justice is primarily a *distributive*
notion, whereas not all violations of rights involve maldistribution.
There are three responses I wish to make to this line of criticism. First,

Mill did *not* say that all violations of rights involve acting *unjustly*. He said they involve doing someone an *injustice*, and that notion is *not* obviously a distributive one. It is, of course, an understatement to say of someone who kills another that the person committed an injustice, but it is equally an understatement to say that the misdeed was the violation of someone's right. In both cases, the language may be too weak, but it does not follow that the statements are false. They are too weak, because someone was *killed*, and the enormity of the misdeed is not fully conveyed by saying an injustice was done the person *or* that the person's rights were violated. (Just try out Quinton's own language: "Smith's rights were invaded and flouted." "Really, how?" "Someone bludgeoned him to death.")

The second point I want to make is that I suspect Quinton is right insofar as there is a current *philosophical* use of "unjust" and "injustice," in which they are applied only in cases of distributive wrongs. This was not true in Mill's day, so far as I can tell, nor is it engrained in everyday usage today. Virtually every major dictionary I have consulted gives "violation of rights" as a meaning for "injustice," and some give it as the first meaning.

Finally, I should indicate that I do not think Mill would be too greatly upset by the criticisms even if the points made were correct. Much philosophizing goes wrong, he thought, because insufficiently precise language is employed. The philosopher cannot, however, merely invent a technical language for those "subjects belonging to the domain of daily discussion." It would be extremely difficult and inconvenient, so the philosopher must retain the existing phraseology, while seeking to improve it:

> This can only be accomplished by giving to every general concrete name which there is frequent occasion to predicate, a definite and fixed connotation; in order that it may be known what attributes, when we call an object by that name, we really mean to predicate of the object. And the question of most nicety is, how to give this fixed connotation to a name, with the least possible change in the objects which the name is habitually employed to denote; with the least possible disarrangement, either by adding or subtraction, of the group of objects which, in however imperfect a manner, it serves to circumscribe and hold together; and with the least vitiation of the truth of any propositions which are commonly received as true.[264]

In the moral sciences, he held, problems of vague usages of words abound, and he specifically mentioned the words "just" and "unjust," when used by ordinary persons, as connoting "little more than a vague gross resemblance to the things which they were earliest, or have been most, accustomed to call by those names."[265] Thus, a *philosophical* treatment would have to clarify such terminology; it would strive to preserve the commonly held truths, but a perfect fit is neither possible nor desirable. If actions that we have some hesitancy in calling acts of "injustice," in fact share important properties with those we do apply such language to, that may be grounds for the philosopher to extend the application of the term.

RAWLS'S CRITIQUE OF UTILITARIAN JUSTICE

A second set of difficulties that a theory of justice such as Mill's must encounter is generated by criticisms of utilitarianism made by John Rawls. Rawls's points have been extremely influential, and it is of some importance, then, to show how Mill's theory fares against them.

Rawls maintains that in utilitarianism, the satisfaction of desire always has value, regardless of what the desire is. Some desires can, of course, be "indirectly" discounted, but only because the overall objective is to maximize desire fulfillment or satisfactions. Thus, a desire could be discounted only if, all desires considered, it would not maximize desire-fulfillment to satisfy that one also. Similarly, the *source* or person who has the desire does not matter; it is *maximization* of satisfaction that is sought. His own theory, he believes, differs from this approach, in that it subordinates the theory of the good to the theory of the right. The principles of justice limit beforehand what satisfactions have value: "Hence in justice as fairness one does not take men's propensities and inclinations as given, whatever they are, and then seek the best way to fulfill them."[266]

According to Rawls, the utilitarian perspective has further problems. By virtue of taking people's desires as given, and making no distinctions among them, all desires are "conflated" into "one system of desire."[267] Rational choice among the system of desires would proceed as if one were choosing for a single person. In the individual case, one simply seeks to maximize one's own desires, sacrificing some for the achievement of others. If, then, one is seeking to maximize the *system* of all person's desires, making no distinctions as to quality or source, some can be sacrificed for the achievement of others. In this respect, utilitarianism does not respect the "separateness" of persons. It fails to incorporate respect for persons as such, whereas his own principles of justice limit desire-satisfaction from the outset, in ways that respect persons as ends in themselves.

Rawls *does* recognize that desires *can* be discounted even as he depicts the utilitarian position. Further, he recognizes that there can be utilitarian reasons for adopting certain rules of justice, or ideals for persons. There are two criticisms he makes, however. The first criticism appears in a discussion of utilitarian reasons for adopting *his* principles of justice. One could argue that self-respect is desired by people, and that this requires the equal basic liberties guaranteed by his principles; but, he argues, such facts present the utilitarian with a dilemma. On the one hand, to continue to insist on the utilitarian principle as defining society's conception of justice would entail the loss of self-respect that his principles safeguard; on the other hand, to go ahead and adopt his principles of justice would be to give up utilitarianism as one's theory of justice:

> We must not lose sight of the publicity condition. This requires that in maximizing the average utility we do so subject to the constraint that the utilitarian principle is publicly accepted and followed as the fundamental charter of society. What we cannot do is to raise the average utility by encouraging men to adopt and apply nonutilitarian principles of justice. If, for whatever reasons, the public recognition of utilitarianism entails some loss of self-esteem, there is no way around this drawback. It is an unavoidable cost of the utilitarian scheme given our stipulations. Thus, suppose that the average utility is actually greater should the two principles of justice be publicly affirmed and realized as the basis of the social structure. For the reasons mentioned, this may conceivably be the case. These principles would then represent the most attractive prospect and . . . would be accepted. The utilitarian cannot reply that one is now really maximizing the average utility. In fact, the parties would have chosen the two principles of justice.[268]

Rawls adds that if there are utilitarian reasons for acceptance of *his* principles, that is merely further ground in support of *those* principles. At a later point, however, he gives a different objection to this sort of utilitarian ploy. He agrees that the utilitarian *can* distinguish among desires on the ground that some promote well-being better than others. He objects as follows:

> Nevertheless, the choice does depend upon existing desires and present social circumstances and their natural continuations into the future. These initial conditions may heavily influence the conception of human good that should be encouraged. The contrast is that both justice as

fairness and perfectionism establish independently an ideal conception of the person and of the basic structure so that not only are some desires and inclinations necessarily discouraged but the affect of the initial circumstances will eventually disappear. With utilitarianism we cannot be sure what will happen. Since there is no ideal embedded in its first principle, the place we start from may always influence the path we are to follow.[269]

It should be noted that Rawls has always indicated that his indictment is meant to catch the "classical" utilitarians, and that he most often mentions Bentham and Sidgwick. He does not include Mill. Mill's moral philosophy is not infected with the faults he picks out. I want to show that Mill's theory does not fall prey to this attack, and that the force of Rawls's criticisms stems from an inaccurate, incomplete, and idiosyncratic portrayal of utilitarianism.

In the first place, Rawls seems to have identified utilitarianism with a particular theory of value, namely, that it is "satisfactions" that have value. In addition, he appears to have identified the maximization of satisfactions with the maximization of desire-fulfillment.[270] But these are *not* the same. People may desire things that will not be satisfying and may be satisfied with things they did not desire. Even *if* utilitarianism could be identified as a theory that requires maximizing satisfaction, it would *not* follow that it is committed to maximizing the fulfillment of *existing* "propensities and inclinations." This was *not* Mill's view at all.

Mill's theory of value does not meet Rawls's depiction of utilitarianism in further important respects. Mill's "naturalism" must be taken seriously. Morality springs from, and is rooted in, human nature. To see how, it is requisite that his account of human nature be taken seriously. Mill's view was that human nature is such that certain things are necessary ingredients of happiness, other things are essentially antithetical to happiness. Thus, the very conception of happiness can provide a basis for rejecting certain desires as a basis for claims. We have seen that he argued, in fact, that the desire for power over others should be discounted. In addition, his account of the requisites of human happiness entails that *certain* needs, desires, interests, carry *special* weight. In particular, he emphasized the value of freedom and autonomy.

It is true, of course, that Mill was no essentialist; he did not hold that somehow these facts about human nature can be read off from the very conception of a human being; but they are not *mere* contingencies either. Creatures who did not desire any of the constituents of Mill's conception of well-being, or who could not be made happier by their attainment would not be fully recognizable to us as humans, he could argue. Indeed, Mill's account of human well-being bears marked similarities to the picture given by Rawls in his extremely important account of the good and of moral psychology in part 3 of his book.[271] I think it can be argued that *if* these *are* facts about human nature, then any moral theory must come to grips with them, as, indeed, Rawls's theory attempts to.[272] Just what role such "facts" can legitimately play in a moral theory is certainly a subject of debate. It was Mill's belief that such "facts" of human nature play a central role—the "bindingness" of any putative moral duty ultimately depends on its furthering essential requirements of human nature. In Rawls's theory, principles of justice arrived at through his analytical device of choice in the "original position" must stand the tests of "stability" and "congruence"—the sense of justice it generates must be sufficiently strong to maintain compliance with the principles, while overcoming (and not generating) contrary inclinations, and the sense of justice itself must be a good to those who have it, in real human society. Of course, *arguments* in support of the eventual stability and congruence of principles of justice arrived at through the analytical device must use premises from general psychology and propositions of general kinds about human nature. Rawls does not object that Mill's account of human nature is false. This, indeed, strikes me as an arguable position that I shall pursue in my concluding chapter. The crucial question, then, is whether the Millean conception of human nature, together with acceptance of maximizing happiness as the goal of life, can generate an acceptable theory of justice. Rawls's first ground for rejecting the utilitarian claims—that the utilitarian can make no distinctions among desires except as contingent, hence, unreliable, facts may dictate—is mistaken.

A second point to make against Rawls is that there is no reason to suppose the utilitarian is barred from recognizing the "distinction between persons." This is supposed to stem partly from the failure of utilitarianism to take account of the *source* of desires; presumably for the utilitarian, there is only a large "pot" of desires—one system—the maximum satisfaction of which is to be achieved. On Mill's view, however, we require the components of dignity in order to be happy, which, I have argued, could be construed to include having the respect of others and self. Moreover, we have, and more and more acquire, desires for the well-being of others. In both cases, it matters enormously *whose* desires are fulfilled or not. In an ideal state of desiring, we saw that Mill maintained that we would not desire for ourselves what could not be shared with others. Although he qualified this claim,[273] to hold it in any form is to argue that we cannot maximize well-being, given human nature, without recognizing that it is *persons* who *have* desires, and that certain desires or needs of theirs cannot be overlooked merely to increase the well-being of others.[274]

Oddly enough, Rawls recognizes that utility may indeed be maximized by promoting respect, even by adopting principles of justice that incorporate and guarantee respect for persons. He argues that to do so is to adopt "nonutilitarian" principles, but then the utilitarian cannot go on to hold that "one is now really maximizing the average utility."[275] Since the premise is that by adopting such principles one *is* maximizing utility, I interpret Rawls to mean that *even if* utility is thereby maximized, one is no longer a utilitarian.

Though it is common in the literature to refer to "nonutilitarian" principles, it is unclear what anyone means by the expression. On the most obvious reading, it simply means any principle that does not specifically state that one should seek to produce utilities. Rawls surely does not mean that the utilitarian cannot adopt *any* other rules. What he is really getting at is explained shortly after the criticism:

> We should note, then, that utilitarianism, as I have defined it, is the view that the principle of utility is the correct principle for society's public conception of justice. And to show this one must argue that this criterion would be chosen in the original position. . . . What we want to know is which conception of justice characterizes our considered judgments in reflective equilibrium and best serves as the public moral basis of society. Unless one maintains that this conception is given by the principle of utility, one is not a utilitarian.[276]

There is much that could be said of this strange view. I note, for example, that if we take it literally, then a utilitarian who regards rules of justice as the superstitious carryover of earlier, indefensible, "intuitionism," and who, as a consequence, believes there are *no* moral rules which are "correct" for a public conception of justice, would *not* be a utilitarian!

Perhaps more importantly, I note that Rawls's rejection of such a "utilitarian" position stems solely from his idiosyncratic definition of "utilitarian." There is an important sense in which a theorist of the sort Rawls considers would *still* be a utilitarian, and it is *that* sense which has traditionally characterized the utilitarian position. As I argued in the preceding chapter, even an *act* utilitarian could urge the strict (and public) adoption of rules on the ground that *by* adopting them strictly, utility is more likely to be maximized than by adopting other rules, less strict rules, or assessing each case individually. As a utilitarian, such a theorist would hold that, as individual acts are *right* according to their consequences, following the rules will maximize the performance of acts that are right. The ultimate standard of right conduct, however, is the principle of utility. Saying this, though, is consistent with the adoption for practical affairs of *intermediate* criteria of right, for example, the rules of justice. Thus, in practice, we may do best to judge conduct by the standards given by those rules. It is, however, the ultimate theory about what properties an act must have to be right that makes such a theory utilitarian.

In this account, I have said nothing about what would be chosen "in the original position," but I can see *no* reason to *define* utilitarianism by reference to that notion. It is ahistorical, misleading, and has odd consequences.

I should also note that I have *not* been arguing that a utilitarian would necessarily adopt any principles of justice in a strict fashion, or accept Rawls's two principles. I have only argued that there is an important sense in which a utilitarian would still *be* a utilitarian, even *if* he or she adopted such principles strictly. While it is clear Mill would find Rawls's two principles attractive, it is not at all clear to me that he would adopt them in the formulations given by Rawls. (I have doubts Mill held Rawls's notion of "basic liberties," but it is, in my view, a weakness in Mill that he did not.) Further, I have doubts he would urge the adoption of any principles on a strict basis. If not, then whatever principles would constitute his conception of principles to govern the choice of substantive principles would have to be qualified by reference to exceptional circumstances, or would have to include the principle of utility, itself qualified to apply in special cases.[277] At no time does Rawls even consider the relative merits of some such set of principles. It is conceivable that a utilitarian who accepts Rawls's analytical framework, and his metaethical conception, could show that such principles do match our considered judgments, and do meet the tests of reflective equilibrium, stability, and congruence, better than his principles. To continue to deny such a theory the status of a "utilitarian" theory, and thereby claim the defeat of the opponent, would be a semantic victory only, as I see it. In any event, Mill, who adopted principles of justice designed in part to preserve the dignity and respect of persons, cannot be faulted as having given up utilitarianism.

I should note, in closing my discussion of Rawls, that there is one further argument he makes that does not rely on his defining utilitarianism with reference to the "original position." With reference to teleological theories in general, he writes:

> If the distribution of goods is also counted as a good, perhaps a higher order one, and the theory directs us to produce the most good (including the good of distribution among others), we no longer have a teleological view in the classical sense. The problem of distribution falls under the concept of right as one intuitively understands it, and so the theory lacks an independent definition of the good.[278]

This is extremely confusing. It is unclear what weights or roles are to be given such phrases as "in the classical sense" and "as one intuitively understands it." If there is an argument here, it is mistaken. No matter how one "intuitively understands" the problem of distribution, if one takes certain distributions as good in themselves, then this is a claim within one's theory of the good; it is *not* a claim about the theory of what acts are right. Indeed, logically speaking, one would still be free to hold that acts are right that *ignore* those distributions. Of course, one would not then be a teleologist, but the *possibility* of such a position shows that accepting distributions as themselves good does *not* commit one to any theory of right. To say a theory is teleological is to say that it defines right action by the good produced by the action (or rules under which the act falls). Thus, a teleological theory is defined by its *structure*; it defines rightness in terms of the production of certain *goals* or *ends*. To call it "teleological," however, is not to say the theory is committed to any conception of the nature, content, or structure of the ends. There may be historical warrant for restricting the term "utilitarian" to theories which take happiness as the end of action, but even here, there are differences among utilitarians as to the nature of that end—the contrast between Bentham and Mill in this matter is a case in point. If one held that certain distributions are intrinsically satisfying in themselves and have a priority ranking over other goods, one could be a "utilitarian" in the historical sense of the term and not give up one's teleological conception of right action. I have not quite interpreted Mill in this way (although his acceptance of equality as good in itself could, perhaps, be so interpreted). He did hold, however, that given human happiness as he conceived it, there are grounds for preferring some distributions over others. I see no reason to accept that he thereby had given up his teleological-goal-directed conception of the right.

The Status of Imperfect Duties

I want finally to consider a difficulty for Mill's theory that I do not believe he ever dealt with in a satisfactory way. Indeed, he appears to have been entirely unaware of the problem. On one hand, he distinguished "perfect" from "imperfect" duties, limiting duties of justice to the former category. Further, he clearly distinguished the "idea of justice" from "moral obligation in general,"[279] and appears to have regarded it as a mistake to "merge all morality in justice."[280] On the other hand, there are places where he seems committed to holding that duties of justice are the only moral duties. I shall explore several proposed solutions to the problem, which I shall reject. I believe Mill *was* inconsistent on this issue. Nonetheless, I shall suggest an alternative solution that fits much of Mill's text, and which is of interest in its own right as a philosophical analysis of an important aspect of morality.

Mill distinguished imperfect duties in two ways. In the less precise usage of "ethical writers," they are duties "in which, though the act is obligatory, the particular occasions of performing it are left to our choice."[281] He mentioned the duty of charity or beneficence, which we need practice toward no definite person at any particular time. The more precise characterization of such duties says that these are duties that do not give rise to *rights* held by any definite person. Some moralists, Mill pointed out, have held that we owe all the good we can do to others; but then, he said, such efforts are *due* to others, and the duty of beneficence is assimilated to a debt, hence, is treated as a duty of justice.[282]

In the paragraph *prior* to that in which perfect and imperfect duties are marked, Mill had maintained that central to the idea of duty "in every one of its forms" is the idea that the individual who has the duty may be compelled to fulfill it. He went on to say: "Duty is a thing which may be *exacted* from a person, as one exacts a debt. Unless we think that it might be exacted from him, we do not call it his duty."[283] In *this* paragraph he distinguished acts which it is one's duty to perform from those that it is desirable or praiseworthy to perform. The former we can compel persons to do, while the latter we can only seek to persuade or exhort them to do. This passage appears to reduce all duties to debts, hence, to duties of justice.

The problem is not alleviated in his other writings; on the contrary, it is exacerbated. In the essay on Comte, he again distinguished duties—acts we can be compelled to perform—from acts of "positive worthiness," which it is morally praiseworthy to perform, but which should not be subjects of compulsion. The reproaches of others, and of conscience, should be reserved for enforcing conduct that consists in not harming others, or interfering with their freedom when they are harming no one else, and in keeping express or tacit agreements. He then added:

> And inasmuch as every one, who avails himself of the advantages of society, leads others to expect from him all such positive good offices and disinterested services as the moral improvement attained by mankind has rendered customary, he deserves moral blame if, without just cause, he disappoints that expectation. Through this principle the domain of moral duty, in an improving society, is always widening. When what once was uncommon virtue becomes common virtue, it comes to be numbered among obligations, while a degree exceeding what has grown common, remains simply meritorious.[284]

Here, Mill was saying that by enjoying the benefits of society, one leads others to expect certain "good offices and disinterested services," namely, those that have become customary. To not provide them is to disappoint those expectations. As we saw earlier in this chapter, the disappointment of expectation was regarded by Mill as a serious wrong, and the basis of such duties of justice as those of promising and fidelity to friendship. However, given *that* analysis, those positive good offices and disinterested services that are customary would be *owed* others, hence, would be duties of justice. Of course, Mill did not *say* all this, and I shall suggest later a way out of the difficulty that would *not* commit Mill in the Comte passage to reducing all duties to those of justice.

In his *An Examination of Sir William Hamilton's Philosophy*, Mill did explicitly hold that punishment "is a precaution taken by society in self-defense." In addition, he maintained that it is a protection of "the just rights of others against unjust aggression by the offender."[285] This appears to limit punishment to enforcing rights, hence, to enforcing duties of justice. Furthermore, I shall argue in the next chapter that the central theme of *On Liberty* is that interferences with freedom are justified only to protect superior rights of others.

These difficulties are compounded by criticisms David Lyons has raised concerning the "imprecise" formulation of Mill's characterization, in which imperfect duties are not owed a particular person at a prescribed time. Lyons considers the example of the duty to be charitable, and he points out that if, given ample opportunity, one rarely performs a charitable act, there is a failing of virtue; one's moral character is deficient, "and one's *overall* behavior may be criticized accordingly."[286] In such an instance, though, no particular acts are required of a person: "Moreover, from the fact that one fails to perform a charitable act on a given occasion, when he has the opportunity to do so and there is no overriding obligation, we *cannot ever* infer that he has breached his moral obligation to be charitable and has acted wrongly."[287] Lyons observes, however, that Mill *did* seem to want to be able to say that one has acted wrongly by breaching a moral obligation, without thereby violating a duty of justice.

The simplest solution to the difficulty is that of D. P. Dryer, who contends that Mill simply "abandoned" the claim that duty in all forms may be enforced by compulsion.[288] Unfortunately, the only evidence for this claim is his statement: "For when it is said that someone has an obligation to be generous, Mill points out that it is not implied that it would be wrong for others to force him to be generous."[289] Of course, Mill never literally *said* this; it involves considerable interpretation on Dryer's part, including his claim that Mill analyzed statements that something ought to be done as implying that others ought to punish or condemn the person for not doing it. *That* seems to me questionable, but, even if true, Mill nowhere says that persons who fail to display generosity do not deserve condemnation, nor is there any reason to suppose that he thought it wrong to assert "He ought to be condemned for his behavior." Furthermore, there are numerous other places where Mill analyzed the notion of duty as connected with the notion of liability to, or deservingness of, punishment. (I have cited several of these in the last few paragraphs of chapter 3. I note, however, that subtle differences among the accounts suggest that Mill had not fully thought through the matter, hence, any interpretation that depends largely on one formulation, as does Dryer's, is somewhat shaky.) Furthermore, at the end of *Utilitarianism*, Mill reasserts the distinction between duties of justice and other kinds, but indicates that the "sanctions" to which the other kinds are subject are less stern.

Lyons's solution to the problem is subtle and complex. I shall attempt to summarize its essentials. He believes that Mill's own examples of charity and beneficence cannot constitute the class of imperfect duties because then, there cannot be cases of acting wrongly but not unjustly. Lyons's solution is that Mill picked out three categories of obligation, two of which are "nonjustice" obligations in that they do not correlate with rights, or do not do so "directly." One of the nonjustice categories is what Lyons calls "good samaritan" obligations, typified by duties to help others in distress. Of these, Lyons gives several arguments in *favor* of the plausibility of saying the person in distress has a *right* to aid. I shall show later that Mill seems committed to this view. Lyons's grounds for treating the category otherwise are that such an obligation "does not seem to be an obligation of justice," and that to treat it as such runs the risk of leaving only the unacceptable categories of charity and beneficence as imperfect duties. But Mill's theory of *rights* seems to *commit* him to saying there is a right in these cases. The individual in danger has an interest in the others' aid which society should enforce. In a letter to Thornton, he went so far as to suggest that one who fails to save the life of another should "be amenable to the criminal law."[290] Furthermore, it is no argument that *these are* imperfect duties to hold that otherwise there would not be an acceptable category of such duties.

The second "nonjustice" category that Lyons picks out consists of those duties involved in doing one's "fair share" in cooperative arrangements. According to Lyons, Mill limited the duty to cases where the cooperation is needed to prevent harms to persons. As a recipient of the benefit, one acquires a "second-order obligation of reciprocity," which correlates with rights the others have to one's compliance. However, the rules of the arrangement *itself* do not correlate with rights. The obligations *they* engender are not rules of justice, and there is no violation of a right *per se* in the violation of those rules. It is the *further* obligation of reciprocity that correlates with rights of others.

It is not clear how this account is supposed to bring the *moral* obligation to perform the acts required by the cooperative practice *out* of the category of a justice obligation. Given the facts of the case, not performing the acts *does* violate the rights of the others to compliance. That the requirement given by the rule of the practice becomes a moral obligation only via the second-order duty of reciprocity seems immaterial. If I *promise* someone I shall abide by a given set of rules and fail to do so, I have breached a promise. That the act is mediated by rules that do not *per se* lay down moral obligations seems immaterial. Lyons does concede that obligations that protect interests that "ought to be considered as rights" are justice obligations. Nonetheless, I showed earlier that Mill's own argument for duties of compliance in these cases was based on the "direct interest which others have in each individual's observance of the practice."[291] Thus, there are grounds for claiming that *this* sort of interest should be protected as a matter of rule, hence, the duty would be a duty of justice. (The point is even stronger if Lyons were right that Mill restricted the duty to practices that prevent harm, but this claim is not clearly true. He favored "Sabbatarian" legislation to enforce a cooperative project, and that is not clearly needed for harm prevention.[292] In fact, he described enforcement as needed in cooperative arrangements in order to "give effect to the wishes of the persons interested," and in that discussion, no restriction whatever on the ends of acceptable projects is given.)[293]

Lyons's treatment is almost surely intended as a "philosophical reconstruction." He does not purport that there is clear textual evidence for all aspects of his interpretation, nor would it be decisive against him that there are passages to be found that are not entirely consistent with that interpretation. On some points, he believes the view he has outlined is superior to things Mill seems to have held. The interpretation for which I shall argue is also a reconstruction. I believe that it is somewhat more faithful to Mill's texts, but, as was the case with Lyons's interpretation, there are aspects of it which Mill nowhere recognized.

The most essential element in my interpretation of Mill's "imperfect" duties are given by Mill himself in the last lines of *Utilitarianism*. He contrasted duties of justice with others as follows:

> Justice remains the appropriate name for certain social utilities which are vastly more important, and therefore more absolute and imperative, than any others are as a class (though not more so than any others may be in particular cases); and which, therefore, ought to be, as well as naturally are, guarded by a sentiment not only different in degree, but also in kind; distinguished from the milder feeling which attaches to the mere idea of promoting human pleasure or convenience, at once by the more definite nature of its commands, and by the sterner character of its sanctions.[294]

There are four points I want to stress from this passage: (a) Mill continued to hold the notion that imperfect duties have associated "commands" and "sanctions"; (b) the moral sentiments associated with the two kinds of duty (presumably expressed in the different kinds of moral judgment), are different in degree and kind; (c) the "commands" associated with imperfect duties are less "definite" and the associated "sanctions" are not as severe; (d) there can be particular cases where an imperfect duty is more imperative than a duty of justice.

The interpretation given by Lyons, in which "good samaritan" duties and duties of fairness or reciprocity constitute the primary imperfect duties, fit these points, or can be made to fit them, rather well. Still, these points seem to take Mill's "choice" criterion as central, while, I have argued, the "good samaritan" duties may, and duties of reciprocity certainly do, have associated rights. Lyons, however, wants to take the rights criterion as central to the notion of a perfect duty. In that case, these duties are less plausible candidates for imperfect duties.

There is little question that Mill accepted the rights criterion of perfect duties; but the final passage from *Utilitarianism* cited above shows that he continued to hold the "choice" criterion as well. These are not in the least inconsistent. If a duty to others is owed to no particular person as a right, then one has a choice as to the individuals with respect to whom the duty is discharged. The duties of charity and benevolence are ideal examples, in that one's failures in respect to these duties give no grounds for complaint by given individuals that something that was *due* them or *owed* them was withheld.

What of Lyons's objection to the choice criterion? He holds that if one fails to be charitable, say, on a particular occasion, that can never give grounds for the assertion that a moral obligation has been violated. There are no particular acts which are required, hence, there are no particular failures which count as wrongful acts. Lyons maintains, however, that Mill seems to have wanted to be able to say that one can act wrongly without thereby acting unjustly.

So far as I can tell, though, the only place where Mill implies that one can act wrongly without acting unjustly is the very place where he marks the perfect-imperfect obligation distinction by the less definite nature of the commands of imperfect duties. By saying that in particular cases a nonjustice obligation can be more imperative, I take him to imply that one acts wrongly if the justice obligation is given precedence. (Of course, it should be noted that in the previous paragraph he said that we "accommodate" our language to the case and say that the act usually required by justice is not just in this case.)

I want to suggest that Lyons has dismissed too quickly the examples Mill himself gave of imperfect duties.[295] Imagine a wealthy oil tycoon. Let us suppose that she informs her associates that she is tired of being bothered by various and sundry charities that keep dunning her for contributions. She has adopted a policy of drawing up a set list of charities—all well known and highly public and publicized—to which she will make yearly contributions. She will make no further charitable contributions. Furthermore, though the list is extensive (it would impress people how many charities she contributes to) the amounts are quite small so that her total charitable contributions are, in light of her great wealth, niggardly. Let us suppose further that after sticking to this policy for some years, she is approached by a poor relative who has fallen on hard times and who is dying of cancer. She needs a few thousand dollars for treatment that will give her extra months of life with improved comfort. The relative asks our oil tycoon for the money, but is turned down on the ground that all the tycoon's contributions to charity are committed.

Some of the appropriate points to be made are given by Lyons. Our oil tycoon's secretary, assuming him to be informed as to all the facts, could claim that the several years of stingy behavior and treatment of the relative show the tycoon to be an ungenerous, uncharitable *person*. The individual's character could be criticized; she could be said to lack important moral virtues. In addition, the overall behavior could be criticized. My own view is that it is perfectly sensible to say that the *course of behavior* was *wrong*. All of the following seem to me to be both intelligible and true statements: "She *ought* to have been more generous than that"; "She *should* have given more money to charity"; "She was *wrong* to limit the amounts of her giving as she did." This last criticism, I note, may well entail that specific acts were wrong. "She was wrong to donate only $100 to that charity." And, if that is not convincing, it seems to me clearly true that the tycoon acted wrongly in refusing to aid the relative. There would be no anomaly in the secretary saying: "She really ought to have given the relative the money; it was quite wrong of her to refuse." I suggest, moreover, that these claims would be true.

It remains to explain *how* such claims could be true, and to give reasons to suppose that Mill could accept such an analysis and fit it into his account of imperfect duties. The first thing to be pointed out is that, given sufficient opportunities to act, the possession of a virtue entails that over a course of time, one *will* display certain behaviors. Failure to display those behaviors will be evidence that one lacks the virtue. In general, if one has a duty to display a given *course of behavior*, failures to act constitute the violation of a duty, if not sufficiently counterbalanced by performances. Sometimes, circumstances are such that a *perfect opportunity* is presented that only someone lacking the virtue, or who fails to recognize the duty, would ignore. In the case of the duty to be generous and charitable, it is plausible to say that the duty to be generous entails that one not pass up perfect opportunities. That is one of the reasons why it makes sense to say the tycoon acted wrongly in not helping the relative. There could, of course, be countervailing considerations that remove the imputation of wrongdoing, for example, if confronted with a *crowd* of persons in need, each does *not* present a perfect opportunity since meeting all would be excessively burdensome.

In addition to implying a duty to exploit perfect opportunities, the duty to be generous may also entail a duty of minimal effort. One point of criticism of the tycoon was that she gave too little. A $100 contribution may be too little help, given her resources, to count as a benevolent act. It shows too little regard for the *need* of the eventual recipients. Again, a *particular* act could be said to be wrong, as a violation of a duty of beneficence.

If these points are correct, then the duties of charity and beneficence are saved as imperfect duties. They imply duties to display a *course of behavior*, and provide a basis for saying a person acted wrongly in a particular case. Furthermore, these are *not* cases where the person involved had a *right* to the benefit. When we criticize the oil tycoon for not helping the relative, we are not saying the relative had a justified *claim* on the tycoon's money, or that the tycoon *owed* it to her. (Of course, there *could* have been prior relationships to justify such a claim, but I have supposed this was not the case.) We are merely saying that this was a circumstance that called for the grant of aid.

How does all this stand with Mill's texts? I note first that he did seem to recognize at least that imperfect duties may imply a duty of "minimal effort." William Thornton had published part of his book on "the claims of labor" in the *Fortnightly*, and Mill sent Thornton some criticisms that formed part of the basis of his own later review of Thornton's book. He wrote to Thornton:

> Again you argue throughout that no question of justice can arise as to the amount for which A hires the labour of B, because A is not bound to hire B at all. Is not this assuming that what jurists call a duty of imperfect obligation, i.e., not owed to an assignable individual, is no duty? A may not be bound to hire B, but if he is bound to hire or to benefit some person or persons at his choice, the amount of the benefit may be an essential condition to his fulfillment of the duty.[296]

We can also sketch an account of the sentiments associated with failures of beneficence. In general, as Mill said, we do not require the help of others as much as we do that they not harm us; but we do sometimes require their help, and life is made easier through the assistance of others. Moreover, having their assistance provides reassurance of their regard for our interests and needs. Thus, it is natural that we are pleased at acts of beneficence, and upset by failures, especially given "perfect opportunities." When we consider such acts from the point of view of the general interests of society, those feelings are given a moral basis—it is moral approval and disapproval we feel. Considerations of the general welfare also argue for inculcating the virtues of beneficence and charity, and this will imply the propriety of urging the correlative behavior on one another, and condemning the failure to display a generous or charitable course of behavior, or the failure to act given perfect opportunities, and so on.

These, then, would be genuine duties; they would have associated "commands" and "sanctions." Further, the moral sentiments associated with these duties would differ in kind and degree from those we feel when someone harms us. In the latter case, it is *resentment* we feel, and a desire for *retaliation*. In the case of the imperfect duties, the feelings involved are simply those attendant on our caring for the interests of others. The former feelings are generally more intense. It would also seem to be possible that there are cases where benevolence is so greatly needed that a failure may be regarded as total disregard for vital interests, and provoke resentment and the desire for revenge. Someone who could have saved the life of another at little or no personal cost, where it is clear the failure was a deliberate omission, may be thought to have thereby disregarded essential interests of the other in a way as inimical to the general welfare as is harming others. (As we shall see in the next chapter, Mill went so far as to hold that we can *harm* others *by* our omissions.) In such a case, it could be argued that the interest we all have in help from others when in such distress is so great that it should be protected as a matter of rule, in which case, we all have a right to such aid. As I pointed out earlier, in his letter to Thornton, Mill indicated he was even amenable to making such a failure a criminal offense. This line of reasoning could, therefore, go to show that *some* benevolent acts are *so* needed that they cannot be left to chance, and should be enforced as a matter of right. I showed earlier that Mill gave such an argument in support of the Poor Laws. (He did *not* explicitly conclude there is a *right* in such a case. That follows from his analysis of rights in *Utilitarianism*, however.) Thus, some acts of positive benefit to others would fall under duties of justice.

I still must account for the apparent inconsistencies in which Mill seems to have been caught. He held in *On Liberty* that only self-protection justifies punishment; he held in *Utilitarianism* that duty implies liability to punishment, going so far as to say that duty can be *exacted* from one as a debt. He maintained in the book on Sir William Hamilton that punishment can be justified to protect just rights. But if no rights are associated with imperfect duties, it should follow that punishment is *not* appropriate, thereby implying that there is no duty present.

So far as I can see, the inconsistencies are real and not merely apparent. I shall suggest a partial resolution based on a suggestion to be found in Mill's own writings. The suggested resolution raises problems of its own that I shall discuss more fully in the next chapter. My suggestion is that Mill, at times, distinguished punishment that consists merely in the expression of condemnation from punishment that goes beyond the mere expression of opinion. This point is difficult to see because he often used the phrase "public opinion" to refer not merely to opinion, literally understood, but also to further acts of disapproval such as withholding goods, removing a person from a job, turning friends against the person, and so on. To cite just one example, he gave public opinion as one of the chief influences on people's behavior in *Utility of Religion*, but he indicated that public opinion operates through the whole range of actions I have described, "sufficient to make life miserable," and "reaching in some states of society as far as actual persecution to death."[297]

There is no question that he sometimes meant to include the expression of negative opinions of certain sorts among the forms of punishment. Though praise and blame are expressions of our feelings, they can also be used to inhibit or encourage conduct. It seems clear that in *On Liberty*, he intended to view such expressions of opinion *as* a form of punishment. Even in that essay, however, there is some evidence that he distinguished the punishment represented by *mere* expression of disapproval from other forms of punishment. In one passage, he listed the sorts of acts "injurious to others" that justify punishment: "encroachment on their rights; infliction on them of any loss or damage not justified by his own rights; falsehood or duplicity in dealing with them; unfair or ungenerous use of advantages over them; even selfish abstinence from defending them against injury." Of the list, he said: "these are fit objects of moral reprobation, and, in grave cases, of moral retribution and punishment."[298] He went on to hold that even the dispositions leading to these acts "are properly immoral, and fit subject of disapprobation which may rise to abhorrence." On the other hand, he held that self-regarding faults "are only a subject of moral reprobation when they involve a breach of duty to others."[299]

In this passage, he held that actual punishment beyond reprobation is justified only when duty has actually been violated and only in "grave cases." The expression of moral disapproval rising "to abhorrence" is justified even of propensities not fully actualized. A further instance where such a distinction in *kinds* of penalties is invoked is in the essay on Thornton on labor. He there considered the charge that labor unions unjustly infringe the liberty of nonmembers by expressing disapproval and reproach for not doing their share in common efforts. Mill wrote:

> We hear much invective against Trades' Unions on the score of being infringements of the liberty of those working men on whom a kind of social compulsion is exercised to induce them to join a Union, or to take part in a strike. I agree with Mr. Thornton in attaching no importance whatever to this charge. An infringement of people's liberty it undoubtedly is, when they are induced, by dread of other people's reproaches, to do anything which they are not legally bound to do; but I do not suppose it will be maintained that disapprobation never ought to be expressed except of things which are offences by law. . . . it must be admitted that the members of Unions may reasonably feel a genuine moral disapprobation of those who profit by the higher wages or other advantages that the Unions procure for non-Unionists as well as for their own members, but refuse to take their share of the payments, and submit to the restrictions, by which those advantages are obtained. . . . All that legislation is concerned with is, that the pressure shall stop at the expression of feeling, and the withholding of such good offices as may properly depend upon feeling. . . .[300]

This passage has important implications for Mill's theory of liberty, which I shall explore in the next chapter. For whatever reasons, he was holding here that moral disapprobation, but no further punishment, is justified in these cases, thus endorsing an important difference in kind between the expression of condemnation and further punishment. Apparently, he thought the former sufficiently less "severe" as not to constitute an unacceptable interference with an individual's freedom. This does, though, give us a basis for distinguishing perfect and imperfect duties. If, on the one hand, he intended the latter to justify only the expression of moral disapprobation and condemnation (and whatever further behavior, e.g., avoidance of the person, that is a natural concomitant of that feeling), then he could maintain, as he did, that the "sanctions" associated with imperfect duties are less "stern" than those deserved by violations of perfect duties; it is plausible to hold that failures of charitableness and beneficence justify condemnation but no further punishment. On the other hand, the expression of moral disapprobation *is* a kind of sanction, hence, the connection between duty and deservingness of punishment is preserved. Mill cannot, of course, go on to say that duty, in *all* its forms, may be exacted as a debt from the person. This account does not resolve all the difficulties with Mill's statements. Of course, Mill may simply have overstated his case, especially since his main objective in the section in which this statement occurs was to characterize duties of justice, of which (he thought) the statement is true. The contrast he made in that passage was, in fact, with supererogatory acts, *not* imperfect duties.

Thus, my interpretation of Mill on imperfect duties preserves a good deal of what he had to say. It reinstates duties of charity and beneficence as genuine duties, and illustrates how they would fit his characterization of imperfect duties given in his summary statement at the close of *Utilitarianism*. It would also (if correct) shed light on the nature and implications of such duties as a matter of philosophical analysis independent of Mill's theory. The account also has implications for his theory of freedom to be discussed in the next chapter.

I should note in closing that retaining duties of charity and beneficence as imperfect duties does not show they are the only kinds. The letter to Thornton indicates that Mill recognized others. Despite my arguments to the contrary, there is some evidence that David Lyons is right in regarding what he terms "good samaritan" duties as imperfect for Mill. In the penultimate paragraph of *Utilitarianism*, for example, Mill appears to *contrast* duties of justice with the duty to save a life, and he gives it as an example of a case when "some other social duty" may "overrule any one of the general maxims of justice."[301] This would not undercut my analysis. Despite what Mill may have *thought*, I believe his analysis of rights commits him to saying the person in trouble has a *right* to aid; even if there are grounds to deny this, the analysis of charity and beneficence would stand, as would the analysis of duties of imperfect obligation that it provides.[302]

The discussion of Mill's theory of justice has been long (and perhaps) tortuous. I believe I have shown it to have considerable power and scope in ways that have not been appreciated in the past. I shall show next how that theory is important in understanding and defending Mill's theory of liberty.

5

THE THEORY OF FREEDOM

Mill's views on freedom, or liberty, have received widespread attention and discussion virtually from the day of their publication in his classic essay *On Liberty*. It was Mill's own judgment that this was likely to be his most lasting and influential work,[1] and I believe it to be the judgment of most commentators that no work of Mill's is more deserving of such reaction. One would think that at this late date, more than a century after its publication, little more can be said of it that is significantly enlightening. Indeed, I believe that much recent commentary on the essay goes quite far in giving us a good grasp of the central themes, and their strengths and weaknesses.[2] Nonetheless, controversy over Mill's theory continues. As an extreme example, we find some readers who accuse Mill of being a sort of "moral totalitarian" whose book was intended to support the freedom only of the rational elite in society, and was designed to convert people to a social ideal to be imposed on society, rather than to free the general run of persons.[3] On the other hand, Professor Himmelfarb reads *On Liberty* as advocating a virtually unlimited libertarianism that makes the individual "the repository of wisdom and virtue," and "the freedom of the individual the sole aim of social policy."[4] Furthermore, criticisms of Mill's doctrines on freedom aim at undermining them entirely as defensible philosophical views. It is alleged that he defended freedom as good in itself, which is held to be inconsistent with utilitarianism, that his argument depends on a distinction between self-regarding and other-regarding acts that cannot be maintained, and it has seemed to many commentators that the incursions on freedom that he recognized toward the end of the essay (and elsewhere) amount to giving up the principle. Even defenders of Millean principles have held him to have been mistaken in some of his applications. Thus, it is said that he did not himself consistently apply the central principle that the essay outlines and defends. *On Liberty*, then, is pictured as a moving rhetorical document, the philosophical significance of which consists of the nonutilitarian insights illegitimately smuggled in by Mill.[5]

To fully attack the important controversies would require a book of its own. In this chapter I can only show how the theories I have thus far attributed to Mill fit in with his theory of freedom. I shall argue that treating his views on freedom as a branch of his theory of justice sheds light on the themes of *On Liberty*. I shall then show how the resulting understanding of his doctrines on liberty can be used to counter some of the more influential criticisms. Though much of what I say has obvious bearings on the views of Professors Cowling and Himmelfarb, I am satisfied that these extreme interpretations have been undermined by others.[6]

I shall begin the discussion of freedom by outlining Mill's objectives in *On Liberty*.

MILL'S OBJECTIVES

In the introductory section of *On Liberty*, Mill set out the most general aims with which the essay was undertaken. He traced the progress of the development of political liberty from the battle for a proper balance between the political freedom of subjects and the authority of government, through the adoption of political rights and of constitutional checks on the ruler, to the institution of political democracy, whereby the rulers become identified with the people. Mill pointed out that despite common talk of "self-government," the truth is that democracy is rule by the majority, "of each by all the rest."[7] This raises the possibility, recognized by others such as de Toqueville, of the "tyranny of the majority." However, Mill did not fear the tyranny of the majority so much in the form of political despotism, that is, the oppression of political minorities by the electoral majority. That fear he addressed through the device of proportional representation (see chapter 4). His concern in *On Liberty* was with nonlegal control of the individual through the medium of "public opinion." Society can enforce the prevailing opinion and feeling by means other than civil penalties, through which "it practices a social tyranny more formidable than many kinds of political oppression."[8] Mill described such social pressures as a fetter to the development of individuals and as producing servility to prevailing custom.

In passages often overlooked by commentators, Mill pointed out that the opinions of most people, hence those that constitute the prevailing opinion, are only partly determined by reason, and often not by reason at all. People's views on right or wrong are as much determined by prejudices, superstitions, their social *feelings*—including antisocial ones, envy, jealousy, arrogance, contemptuousness, and "their desires or fears for themselves—their legitimate or illegitimate self-interest."[9] The result is that the prevailing "morality" often represents the mere likings and dislikings of society. Opinion then, for the most part, enforces the strongest feelings and personal preferences in society. And Mill criticized the leading intellectuals for concentrating on the question of what things society ought to like or dislike without asking "whether its likings or dislikings should be a law to individuals."[10] *Part* of the objective of the essay, then, is to show that this is false. There is a limit, Mill asserted, to the extent of control of the individual that "collective opinion" may exercise, "and to find that limit and maintain it against encroachment, is as indispensable to a good condition of human affairs, as protection against political despotism."[11]

As outlined in the essay, Mill's objective was to assert and defend a principle or rule which could provide a basis for determining what freedom individuals are to be accorded, rather than for that to be determined by the dominant likings and dislikings in society. As was his objective in morality in general, he wanted people to base their actions on rational principles, rather than on their feelings, sentiments, or varying "intuitions" concerning an act's propriety or acceptability. The problem of the essay is that of the limits of social control of individual behavior; the objective is to provide and defend a principle that marks that limit and can provide a rational basis for permitting or suppressing modes of action through the coercive instruments of society. Just what those "instruments" are is a matter of some importance. Though Mill *did* regard the expression of opinion as sometimes employed for punitive ends, he also thought of it as a direct expression of our attitudes independent of any further punitive function. As I argued in the last chapter, he also distinguished in a number of places the punitive role of expressions of opinion from that of further penalties. I shall take up in a later section the *forms* of control that he thought of "public opinion" as taking. It is helpful to bear in mind that in *On Liberty*, it is as often these *further* instruments of control that Mill was referring to in using the phrase "public opinion."

Now, the principle, or principles, that Mill defended are abstract and stated in terms meant to rule out certain *grounds* for interfering with the freedom of others, or to rule out certain kinds of conduct as fit objects of social control: only to prevent harm to others may society interfere, and then only if the conduct directly harms others. Conduct that harms others "through" the actor, for example, because the others care about the person, or by virtue of the example the actor sets, does not warrant interference. Put this way, the essay essentially is directed at establishing a negative thesis concerning freedom itself. This is misleading, however, and the most important and distinctive feature of the work may be missed or undervalued if Mill's own statement of his objective is taken as totally definitive of the thrust of *On Liberty*. In writing *about On Liberty*, it is clear that he viewed the essay as asserting (what I regard as) a powerful, somewhat innovative, positive doctrine that has important practical consequences, and which is crucial to the ultimate defense of his theory of freedom. This is the doctrine of the importance to human well-being of individual self-development, or, as I prefer to call it, autonomy. In his *Autobiography*, Mill described *On Liberty* as "a kind of philosophical textbook of a single truth"—"the importance, to man and society, of a large variety in types of character, and of giving full freedom to human nature to expand itself in innumerable and conflicting directions."[12] In the next paragraph, he referred to "the doctrine of the rights of individuality, and the claims of the moral nature to develop itself in its own way," in a fashion that makes it clear that he regarded this as the central theme of the essay.[13]

The interpretation I shall present takes this characterization by Mill of his central concern very seriously. Moreover, I shall argue that his reference to "the rights of individuality" was also to the point. The essay is aimed at providing a rule of conduct for society that is designed to protect what Mill regards as a vital interest of persons—autonomous development and activity. Given the theory of rights that I discussed in the previous chapter, it will follow that people have a right to individuality. Mill's theory of liberty, then, is an application of his theory of justice. I shall outline and argue for an interpretation along these lines, and I will show how it sheds light on controversial aspects of Mill's theory.

FREEDOM, RIGHTS, AND HAPPINESS

On Liberty was concerned with setting out a rule that would give freedom appropriate protection. It sets out the sorts of considerations that are relevant or irrelevant when issues of freedom arise, and what burdens of proof fall on those who would restrict freedom. I want to show that his theory of liberty is best understood as a defense of a right to freedom that is itself defended in terms of a right to autonomous activity. I shall start with the right to freedom.

Some commentators have thought that Mill was not entitled to defend a right to freedom, or have thought it inappropriate to interpret him in this way,[14] since he explicitly said in the introduction: "It is proper to state that I forego any advantage which could be derived to my argument from the idea of abstract right, as a thing independent of utility." This disclaimer does not reject *all* talk of rights, only of "abstract" rights that are not grounded in utility. Though he did not systematically express his theory of liberty in terms of rights, Mill sometimes did so in *On Liberty*, and I have already quoted him as saying the essay deals with the "rights of individuality." As I showed in the last chapter, Mill had a conception of rights and justice that *are* grounded in utility, which played an important role in his thinking about social, political, and economic issues. I shall sketch how the principle of liberty can be fitted into the framework of his theory of justice.

As I argued earlier, Mill held that someone has a right to act in a certain way or be treated by others in a certain way if and only if society has a duty, specified by a rule, to protect the person's interest in acting in that way, or to be treated in that way. Mill's position on freedom was that people have an interest in freedom that should be protected as a matter of rule. It would follow that everyone has a right to freedom.

This statement may not be entirely accurate. One influential philosopher has denied that there is any general right to freedom as such, and the basis of his argument *may* have been acceptable to Mill. Consequently, the claim of a right to freedom will have to be examined more clearly later to see how it is to be understood, and what limitations to it Mill may have been willing to accept. As a preliminary statement of his theory, however, I think the claim of a right to freedom captures something essential. Moreover, it will be extremely useful to bring out in further detail just how Mill understood the argument for the proposition.

To understand adequately Mill's argument for the importance of the interest in liberty, it is necessary to recall how he saw freedom to be connected to human well-being, or happiness. Happiness for people, according to Mill, is tied to the "elevated faculties" of humans. Creatures with such faculties cannot be fully satisfied or fulfilled to the extent that the higher faculties go undeveloped and unused. The development and use of these faculties is requisite to the "sense of dignity," which derives in part from "the love of liberty and personal independence."[15] Freedom, then, is an essential element of human well-being; it is of value in itself, as well as for the other goods it facilitates our achieving. Mill's conception of the rules of justice, we saw, took these rules to be of such great importance to us precisely because they protect interests that "are more vital to human well-being" than other sorts of rules. Further, these rules of justice "forbid mankind to hurt one another (in which we must never forget to include wrongful interference with each other's freedom)."[16] Thus, Mill explicitly brought the principle of freedom under the theory of justice by virtue of the inclusion of freedom among the essential interests of persons.

Therefore, even though Mill only occasionally framed his theory of freedom in terms of rights, certain essential aspects of his theory are captured by that formulation, and Mill himself explicitly indicated that the rule that defines "wrongful" interferences with liberty is a rule of justice that confers a right on individuals. In *On Liberty*, immediately following the disclaimer of an appeal to abstract rights, he added: "I regard utility as the ultimate appeal on all ethical questions; but it must be utility in the largest sense, grounded on the permanent interests of man as a progressive being."[17] Mill did have a theory of human progress—that there are tendencies in human nature that make for greater cooperation and the development of sociability, and that the resulting trend toward greater civilization itself creates tendencies which, taken together with the essential needs of persons as such, gives greater stress to the principles of equality and freedom. People, *as such*, have interests that are, in that sense, permanent, and to which the progressive trends in human history give a priority.

In the last few paragraphs, I have given a sketch of the interconnections among Mill's conceptions of happiness, justice, and freedom. If this account is correct, then *On Liberty* was not a work independent of his general moral philosophy, as some have contended, nor did his defense of freedom abandon his utilitarianism. The above account makes his general theories of happiness and morality crucial to understanding *On Liberty*, and explains how Mill could defend freedom as both *intrinsically* valuable, and as a *means* by which other goods are achieved.

The account thus far has only been a sketch, however. We need to be clearer on how Mill understood freedom, and what limitations to a right to freedom he acknowledged, or which would be consistent with his general position. I have already indicated that central to his views on freedom was his defense of autonomy or individuality. In the next section, I shall turn to elucidating that notion in Mill; I will then show how it *is* central to the doctrine of *On Liberty*, and how it helps to explain and justify important aspects of that doctrine.

AUTONOMY, INDIVIDUALITY, AND FREEDOM

In *On Liberty*, Mill divided his consideration of the principal forms of liberty between freedom of the intellect, and freedom of action. The first encompasses the freedom to entertain, formulate, and settle upon beliefs according to one's own judgment, together with the cognate, implied freedoms of expression and of access to expressions of belief. The second consists in the freedom to act in accord with one's desires and beliefs. Of the first set, Mill took a strong stand for unrestricted freedom, though only to a limited extent did he recognize that the freedoms involved in expression create some very thorny problems, and, where he did recognize this (e.g., in connection with cases of "incitement"), his position may not be as liberal as many would like.[18] The second set of freedoms is itself divided into two parts, the first consisting in acting according to one's own plan for life, and the second consisting in the derivative freedom to combine with others to achieve common purposes. Mill thought that there are only a few respects in which the latter freedom cannot be treated in the same way as the freedom to act as one wants, and so there are only brief discussions of the subject in the book.[19] I shall argue later that this issue is somewhat more complicated than Mill supposed, and that it raises serious problems. Since Mill did not see its significance, however, he devoted most of his attention to freedom of action for the individual. Unlike the case of freedom of speech, with respect to freedom of action a principle to determine justified interference is important since "no one pretends that actions should be as free as opinions."[20] His discussion of freedom of action is found in chapter 3, entitled "Of Individuality, as One of the Elements of Well-Being," thus indicating that it is in connection with individuality that his primary argument for his principle of freedom occurs.

Unfortunately, Mill's discussion of individuality is not very precise, even given his own somewhat loose standards of exactitude. On one hand, his use of the language of "individuality," "originality," "spontaneity," together with his emphasis on individual "tastes and modes of life," and "experiments in living" has led some to suppose that he was extolling "the virtue of eccentricity."[21] On the other hand, he described his conception also with the phrase "self-development," which carries somewhat different connotations. Thus, commentators have concluded that Mill did not have a unitary conception of individuality.[22] Mill himself, however, referred to his central thesis using *both* the notions of individuality and self-development,[23] in a way that suggests these are interrelated in a single thesis. In one place in the essay he wrote that "Individuality is the same thing with development," again implying at least a close relation.[24] I shall seek to ferret out from Mill's discussion of individuality a somewhat complex conception that gives play to the diverse emphases within his work, but which can be regarded as a unified conception of what I believe we now more commonly refer to as "autonomy." He himself used this very term in referring to his central doctrine in at least one place.[25] I am not trying to show that Mill saw himself as presenting a clearly articulated conception of individuality that would satisfy the critics; rather, I am concerned to show that from his discussion such a view can be constructed, and that if his thesis on freedom is understood in terms of this conception, it is more readily explained and is more defensible.

Mill began his account and defense of individuality with his claim that it is both an *ingredient* of the good life and a *necessary condition* for the achievement of the other components of well-being. Failure to recognize this, he saw as a crucial problem for the defense of freedom:

> If it were felt that the free development of individuality is one of the leading essentials of well-being; that it is not only a co-ordinate element with all that is designated by the terms civilisation, instruction, education, culture, but is itself a necessary part and condition of all those things; there would be no danger that liberty should be undervalued, and the adjustment of the boundaries between it and social control would present no extraordinary difficulty. But the evil is, that individual spontaneity is hardly recognised by the common modes of thinking as having any intrinsic worth, or deserving any regard on its own account.[26]

In large measure, Mill's understanding of individuality is to be found in the contrast he continually made with the person who *lacks* it. In drawing that contrast, he wrote that where tradition or custom alone determines conduct, "there is wanting one of the principal ingredients of human happiness."[27] The person who does *not* live autonomously lives according to custom, allows his or her behavior to be settled by social tradition, rather than on the basis of the person's own judgment, and independently of the person's own needs, desires, personality, and interests. Mill gave a vivid description of the sort of nonself-determining person he feared that society was mass-producing:

> In our own times, from the highest class of society down to the lowest, every one lives as under the eye of a hostile and dreaded censorship. Not only in what concerns others, but in what concerns only themselves, the individual or the family do not ask themselves—what do I prefer? or, what would suit my character and disposition? or, what would allow the best and highest in me to have fair play, and enable it to grow and thrive? They ask themselves, what is suitable to my position? or (worse still) what is usually done by persons of a station and circumstances superior to mine? I do not mean that they choose what is customary, in preference to what suits their own inclination. It does not occur to them to have any inclination, except for what is customary. Thus the mind itself is bowed to the yoke: even in what people do for pleasure, conformity is the first thing thought of; they like in crowds; they exercise choice only among things commonly done: peculiarity of taste, eccentricity of conduct, are shunned equally with crimes: until by dint of not following their own nature, they have no nature to follow: their human capacities are withered and starved: they become incapable of any strong wishes or native pleasures, and are generally without either opinions or feelings of home growth, or properly their own.[28]

This fear of a mass-produced personality is to be found elsewhere in Mill (most notably, in his essays on de Tocqueville), and it is surely a forerunner of similar fears expressed in our own day, sometimes by critics at odds with liberalism.[29] I shall have more to say about such fears later. For now, what should be stressed in this passage is Mill's view that people *have* individual needs, desires, and capacities peculiar to their own natures. Further, that a person's nature can atrophy and die out if not developed and given a chance to be tried out. Mill ended this paragraph with a rhetorical question meant to indicate that he thought such a life-style of conformity to custom is undesirable. To stress this, however, would miss his essential point. Later, he reiterated the claim that people differ in their natures, and in the way the social environment affects them, so much so "that unless there is a corresponding diversity in their modes of life, they neither obtain their fair share of happiness, nor grow up to the mental, moral, and aesthetic stature of which their nature is capable."[30] Here, the central point is that people cannot attain their highest measure of well-being without the development and exercise of that which is individual to them. Mill's references to the value of "eccentricity" were not intended to make *that* a good in itself, but, rather, were an indication that to the extent a person is true to his or her own nature, the person will be happier. Moreover, he held that the diversity of life-modes in society is a good to society by opening up to people the various possibilities for human existence.

Mill did not rest his argument for individuality solely on the intrinsic desirability of developing what is individual to a person, and his conception of autonomy and self-development would be incomplete if left at that. He did not think a person can, or should, live apart from the impress of custom and tradition. One's nature is always a nature that has been influenced and modified by the culture, and custom encapsulates the experience of others from which one can benefit. Nonetheless, he held:

> The traditions and customs of other people are, to a certain extent, evidence of what their experience has taught *them*; presumptive evidence, and as such, have a claim to his deference: but, in the first place, their experience may be too narrow; or they may not have interpreted it rightly. Secondly, their interpretation of experience may be correct, but unsuitable to him. Customs are made for customary circumstances and customary characters; and his circumstances or his character may be uncustomary. Thirdly, though the customs be both good as customs, and suitable to him, yet to conform to custom, merely *as* custom, does not educate or develop in him any of the qualities which are the distinctive endowment of a human being. The human faculties of perception, judgment, discriminative feeling, mental activity, and even moral preference, are exercised only in making a choice. He who does anything because it is the custom makes no choice. He gains no practice either in discerning or in desiring what is best. The mental and moral, like the muscular powers, are improved only by being used. The faculties are called into no exercise by doing a thing merely because others do it, no more than by believing a thing only because others believe it. If the grounds of an opinion are not conclusive to the person's own reason, his reason cannot be strengthened, but is likely to be weakened, by his adopting it: and if the inducements to an act are not such as are consentaneous to his own feelings and character (where affection, or the rights of others, are not concerned) it is so much done towards rendering his feelings and character inert and torpid, instead of active and energetic.[31]

This is an important passage because it shows that on Mill's view, there are two kinds of faculties, capacities, and corresponding needs and desires that form the basis of a person's "character," and the development and exercise of which are requisite for a person to be fully self-developed. First are those which a person possesses by virtue of being human. The ones that he lists, involving the mental capacities, converge nicely with his account in *Utilitarianism* of people's "higher faculties,"[32] and here he refers to these faculties as "the distinctive endowment of a human being."[33] In order to *act* autonomously, one must possess the faculties of perception, judgment, and so on, and the exercise of those faculties is requisite *for* them to be fully developed. Second, each person differs from all others in having unique capacities, sources of pleasure and pain, and hence unique kinds or combinations of desires, enjoyments, and so on. Thus, individual well-being requires the development of the whole person, and freedom to be self-determining is a requisite of this full development.

It is also important to stress Mill's view that faculties and capacities can wither and fade if left unexercised. Moreover, one cannot *induce* the full-fledged capacities of foresight, discrimination, judgment, and choice without giving them room for independent exercise. The attempt to impose a way of living will, therefore, necessarily thwart the development of one's nature:

> Human nature is not a machine to be built after a model, and set to do exactly the work prescribed for it, but a tree, which requires to grow and develop itself on all sides, according to the tendency of the inward forces which make it a living thing.[34]

Similar themes are found throughout Mill's writings. In his second essay on de Tocqueville, for example, he made the point that the chief part of a person's education is not through books; "life is a problem, not a theorem," and "action can only be learnt in action."[35] Thus, he argued for political participation as promoting the development of the faculties through their exercise. In his *Considerations on Representative Government*, he made the point that "whatever invigorates the faculties . . . creates an increased desire for their more unimpeded exercise."[36] Thus, while there are elements of a "character-ideal" in Mill's conception of the autonomous person, such an ideal is not possible for a person who is not given freedom to live the life the person wants as it suits the individual's nature.[37]

Mill, in fact, took his analysis of human character a step further, and held that a person whose life-mode is not autonomously determined does not *have* a character:

> A person whose desires and impulses are his own—are the expression of his own nature, as it has been developed and modified by his own culture—is said to have a character. One whose desires and impulses are not his own, has no character, no more than a steam-engine has a character. If, in addition to being his own, his impulses are strong, and under the government of a strong will, he has an energetic character.[38]

Mill carried this view even further, arguing that one has greater character to the extent one's impulses and desires are strong, and to the extent that one's nature is "energetic." At best, this seems a mistaken way to express a truth that he was suggesting; while at worst his view here seems just wrong. Some people appear by nature to be complacent, unenergetic followers of the crowd. Or, more sympathetically, some people take greater pleasure in contemplative reflection, deep appreciation of experience, and observation of the flow of human events. Modes of living that feature and foster such experience over energetic activity are as much human ways of being as Mill's favored active personality. A person may well find his or her own individuality in such a way of being.[39]

Perhaps Mill could claim that a person whose ways of feeling, thinking, acting are largely the result of custom has no *individual* character. Such a person is like a piece of machinery stamped out to be a certain fixed way. The person *has* a character, but it is one formed by society. Still, one could *be* an individual and not display the active personality that Mill claimed was requisite to individuality. One may perfectly well choose or knowingly acquiesce in the alternative life-styles described above, *as* perfect expressions of self. There is not, then, a conceptual connection between individuality, autonomy and having an active, energetic nature.

Mill's thinking may be illuminated somewhat by considering points he made elsewhere that undoubtedly played some role in the ideas worked out in *On Liberty*. In a number of places, he expressed fears of the loss of individuality as society becomes increasingly a "mass" society. In "Civilization," he expressed the view that as civilization advances, power more and more passes to the masses with the result that the individual is lost "and becomes impotent in the crowd," while individual character "becomes relaxed and enervated."[40] In a totally different context, Mill pointed out that a person generally does not resist public opinion ("unless when under the temporary sway of passionate excitement"), unless "from a preconceived and fixed purpose of his own," which is "evidence of a thoughtful and deliberate character" and which "generally proceeds from sincere and strong personal convictions."[41] The claim that *this* suggests is that in mass society, a measure of strength of feeling is requisite to be autonomous to the extent that it is needed to resist the contrary pressures of public opinion. To say *this* is not to exalt an energetic character indefensibly; it is compatible with adopting *for oneself* a phlegmatic mode of being that is in fact rarely at odds with society; but it preserves Mill's insight that in a society of "crowds," an independent mode of existence *may* require considerable strength of character and desire in order to be maintained.

From this account we can outline Mill's conception of the person who *is* self-developed: (a) the person's desires and impulses are expressions of his or her own nature, not acquired solely through the pressure of society, (b) the manner of the development of the person's character—desires, dispositions, pattern of life—are, in large measure, a result of the person's reflection, judgment, knowledge, personal experience, and choice, (c) the person's unique capacities and potentialities have been developed and fulfilled, or at least explored and tried out, and (d) the person has whatever strength of character is needed to resist contrary social pressures.[42] We should quickly add that the person who *is* self-determining, who lives an autonomous life is *actively engaged* in a life-mode that expresses the person's individuality. Hence, freedom from the control of others is implicit in the idea of living autonomously, and living in that way is requisite for human happiness.

There is one further point I want to make about Mill's conception of self-determination. It is not given in *On Liberty*, but, as I argued in the last chapter, it is more than hinted at in *The Subjection of Women* and elsewhere. This is the view that freedom and equality imply one another; in this context, it means that living an autonomous life entails that one enjoys the status of an equal with others. As I pointed out, Mill stressed that lack of freedom to determine one's own life results in a lessened "sentiment of personal dignity," for one lacks a sense of having an entitlement as a human being "like any other" to choose one's own life.[43] Furthermore, Mill emphasized the contrast between the desire for freedom and the desire for power over others. These, he described as "in eternal antagonism," and he held that the latter "can only cease to be a depraving agency among mankind, when each of them individually is able to do without it: which can only be where respect for liberty in the personal concerns of each is an established principle."[44] In other passages, he emphasized that power over others, manifested in relations of "command and obedience," while "unfortunate necessities of human life," will give way as society progresses, and "become exceptional facts in life, equal association its general rule."[45] The point I wish to stress in this is that self-determination requires that one be an equal of others, that in choosing one's mode of existence, one not be subjected to the control of others.

The arguments that I gave earlier to show that Mill's views on freedom, together with his conception of rights, yield the conclusion that everyone has a right to freedom (subject to qualifications), can also be appealed to in showing that everyone has a right to lead an autonomous life; or, in his own terms, a right to "individuality" and to "self-development." Furthermore, I shall argue that *this* doctrine is *the* central thesis of *On Liberty*, and helps to explain the extent of, and various limitations on the right to freedom that he accepted. There is, of course, a major stumbling block in the way of such a demonstration: Mill *stated* his central thesis, and this was not it. Nonetheless, I believe I can support my claim by examining Mill's own statement, and by showing how its central features are either explained or follow from the thesis I claim is central. In claiming it is central to *On Liberty*, then, I am making a claim about its explanatory power.

In what follows, I shall quote Mill's own statement of his thesis, then I shall cite his own additions, elaborations, or explanations of the thesis. Finally, I will show how the positions he took can be argued for and expressed in terms of the right to self-development, and his theory of justice.

Mill's own statement of his view is as follows:

> The object of this essay is to assert one very simple principle, as entitled to govern absolutely the dealings of society with the individual in the way of compulsion and control, whether the means used be physical force in the form of legal penalties or the moral coercion of public opinion. That principle is that the sole end for which mankind are warranted, individually or collectively, in interfering with the liberty of action of any of their number is self-protection. That the only purpose for which power can be rightfully exercised over any member of a civilized community, against his will, is to prevent harm to others. His own good, either physical or moral, is not a sufficient warrant. He cannot rightfully be compelled to do or forbear because it will be better for him to do so, because it will make him happier, because, in the opinions of others, to do so would be wise or even right. These are good reasons for remonstrating with him, or reason-

ing with him, or persuading him, or entreating him, but not for compelling him or visiting him with any evil in case he do otherwise. To justify that, the conduct from which it is desired to deter him must be calculated to produce evil to someone else. The only part of the conduct of anyone for which he is amenable to society is that which concerns others. In the part which merely concerns himself, his independence is, of right, absolute. Over himself, over his own body and mind, the individual is sovereign.[46]

Following this statement, Mill added that the principle is meant to apply only to adult human beings, and only to such as live in sufficiently advanced societies. "Barbarians," he held, live in a backward state in which the entire society "may be considered as in its nonage." I shall return to these exclusions later, as they are almost universally ignored, but, I believe, they reveal important aspects of Mill's conception of autonomy and its relation to freedom.

Further, Mill went on to explain that not only can freedom be interfered with to stop people from harming others, but people may be compelled to perform "many positive acts for the benefit of others," in which he included saving someone's life, protecting the defenseless, giving evidence in court, and anything else that is necessary to the social good for which one "may rightfully be made responsible to society for not doing." Further he held that, in these cases, one causes harm to others by inaction, and so is responsible for the injury.[47] This also raises difficulties that must be explored later.

Finally, Mill explained that one is responsible to society, according to his doctrine, only when one's conduct affects others "directly, and in the first instance." One may harm others "indirectly" or "through himself," to wit, if the others are upset by harm to oneself, or by way of example. His thesis about freedom, then, is that indirect harms to others do not provide a ground for interfering with an individual's conduct.

It is evident that Mill's doctrine of liberty is neither simple, nor is it properly stated as "one" principle. Immediately following its statement, he limited its application, elaborated on some of its concepts, and extended its application to justify interference to require "positive acts." Later in the book, he described the doctrine as consisting of *two* principles.[48] Further, the doctrine as stated by Mill begins with an account of the *reasons* or *purposes* for which conduct may or may not be interfered with, while the last part of Mill's statement specifies the *kind of conduct* that may or may not be interfered with. However, the passage does not explain how these two parts are to be tied together (e.g., as jointly necessary conditions for justified interference).

I want to start my discussion by addressing Mill's conception of "self-regarding" acts, and show how the notion of self-development dictates protection for them. This is a highly controversial matter, however, and I do not pretend that my account solves all its problems. Some philosophers have held that there really is not a distinction to be made between self- and other-regarding conduct, and thus that the principle of liberty falls apart.[49] And some of Mill's more sympathetic interpreters seek to defend his general position without the distinction. C. L. Ten, for example, argues cogently that what is crucial to Mill's position is a distinction between the *grounds* or *reasons* for justified coercion, thus emphasizing the first part of Mill's statement of his principle.[50] In fact, Mill *did* assert such a distinction, as we saw in an earlier chapter. It was part of his intellectual inheritance, and, *if* it can be maintained, it would go a long way toward explaining and justifying Mill's doctrines on liberty. Moreover, I am not entirely convinced by the grounds given for its rejection, so that even if there is a less problematic approach to these matters, it remains of interest to see what can be made of Mill's account.

First, I want to try to understand the distinction. Mill said that actions can affect others directly "and in the first instance," or, by way of contrast, indirectly and "through" the actor. Later, he explained:

> I fully admit that the mischief which a person does to himself may seriously affect, both through their sympathies and their interests, those nearly connected with him and, in a minor degree, society at large. When, by conduct of this sort, a person is led to violate a distinct and assignable obligation to any person or persons, the case is taken out of the self-regarding class, and becomes amenable to moral disapprobation in the proper sense of the term.[51]

In this same chapter, Mill was also unwilling to admit among "direct" effects the feelings of distaste or resentment people have merely at the knowledge that certain actions are engaged in.[52] He further excluded from direct effects the harms produced by way of setting a bad example.[53] Nonetheless, in the final chapter of the book, he conceded that acts which otherwise directly affect only the agent may be "violations of good manners," and cause offense if done in public, and may therefore be interfered with. From these statements, and Mill's various examples of interferences that breach the distinction, we can formulate what Mill appeared to have intended. An indirect effect of an act is caused solely by the effect of the act on the *actor*; in this sense, it operates "through" him. If I am saddened at the drunken state of my friend, the sole cause of *my* pain (so far as *his* agency is concerned) is the

perceived effect of his drinking on him. On the other hand, his being
drunk may cause him to do or fail to do certain things that do directly
affect me, for example, failing to pay a debt, or keep an important
appointment. The ill effect is produced by something he has done or
omitted, not merely by the effect on him. Similarly, if my friend reels
drunkenly on the sidewalks, smelling of alcohol, and so on, he *has* done
something further that produces the bad effects—he has *intruded* his
state on the public consciousness. The effects are not merely the result
of his being in that state, combined with the causal efficacy of the
others' beliefs, feelings, sympathies, or antipathies. Here, greater
causal responsibility lies with the agent who has *forced* the display on
those having these sensibilities.

It is extremely important to bear in mind that Mill's distinction was
drawn for the purpose of *excluding* certain kinds of effects as relevant
when considering issues of freedom, namely, indirectly caused effects.
In allowing as relevant those effects that are caused by intruding on
others, however, Mill must not be taken to have given a blanket endorsement to *any* intervention based on such effects. I shall discuss this
point later. Further, it is important to bear in mind that Mill was *not*
claiming these effects can be ignored because they are not really effects
or because they do not really harm others. His claim was that these *are*
distinguishable *kinds* of harms, and that, on grounds of the need to
protect freedom, these are not harms from which people can legitimately expect society to protect them. Moreover, it should be noticed
that if Mill could make out the last part of this claim, then it will follow,
given his theory of rights, that people do not have a *right* to protection
from indirectly produced harms; it is not in the general interest, as a
matter of rule, to protect systematically people's interests in not being
angered, feeling resentment, and so on, over self-regarding conduct.

There are two sorts of objections I want to take up at this stage: that
Mill's distinction does not hold up; and that Mill is not entitled to
exclude such harms from consideration. Discussion of the first objection can help clarify the distinction, while discussion of the second will
help show how Mill's theory of justice applies, and how the right to live
autonomously forms the basis of Mill's defense of freedom.

The argument against such a distinction usually takes the form of
what I term a "but what if" argument. An example is given of a
supposedly "self-regarding" act; the critic than asks: "But what if—,"
where the blank is filled in with a description of further circumstances
where others are affected. Scratching my left ear at home alone in bed
appears to have no effects on others, but what if my shade is open and

my confederate is awaiting my signal across the street—consisting of my scratching my left ear in bed—to go ahead with our joint plot to murder my next-door neighbor. An apparent example of such an argument was given by Lord Devlin:

> You may argue that if a man's sins affect only himself it cannot be the concern of society. If he chooses to get drunk every night in the privacy of his own home, is any one except himself the worse for it? But suppose a quarter or a half of the population got drunk every night, what sort of society would it be? You cannot set a theoretical limit to the number of people who can get drunk before society is entitled to legislate against drunkenness.[54]

The two examples illustrate the common deficiencies of such arguments. The act of signalling a confederate in a murder plot is significantly different from that of *merely* scratching one's ear, and the machinery for drawing that distinction (e.g., in terms of differing intentions, intended connections with other acts, etc.) is as open to a utilitarian as to any other philosopher. To be a self-regarding act it is not requisite that the act be of a kind that is *always* self-regarding no matter what context. Mill's claim that *public* performance can remove an act from the category implies as much. Devlin's example shows that these arguments are generally non sequiturs. His "but what if—" question invites the response "yes, *so what if.*" What *exactly* are we to imagine— one quarter of the population drunk each night, but failing not at all in the performance of duties to others? If no *further* acts or omissions occur that significantly or directly affect others, it is hard to see that the case is problematic for Mill. (I ignore here what seems to me the fact of the matter—there are numerous well-functioning communities in which sizable parts of the population *are* drunk every night!) On the other hand, if the circumstances are that people are made incapable of bearing their responsibilities to others, condemnation and even compulsion may be justified with respect to *each* such person. There is, of course, the problem of when it is appropriate to enlist the sanctions of *law* for such problems; but *that* problem does not arise out of any defect in the self-/other-regarding distinction. On the contrary, it is precisely because we think that drinking largely *is* a private matter that we are concerned with invoking legal penalties when some such acts are carried out of the purely self-regarding class.

The self-regarding/other-regarding distinction is sometimes phrased as a distinction between the "private" and the "public." The language, of course, is suggested by Mill's claim that acts done publicly are to be treated as other-regarding. Some liberal writers, however, use the terminology of the public and private in place of Mill's self-/other-regarding distinction, and this has caused some confusion. David A. Conway has criticized such attempts, arguing that the public/private distinction cannot be defended, and he holds with an "extreme libertarian" position that makes no such distinction and requires of one who would suppress conduct that it be shown that actual harm is likely to result from that conduct.[55] Conway's arguments are directed against the position of H. L. A. Hart, but a central argument he gives appears to apply also against Mill's distinction between nuisance acts and those done in private.[56] I have clarified this issue earlier by pointing out that the public act *intrudes* on the consciousness of others. This could also be explained by saying the conduct was *foisted* on the others. Conway argues, however, that there is no defensible way of discriminating the public and private by this concept. Conway agrees that public actions may force the offense on others by making it difficult or impossible for the others to avoid the offense; but, he claims, so-called private actions may be equally "unavoidable" to the person who is offended at the mere knowledge of the existence of such acts:

> the question at issue is whether a distinction can be made between public and private actions, and the situation . . . is not very different from what it is in the case of private actions. In fact, it may be more difficult to avoid the offence resulting from merely being aware of private immorality. For instance, the person greatly offended by the mere fact that homosexuals inhabit the house three doors away and there nightly indulge in their 'abominable practices' may be virtually incapable of ridding himself of such thoughts. There is no equivalent here to shutting one's eyes or looking the other way. So this person is at least as much, if not more, the unwilling victim as is the potential spectator of a public act. It does not appear that a public-private distinction can be based on the claim that only public actions are forced to the attention of the unwilling participant.[57]

I should note that this argument need not undercut the Millean position on freedom. So long as Conway will allow that people's dislike and disapproval of actions alone cannot count in favor of interfering with freedom, the gist of Mill's account will survive, even if his willingness to interfere with indecent behavior would not. Conway's description of his own position suggests that this is his own view. There is, however, some unclarity, as he gives no reason to think the anguish caused by mere knowledge is not harm. Moreover, if Conway's argument as quoted is accepted, it is hard to see that Mill's "direct-/indirect-harm" distinction will hold up. If, then, the conservative need only show that such distress is caused by mere knowledge of such activity, Conway's requirement of a showing of harm may permit considerably greater interference with freedom than one (even he) may suppose.

There is, however, no reason to accept Conway's argument. He has taken as the *criterion* of foisting offense on others the avoidability of the feelings of distress, and so on. Of course, if one is distressed at mere knowledge of the existence of such conduct (how about the mere *suspicion* that it takes place?), one will find such distress quite unavoidable; but this has *nothing*, essentially, to do with whether the actor *foisted* the behavior on one. The reason for this is that the avoidability of the feelings may not be a function of the *actor's* behavior. This is readily seen in the example Conway gives. Surely, whether the alleged homosexuals *foisted* their behavior on the "unwilling" participant depends on what *they* did. But Conway's discussion ignores this question entirely. Doesn't it, for example, matter *how* the offended person came to this knowledge? Let me describe a possible scenario. The offended person noticed that both men in the house wear somewhat long hair, and guessed they were homosexuals. At night, he sneaked up to the window of a bedroom in their house and, using wires pushed through the screen, opened the venetian blinds enough to see in, and spied a sex act taking place.

Surely, it would be a misuse of language to claim the homosexuals had *foisted* the offensive experience on that person, despite the fact that it was direct observation of their behavior that *caused* the offense. The point is *they* did nothing to *force* it on the offended person's consciousness. Indeed, the person may well experience the distress *whether or not* they engage in homosexual acts, if, for example, the person has merely been *told* by someone else that such behavior is engaged in (e.g., by another neighbor, or a "voice" in the night). Here, it is the offended person's beliefs, fears, and so on, that cause the distress, not any acts committed by the (alleged) homosexuals. Conway responds that we can also say of the person offended by the *public* performance of such acts that it is the offended person's "fault that he finds this offensive."[58] This misses the point, however. It was *not* his fault alone that he *experienced* the offense; that is causally tied to the offender's having brought it out in the open. Had that *not* been done, there would have been no offense given over and above what is experienced from merely believing such acts occur.

I have defended Mill's position on "nuisance" behavior in order to show that it is not inconsistent with his distinction between direct and indirect effects, and that such nuisance behavior can be regarded as producing *direct* ill-effects even though these are also produced by the thoughts, beliefs, sentiments of the offended persons. All that follows, however, is that such harms are not ruled out as protected by the liberty principle. It does *not* follow that all such offensive behavior *can* be interfered with. In order to decide when and if that *is* the case, we shall need to know what considerations are relevant to determining when directly harming others *does* provide a basis for intervention by society. One *could* agree that nuisance behavior *does* directly harm others and still insist that it ought not to be prohibited or punished. As I shall argue, there are very strong grounds, based on the requisites of individuality, to hold that *some* kinds of public behavior that give offense to others ought not to be interfered with. To show how this can be argued for, it will be useful to turn to the second objection: that Mill cannot *consistently* rule out feelings of disgust, resentment, and so on, as a basis for restrictions on freedom.

The argument to which I shall respond can be outlined as follows. As a utilitarian, Mill is concerned with promoting human well-being and minimizing suffering, pain, and misery. Mill does admit that so-called "self-regarding" acts can play a causal role in producing suffering of a psychological kind. Since the act can have such a consequence, then, whether or not it is likely to is relevant to whether or not it should be done, and is relevant, therefore, to whether or not society should prohibit or punish it. If the pain it produces is greater than the good produced, prohibition or punishment should be appropriate. Since there *could* be cases where this is so, it is not open to the utilitarian to rule out such effects. C. L. Ten has expressed the problem well. He points out that offended persons may very well be brought to the point of illness:

> What the utilitarian needs to show is that such a prohibition is never the most economical or effective way of preventing the illness, or that the cost in utilitarian terms of such prohibition will always outweigh the evil of the illness. These he may or may not be able to show.[59]

The argument in response has two parts. First, it will be shown that, given Mill's conception of human well-being, the interest an individual has in living autonomously is considerably stronger than the interest a person has in not being offended by conduct that is not foisted on him or her. Second, it will be demonstrated how this establishes a right that can hold even in the exceptional case where the offense taken is great.

Mill maintained that individuality—living an autonomous life—is "one of the elements of well-being," and it was shown that this requires freedom to choose one's own life-mode and develop one's own capacities to reason and choose, and to live according to self-developed desires and needs. Moreover, this requisite of happiness is constantly being thwarted and endangered (he held) by people's allowing or interfering with freedom merely by their likes and dislikes of conduct. He conceived the need of a liberty *principle* as a need to protect autonomy *from* such feelings. Clearly, if a person's lifestyle could be dictated by the mere likings and dislikings of society, protection could not be given to a central requisite of happiness while at the same time giving systematic protection to these likings and dislikings. There *is*, then, a right to be self-determining, and this entails that there cannot be a right to protection from the distress caused merely by knowledge of the existence of conduct, and so on. Even if a person is distressed at the idea that others behave differently, the person is still free to lead his or her own life as self-chosen. Thus, the evil of interference with self-regarding conduct, and the evil of having caused distress to another because the other is distressed at the mere fact of one's behavior are not on a par. The one evil involves a denial of a basic constituent of well-being, something to which everyone has a right, whereas the other evil is not tied to an essential element of happiness, and it is one from which we can have no right to protection. Thus, Mill wrote that "there is no parity between the feeling of a person for his own opinion [concerning what sort of life to lead], and the feeling of another who is offended at his holding it; no more than between the desire of a thief to take a purse, and the desire of the right owner to keep it."[60]

It might be objected that this still does not quite meet Ten's objection since the harm done to the offended person is, after all, harm, and how can the utilitarian *guarantee* that in each and every case it is on the whole better that such feelings not be protected? The reply must repeat points made in chapters 3 and 4. Since the device of rights is meant to give *special* protection to vital interests, it will rule out case-by-case meddling with the rules that assign those rights. Where there is an interest that is part of the very idea of human well-being that is at stake—our interest in being autonomous persons—this requirement must be especially strong. Where the interest is strong, and the threats great, it is perfectly rational, in pursuit of the goal of the general well-being, to erect a near-impenetrable barrier. Just *how* impenetrable a barrier will obviously depend on a number of difficult matters to assess. If this is Ten's point, it is one that is, perhaps, well taken; but there would be no *inconsistency* in the utilitarian holding that the barrier should be absolutely strict. One may question if too high a value has been placed on individuality, or if the threats to autonomy have been exaggerated, but these are questions concerning the *truth* of premises in the argument for the absolute prohibition; they do not address the question of consistency.[61] There is, of course, the further question of whether Mill adopted an absolute principle of liberty. I shall argue later that he did not, but here I am only concerned to argue that it was not inconsistent for him to adopt absolutely a prohibition against consideration of certain indirectly produced harms to others.[62] The right to self-development can also explain Mill's position that freedom may not be interfered with for the agent's own good. Mill presented several reasons for thinking that society is not generally competent to decide or judge for the individual—this, in large measure, because the person *is* individual and unlike all others in important ways. Thus, on the grounds of the likelihood of error by society, he thought the moral rule should be noninterference.[63] His conception of self-development, however, implies a stronger argument still. Even where the societal judgment is correct, society necessarily impinges on the development of the person's own powers when it forces conduct on him or her. The interference deprives the agent of judging for self, of testing judgment, of employing the powers of choice in balancing one's own needs and desires. Of course, it is possible that any such assessment or self-development is ruled out in the particular case, for example, because the person is incapacitated, or lacks the relevant powers. It is possible that any further good to the agent is ruled out by the nature of the choice, for instance, if the choice is to enslave oneself. In these cases, Mill warranted intervention (more on this later); but so long as the agent can benefit in terms of self-development, the general rule must be nonintervention by others to overrule the agent's choice for self. We should note that this sort of argument—one that appeals in part to "strategy" considerations as well as the evils of intervention—is compatible with admitting that there may be cases where greater autonomy would be produced by intervention. What the Millean position denies is that society is likely to make that judgment wisely. Autonomy has its risks, but to allow society to guard against these—even in the name of promoting greater autonomy—entails even larger risks, along with the evils that always attend overriding individual choice.

I indicated earlier that Mill did not believe that the fact that an act directly harms others is a *sufficient* basis for limiting freedom. It clearly is necessary, but is not sufficient. If, by holding hands in public, an interracial couple causes feelings of disgust in bigoted observers, Mill will have to regard the harm as produced in part by the public aspect of the behavior, hence, as a direct effect. Further, in pursuing our goals, or living in desired ways, we often cause harm to others that is unavoidable, and which is not merely the result of their opinion of us or the way we live. Competitive relations abound in this sort of thing. By pushing up my store's profits, I, a grocer, may cause the profits of competitors to decline. By marrying the love of my life, I may deprive her numerous other suitors of a hoped-for companion, and cause them considerable disappointment or even grief. It is not that they dislike *my* way of living or the nature of my conduct, but that they suffer from the resultant deprivation. The situation is very conveniently expressed in the language of rights. Being able to enter into the full intimacy of marriage is something for which society deems it worthy to provide both social protection and legal safeguards, and having the right to engage in such behavior entails that protection cannot systematically be given from broken-hearted disappointment. Thus, even directly produced harms warrant interference with conduct *only* when the harm is one from which society ought systematically to protect individuals, that is, only when the harm is such that the individual has a *right* that is violated by the conduct. In this way, the theory of rights provides a useful way of expressing Mill's view. Some evidence that Mill in fact thought in these terms is given by the fact that he himself expressed his position, using the language of rights:

> It must by no means be supposed, because damage, or probability of damage, to the interests of others, can alone justify the interference of society, that therefore it always does justify such interference. In many cases, an individual, in pursuing a legitimate object, necessarily and therefore legitimately causes pain or loss to others, or intercepts a good which they had a reasonable hope of obtaining. Such oppositions of interest between individuals often arise from bad social institutions, but are unavoidable while those institutions last; and some would be unavoidable under any institutions. Whoever succeeds in an overcrowded profession, or in a competitive examination; whoever is preferred to another in any contest for an object which both desire, reaps benefit from the loss of others, from their wasted exertion and their disappointment. But it is, by

common admission, better for the general interest of mankind, that persons should pursue their objects undeterred by this sort of consequences. In other words, society admits no right, either legal or moral, in the disappointed competitors to immunity from this kind of suffering; and feels called on to interfere, only when means of success have been employed which it is contrary to the general interest to permit—namely, fraud or treachery, and force.[64]

Insofar as we can now formulate the only condition sufficient for interference with a person's freedom, we have really come to the core of Mill's principle of freedom: Interference with freedom is justified when the exercise of that freedom does (or would) infringe a superior right of someone else. Having already established that there cannot be a right not to be harmed indirectly, and that no one has a right to interfere for another's good, it will follow that society can interdict freedom only to protect the interests of other person's. We have, then, the necessary and sufficient conditions for proscription of freedom, and have seen how they are developed from the "rights of individuality," that Mill claimed to be the chief subject of his essay.

At this stage of my interpretation of Mill's theory of liberty, it will be useful to say something about the notion of freedom in Mill and to add some important qualifications to the right to freedom. There has been considerable recent discussion of a contrast drawn between "negative" freedom and various conceptions of "positive" freedom.[65] Negative freedom consists in the absence of external constraints on behavior, and some political thinkers believe that this concept of freedom is inadequate to capture the important ways in which social, political, and economic institutions impede the "true" freedom of individuals, apart from coercive restraints on behavior. On the one hand Mill wrote that "liberty consists in doing what one desires,"[66] and he said that "all restraint, *qua* restraint, is an evil."[67] This makes it look as if his was the negative conception of freedom. On the other hand, Mill's conception of self-development, or autonomy, has many features that some advocates of a "positive" conception of freedom emphasize, and there are passages in Mill to indicate that sometimes in referring to "freedom," he intended the larger notion.[68] So far as I can see, however, the dispute will turn out to be largely verbal in Mill's case. Whatever advantages are to be obtained through a conception of positive freedom are available to the Millean through the concept of autonomy or individual self-development. Moreover, there may well be important advantages to insisting that the latter concept goes beyond that of freedom. I think it best, then, to accept Mill's statements that imply that he conceived of freedom in terms of the absence of external constraints. To accept this view, together with the claim that there is a right to freedom, raises a serious problem, expressed in the criticism of Professor Dworkin.[69]

Dworkin maintains that for a right to play a significant role in political argument, it must be conceived in a "strong" sense, namely, as implying that it is wrong for government to deny it to the person who has the right even if it would be in the general interest to do so. While Mill might not have accepted particular aspects of this claim, the theory of rights I have attributed to him rules out appeal to the general interest in particular cases (except in exceptional circumstances, which Dworkin may also be willing to accept). Dworkin argues, however, that there is no right to liberty in this strong sense since laws regulating traffic, for one example, deprive individuals of liberty, but are justified merely on the ground of the general interest; of course, it would be easy to extend the example to numerous others.

Mill's principle of liberty, as I have explicated it, permits interferences with liberty only to protect superior rights of others, but this is consistent with, indeed implies, that any particular claim to liberty may be relatively weak or strong. The right to drive in any direction one chooses may be fairly weak. Moreover, we may all have a right to protection from the dangers posed by persons exercising free choice as to where they will drive. It is not clear, then, that Dworkin is right in maintaining that such legislation is based solely and simply on a calculation of the general interest, and in a way that undercuts a right to liberty.

Still, the reply presupposes that one has a criterion for ordering claims to liberty, and for ordering the strengths of conflicting rights. Such a criterion, I believe, is implicit in Mill's theory, and there is an important passage in his *Principles of Political Economy* where he explicitly utilizes it. That criterion is the very one I have argued is central to his theory of freedom. The freedoms we may wish to exercise are not all on a par, with respect to exercising our individuality. Insofar as physical safety is a prerequisite for anyone's living autonomously, it has a high priority. On the other hand, being required to drive in one direction only on a given street normally makes negligible difference to the sort of life-mode one leads. Thus, one could say that the right to this particular freedom is weak compared to the right people have to protection on the streets. Alternatively (what seems more plausible), one could say that the interest in this particular freedom is so weak relative to the protection of autonomy that there is no right involved at all. It is simply not an important enough freedom. On the latter view, it would be perfectly plausible to hold that the incursion on freedom a restrictive traffic law represents is one that *can* be justified by a simple appeal to the general interest. What is important, however, is that on *either* position, we have a right to freedom only to the extent that freedom is requisite to, or important for the exercise of an autonomous life-mode. Restrictions on freedom that leave us free to live the sort of life we want, despite ruling out *certain* choices, are not interdicted by the liberty principle.

While Mill never quite adopted such a view wholesale, it is strongly suggested in his *Principles of Political Economy*, in a section that summarizes important aspects of his theory of freedom. When discussing objections to government intervention in social affairs, he made the point that there is a limit to such interference "which no government . . . ought to be permitted to overstep: there is a part of the life of every person who has come to years of discretion, within which the individuality of that person ought to reign uncontrolled by any other individual or by the public collectively." This domain he marked out by appeal to conduct that affects no one but the agent, or if it affects others, does so only by the influence of example. He then went on to hold that even when conduct directly affects others, the burden of proof is on the advocate of restraint, and "a merely constructive or presumptive injury to others" will not justify interference. Being prevented from doing as one wishes, "always tends, *pro tanto*, to starve the development of some portion of the bodily or mental faculties," and thus, only a strong necessity "will justify a prohibitory regulation." Unless the individual can be convinced of the necessity, the restraint "partakes, either in a great or a small degree, of the degradation of slavery"; but when government merely provides funds or other means to achieve an end, "leaving individuals free to avail themselves of different means if in their opinion preferable, there is no infringement of liberty, no irksome or degrading restraint." Mill then went on to add that compulsory taxation, required usually to provide public support for projects, does involve a limitation on liberty.[70] However, it must be recalled that his scheme for taxation *permitted* near-confiscatory taxation of income beyond that requisite for "comfortable independence" (in the case of income from bequeathal), when the income had not been earned, or was not proportionate to effort. Apparently, then, he felt that taxing a person, but leaving the individual free to live a comfortable life was not a degrading interference with freedom.

The appeal in these passages of Mill's is consistently to the notion of what is requisite to the exercise of individuality, and his position explicitly recognized that not all interferences with an individual's choices equally affect the person's autonomy. Thus, I conclude that Mill's position on the right to freedom is best summarized in the statement that everyone has a right to freedom in proportion as that freedom is requisite to, or important for the exercise of an autonomous way of living. This may entail, as Dworkin argues, that there is no right to liberty as such, but, rather, to that which justifies the liberties to which we do have rights. In Mill's case, that to which we have a strong right is autonomy.

DUTY, FREEDOM, AND MORALITY

I have outlined the chief features of Mill's theory of liberty, explaining them in terms of his conceptions of happiness and justice. In this section, I shall consider how his views on freedom relate to his general position on the nature of moral duty. Some important recent work has been done on these matters, and the issues have some significance for the contemporary debates over the limits to the right of society to enforce morality through punishment, and over the alleged right of society to engage in paternalistic intervention to protect persons from harming themselves.

THE ENFORCEMENT OF MORALITY

Professor D. G. Brown has published a paper that offers a comprehensive account of Mill's theory of liberty and that draws important connections between that theory and Mill's theory of morality. Brown's work has spurred considerable further research (including my own), and has elicited significant commentary. One important conclusion he has drawn is that Mill was committed to a principle that conduct can be interfered with if, and only if, it is morally wrong. As this appears to commit Mill to acceptance of a thesis favoring the enforcement by society of morality, while he has usually been taken as arguing *against* such a claim,[71] it is of some interest to explore Brown's interpretation. Doing so will also unearth important difficulties for Mill's theories.

Brown's interpretation attributes to Mill the following four propositions:

1. The liberty of action of the individual ought prima facie to be interfered with if and only if his conduct is harmful to others. (Brown calls this "The Principle of Liberty.")
2. All interference with the liberty of action of the individual is prima facie wrong.
3. Conduct which is harmful to others ought actually to be interfered with if and only if it is better for the general interest to do so.
4. The liberty of action of the individual ought prima facie to be interfered with if and only if his conduct is prima facie morally wrong. (Brown calls this "The Principle of Enforcing Morality.")[72]

I have earlier given my reasons for wanting to phrase Mill's theory of liberty in terms of rights, so there is little to be gained by arguing again for the superiority of my formulation to Brown's Principle 1. Moreover, we are not necessarily far apart, since he takes that principle as clearly laying down a *necessary* condition for interference—that the conduct be harmful to others—whereas the "prima facie" clause leaves it open as to *when* harmful conduct does warrant intervention. I shall explore further the defensibility of the necessary condition given in Brown's formulation.

If Brown's four principles do summarize Mill's theories of freedom and morality, it follows that Mill thought of Principle 1 and Principle 2 as asserting the coextensionality of the predicates "causes harm" and "is morally wrong." Brown argues that Mill could not consistently hold this, however, since *some* of the acts Mill regarded as wrong do *not* cause harm to others. It should be recalled that Mill had said that people may be rightly compelled to perform positive acts for the benefit of others, such as:

> to give evidence in a court of justice; to bear his fair share in the common defence, or in any other joint work necessary to the interest of the society of which he enjoys the protection; and to perform certain acts of individual beneficence, such as saving a fellow creature's life, or interposing to protect the defenceless against ill-usage, things which whenever it is obviously a man's duty to do, he may rightfully be made responsible to society for not doing.[73]

Mill went on to say that the principle of liberty does not rule out compulsion in these cases, since "a person may cause evil to others not only by his actions but by his inaction." Thus, we get in this passage not only the examples Mill had in mind, but his identification of causing harm with violating moral duty, as well as a statement of the appropriateness of social enforcement of moral duty.

Brown argues, however, that the examples will not pass muster as cases of "causing harm." He writes:

> If I do not save a fellow creature's life, or do not protect the defenseless against a third party, even in the circumstances in which I could be required to do so, it does not follow that in every such case I cause harm to the neglected person or to anyone at all. It is sufficient to preclude such an inference, and in general to preclude any inference from not preventing evil to causing evil, to consider the agency of other people. A drowning man may have jumped or may have been pushed, and quite ordinary circumstances may require us to assign the agency of some other person than myself as the cause of the evil.
>
> What is still more doubtful is whether Mill can include under causing harm to others the breach of one's responsibilities to society at large. . . . That the individual is necessarily injuring others by not bearing his share of protecting them from injury is a relatively arguable if dubious claim. But that he is necessarily injuring them by not bearing his share of any joint work necessary to the interest of the society seems to be a much stronger claim and an indefensible one. There can be no guarantee that joint works necessary to the interest of society will not include institutional care for the mentally defective, urban redevelopment, or foreign aid to countries whose economic condition might otherwise lead to war. I cannot see how refusal to co-operate in such efforts toward alleviation of existing problems could be shown to constitute causing harm to others.[74]

Professor David Lyons, in a recent paper,[75] has argued that Brown's concern is unjustified because, though the crucial passage is "equivocal," Mill is most consistently (or best?) read as *not* holding to the view that conduct may be interfered with if and only if it is harmful to others, but, rather, that "the prevention of harm to other persons is a good reason, and the only good reason, for restricting behavior."[76] On this reading, Mill's examples are not problematic, since each *could* be regarded as a case of behavior required to protect important interests of others, even if they cause no harm. That Mill's position is thereby more defensible is some reason to think Lyons's formulation comes closer to his intentions. Lyons's treatment of the textual evidence, however, does not seem to me entirely satisfactory. Lyons cites Mill's own statement:

> A person may cause evil to others not only by his actions but by his inaction, and in either case he is justly accountable to them for the injury. The latter case, it is true, requires a much more cautious exercise of

compulsion than the former. To make any one answerable for doing evil to others, is the rule; to make him answerable for not preventing evil, is, comparatively speaking, the exception. Yet there are many cases clear enough and grave enough to justify that exception.

Of the passage, Lyons comments:

> This passage shows that Mill acknowledges the very distinction that, on Brown's reading, he is supposed to neglect—between conduct that causes harm and conduct that fails to prevent harm to others. Furthermore, in employing the distinction as he does, Mill seems to be saying that he would allow interference not just to inhibit harmful conduct but also to elicit acts that prevent harm to others.
>
> In other words, the evidence offered by this passage is equivocal. Mill's initial comment on causing evil by inaction suggests some confusion about the character of his own examples, as if he wishes to limit interference to conduct that causes harm to others. In the continuation of the passage, however, he explicitly extends interference to conduct that does not cause harm, but that fails to prevent harm, as his good samaritan examples require.[77]

So far as I can see, however, Lyons is not justified in making this final remark. Mill *did* make a verbal distinction between "doing evil" and "not preventing evil," but he did *not* say that the latter case is not a case of causing evil. *This* sort of case he picked out as one in which an individual causes evil *by his inaction.* "Doing evil" involves positive acts, "not preventing evil" involves an omission, but both cases are explicitly described as causing evil. Unfortunately, the passage is *not* equivocal, and it supports Brown's claim.

There is considerable further evidence that Mill consistently thought of the failure to provide aid as a form of causing harm. As I pointed out earlier, his own statement of his principle of liberty begins with laying down the only *reasons* for interference with liberty, while the second part describes the sort of *conduct* that can be interfered with—it must "produce evil to someone else."[78] Furthermore, in his discussions of duty in *Utilitarianism*, he traced the moral sentiment consisting in the desire for punishment to the desire for revenge for "hurts," "injuries," and "damage," and he spoke of "the desire to punish a person who has done harm." In the case of a violation of a duty of justice there has been "a hurt to some assignable person." As I showed in the last chapter, he *also* held a positive principle of "good for good," and he tried to argue that though it has no "obvious connection with hurt or injury," it really does by disappointing the expectations of the person who is denied the benefit.[79]

I argued, in chapter 4, that Mill *also* held that we naturally desire good for others and that this sentiment can be "moralized" as well as can the desire for retaliation, and I indicated that such facts could be used to resolve another problem Mill appears not to have seen—that of fitting imperfect duties into his account of morality. I have argued, however, that some goods are *so* needed; that some failures to provide aid represent *such* a gross disregard of others' interests that they rightly provoke resentment and a desire for punishment; and that, in this way, there can be a *right* to aid. If this line of argument had ever been clearly accepted by Mill, and made the basis of duties to aid, Mill would not have had to identify all cases of failing to provide benefits as cases of causing harm.

I should add that I do not think it can be sustained that failing to prevent harm is always a case of harming others. Though the issue is being hotly debated and it cannot be taken as settled, I am unconvinced. Mill may have been right in holding that omissions *can* cause harm *via* disappointment of expectation, or even in other ways. In cases of failure to perform cooperative duties, for example, the observation of one's failure can cause insecurity in others, and through that endanger the scheme itself and its benefits. Moreover, the rights of the others are violated, harming them in this way; but this simply will not work in the case of a drowning person whom we could but do not save. We may grant that others may be made less secure, even that the drowning person, *if* aware of our inaction, will be caused (momentary) disappointment, but this is *not* the evil of our inaction; it is *not* the basis of the ill-will others will feel toward us. *That* is much better captured by Mill's own formulation, when he referred to acts that are "wanting in due consideration for" the welfare of others.[80]

The upshot of the discussion is that Mill's view should have been that freedom can be interdicted only of conduct that either harms others or that shows insufficient regard for the interests of others; and, as I have argued, the conditions that explain when causing harm justifies punishment, and when conduct insufficiently cares for the interests of others, are best expressed in the language of rights. Those interests only to which persons have a right to protection are to be figured in, and positive beneficial acts can be compelled if, and only if, people have a right that they be performed.

But what of Brown's claim that Mill was committed to the Principle of Enforcing Morality; that conduct ought to be interfered with if, and only if, the conduct is morally wrong? In the first place, moral wrongness could not be, for Mill, a necessary condition for justified punishment *in general*. It *must* be kept in mind that the principle of liberty was a secondary principle for Mill that was limited in application. It did not apply to children and "barbarians," and Mill explicitly said elsewhere that it is permissible to punish children, for example, for their own good.[81] Even of mature adults, he permitted exceptions, holding that it is permissible for society to refuse to enforce a contract that makes a slave of a person, even if the individual agrees to it.[82] Here, the person is not acting wrongly—he or she harms no one else—but societal interference with the person's choice is justified. This last example, it must be admitted, is controversial, with some commentators holding that Mill was simply inconsistent on this point, while others hold there is no genuine infringement of freedom involved. I shall examine these claims below. Still, the children and barbarian examples make the point that his *general* position was not that wrongful action must occur (or be likely) before interference is justified.

Professor David Copp has argued that Mill did not hold that *social* enforcement is always appropriate for wrongful behavior, since he had said that circumstances might render legal or social enforcement inappropriate, in which case the individual's conscience should fill in.[83] This would, of course, take some of the sting out of the claim that Mill favored the enforcement of morality, since the mode of enforcement need not be that of law or social action. Still, Mill did not *always* summarize his theory in such a way that conscience would figure as the ever-present enforcer of duty; an argument could be made out that there is always a connection between moral duty and the *deservedness* of social punishment, even if, on balance, in a particular case only conscience should apply.[84] Thus, there would be no moral duty which, in principle, was immune from social enforcement. Perhaps Brown was right, then, in claiming that (at least for civilized adults), the fact that a person has violated a moral duty, or will do so, is always a (prima facie) sufficient ground for interfering with the liberty of that person.

Would it follow that Mill is wrongly cited by contemporary liberal philosophers as an ally in their position that the law should not enforce "morality as such?" The answer seems to me clearly to be that Mill would agree with the thrust of the liberal position. What has been at stake in the contemporary debate has been the issue of whether society has the right to enforce its beliefs about how people should behave, whatever those beliefs may be, and whatever may be the basis of those beliefs. The question, then, is whether the majority's conception of morality is entitled to enforcement merely by virtue of the fact it is the dominant view. On this issue, Mill's position was with the liberals—

only in those cases where the conduct is of a kind that directly harms others in ways to which the others have a right to protection from, and then, the justification in terms of rights must take full account of the requirements of individuality. Thus, there is no right to protection from disgust, shock, and indignation felt merely in knowing of the conduct of others. Nor does acceptance of the right to individuality permit interference with freedom for the actor's good alone. These claims are the very heart of the liberalism espoused by contemporary philosophers.

I shall turn next to consider the views of a critic of the liberal positions on the enforcement of morality—Lord Devlin—in order to illustrate how Mill's position can deal with conservative criticism. I shall then attempt to reformulate what I take to be a central theme in the conservative position, because I believe that Mill's view is vulnerable to the reformulated version. I do not believe the sort of difficulty Mill would have to face has been explored thoroughly in the literature, so there would seem to be some importance to this discussion. It will also help to bring out the different sorts of claims liberalism will need to support to respond adequately to a reformulated conservatism.

Devlin's view can be summarized in the following propositions:

1. A society is a community of ideas, including its moral ideas.
2. Without a shared morality, a society cannot exist; so that, when common agreement is gone on politics, morals, and ethics, a society will disintegrate.
3. Since a society may properly use the law and its punitive apparatus to preserve itself, it may use the law to maintain its morality.
4. Furthermore, no line can be drawn between so-called "private" and "public" morality—any sort of conduct *could* have social effects, hence, there can be no theoretical limit drawn as to the sort of conduct that society can proscribe.
5. Still, there *is* a right to freedom that society should respect and to which the widest possible play should be given; thus, only that conduct should be suppressed that engages social reaction to an extreme extent—only when the conduct is met with "intolerance, indignation and disgust," and then, the interference should respect privacy as much as possible.[85]

It is of some further importance to stress Devlin's conception of morality. A moral judgment, he explained, unless purporting to be divinely inspired, "is simply a feeling that no right-minded man could behave in any other way without admitting that he was doing wrong."[86] The "right-minded" person, for Devlin, is the equivalent in morality of the "reasonable man" in the law—"the man in the Clapham omnibus."[87] I cite Devlin's depiction of morality not because it is bizarre (which it is), nor because it is a logically empty conception (how are we to explain the "right-minded" person's feeling that he would be doing *wrong* if *that* judgment is just a feeling that every right-minded person would judge it *wrong?*), but because it emphasizes a strong role for feeling in the very idea of a moral judgment.

Much has been written of Devlin's argument and the claims he made.[88] Professor Hart has pointed out that there is a crucial ambiguity in Devlin's claim that society will "disintegrate" if its shared morality loses its consensus. On the one hand, Devlin appears to regard it as an *a priori* thesis, in which case if a society were to *change* its moral views, it would have to be taken as having disintegrated. On the other hand, Devlin *may* have meant that if the social morality is unenforced and it begins to lose allegiance, then genuine social upheaval will result— disorder, chaos, and so forth. Hart points out that Devlin seems "indifferent to the question of evidence."[89]

I do not believe that Devlin ever adequately clarified his position; indeed, his attempt to do so betrays his failure to grasp the force of the objection.[90] Indeed, I think that this failure creates chaos with respect to the reasonableness of the whole list of claims he endorsed. Devlin maintained that society should *not* enforce its moral code unless the conduct interfered with is met with "intolerance, indignation, and disgust." This limitation was intended to reflect his concern for the right of freedom. It marks a limit within which freedom is properly operative. However, if the right of society to defend itself from disintegration (in a nontrivial sense) is the basis of his claims, then the criterion he gives is reasonable *only if* conduct solely of the kind that provokes such reaction is likely to threaten society's existence. Moreover (as Mill would insist), he must also assume that the deterrent effect of social displays of intolerance, indignation, and disgust is insufficient without adding legal penalties. Neither of these assumptions seems at all plausible as generally true factual claims about society. Further, if conduct that society is *indifferent* toward really *would* endanger society, then he has been far *too* liberal in setting out the criterion of justified interference, since society's reaction alone determines when interference is justified.

The feeling criterion *would*, perhaps, be more sensible if one were to stress Devlin's conception of morality. If morality *consists* in sets of feelings, then it may be sensible to take as central to a society's morality those judgments that reflect the strong feelings of society. Then, however, the criterion protects the society's *morality*, not its *existence*, and the argument as to why it has a right to do that cannot appeal to the need to protect its existence, unless some further strong claim can be supported to the effect that society will likely disintegrate (in the nontrivial sense) if its strongest feelings are not enforced by law as well as by the strong negative expressions of intolerance, indignation, and disgust. Again, this seems implausible, and Devlin, in fact, stepped away from such a claim in the introduction of his book, when seeking to dispel the image of an antilibertarian. He there explained that because there must be toleration of maximum individual freedom, only when the intolerance and disgust of society is the result of "calm and dispassionate consideration," is there a right to enforce the moral code.[91] This is surely the wrong criterion to use in determining when deviation from the moral code will provoke genuine social disorder and disintegration.

The difficulties involved in Devlin's position highlight the strength of Mill's views. Mill emphasized the fact that social feelings, no matter how widespread or strongly held, may reflect prejudice, fear, superstition, and so on, and that they pose a threat to an essential aspect of well-being—human individuality. Opponents, then, must establish a right for society to go beyond the "natural" concomitants of holding such views—the expressions of disapproval, rejection, and so on—to enforce them through social punishment. Since Mill's theory *permits* intervention when conduct threatens genuine social disorder, the burden on the conservative is far greater than many seem to recognize.

It is possible, however, to stress other aspects of the conservative position that address *weaknesses* in the Millean position, and which must be dealt with by any liberal opponent of a strong "enforcement of morality" thesis. The essence of the conservative position consists in a fear of ultimate or long-range effects of (apparently) self-regarding acts. At least this seems to be central to any position that is not reducible to the view that society may enforce its strongest feelings about conduct regardless of *any* effects of that conduct. The conservative foresees a *train* of events, perhaps a complex process, of which the (apparently) self-regarding acts are an early stage. A society *filled* with gambling, drunks, and homosexuals may be the ultimate horror imagined. In more reasonable terms, the picture could be of a community weakened by too much time spent gambling, many individuals who no longer control the gambling urge, in which the poor are exploited, spending needed dollars at the bookie joint, filling the pockets of an extended criminal establishment, and so on. While some persons, even many, are able to assimilate gambling as a pleasant recreation, a great many cannot. Given such a possible scenario, the conservative holds that there can be no *principled* ground for nonintervention in *any* sort of conduct, even if engaged in private, since it may well be desirable or necessary to intercede in the earliest stages of the process.

Something like the above argument may have been what Lord Devlin really had in mind. In a later part of his book, for example, he wrote:

> It is obvious that an individual may by unrestricted indulgence in vice so weaken himself that he ceases to be a useful member of society. It is obvious also that if a sufficient number of individuals so weaken themselves, society will thereby be weakened. . . . If the proportion grows sufficiently large, society will succumb either to its own disease or to external pressure. A nation of debauchees would not in 1940 have responded satisfactorily to Winston Churchill's call to blood and toil and sweat and tears.[92]

From the point of view of the theory of freedom, it will not do to object to such arguments on the grounds of being "slippery-slope" arguments. Contrary to the impression one sometimes gets from critical reasoning textbooks, not all "slippery-slope" arguments are fallacious. Sometimes, starting along a path of conduct is very likely to lead to complex, wide-ranging evils. Most liberal arguments in favor of a permissive view of freedom of expression involve a slippery-slope argument, and there, the conduct for which interference is proposed is often conceded to have harmful effects. More important, if we accept this conservative line of reasoning, we shall have to reject the self-/other-regarding distinction, and, perhaps even more importantly, we shall lose the sort of protection for individuality that Mill's principle was designed to ensure.

The first point I want to make against the conservative claims is that the argument shows the danger of reducing the self-regarding/other-regarding distinction to that of the public/private distinction. Mill's distinction turns on the different *ways* in which conduct is likely to affect others. The person who gets drunk at home alone at night, and who otherwise functions as the model citizen is engaged in purely self-regarding conduct even if the rest of society is going to hell through drink. The solitary drunk, on the other hand, who can no longer meet his or her obligations to others as a result of drinking, has carried the behavior out of the self-regarding class, and Mill explicitly held it to be no illicit violation of the freedom principle to interdict or penalize such a person's imbibing.[93]

The question that becomes crucial in the argument then—and I am afraid that it has been generally lost sight of in the heat of the debate—is the appropriate limit to *preventive* intervention by the state when apparently self-regarding conduct *can* develop into conduct directly harmful to others. Mill addressed this problem and took a strongly liberal position on it. His view was complex, interesting, and important, and has, for the most part, been ignored in the literature.

Mill raised the issue of "the preventive function of government," in a passage that has been widely cited and studied because of an example given in it that has import for the issue of paternalism.[94] In fact, however, the issue addressed is much wider. He began by pointing out that the preventive function is easily abused, "for there is hardly any part of the legitimate freedom of action of a human being which would not admit of being represented, and fairly too, as increasing the faculties for some form or other of delinquency."[95] Where there is a *certainty* of danger, there is no question of rightful intervention—if one sees another about to commit a crime, or if one sees another about to cross an unsafe bridge and cannot warn the person, interference with the conduct is justified. The bridge-crossing example is often referred to, but I have never seen *Mill's* conclusion drawn from it. He said further that "when there is not a certainty, but only a danger of mischief, no one but the person himself can judge of the sufficiency of the motive which may prompt him to incur the risk."[96] Thus, he concluded that the individual should only be warned, if possible. By way of analogy, he held that though poisonous articles can be abused, to ban the sale outright would make legitimate use impossible. Similarly, registration of purchasers, including a statement of intended use, would be permissible. So long as regulation of the sale and purchase of such articles is "no material impediment to obtaining" them, he appears to have regarded such limitations on freedom as leaving individuals free to live their lives as they choose. (This is an interference with freedom that does not undercut autonomy.) The position taken, then, was that so long as the danger is remote and not certain, society may not ban the activity entirely; it may regulate it only to the extent such regulation can facilitate dealing with abuses, and only so long as the regulation does not interfere with the ability of persons to live in self-chosen ways.[97] Furthermore, he was willing to make regulation fairly intrusive; for example, the licensing of persons who engage in the sale of dangerous articles could be limited to "persons of known or vouched-for respectability of conduct," and he was willing to have hours of sale set that maximize "public surveillance," and to sanction license withdrawal if breaches of the peace occur, or if the place "becomes a rendevous for concocting and preparing offences against the law."[98]

Mill's position—that only a certainty of harm to others justifies intervention—contrasts well with Devlin's. The value of autonomy is taken as so strong, and the threat to freedom as sufficiently great that *no* slippery-slope arguments have a foothold. No matter how widespread the likely damage will be, or how compelling the evidence that the slide down the slope has started for a great many people, the position taken by Mill limits society's response to the expression of its attitudes, and such regulatory devices as leave people free to choose to take the first steps. Of course, society *can* step in to deal with the abuses, that is, to enforce people's obligations, and this must not be forgotten. Still, to the conservative critic, this intervention appears to be too late. Of course, it is conceivable that in particular cases, the conservative could be right. Thus, the strong liberal position I have attributed to Mill seems to leave society inadequately equipped to protect itself from insidious harm that is the upshot of a chain of influences that begins with conduct that, viewed out of that context, appears to harm only the agent.

The liberal *can* respond, as I suspect Mill would, that autonomy is so precious, and the dangers of weakening the permissible grounds for societal intervention are so great, that it is best that we risk such harms. In other words, to *be* free, we must risk some dangers such as these. To others, however, it may not be clear that autonomy has *so* much value, or that the risks of weakening the principle of liberty are so great; but for the liberal to adopt an interpretation of the principle of liberty that is weaker than Mill's runs the risk of making the position indistinguishable in principle from Devlin's. The liberal can insist, for example, that there must be *strong* evidence that engaging in the suspect behavior leads a *high* percentage of people to do *very* bad things, and that it is *extremely* unlikely that regulation alone can adequately deal with the likely tide of abuse. Then, however, an argument is needed to show that *that* position is more defensible than a somewhat *less* liberal position, and so on. I do not mean to suggest that a liberal position cannot be defended, or even that Mill's strong view is indefensible. I mean only to point out that the conservative challenge must be met by defenders of the principle of liberty, whereas it is not clear that the problem has been significantly on the liberal agenda at all.

PATERNALISM

It will be useful to consider next Mill's views on paternalism—the use of compulsion for the agent's own good. There are important interpretive problems, and a brief look at the work of other commentators will help bring out significant features of Mill's theory of liberty.

The chief interpretive problem has been posed by Mill's treatment of examples in the concluding chapter of *On Liberty*, as many commentators have thought that his discussions there are not entirely consistent with his strong antipaternalistic stance in the earlier chapters. Especially vexing to liberal interpreters is Mill's treatment of contracting into slavery. He held that an agreement to become a slave may be regarded as null and void by society, and he said that the ground for interfering is a concern for the agent's freedom: "It is not freedom, to be allowed to alienate his freedom."[99]

Professor Gerald Dworkin, in an essay that has been extremely influential in the contemporary discussion of paternalism,[100] has taken Mill's discussion of the contract into slavery case as providing a crucial insight into Mill's thinking on the issue of paternalism. Dworkin first notes that there is a conception in *On Liberty* of an autonomous agent who has an independent status. He sees that freedom is noncontingently connected to that concept of being autonomous. (He regards the resulting argument against paternalism as "nonutilitarian"—a view I do not share.) What is preserved, then, when society refuses to enforce the slavery contract is the agent's status *as* a free agent. Thus, Dworkin holds, Mill's discussion suggests a very limited paternalistic principle: "Paternalism is justified only to preserve a wider range of freedom for the individual." This principle, Dworkin recognizes, can be employed to justify widespread limitation of liberty, and he explores the sort of further principles needed to fully justify compulsion. His own view stresses the role of consent, holding that those limitations of freedom are justifiable that rational persons would consent to. For society to generally permit such paternalistic regulation is like taking out an insurance policy against our own (presumably dangerous) momentary whim, irrationality, or emotional state.

Dworkin's reconstruction of Mill's position has been rejected by a number of philosophers both as an interpretation of Mill and as a substantive position on paternalism. John Hodson, for example, takes a point (first made by Joel Feinberg)[101] as undercutting Dworkin's view—that many employment contracts require extensive limitations on the liberty of employees (even in such otherwise personal matters as mode of dress) in order for the employees to obtain other benefits. Thus, he argues, if preservation of a wider range of freedom were sufficient to warrant intervention, these agreements could be declared null and void also, which, presumably, shows that too wide a range of interference would be permitted.[102] Richard Arneson has carried this point a step further, arguing that if freedom-maximization is the goal, then society would be justified in banning cigarettes and fried foods on the grounds that these result in shortening life, with a net loss in freedom.[103] Hodson also rejects Dworkin's appeal to hypothetical consent on the ground that it involves a substitution of the "rational will" for that of the agent, which fails to capture Mill's strong antipaternalism.

Though I am not persuaded that these are entirely effective criticisms of a position on paternalism such as Dworkin's, I think it is clear that Dworkin's view was not Mill's. Let us turn, then, to the positions of Hodson and Arneson. Though neither purports to be giving precisely Mill's view, they both claim to be defending the strong antipaternalist stance of the earlier chapters of the essay on liberty.

Hodson proposes the following principle: Paternalistic interventions are justified if and only if: (1) there is good evidence that the decisions with respect to which the person is to be coerced are "encumbered" (i.e., made in circumstances that sometimes lead to regretted choices); and (2) there is good evidence that this person's decisions would be supportive of the paternalistic intervention if they were not encumbered.[104]

Arneson distinguishes between freedom—doing what one wants—and autonomy, which he defines as follows:

> Let us say a person lives *autonomously* to the extent that he is not forcibly prevented from acting on his voluntary self-regarding choices except when his prior commitments bind him to accept such forcible preventions.[105]

He elaborates on this definition with "stipulations" that entail that the more important a desire is to a person, the greater the loss of autonomy that would result from an interference with its fulfillment. Moreover, it is "stipulated" that a forcible interference with a person's course of action, designed to prevent future bad consequences, "always lessens autonomy." The "stipulations" must be added, since they do not follow from the definition, and they *do* guarantee that *every* interference with a self-regarding choice lessens autonomy. (One may, indeed, wonder what it *is* that is so lessened, since it is *not* living autonomously as defined above. Lots of conceivable interventions could result in greater autonomy in *that* sense.) Frankly, I cannot find the slightest textual evidence that Mill ever held such a conception, and I shall cite reasons to think he would reject it. What I want to stress at this stage is Arneson's way of dealing with Mill's own discussion of justified intervention in the concluding chapter of *On Liberty*.

With the exception of two kinds of cases that must be discussed, he believes the examples can be fitted in by viewing them as not representing a *voluntary* choice of the agent. He glosses this as follows: "we may say that a person acts voluntarily if and only if his choice of the act (a) would not be abandoned if he were apprized of all the act's unforseeable consequences, (b) does not proceed from an emotional state so troubled as to preclude the full use of the reasoning faculty, and (c) does not occur under conditions of external coercion or compulsion."[106] Thus, short of acting from ignorance, compulsion, or a virtually unreasoning state, the agent is left free to make his or her own mistakes, shouldering full responsibility for the consequences.

Both positions—Hodson's and Arneson's—stress impairment of the choosing process or agent as the ground of justified interference, and each runs aground on the example of contracting into slavery, since the person who chooses to do this need not be in an impaired or uninformed state. Arneson chooses to reject the position Mill took on slavery contracts (and also his opposition to contracts "in perpetuity") on the ground that Mill's position cannot "cohere well with his overall position," since it stresses, he claims, maximizing freedom. I want to show that Mill's view here *does* cohere with, indeed, that it illuminates his general position.

Hodson deals with the contract into slavery by arguing that the action of the state is simply that of refusing to enforce a contract. The state does *not* thereby coerce anyone to do anything, hence, there is no violation of the freedom principle. This is an important point, since, at the very least, it shows that a legal system can *enlarge* the range of freedom, and can enlarge the range of life-modes open to people, by *creating*, or permitting them to create, enforceable relationships among them that would otherwise not exist. It should be borne in mind, however, that *when* the state recognizes agreements, it *also* recognizes that the *legal* relations among the contracting parties are altered, and attaches or removes penalties for future conduct as a consequence of that recognition. Normally, Smith cannot take Jones's car without Jones's permission. If Jones lends Smith his car, the law will enforce its return whenever Jones demands it, no matter what length of time it had been loaned for. If, however, Jones signs a contract with Smith, giving him the use of the car in exchange for services, the law may *force* Jones to keep his part of the bargain. If Jones signs a contract with Smith to become Smith's slave, that contract may contain provisions that Smith (or his private police force) may do things to Jones (e.g., whip him, or take his property) that are otherwise illegal. The *refusal* of the state to recognize the contract means that the state *will* force *Smith* to behave in certain ways (and Jones as well). Thus, the refusal of the state to recognize an agreement may entail that the state will force people to do things against their expressed will, since the point of seeking legal recognition of the agreement is precisely that of altering their legal relations so as to engage new penalties or release from old legal penalties for performing certain acts. A person cannot enslave himself or herself knowing that a later change of mind will have no effect, since the law *will* act against the slave-holder if that party seeks to continue the relationship. By depriving the slavery contractors of the possibility of an enforcement process, *either* private or legal, they are both forced to maintain the relations of equals, in opposition to their own wills. Mill described the antislavery contract position as limiting a person's "power of voluntarily disposing of his own lot in life," and thus as an infringement of liberty.[107]

It may well be that this argument is defective in that the state is not depriving the parties of some freedom they already had (Hodson makes such a claim); but this is misleading. Without state action, the parties *would* be able to agree to and arrange *private* enforcement. However, the state does *not* merely step back from enforcing the contract itself; it will not permit *anyone* to enforce such a contract. Thus, while people may be free to engage in all sorts of relationships that are not given legal force, they are not *permitted* to enslave themselves in the full sense of that notion. They may *play* at it, or *pretend* to that status, but when really *being* a slave matters (when the slave wants out), the refusal of the state to recognize that arrangement commits it to enforcing laws that make the continuance of the relationship null.

For *my* purposes, however, it is not necessary that Mill should have been right in holding that the refusal to enforce slavery contracts constitutes an interference with freedom. He thought this to be the case, so what is of importance is his reason.

Dworkin, Arneson, and Hodson have supposed that Mill's statements on the slavery contract commit him to the position that freedom may be interfered with whenever doing so will result in greater freedom; but he did *not* say this. The slave does not merely have *less* freedom; the slave has given up freedom (as autonomy) *entirely*. It will be recalled that in discussing the bridge-crossing example, and others, Mill had argued that *only* when there is a *certainty* of harm can a rational adult be forced to act against his or her chosen act (or, if the agent's capacities are radically impaired). He did not say that freedom may be denied for the sake of greater freedom, but in order to preserve the *possibility* of being free.

Mill's overall position can be illuminated by reconsidering the fact that the liberty principle had limited application for Mill; it was not a general principle of morality that dictates our duties to all sentient creatures. Children and "barbarians" were excluded; but why? Certainly, *both* are *capable* of acting freely, in the sense of doing what one wants. At least the barbarians (perhaps also children) are capable of acting autonomously in Arneson's sense. When one looks at Mill's treatment of savages, slaves, and children elsewhere, however, it is clear that they are not capable of acting autonomously in the sense of that term which I have attributed to Mill. In his essay "Civilization" (and also in *Considerations on Representative Government*), he held that the savage lives by impulse, and is unable to frame fixed purposes, or to live by a fixed rule.[108] The savage, he thought, cannot exercise self-control; slaves (at least in a rudimentary state of development) minimally have the habit of obedience; but neither is capable of self-government. Children may also be viewed as suffering these disabilities to a greater or less degree, and neither children, slaves, or savages have yet the capacity to formulate or conceive long-range plans of action, or to exercise the discipline needed to carry such plans through. Moreover, they lack the developed capacities to acquire knowledge, foresee the consequences of acts and weigh them, and to make choices that give weight to past mistakes of their own and others, and so on. However mistaken he may have been, he described undeveloped persons as not "capable of being improved by free and equal discussion," and as *requiring* even "despotism" in order to overcome "the difficulties in the way of spontaneous progress."[109]

This suggests two points. One is that *being* an autonomous person requires that one already have (somewhat) developed faculties. Children and barbarians are in such a rudimentary state that even if they *have* freedom, they cannot live the sort of life that engages *all* the faculties, including the higher ones, and cannot develop for themselves an independent and individual mode of being that is the mark of the self-developed, autonomous person. The self-developed person *can* be left free to make his or her own mistakes, including those that result from impulsiveness, irrational choice, or ill-consideration, because such a person has developed capacities with which to learn from those experiences. A presupposition, then, of the application of the liberty principle is that the agent have the capacity of acting autonomously. Thus, given that a person *is* developed, there is always the possibility that freedom will make *some* contribution to well-being, and, of course, it is necessary to the attainment of the highest states of well-being. This suggests the second point that Mill's position seems to make. In the case of developed adults, there is a general presumption that freedom will (in the long run) be of benefit. The general incapacities of children and savages defeats this presumption. Furthermore, particular incapacities of civilized adults can defeat the presumption (e.g., if one is "delerious, or in some state of excitement or absorption incompatible with the full use of the reflecting faculty").[110]

These points fit in well with the discussion of slavery contracts. Mill's point there was that *all future* freedom is foregone ("he foregoes any future use of it beyond that single act"), and the agent is "in a position which has no longer the presumption in its favour, that would be afforded by his voluntarily remaining in it."[111] In other words, *this* exercise of freedom cannot possibly contribute to autonomous development; the presumption is defeated with certainty.

Arneson argues for *his* conception of autonomy as having been Mill's on the basis of Mill's treatment of polygamous marriage among Mormons. He takes Mill to have regarded such marriage as much like a contract into slavery since each wife relinquishes her future freedom; but Mill would *permit* polygamy. Given Arneson's definition of (and gloss on) "autonomy," the wives can be said to live autonomously, though not freely. However, Mill's discussion does *not*, in fact, bear out Arneson's interpretation, and a close look shows Mill's treatment there to be precisely the position he took with regard to slavery contracts. While I also read Mill as having argued against punishing such practices, he added that living this way should be open to people "provided they . . . allow perfect freedom of departure to those who are dissatisfied with their ways."[112] The proviso here guarantees that the wives do not give up freedom irrevocably, and that if they come to see the harms to themselves through experiencing that way of life, they can still choose another way of being. Thus, being an autonomous person (as I understand Mill to mean it) is still open.

In the next section, I shall extend the discussion of the role of Mill's conception of individuality in his theory of freedom to his views on freedom of expression.

FREEDOM OF EXPRESSION

Mill's position on freedom of expression has been widely read and discussed. Though there continue to be some quarrels over particular points (e.g., over the interpretation of his claim that censorship entails an assumption of infallibility), this part of *On Liberty* has not spawned the large-scale reworking of Mill scholarship that has resulted from rereading other parts. Mill's arguments were relatively straightforward, and he summarized them himself. He held that: (a) a censored opinion may well be true, so society risks losing a truth; (b) even if wrong, the censored view may contain a part of the truth, so that, again, society risks losing truth through censorship; (c) even if the accepted opinion is wholly true, it will be held as a dead dogma or prejudice if those who accept it have not adopted it through rational debate over alternative views; and (d) as a dead dogma, the full meaning of the received opinion will be lost, and its effectiveness will be lessened insofar as it will not be the result of personal conviction and live inquiry.

Mill's arguments combine consequentialist and "strategy" considerations to support a strong position against interference with freedom of expression. The chief arguments against such a position capitalize on (what seems to be) the fact that in particular cases, the relevant utilities may favor suppression of expression, hence, as a utilitarian, it is held that he is not entitled to so strong a position against censorship. I am inclined to think, however, that if one stresses the "strategy" features of Mill's arguments, and also sees his position as an argument to support a *right* of promulgating and receiving communications, it will be evident that Mill's arguments are stronger than the critics suppose.[113]

I shall not pursue that line, however, as aspects of that defense have been given convincingly by others. Moreover, I wish to develop an alternative element in Mill's theory that has been overlooked, and which gives a basis for a stronger prohibition on censorship. I shall start by citing an interpretive point made by C. L. Ten, who came very close to recognizing the argument in Mill to which I want to draw attention. Ten emphasizes a distinction Mill made between having true beliefs and *knowing* the truth. The former can be the result of teaching, indoctrination, manipulation of the media, and so on. The latter, which involves understanding the *grounds* of the view, entails that rational inquiry has been the basis of the belief, and this requires free expression. Ten argues for the desirability of knowing the truth as follows:

> The value of having true beliefs lies in the good consequences produced by the beliefs. True beliefs promote progress and improve the welfare of men. But a man's views on morality, politics, and religion are intimately linked to his personality. The beliefs he has, and the way he holds them, help to define the sort of person he is. The mere fact that he has true beliefs is not enough. We do not think much of a person who simply holds on to true beliefs but has no clear understanding of them or of the reasons for holding them. In assessing the type of person he is, or whether his life is worthy of imitation, we will look at his personal qualities, and these include the way he holds his views about what is and what is not desirable, the influences these views have on his daily life as displayed in the manner he applies them to particular situations and the way he reacts to changing circumstances. For Mill, it really is important not only what beliefs men hold, but also what manner of men they are that hold them.[114]

As Ten points out, if freedom of expression, on the one hand, is defended *solely* for its contribution to the promotion of true beliefs, it can be abandoned whenever those beliefs are better produced through (say) indoctrination; true beliefs may, in fact, sometimes be best maintained through censorship. If, on the other hand, free expression is defended as integral to *knowing* the truth, then freedom cannot so readily be foregone.

There is, however, a further point that Ten has foreshadowed, but not developed. He has seen that what sort of person one is has an intimate connection to the individual's mental history—the sorts of intellectual influences one is exposed to, and the *manner* in which one's world view has come to be constructed. He goes on to say merely that the person who *knows* the truth has a more desirable nature, and that Mill "admires rational and intellectually active men," and freedom of discussion is necessary to produce such persons.[115] In saying this, he cites Mill's claim that freedom of expression provides an impulse that raises "even persons of the most ordinary intellect to something of the dignity of thinking beings."[116] However, Mill did not merely admire intellectual activity in persons; he held it to be both a prerequisite for, and a constituent of leading an autonomous life. Insofar as human beings *as such* require the development and use of their higher faculties, *everyone* has an interest in the requisites of determining beliefs for oneself; and, insofar as leading the sort of life that provides the greatest fulfillment for persons requires that one determine reality by one's own lights, that interest will be strongly connected to an essential element of well-being. This gives a strong underpinning to Mill's claim that not only is freedom of expression needed to produce great thinkers to unearth and promulgate truths, but also "it is as much and even more indispensable, to enable average human beings to attain the mental stature which they are capable of."[117] As indicated earlier, to the extent this is achieved, each person attains the "dignity" of a thinking being.

Mill did not emphasize these points. The bulk of his discussion stresses the general good consequences of free expression in promoting truth. His views on individuality come in the following chapter. Apparently, he was satisfied that the appeal to its contribution to discovering living truth was sufficient to defend free expression. He does not appear to have realized that a *stronger* defense could be made in terms of the right to self-development, in that the latter is seriously compromised to the extent that restrictions are placed on receiving and exchanging ideas. Freedom of expression is intimately connected to the processes of learning about the possibilities of human existence, of ways to organize experience, of modes of relating to one another, of the range of feelings, emotions, attitudes of which persons are capable, and of the possible consequences of these. We can "try out" in imagination styles of existence that are communicated to us through the various expressive instruments ranging from historical accounts to newspaper reports, novels, short stories, and (in our own day) movie and television portrayals. In a sense, to some extent, we "live" through the communications we receive, and we live in a self-determined way by assimilating these communications to our own needs, by utilizing the information as we see fit, by determining our courses of behavior on the basis of *our* understanding of the reality we construct from the communications, and by assessing that reality from our own point of view. Our ability to express our views to others—to search out their criticism, to seek to persuade them, to influence others, to communicate and share truths or feelings—is intimately tied to our conception of ourselves as independent sources of intelligence, as equals to others as sources of opinions, as well as being instrumental to our *further* inquiry for truth. Thus, censorship not only interrupts the search for truth, it interferes with our capacity to be self-determining, and it is a denial of our status as equals.[118]

The only point to add is that such a position can be expressed in a cogent version in terms of the Millean theory of rights. The above considerations provide a ground for the claim that individuals have an interest in freedom of expression that derives from an essential aspect of human well-being. Given the weight of that interest, and the threats to it that censorship presents, it is an interest that should be protected and respected by society as a matter of strict rule. Thus, there is a right to freedom of expression, and the fact that our status as equals is partly defined by *having* this right entails that every act of censorship has *some* disutility as an assault on our dignity as equals. Such an argument, taken together with the ones Mill gave in *On Liberty*, would seem to provide a powerful argument for freedom of expression that is both utilitarian, and would support a near-absolute prohibition on censorship. There are, of course, hard problems in the philosophy of free expression that must be dealt with—the status of libel law, the proper treatment of pornography and other expression (such as that of Nazis) that degrades or humiliates women, or blacks, or Jews—but the philosophical rationale we provide for the right of free expression makes a very great difference in our approach to these problems.[119] Thus, it is important that we see how this *other* element in Mill's theory—grounded in the right to self-development—can provide a strong basis for free expression.

I shall turn next to a consideration of some matters touched on earlier that have yet to be developed. These concern Mill's conception of the relation of the individual to society in light of his theory of freedom and the right of individuality.

MILL'S INDIVIDUALISM

On Liberty has been hailed through the years as a stirring defense of the freedom of the individual, and Mill's views are sometimes associated with a kind of individualism that is, in reality, inconsistent with his own views on human nature, and with his conception of the relation of the individual to society. The concept of self-development appears to be morally neutral (a person's nature *could* be of *any* sort), and Mill's doctrine on self-development appears to permit the development of injurious aspects of personality, since society must leave the individual free until he or she actually harms someone else or poses a real threat to someone. This, we saw, was a significant fear of those who, like Lord Devlin, oppose the notion that there is such a thing as self-regarding conduct that it is beyond the right of society to control. To such persons, Mill's doctrine appears to leave society defenseless until it is too late to counteract the folly of its own "hands off" policy. Individualism appears as a kind of anarchy of personality development, hedged in only by the right to protection when it may be too late.

Furthermore, if one takes Mill's well-known defense of laissez-faire economics as an extension of his doctrine of individualism, it is easy to associate him with a kind of "rugged individualism" that holds persons to be independent, self-interested units struggling against a freedom--destroying society. On this view, society (or the state) is a necessary evil, required to provide protection from harms, but not in any other way integral to the very notion of the individual as human. Society is seen as a useful association, but one that has to be kept in check to assure it does not exceed its bounds and destroy the "natural" freedom of persons. Such a set of views has been held to be misconceived, socially destructive, and immoral. No part of it, however, was endorsed by Mill. I shall try to show that Mill's theory of freedom cannot be fully appreciated without understanding that he thought of the doctrine as needed, in part, *because* people are social creatures, because human life cannot exist except in a social context, and because there are powerful tendencies in the nature of persons that produce conformity to social practice, and that gives public opinion an extreme influence in determining the behavior of individuals.

In chapter 1, I discussed at some length Mill's conception of persons as *by nature* social. Sympathy and the desire to be in unity with others, he held, are natural sentiments that, together with the necessities of life, impel us more and more to the social state. His view was that "the social state is at once so natural, so necessary, and so habitual to man, that, except in some unusual circumstances or by an effort of voluntary abstraction, he never conceives himself otherwise than as a member of a body."[120]

Though Mill made the point in *On Liberty*, he emphasized even more in "Utility of Religion" that the desire to be in accord with public opinion takes a number of forms that exert a very great pressure on people to conform. Some of the strongest passions in human nature, he held, are derived from a concern with public opinion. Among these passions, he included "the love of glory; the love of praise; the love of admiration; the love of respect and deference; even the love of sympathy."[121] Moreover, the concern with public opinion promulgates fears associated with violating opinion that act as a deterring power—"the fear of shame, the dread of ill-repute, or of being disliked or hated."[122] Even our self-esteem, he held, is largely dependent on the opinions of others; and he maintained that ordinary people thus find it extremely difficult to resist when others disapprove of their behavior or think it wrong.

For this reason, Mill did not think his principle of freedom would leave society defenseless until it was too late, when self-regarding abuses would develop out of hand. Not only are there strong pressures to conform that arise out of our social natures, but society has the early training of the individuals in it under its control, so that "if society lets any considerable number of its members grow up mere children, incapable of being acted on by rational consideration of distant motives, society has itself to blame for the consequences."[123]

Furthermore, Mill maintained that in the exercise of our *own* individuality we have a right to express our own distaste for, or abhorrence of, the self-regarding faults of another, and may avoid the person, or warn others of him or her, and so on; in such a case, all the devices of exhortation and persuasion are appropriate. The reactions we have to the ill-use people make of themselves, especially when we care for them, are "natural" and "spontaneous" consequences of their behavior, and the principle of liberty does not forbid the expression of these. Clearly, given the deference people show to public opinion, Mill thought these reactions would function to make deviant behavior less likely. Moreover, if we seek to go beyond such expression and coerce the individual, "vigorous and independent characters . . . will infallibly rebel against the yoke."[124]

Some commentators have thought that in permitting these "natural" reactions, Mill may have made his case stronger in one respect, but that he weakened the principle of liberty too much, for the "natural" ill-consequences of self-regarding behavior *can* be as severe as imposed penalties (a point Mill admitted). I think, however, that Mill was right to insist that there is a great difference between statements and behavior that express *dislike* of the behavior of others and those that express *resentment* at the behavior of others. Insofar as our self-respect is a function of the attitudes others display toward us, it makes a great deal of difference if their behavior evinces merely that they dislike us, or what we are doing, or how we live, or, alternatively, if it shows that they regard us as endangering the interests of others in a way that justifies society in inflicting harm or deprivation on us. Our dignity as persons is undercut to the extent we are viewed by others as fit objects of punishment. The difference in attitudes expressed is just the difference in the *moral status* that we perceive others accord us.

Mill's fear was that society does not stop at the expression of opinion when it strongly disapproves of behavior. I have argued earlier that by "public opinion," he often meant to include reactions of people that go beyond the expression of spontaneous reactions. In *Utility of Religion*, after listing the fears to which a concern for public opinion leads, he wrote:

> But the deterring force of the unfavourable sentiments of mankind does not consist solely in the painfulness of knowing oneself to be the object of those sentiments; it includes all the penalties which they can inflict: exclusion from social intercourse and from the innumerable good offices which human beings require from one another; the forfeiture of all that is called success in life; often the great diminution or total loss of means of subsistence; positive ill offices of various kinds, sufficient to render life miserable, and reaching in some states of society as far as actual persecution to death.[125]

In *On Liberty*, he made this same point, that public opinion manifests itself in the form of penalties that go beyond mere expression:

> In respect to all persons but those whose pecuniary circumstances make them independent of the good will of other people, opinion . . . is as efficacious as law; men might as well be imprisoned, as excluded from the means of earning their bread. Those whose bread is already secured, and who desire no favours from men in power, or from bodies of men, or from the public, have nothing to fear from the open avowal of any opinions, but to be ill-thought of and ill-spoken of, and this it ought not to require a very heroic mould to enable them to bear.[126]

Even when legal penalties are provided for behavior, he held that public opinion is so powerful that its strong expression can render the penalties null. In one of the essays on De Toqueville, he pointed out that the American experience showed that the law may be flouted if public opinion will not permit its enforcement.[127]

The points I have been making place Mill's theory of liberty in perspective. He did *not* exalt individual self-development as the only end of value, nor did he sanction freedom as a tool of "atomistic" units seeking to resist collectivized society. He saw people as social beings by nature, whose social nature creates great pressures for homogeneous personality and behavior; but he also held that our natures have both human and individual tendencies, the fulfillment of which requires that we exercise individual choice of life-mode, if we are to achieve the greatest well-being of which we are capable. The problem as Mill saw it was to protect individuality in a context in which *society necessarily and naturally exerts enormous pressure for conformity*.

Thus, Mill's theory of freedom is not something apart from his social conception of human nature. The sociality of persons was something taken as a given by Mill, and the meaning, force, and necessity of the doctrine of liberty cannot be fully grasped without placing it in that context.

6

A CRITICAL ASSESSMENT

There are many unresolved problems to be faced by a utilitarian holding views such as those of Mill. While I believe the theories I have attributed to him are considerably stronger philosophically than those with which he is usually saddled, there are a great many further difficulties that can be raised. In this concluding section of the book, I shall sketch some of the chief ones. These are problems that I regard as important either to Mill's version of utilitarianism, or to utilitarianisms of all kinds.

THE "NATURALISTIC" FOUNDATIONS OF MORALITY

I shall begin by pointing out that Mill had a conception of moral justification that he supposed to be true, but for which he gave no arguments. He assumed that a moral theory can be argued for only by showing that its dictates somehow recommend themselves to aspects of human nature. Prior to his "proof" of the Principle of Utility, he held that all that one can do by way of proof in ethics is to present "considerations . . . capable of determining the intellect either to give or withhold its assent to the doctrine."[1] I argued in chapter 2 that for Mill these "considerations" must always ultimately show that the actions prescribe further ends that are deeply embedded in human nature. In other words, Mill held that justification of an ethical theory must ultimately be teleological in form. There was really no *argument* for this conclusion, however. There are only brief mentions of alternative conceptions, and his discussions are unsatisfactory. One alternative, for example, is the view that morality can be derived from reason. Mill was familiar with the claims of Kant as an exponent of such a view, but he attempted no systematic refutation, and gave a two-sentence argument that may represent a serious misconception of Kant's theory.[2]

Perhaps one can excuse his failure to consider the view that a philosophical justification for a moral theory consists in showing that theory to derive from an analysis of the concepts of morality. Such an overall position did not become popular until well into the present century. However, a significant part of Mill's own account of morality consisted in conceptual analysis, such as considerations of the meanings of "ought," "wrong," and "duty." At no time, though, did he assess the role that such analytic considerations should play in the derivation of a moral theory.[3]

One also could not find Mill entirely at fault for not considering the possibility of arguing for a moral theory by a process such as that described by Professor Rawls, in which theories are tested against practical judgments, and vice-versa, until one (or more) finally stands up as best assimilating the diverse "considered" judgments we make. Various sorts of "coherence" tests can be proposed, and an argument is needed to show that, rather than one of these, a teleological account is superior. The economist John Elliot Cairnes did write Mill that his proof was not decisive against the intuitionists—they would agree that we desire only happiness, but would hold that "the moral faculty" is nonetheless superior in authority—and Cairnes suggested an approach that is similar to a "coherence" argument. Mill responded that "the mode of treatment . . . is very much to the purpose," and that he would like to see the question handled in that way by Cairnes or some other "competent" person.[4] Again, it is clear that he was aware of alternative approaches.

The problem of justification is crucial for Mill's position, as so much turns on it—his "proof" of the Principle of Utility, his account of the ultimate structure or form of practical reasoning, even aspects of his account of the meanings of moral statements; and his "naturalism" is not self-evidently true. Mathematical theory can also be explained as arising out of basic human needs, desires, and ends, but the question of *justification* of claims within mathematical theory does not, in the view of many philosophers, appeal to those ends and goals. There *are* philosophers, to be sure, especially within the pragmatist tradition, who hold otherwise, but they *argue* for their positions. Even if one thinks that human nature is important in determining moral duty, it is not obvious that it imposes anything other than *limits* to moral duty, that is, that nothing can be a duty that is not *possible* for persons. This is different from deriving duties from the nature of persons.

While all moral theories must ultimately face the issue of justification, the naturalism that is basic to Mill's theory is *not* thereby basic to utilitarianism as such. Rawls's coherence procedure, for example, could conceivably yield a utilitarian theory, and R. M. Hare, an adherent to an analytical approach to moral philosophy, has held that analysis supports a kind of utilitarianism.[5]

There are a number of difficult problems that attach to Mill's conception of happiness. Some of these are discussed earlier in this book, and some are found in the existing critical literature on Mill. There are, however, a number of problems—some that go to the very heart of the conception of utilitarianism—that I do not believe have been given sufficient attention, or even recognized.

THE CONCEPTION OF HAPPINESS

Mill's conception of happiness as I have explicated it is extremely complex, and partly for that reason it raises numerous questions. I shall start with two points that have been alluded to and discussed somewhat in earlier sections of this book. The discussion brings out how important Mill's teleological conception of moral theory is.

In the first place, Mill's conception seems not to be the ordinary notion of happiness. In the second place, it would appear that in his view, people can, and do, pursue things that are *not* conceived as leading to, or promoting, their happiness. People envisage ideals of life beyond their happiness. Indeed, Mill himself admitted this very point when he granted the possibility of martyrdom, that is, of persons who sacrifice their own happiness for the sake of others.[6]

The points are connected with one another, for one of the grounds for denying that people always desire only happiness is that, given the ordinary notion of happiness, there are things which are desired, or ways of living that do not promote happiness in that ordinary sense. The sorts of facts appealed to against the Millean conception of happiness consist in pointing out that people sometimes undertake ideals of life that require self-abnegation and sacrifice. Sometimes these ideals do not look to the happiness even of others. Integrity to the ideal of not taking human life might require refusing not to kill another even *if* doing so were to promote the maximum of happiness for others. In chapter 2,

I discussed how this would be possible, given Mill's theory of human motivation.

In addition, the Millean conception of happiness has a specific content—it requires development of intellectual and other "higher" faculties. This conception is contrasted by Mill with the idea of contentment. Nonetheless, many persons do *not* seek the sort of life-style Mill describes, and he even conceded that many have reached a stage in their individual development that they *cannot* be brought to desire any "higher" mode of living. Such persons may be perfectly contented with their lives, and would, in conventional terms, be called "happy" if satisfied.

This last point runs less deep since it depends essentially on common usage, whereas Mill surely did have a somewhat special notion of happiness in mind. That this is so must, indeed, be conceded, if his remarks on martyrdom are to be taken as consistent with other aspects of his conception of happiness. In the conventional sense of the term, to sacrifice *individual* happiness just *is* to sacrifice happiness.

I have held that the underlying conception of happiness in Mill is that of a sense of fulfillment of one's capacities, talents, and so on. I have argued that he conceived these as falling roughly into two classes— those possessed by virtue of one's nature as a person, and those specific to the individual. I have also held that Mill's criterion for picking out the former consists in appeal to what experienced persons prefer. The only way to tell what fulfillments are needed by persons as such is to see what people over history *have* required. It is worth exploring what connection this conception has to the notion of contentment, and the conventional sense of happiness.

We should note that there is an important sense in which contentment with one's life can be unstable. A person who is contented with his or her style of life may be exposed to alternatives by comparison with which the present life-style pales. The contented housewife may come to question the satisfactoriness of her life-style upon exposure to that of an independent, self-sufficient woman. She may, indeed, lose her sense of contentment with her life-style, and come to desire a change. She might decide she can no longer be happy living the old way. It would, I think, be perfectly proper—not a misuse of language—for her to say she *had* been happy in that life-style, but no longer can be. While this usage does not imply it, it is consistent with a notion of happiness that equates happiness and contentment. Still, it would also not be a misuse of language for her to say "I was not *truly* happy," or "I am more truly happy in my current life-style," or even "I am happier now." Such statements do not merely mean "I am more contented now." Indeed, she may well have been more *contented* in her old life-style; that may have been one of its drawbacks—by virtue of its contentedness, it offered less challenge, required less of her, provided less excitement, engendered fewer risks.

That this second set of statements does not *violate* ordinary language, and that it does not imply a conception of happiness as contentment, shows either that ordinary uses of the term *happy* embody fundamental unclarities, or mask several somewhat distinct conceptions of happiness, or both. This fact, of course, would not show that *Mill's* conception is one of them. What *would* show this would be the sorts of *reasons* the woman would cite for her claims, and it is surely plausible that these reasons would have some relation to a greater sense of the development and exercise of her capacities and abilities, including those human capacities that Mill cited as composing a sense of personal dignity—the sense of control over one's own life, and the exercise of freedom of choice. Mill's conception of happiness is, then, consistent with certain tendencies in the language of happiness, and, perhaps, with a full-fledged conception of happiness that is reflected in certain uses of that language.

The second difficulty for Mill's conception is greater for two reasons. First, Mill's resolution of the difficulty is extremely complex, and ties in with several strands of his thinking about human nature and morality. Second, Mill *agreed* that things other than happiness can be sought, not only without giving thought to happiness, but *also* at a sacrifice of the individual's happiness.

It is important to note at the outset that while Mill held the view that there are certain ways of being that people find fulfilling and, if given an informed choice, would persistently prefer, he also seemed to believe in the near-complete malleability of human nature.[7] He seemed to believe that virtually any propensity in persons could be developed or obliterated through training and social influence. The very notions of dignity and desire for independence can, indeed, be found lacking in persons who have been accustomed to servility and slavery, and this is one of the things wrong with such social relations. Mill would not deny this. In claiming there are certain capacities, needs, and so on, the satisfaction of which is requisite for happiness, Mill was maintaining two theses: (a) there *are* some such capacities and needs which humans typically have as strong propensities; and (b) the history of humankind shows that when experienced in various ways of being, persons tend consistently to prefer a life in which *these* capacities and needs are fulfilled over all others.

These claims are consistent with the thesis of the malleability of human nature. They are even consistent with there being in fact large numbers of people, perhaps even an overwhelming majority, who are no longer capable of appreciating the sort of life-style Mill urged. Mill held the view that these capacities can atrophy through nonuse.[8] Where this has happened, persons may be perfectly contented leading a contrary life-style, and may even feel threatened by alternatives. This is all consistent with Mill's claim that *had* these persons been trained differently, or been exposed to a different social milieu, they would have had a more truly happy life (in the sense of more fulfilling) than the sort of life they now live. Indeed, Mill could give an explanation of what's wrong with the sort of training, and subsequent life-style, such people have received—it renders them no longer capable of achieving a kind of life that would be more fulfilling and satisfactory to them.

There are notorious problems with such claims. What gives Mill grounds for his view that one sort of life which is *not* desired by such persons is more satisfactory, is his view that persons who can experience both prefer the one; but *these* people *cannot* fully experience both, and can have no grounds for rating the life they do not want over the life-style they lead. Moreover, it is claimed, if you *are* the sort of person who requires dignity, freedom, and so on, to be happy, then you do *not* appreciate the satisfyingness of the alternative life-style. Given different capacities, there can be no real comparability. To cite an extreme, the intellectual is said to be simply incapable of appreciating the life of complete sensual debauchery.

The first of these criticisms seems to me true, but irrelevant. The second, though it is often taken as knock-down against Mill, seems to me, on reflection, to be simply false. It is true that someone whose capacities for the "higher" life-style have been starved out can have no reason to rate a "higher" life-style over his or her own, at least not as a life-style for that person to adopt. This fact is irrelevant to Mill's claims, however, for it may still be true that this person *would* have been happier had his or her development been different. Now, *this* claim would be trivial if the second criticism were sound, since, if there can be no real comparability across life-styles, the greater happiness claim could only mean that with the person's *new* capacities he or she couldn't be happy with the *old* life-style.

It seems to me, however, that the incomparability claim is false, at least with respect to all but the most extreme cases. The facts are that: (a) It is not *equally* easy to starve out human propensities; desires for freedom and dignity seem to survive for many persons even *in* conditions of extreme servitude, so it is, in fact, rare to come up with persons *totally* incapable of appreciating alternative life-styles; and (b) Mill was surely right in claiming that there *have* been persons who have tried living alternative life-styles. Most of us in fact at various times of our lives have experimented in one direction or another. In other words, most people in fact have a fair diversity of propensities which make us capable of appreciating a diversity of life-modes. Mill's claim was that history shows that whatever life-modes we tend to choose, we tend to prefer ones which incorporate certain elements, if given a chance to develop and try these. Moreover, if it is true that most persons can continue to develop the capacities Mill spoke of, and that the resultant mode of life would be preferred, then most persons would have some reason to rate such a life over their present ones.

The stress throughout the discussion thus far has been on the *individual's* development of *his or her* capacities, and on the achievement of a sense of *self*-fulfillment. If this stress were combined with Mill's claim that all things sought are sought *as* a part of happiness, then it would be difficult to explain a concern with the *general* happiness, and it would be hard to understand how Mill could consistently admit that individual happiness can be foregone for the sake of others. In addition, it would be hard to explain how people could come to adopt ideals of self-sacrifice and self-abnegation, which incorporate no appeal to happiness whatever—either that of the individual or that of society. It is not enough for Mill to have said such modes of existence are not desirable if they do not promote happiness, since part of his argument for this claim rested on his claim that happiness is the test of desirability since happiness is the end of conduct.

However, I explained in chapter 2 how, by virtue of the contribution that inculcation of such ideals can make to the general happiness, "strategy" considerations would make rational the adoption of them in general, and for the individual also, despite some risk that might be involved. To say this, of course, is to concede the point that individuals *can* seek ends other than the general well-being. The explanation only tells how this is possible, given the basic fact of human motivation— that people seek happiness. One can become a martyr because (by way of explanation) one desired happiness, but, Mill held, once one has become a martyr, the person acts because pained at the idea of sacrificing the well-being of others to preserve one's own well-being. In the same way, *any* useful ideal can be inculcated in persons; but what is the argument to show that these *ideals*, or some set of them, do not *constitute* morality? Presumably, Mill's answer would have to be that justification can *only* come by reference to ultimate ends, whereas these ideals are derived from the desire for happiness.

A further set of problems arise from trying to reconcile Mill's conception of happiness with the arithmetical notions he sometimes sought to apply. He spoke of "calculating" happiness, and of the "sum" of happiness, and of "maximizing" well-being. It is not clear these are sensible notions to begin with, and not at all clear they have any simple sense on Mill's conception of happiness. Mill gave no argument to show that *maximizing* well-being is desirable.[9] If one thinks of happiness as consisting of indistinguishable units of, say, pleasure, the notion of maximizing it at least makes sense. Even then, however, it does not follow that it is desirable. I may desire a quantifiable end, for example, money or genital stimulation, but not want any beyond a certain amount. Even more telling for Mill is the fact that happiness clearly was *not* a mere accumulation of pleasures in his theory. Maximization cannot be defined in terms of an accumulation of goods. The goods that make up happiness for Mill are diverse, and do not consist of units of any one thing (even though all may be said to be pleasures). Furthermore, there is what I call the "meshing" problem for Mill. Happiness, both individual and social, requires the appropriate "mix" of the elements of well-being. A life with a great deal of physical pleasure *may* be lacking in intellectual fulfillment and would, therefore, not be the "greatest" happiness open to the person. As I suggested in chapter 2, there is the problem for Mill of how to determine the proper "mesh" or "mix," and the proper weightings of the "elements" of well-being. However, since there *is* such a problem, it follows that happiness is not an arithmetical "sum" of discrete units of something (as Mill's resort to Benthamic language sometimes suggests).

The notion of "maximization" that the meshing problem suggests is that in which the "greatest happiness" has the sense of "the most nearly complete happiness," meaning by that, "a harmonious mix of goods at the highest possible level of fulfillment." While this would give sense to the notion, it is not clear why maximization in this sense is desirable. I may require close friendships in life, but it does not follow that I would be happier still if I added a few more. (Of course, I might be quite *un*happy if I added a *lot* more, but this would, presumably, upset the harmonious "mix" of goods.) Perhaps the position can be saved by saying that the desire for friendships has built-in limits; it is a desire for a *measure* of satisfying friendships, hence, it *is* maximized by having some; but then, the notion of "maximizing" the goods that comprise happiness loses all force. The desires for goods are fulfilled by something short of a maximum of them.

Mention of the "meshing" problem suggests another. I explained a possible solution in chapter 2 by appeal to Mill's "decision-procedure" in the theory of value. The question of the right mix of the elements of well-being can be resolved by appeal to the preferences of competent judges. For Mill, the only way to tell what is required for creatures to be happy who have the natures of persons is to ask "competent" judges— persons *with* those capacities who have tried out and experienced the respective proposed elements. But what is the nature of this process? What sort of *judgment* is being made by the "competent judge?" Presumably, the competent judge expresses a *preference*, given his or her experience. One may suppose that such a preference reflects the sense of fulfillment derived from the one rather than the other way of living, and that *this*, in turn, reflects some tendency in the nature of persons. Only such suppositions make sense of Mill's procedure. Then, however, the procedure looks suspiciously like the procedures of the intuitionists whom Mill rejected. We can grant that Mill's process is not intended to reveal "moral truths" embedded somehow in the minds of persons, but if we take the process seriously, we shall be deciding important moral questions by appeal to the preferences of persons. In this respect, then, Mill's views offer no significant improvement over an intuitionistic approach to ethics. If someone denies that freedom or autonomy has the great weight for human happiness that Mill claimed, and that security is far more important than Mill supposed, the dispute can ultimately be resolved only by appealing to the preferences of competent judges. It is not at all clear, though, that all such judges would affirm Mill's weightings, and in that case, we are left with conflicting preferences, and no apparent means of resolution. Mill himself seems to have supposed that history has tended to confirm his own conception of the requisites of human nature, and throughout his writings (e.g., in *On Liberty*), he appears to have taken it as unquestionable that his ideal of the energetic personality, leading an autonomous, active, intellectually engaged life is more fulfilling to persons as such than, say, the eastern modes of life that he continually described as having atrophied. What is needed is an argument to show that his was not merely an intuitionistic preference, derived largely from his own experience in a developing industrial economy, geared in large measure to entrepreneurial vigor as a chief value.

Mill's decision-procedure in his theory of value presents another problem that he appears never to have recognized. Mill's moral theory is complex in that it has some of the features of theories that are usually thought of as quite distinct from one another. For example, a distinction is sometimes made between "want regarding" and "ideal-regarding" theories.[10] The former holds that the wants or desires of persons are to be taken as given, and the principles of the theory are concerned with the satisfaction of those wants or desires. In such a theory, the *actual* preferences of people are basic. An ideal-regarding theory holds that there is some basis *other* than the actual desires of persons for ethical principles. Mill's theory has a place for *both* types of considerations. I argued in chapter 2 that Mill conceived happiness as consisting in whatever is requisite to the fulfillment of creatures with the distinctive capacities and needs of human beings. Further, he thought there are and have been persons who are more or less competent to judge this, and that the *actual preferences* of such persons throughout history have been for a sort of life involving development of the "higher" nature, and so on. Mill's "decision-procedure" in his theory of value commits him to accepting the actual preferences of competent judges. Presumably, though, what their preferences reveal is the ideal state of persons as such. Actual persons may not, in fact, desire just exactly the sorts of things Mill supposes would make them happy. By virtue of *not* being competent judges, most people's actual desires could be quite discrepant with the ideal mode of existence which would make them happiest.

This means, however, that there can be conflicts between what ought to be done, given the requisites of the ideal state for persons, and what should be done, given the actual wants of persons. This would also seem to open the door to a sort of despotism, if the requirements of those with more developed "higher" natures are to be given precedence in cases of conflict. After all, the rights of persons are to be grounded in their "permanent interests" as "progressive" beings.[11]

Mill appears to have been led by two sorts of considerations from realizing the significance of this problem. In the first place, he appears to have had what may well have been an overly optimistic view of the extent to which most people in fact desire the most central aspects of his conception of happiness. For example, in *The Claims of Labour*, he wrote:

> the spirit of equality, and the love of individual independence, have so pervaded even the poorest class, that they would not take plenty to eat and drink, at the price of having their most personal concerns regulated for them by others.[12]

The second reason for downplaying the concern is that Mill thought that the chief ingredient of well-being—leading an autonomous life—necessarily gives fair play to the actual desires of persons. These are to be scrupulously respected so long as the individual does not violate the rights of others. The first ground may simply reflect too sanguine a judgment on Mill's part, while the second fails to meet the problem head-on. It *presupposes* that people *do* desire autonomy, with the equal rights that notion implies that all persons must have. If people in fact desire a different sort of society, if they favor greater paternalistic intervention (e.g., because they prefer security to freedom, or because they want to make others live in acceptable ways, etc.), then to insist on a general right of autonomy is to override the actual desires of these people. Even if it were not problematic to claim they would all be happier *if* autonomous, it is not clear that it follows from *that* that society should be organized around a principle that guarantees autonomy, against the wishes of, say, the majority in that society. The closest Mill came to recognizing and addressing the issue was his insistence that laws and government must not "violently shock the preexisting habits and sentiments of the people," nor shall they require qualities of mind, or an interest and care for the institutions of the society which are "unlikely to be really found in them."[13] And the theme runs throughout *Considerations on Representative Government* that "governments must be made for human beings as they are, or as they are capable of speedily becoming."[14] However, this does not recognize the full significance of the problem of the conflict between the actual and the ideal, and it does not provide a *principle* to decide these conflicts.

THE THEORY OF JUSTICE

To many philosophers, Mill's theory of justice will continue to elicit widespread criticism. As a utilitarian theory, critics will no doubt attribute to it all the faults thought to infect the genre. In its full development, as presented in chapter 4, I believe it to be a stronger, more interesting theory than that with which Mill is usually credited.

There are, however, too many hard questions Mill never addressed, so that it can only be taken as a *sketch* of a theory of justice. I tried to show in chapter 4 that that sketch is more detailed than has been realized—he upheld a set of coherent, substantive principles of justice—but he did not resolve all the difficulties of a utilitarian theory. To my mind, one of the most serious difficulties in Mill's account consists in its incompleteness, and it is that critical point that I wish to stress first.

It is striking that Mill never attempted to account for the various uses of the language of rights, or to discuss the various sorts of rights.[15] At times, he spoke of "constituted" rights, meaning by this, that some rights are *recognized*, but it is unclear what moral weight such recognition is to have. In various of his writings, it would appear that they create at least *prima facie* duties. Is this to be understood, though in a sense such that *any* right-conferring rule that society promulgates imposes a moral obligation (perhaps a very weak one), or are there limits built into the notion of a right (or, perhaps, into the notion of a "moral" rule that confers rights)? In at least one place, Mill came close to suggesting that not any recognized right-conferring rule imposes an obligation. In *On Liberty*, when describing the rights that are enforceable, he said that there are "certain interests, which either by express legal provision or by tacit understanding, ought to be considered as rights."[16] This is closer to what one would expect—it is the *interests* that *ought* to be protected that generate obligations. In that case, recognized rules impose obligations that are the correlatives of enforceable rights only when they protect those interests. One must, of course, take account of the sociological fact that an act violates a constituted right, which can affect the consequences of the act. However, this is not the same as considering that some vital interest that society must consistently protect is at stake. Mill never clearly took this position, so one cannot say to what extent he would endorse it. It would have helped clarify the status of rights in his moral theory had he addressed the issue.

A related omission has to do with the fact that Mill did not explicitly speak to the issue of the question of the connection of rights to human dignity. In *Utilitarianism*, where his theory is sketched, rights appear merely as a device that protects crucial interests. By virtue of the consistent protection for those interests provided by society, they are rendered secure. There is a "strategic" gain: the interests themselves are protected, and the *systematic* protections enhance security; but Mill did not develop the notion that our *dignity as persons* is bound up with rights.

As a consequence, his theory fails to capture the full importance that many writers give to the notion of a right in morality. Though Mill often used the language of dignity, he did not seek to analyze that notion. In *Utilitarianism*, he appears to connect the concept with that of the higher faculties, especially with those associated with leading an autonomous life.[17] There is, however, no systematic development of this theme to be found in his work. Though the suggestion is there, we are not given an account of how a utilitarian theory can begin to deal with such notions as treating others as ends-in-themselves, as having worth *as* human beings, and so on, which are captured in part by the notion of dignity. If it is, indeed, interests connected with dignity in this enlarged sort of sense that certain rights protect, then the utilitarian theory is thereby strengthened. Further, had Mill sought to develop this connection, he might have been led to see that there is a notion of *basic* rights that his theory could support, which could be important for his substantive views on justice. Those rights that provide protection for the essential elements of well-being would have a status that is central to that substantive conception. In discussing the substantive principles of justice that Mill employed, I did select those that would undoubtedly be regarded by him as having such a central status. Still, it should be borne in mind that the notion of basic rights was not developed by Mill himself, nor did he explore the complex ways in which basic rights are related to other kinds.

I mentioned that, for the most part, Mill's conception of rights appears to have been generated by "strategy" type considerations. Even as such, however, it is somewhat problematic. The arguments for relatively strict adherence to rights presuppose that all rights will justify a similar strategy for all persons. That is, the arguments have to do with relative lack of knowledge of long-range consequences of acts, with the dangers of general noncompliance with the rules, and so on. Sometimes, however, we *do* have better knowledge than at other times; sometimes the predictable loss is not great, or *we* may be especially knowledgeable persons, or especially strong in character so that we know that *our* violation of the rule on *this* occasion will not weaken our resolve in the crucial cases. What these points suggest is that as a utilitarian, Mill should have considered that a *weaker* strategy might be justified toward some rules, or for some persons. Rather than relatively strict observance of the rules of justice, for example, perhaps a mixed strategy could be supported, depending on the circumstances, or on *who* is doing the "calculating" as to how to act. In fact, there *are* places in which Mill suggests as much. The appeal to rules, and the strong role given them in morality, was justified in part by Mill's arguments for the necessity of what some regard as "indirect" utilitarianism. Mill had argued that happiness is best achieved by not seeking it directly. He urged this in *Utilitarianism*, and in his essay "Bentham," he urged such considerations as the reason for the importance of secondary rules. However, in the *Autobiography*, he also said of the notion of the indirect pursuit of happiness: "I still hold to it as the best theory for all those who have but a moderate degree of sensibility and of capacity for enjoyment, that is, for the great majority of mankind."[18] In an early essay on marriage and divorce, he made the point that persons with higher natures do not require strict rules; they can serve utility better by following their inclinations than by strict obedience to rules, since the latter are always imperfectly adapted to circumstances. "Where there exists a genuine and strong desire to do that which is most for the happiness of all," he wrote, "general rules are merely aids to prudence, in the choice of means; not peremptory obligations."[19] Such considerations, had he systematically pursued them, would lead to the sort of "mixed" strategy or "strategies" that I indicated. This would be a consistent utilitarian position, and it is a version of a utilitarian theory of rights that is open to utilitarians to adopt. It contrasts markedly, though, with the theory that grounds rights (at least partly) in the interests we have in the requisites of human dignity. Respect for rights *as such* would be required, and that would not justify such "strategy" considerations. Elements of both approaches are found in Mill, but it is of great theoretical importance to adopt one or the other, as the two approaches will give a very different role for rights, and contrasting versions of utilitarianism.

The final critical points I want to make concern the special application of Mill's theory of justice to his theory of liberty. I shall discuss them as points concerning his theory of freedom.

THE THEORY OF FREEDOM

A significant difficulty for Mill's theory of freedom arises because of unclarities in his theory of justice. I argued in chapter 4 that it was an important insight that Mill had that he recognized something like a duty of fair play in cooperative projects such as Professors Hart and Rawls argue for. However, I also pointed out that he did not discuss the appropriate *limits* to such duties or the conditions under which they do or do not hold. Some of the positions he took could be extended in ways that threaten to undermine his opposition to the enforcement of morality.

Professor Lyons holds that Mill limited such duties to those cooperative arrangments necessary to prevent harm to others.[20] The evidence cited by Lyons is a passage in *On Liberty* that summarizes Mill's view on the justified grounds for interference with conduct. He wrote that living in society requires that we act in certain enforceable ways toward others, and this includes "each person's bearing his share (to be fixed on some equitable principle) of the labours and sacrifices incurred for defending the society or its members from injury and molestation."[21] Assuming that implicit in this limitation is the further restriction that the "harms" to be prevented must be direct harms, the advocate of the enforcement of morality seems to get no foothold here.

It must be remembered, however, that Mill appears to have held (contrary to Lyons's claims) that denial of benefits *is* a form of harm. Furthermore, there are other places in which Mill did *not* clearly limit cooperative duties to projects that prevent harm. In first stating in *On Liberty* that living in the social state imposes cooperative duties, he wrote "there are also many positive acts for the benefit of others," that one can be compelled to perform, in which he included "to bear his fair share in the common defence, or in any other joint work necessary to the interest of the society of which he enjoys the protection."[22] Also, in his essay on Comte, he indicated that we can be compelled to perform whatever beneficial acts are expected by others by virtue of their being customary, since failure to perform them will disappoint expectations.[23]

A recurrent example of such cooperative duties in Mill's work is that of an enforced rule to safeguard a day of rest for workers. To this extent only he was willing to enforce "Sabbatarian" legislation,[24] and he described the practice which is thereby enforced as "a highly beneficial custom."[25] If some workers were to labor on the day in question, they would make it necessary for the others to do likewise, so each has an interest in the others not working, and it is this interest that is protected. In his *Principles of Political Economy*, he described the enforcement as necessary to make the choices of the participants effective. This suggests that those subject to the restrictions must be voluntary participants in the general project, even if they come to desire to violate particular rules once it is established. As I argued in chapter 4, though, the evidence for this is ambiguous. Moreover, if enjoying the protection of society is enough to obligate one to adhere to whatever requirements further the interest of society, such a restriction will not always be available.

This unclarity in Mill's treatment of cooperative duties could, perhaps, be extended in a way that would permit the enforcement of morality. Conservatives sometimes argue that the majority has a right to seek to create and maintain the sort of environment, social and "moral," that is requisite for a "decent" life. The way in which others behave is part of the environment within which one must lead one's life, and this environment can influence in both positive and negative ways the conditions that make one's life-mode possible. A solid and secure existence in which the social milieu that one deals with and confronts is relatively stable, in which the behavior of others follows regular norms, in which the shock of the unusual or bizarre is rarely experienced, and so on, may be strongly preferred by many. Moreover, it may be more difficult to raise the young to "decency" in a milieu that informs them of the existence of "indecent" conduct, and which confers attractiveness on behavior that is not condemned as beyond the pale. Further, it can be argued that there is almost always *some* public presence of the sort of behavior the majority condemns. Life-modes in which people are caught up are usually shared; there are gathering places for the devotees, articles of sale used by the persons, literature extolling such behavior, and so on.

The U.S. Supreme Court, for example, seems to have been impressed with such an argument as a basis for censorship of pornography. It quoted with favor the argument of the late Professor Bickel:

> It concerns the tone of the society, the mode, or to use terms that have perhaps greater currency, the style and quality of life, now and in the future. A man may be entitled to read an obscene book in his room, or expose himself indecently there. . . . We should protect his privacy. But if he demands a right to obtain the books and pictures he wants in the market, and to foregather in public places—discreet, if you will, but accessible to all—with others who share his tastes, then to grant him his right is to affect the world about the rest of us, and to impinge on other privacies. Even supposing that each of us can, if he wishes, effectively avert the eye and stop the ear (which, in truth, we cannot), what is commonly read and seen and heard and done intrudes upon us all, want it or not.[26]

An argument such as this sees the majority (or a substantial minority? are there *limits* to rights of this sort?) as seeking to maintain a social arena for "decent" modes of life which is endangered by tolerance. It is not possible to fully enjoy the modes of life these people desire in a social world that permits alternative practices. It is not merely that they do not *like* the deviant conduct. That conduct, insofar as it has public manifestations that are unavoidably connected with it, destroys the "moral environment" requisite for the choice of life-mode these people choose for themselves and their families.

It is easy enough to see that such an argument could justify suppression of *any* sort of behavior of which the majority disapproves, and Mill would rightly reject the argument on that ground. However, it is not clear that such a rejection would be entirely consistent with his acceptance of duties imposed by cooperative arrangements. If people can be forced to go along with useful projects, by what *principle* can the majority be denied the right to pursue its own chosen modes of being that are compromised by the aberrant, deviant behavior of others? To the extent that it can be argued that the harms caused are not caused merely by the dislike or disapproval of the others, the argument seems to gain a foothold.

I do not mean to suggest that a Millean has no response open. One cannot, for example, build into one's desired life-mode the requirement that others help maintain it by conforming to it, and claim a right, based on the right of autonomy, to suppress the modes of life chosen by the others. Nor is it at all clear that there is any plausibility in actual cases to the claims that the public manifestations of the alternative ways of living of others compromise the life-modes of the majority. (Bickel's claims about pornography, for example, seem to me to be arrant nonsense.) My point is that further work is needed to specify the principles that pick out sound arguments for cooperative duties from those that are sham.

The final difficulty I want to mention for Mill's theory of freedom is a variant of earlier criticisms. His arguments rest on the assumption that freedom, or autonomy, is so crucial to human well-being that it must be given a priority weighting in determining the principles to govern society. While I am inclined to agree with Mill's assessment of the importance of autonomy, it is certainly not a self-evident proposition; it is not even evident. It must be kept in mind that opponents of liberal principles—those who favor paternalism and the enforcement of morals—also typically reject that assessment of liberty. Mill's theory of liberty is strongly connected to his theory of value, and, as I have argued, to his theory of justice. These represent complex, interconnected aspects of his moral and political philosophy. This gives a coherence to his views that helps provide internal support for one another of his positions on these subjects. This is a strength to be claimed for Mill, but it is also a weakness, insofar as the acceptance of his views in one area (e.g., his theory of freedom) may be jeopardized by shortcomings in another (e.g., his theory of value, or happiness).

It is of some interest to note, in closing, that many of the problems Mill's theories face are due to the fact that there are alternative positions open to the Millean, with respective strengths and weaknesses. This reveals something of great importance about utilitarian theory itself. There are a wide range of positions consistently open to a utilitarian on many of the crucial issues of morality. The usual depictions of utilitarian theory in the textbooks oversimplify it in ways that mask the range of views that can legitimately be called utilitarian, and they fail to recognize the subtlety and complexity that can be accommodated within utilitarianism.

MILL'S LEGACY: HIS CONTRIBUTION TO CONTEMPORARY PHILOSOPHY

It should be clear that I do not believe we can solve the important problems of contemporary moral and political philosophy by merely rereading Mill, even as I have interpreted him. There remain too many unclarities, unresolved difficulties, gaps in the argumentative support, for the Millean position to be taken as a definitive resolution of the chief issues it addresses.

Thus, the question arises as to what the significance is for modern philosophy of the system of moral and political thought we have inherited in his work. Assuming that Mill's was a high-level and lasting contribution in these areas, it is undoubtedly true that each age must reassess that contribution in light of its own problems. Perhaps, considerable distortion of Mill's own intentions, concerns, and emphases must occur in order to make the connection between generations. Nonetheless, a substantive justification for studying the ideas of long-dead philosophers is the light they can shed, the insights that can be gleaned from them, for present concerns. In such matters, then, the assessment of a given philosopher's contribution to today's debates can only be made by taking up the present-day issues and working through them in light of the historical figure's views.

Though I have attempted throughout the book to relate Mill to contemporary debate, either by way of comparison or by addressing a particular issue, this cannot count as an attempt at a full assessment of the contemporary significance of Mill. My discussions have been sporadic and incomplete. I have been more concerned with suggesting possible routes the Millean might take to resolve the difficulties than I have been in seeing if an ultimate resolution is possible. Furthermore, though I have related Mill to some of the contemporary literature, there have been major omissions. For example, I have said little about a major concern of some writers over so-called "agent-centered" considerations, such as ones that refer to restrictions on seeking to maximize good consequences that arise from such special relations as friendship, being a parent, or spouse, or child, of someone,[27] or that arise from considerations of moral integrity.[28] I have explored some of these matters elsewhere, invoking the Millean point of view.[29] I believe, however, that a great deal more needs to be said.

I also have said nothing about the growing literature on utilitarianism that derives from the work of social choice economists, as in the work of John Harsanyi and Amartya Sen.[30] There are three reasons for this omission. For the most part, that literature has defined utilitarianism in a narrow way that identifies it with a simple Benthamite view of utility as desire or preference satisfaction. A theory such as I have ascribed to Mill would be taken as "beyond utilitarianism," and Mill turns out not to be a utilitarian on this conception. Thus, Sen and Bernard Williams write in the introduction to their collection, *Utilitarianism and Beyond*, that valuing the capacity to choose "belongs to an approach altogether different from utilitarianism."[31] Though I would quarrel strongly with the historical accuracy of taking the narrow Benthamite approach as constitutive or characteristic of utilitarianism *per se* (G. E. Moore's "ideal utilitarianism," for example, also turns out to fail as a version of utilitarianism), the problem here is one largely of terminology, not of substance, and an alternative vocabulary exists for the discussion (e.g., one could talk of "consequentialism" where needed). Sen, for example, has given an argument for a certain treatment of rights as having value in themselves that could readily be accommodated within a Millean framework that views rights as integrally bound up with human dignity.[32] (Such an approach was sketched in chap. 4.) However, much time would have to be devoted to clarifying the terminological confusions.[33] Also, much of the social choice literature involves debates over technical matters concerning the computation of social welfare functions with which I have little competence. Finally, though I think the Mill I have described in these pages has much to say that is relevant to social choice theory, the specific application of Mill's views in this area is being pursued, to a more complete extent, by others.[34]

I think it is obvious, therefore, that a full assessment of Mill's significance can only come by means of a deeper, more systematic survey than could reasonably be attempted here. Nonetheless, I believe that some remarks concerning the *general* value of Mill's work for today's philosophers can be put forth in light of the reinterpretation of his theories that I have given.

In my opinion, Mill's continuing relevance to moral and political philosophy has two chief sources. The first of these consists of a number of concepts or principles that were central to his own thinking, but which also have a role to play in the considerations of any moral or political theory. Foremost among these is his enlarged conception of human well-being, that includes such notions as autonomy and dignity as essential, and not mere by-products of, or means to, happiness. Mill's views on these matters are reflected, for example, in the important contemporary work of John Rawls. This enlarged conception of human welfare can play a role in the arguments for rights, for freedom, and for equality in virtually any theory, whether utilitarian or not. In this connection, it is fitting that his principle of freedom is as subject to discussion today as it was when he enunciated it. In part, Mill has been brought into the contemporary debate because of unclarities in his exposition and argument; but the currency of his principle is also due to the fact that it admits of formulations that will appeal to anyone who values individual choice, self-development, and the autonomous working out of one's own life. The connection of autonomy with happiness that, I have argued, was part of Mill's theory, makes his espousal of the principle of liberty more defensible. At the very least, it poses a challenge to any who would reject his principle. I would further add that the conception of autonomy that Mill held will have increasing importance in a world that seems divided into corporate capitalist states and those that consist of state socialist regimes. In both cases, large-scale forces beyond the influence of popular control seem increasingly to determine the features of importance in the lives of persons.[35]

The second, and most important contribution I would claim for Mill's writings on ethics and political theory may strike some readers as paradoxical. Mill's utilitarianism is, according to the once-dominant orthodoxy, an amalgam of contradictory elements. He assuaged his humanistic, freedom-loving, justice-principled inclinations by adding features to his views that simply undermine a consistent utilitarian framework. Thus, it was held, his defense of liberalism was a clear showing of the incapacity of utilitarianism to provide an adequate basis for liberalism.[36]

My own view is that Mill's most lasting legacy consists in his having given us a coherent, interconnected set of doctrines that encompass a comprehensive psychology, theory of morality, justice, and freedom. I do not mean to suggest there are no gaps or inconsistencies in Mill's work. On the contrary, I have pointed to instances of both in the text. What I mean to assert is that these have not been shown to be difficulties that necessarily undermine Mill's entire utilitarian project. Furthermore, part of the significance of Mill's work consists in the fact that there are various ways in which the difficulties may be reconciled. Thus, Mill's theories provide us with a framework, of a general and comprehensive nature, of moral and political thought, the details of which can be adjusted in various ways to yield competing utilitarian theories, or liberal principles, with their respective advantages and disadvantages. In this respect, Mill's work opens up to us an array of theories that demonstrate the resiliency and possibilities for utilitarian and liberal thought, and in terms of which these systems of thought can be assessed.

If this assessment is correct, then Mill accomplished for utilitarianism what I believe John Rawls has accomplished in our day. Both have given comprehensive accounts of morality and justice that permit and facilitate consideration of alternative theories and principles. Moreover, each has its distinctive criteria for relevant modes of argument that are themselves subject to debate, and on which they appear to part company.

If Mill's work has the contemporary significance I attribute to it, then the attempt to trace out the systematic connections among the basic concepts and principles is itself an important project. To the extent that I have been successful in showing his views on happiness, justice, and freedom to be interconnected, and to justify the moral and political principles that define his utilitarianism and liberalism, I shall have succeeded in showing Mill to have been an important moral philosopher, deserving of being taken seriously in our own day as a true advocate of a genuine and enlightened liberal vision of society.

NOTES

1: Psychology and Morality

1. Mill's most important discussions of his psychological theory are in: *A System of Logic: Ratiocinative and Inductive*, Vols. VII and VIII of *Collected Works*, ed. J. M. Robson (Toronto: Toronto University Press, 1973), 849–860; "Bain's Psychology" in Vol. XI of *Collected Works*, 339–373; and in his own footnotes added to his edition of his father's *Analysis of the Phenomena of the Human Mind*, Vol. II, ed. John Stuart Mill (London: Longmans, Green, Reader and Dyer, 1869). Though often overlooked or misinterpreted, the essay *Utilitarianism* also contains most of the centrally important views. (Further references to the *Collected Works* will be abbreviated as "*CW*"; see the list at the head of the bibliography for complete reference information for the volumes in the *Collected Works*.)

2. *Logic*, p. 852.

3. This is the account given in *Logic*. "Bain's Psychology" explicitly cites only the Laws of Contiguity and Resemblance ("Bain's Psychology," p. 347).

4. Mill's argument against the reduction of psychology to physiology is interesting. He makes the practical point that *in fact* no such science of physical-mental causation is available. He also points out that the only means we have of studying the causal relations in question is through prior knowledge of the relations among mental events, since we can *identify* the physiological states as the same or different only by reference to the mental states with which they are associated. This is an important point which anticipates contemporary critiques of psycho-physical reductionism. Mill did not develop the point further, however (*Logic*, p. 851).

5. *Logic*, pp. 852–853.

6. Though this is not the place to explore it, there is an important discussion by Mill of the sort of "proof" which is available for the associationist theory, and the role of *a priori* and empirical elements in it. See "Bain's Psychology," pp. 349–352.

7. *Logic*, pp. 857–859. In his *Autobiography*, he indicated that all pleasures and desires built solely on association can be undermined by analysis, "except the purely physical and organic" (*Autobiography*, *CW*, I:143).

8. "Bain's Psychology," p. 354.

9. *Analysis* II:258; *A Fragment on Mackintosh* (London: Longmans, Green, Reader, and Dyer, 1870), pp. 389–390.

10. Ibid., II:190–192.

11. "Remarks on Bentham's Philosophy," *CW*, X:12–13.

12. Ibid., p. 13.

13. See *Autobiography*, p. 207; also, J. M. Robson, "Textual Introduction," in *CW*, X:cxvi–cxvii.

14. "Bentham," *CW*, X:95–96. The passage reads: "Nor is it only the moral part of man's nature, in the strict sense of the term—the desire of perfection, or the feeling of an approving or of an accusing conscience—that he overlooks; he but faintly recognises, as a fact in human nature, the pursuit of any other ideal end for its own sake. The sense of *honour*, and personal dignity—that feeling of personal exaltation and degradation which acts independently of other people's opinion, or even in defiance of it; the the love of *beauty*, the passion of the artist; the love of *order*, or congruity, of consistency in all things, and conformity to their end; the love of *power*, not in the limited form of power over other human beings, but abstract power, the power of making our volitions effectual; the love of *action*, the thirst for movement and activity, a principle scarcely of less influence in human life than its opposite, the love of ease: —None of these powerful constituents of human nature are thought worthy of a place among the 'Springs of Action;' and though there is possibly no one of them of the existence of which an acknowledgement might not be found in some corner of Bentham's writings, no conclusions are ever founded on the acknowledgment. Man, that most complex being, is a very simple one in his eyes."

15. *Logic*, p. 842.

16. *Analysis* II:307–308.

17. Ibid., II:379.

18. Ibid., p. 381.

19. *CW*, X:238.

20. James Mill had written: "The term 'Idea of a pleasure,' expresses precisely the same thing as the term, Desire. It does so by the very import of the words. The idea of a pleasure, is the idea of something as good to have. . . . The terms, therefore, 'idea of a pleasure,' and 'desire,' are but two names; the thing named, the state of consciousness, is one and the same" (*Analysis* II:191–192). As we have seen, the younger Mill rejected his father's account, claiming that desire is "the initiatory stage of Will," including a tendency to act, along with the idea of a pleasure (*Analysis* II:194–195). It would be a short step to take to hold that an impetus to act which is the result of the force of habitual desiring is a limiting case of desire. I do not believe that Mill ever fully removed the apparent contradiction between: (a) desiring something just is thinking of it as pleasant, and (b) cases of habitual willing involve desiring something because willed, *without* any

thought or sense of pleasure. It *may* be that he was groping to maintain (a), while dropping the idea that a desire is involved in habitual willings. He may have been maintaining (what he virtually says in some places) that actions are sometimes produced by motives *other* than desires, e.g., by "fixed purposes." Thus, pleasure would be inextricably associated with desire, but not the only object of volitions, not the only thing sought. I believe that something like this is maintained by G. W. Spence, in an important contribution to Mill scholarship (see "The Psychology Behind J. S. Mill's Proof," *Philosophy* 43 [January, 1968], 18–28). However, the passages Spence cites, taken with other passages in Mill, do not unequivocally support such an interpretation. It is *also* possible that Mill was maintaining that habitual acts are desired, but not for their own sakes, i.e., only out of habit. This would explain, in part, Mill's statement to the effect that nothing is a good to a man unless it is pleasurable, goods being those things desired for their own sakes. *If* one of these interpretations is correct, my claim will still stand up that Mill did not hold that people always *seek* pleasure as the object of all their actions.

21. *Utilitarianism*, *CW*, X:238

22. "Bentham," *CW*, X:98.

23. *On Liberty*, *CW*, XVIII:264.

24. Aristotle, *Nicomachean Ethics*, Bk. II.

25. Henry Sidgwick, *Outlines of the History of Ethics* (London: Macmillan and Co., Ltd., 1931), p. 59.

26. *Analysis* II:217–218.

27. "Remarks on Bentham's Philosophy," *CW* X:13–14.

28. *Analysis* II:309. J. M. Robson pointed to this difficulty in interpreting Mill. See his discussion in J. M. Robson, *The Improvement of Mankind: The Social and Political Thought of John Stuart Mill* (Toronto: University of Toronto Press, 1968), p. 133 n.

29. "Sedgwick's Discourse," *CW*, X:60.

30. Ibid.

31. "Whewell on Moral Philosophy," *CW*, X:184n.

32. *Utilitarianism*, *CW*, X:231.

33. "Utility of Religion," *CW* X:411.

34. *Utilitarianism*, *CW*, X:231.

35. "Sedgwick's Discourse," *CW*, X:60.

36. In a note added to his edition of his father's *Analysis*, he wrote: "The class of feelings called moral embraces several varieties, materially different in their character. Wherever this difference manifests itself, the theory must be required to show that there is a corresponding difference in the antecedents. If pleasurable or painful associations are the generating cause, those associations must differ in some proportion to the difference which exists in what they generate" (*Analysis* II:324).

37. Ibid., p. 326.

38. Ibid., p. 325.

39. *Utilitarianism*, *CW*, X:246.

40. *Later Letters*, *CW*, XV:649. Mill's position has led to some possible misunder-

standings. Alan Ryan thinks that Mill's analysis of "ought" commits him to saying that a person who lacks the appropriate sentiments *has no* obligations. This does not necessarily follow, however. Mill may have held only that a person who lacks the moral sentiments expresses no genuine moral judgments. Ryan's criticism might apply to the subjectivist interpretation, according to which every moral judgment *states* that the speaker has a certain feeling. If the speaker does not have that feeling, the judgment is false (actually, only *part* of the judgment would be false on this ground, so it is not clear Ryan is right even on this interpretation); see Alan Ryan, *The Philosophy of John Stuart Mill* (London: Macmillan, 1970), p. 209. This should be contrasted, however, with pp. 187—192, where Ryan clearly leans toward the noncognitivist interpretation. F. H. Bradley, stressing a different aspect of Mill's theory of the moral sentiments, fell into a similar confusion; see his *Ethical Studies* (London: Oxford University Press, 1962), pp. 123—124. I take up the distinction further in the next few paragraphs.

41. *Logic*, p. 949.

42. A. J. Ayer, *Language, Truth and Logic*, 2d ed. (New York: Dover Publications, Inc., 1946), pp. 109—110; C. L. Stevenson, *Ethics and Language* (New Haven, Conn.: Yale University Press, 1944). In Stevenson's case, the difference comes out most strongly in his distinction between what a term *means* and what it *suggests*. See, e.g., *Ethics and Language*, pp. 85—86.

43. *Analysis* II:323.

44. Ibid., pp. 325—326; *Utilitarianism*, *CW*, X:248.

45. The account given in the text follows Mill's treatment in *Utilitarianism*. In his discussion in *Analysis*, however, which is quoted earlier in this section, he says that the desire to retaliate must be conformable to the utility of inflicting punishment. Though not necessarily incompatible, these are different theories. The account in *Utilitarianism* makes the feeling a function of the immorality of the crime. The paragraph in *Analysis* makes the feeling a function of the utility of punishment. If the utility of punishment is itself a function of the immorality of the act, there is no problem. Moreover, there is much in Mill to suggest he really did believe that an act is immoral if, and only if, it would be in the general interest to punish it.

46. *Utilitarianism*, *CW*, X:249. The sentiment of justice was further distinguished from other moral sentiments by Mill. This will be discussed in a later chapter.

47. *Auguste Comte and Positivism*, *CW*, X:337.

48. Ibid., pp. 337—338.

49. Ibid., p. 339.

50. *Analysis* II:323—324.

51. *Utilitarianism*, *CW*, X:231—232.

52. "Civilization," *CW*, XVIII:129ff.

53. *Utilitarianism*, *CW*, X:232; also "Comte," *CW*, X:339.

54. This seems to be the gist of his criticisms of those who seek to find in nature a standard of morality. "Nature," *CW*, X:373—402.

55. "Civilization," *CW*, XVIII; and "De Tocqueville on Democracy in America [II]," *CW*, XVIII, esp. pp. 194—200.

2: MILL'S CONCEPT OF HAPPINESS AND THE PROOF OF ITS DESIRABILITY

1. *Logic*, *CW*, VIII:951.

2. See J. M. Robson, *The Improvement of Mankind: The Social and Political Thought of John Stuart Mill* (Toronto: University of Toronto Press, 1968), p. 158. In his *Autobiography*, Mill mentioned *Utilitarianism* in a one-sentence paragraph. In various places, he treated objections to the work in a surprisingly cavalier manner, putting subsequent commentators and defenders at a great disadvantage.

3. The interested reader may consult the following (among numerous others), as illustrations of critical interpretations of this sort: T. H. Green, *Prolegomena to Ethics* (New York: Thomas Y. Crowell Co., 1969), pp. 168–178; George H. Sabine, *A History of Political Theory*, 3d. ed. (London: George G. Harrap, 1963), pp. 705–709, H. J. McCloskey, *John Stuart Mill: A Critical Study* (London: Macmillan, 1971), pp. 58–72.

4. The journal literature is too voluminous to mention. Among the better book-length works are: J. M. Robson, *The Improvement of Mankind*; and Alan Ryan, *The Philosophy of John Stuart Mill* (London: Macmillan, 1970).

5. *CW*, X:210.

6. Ibid., p. 237.

7. Ibid., p. 235.

8. Ibid., p. 236.

9. Ibid., p. 238.

10. *CW*, X:xciii–xciv.

11. It is possible that Mill did not consistently hold only one view as to the nature of the ultimate criterion of value. He may have been caught up with the notion that pleasure alone has value, and, having said that, thought he could consistently go on to make qualitative distinctions among pleasures. *Were* that the case, there is *also* a more sophisticated doctrine to be found in Mill's work, which, to a certain extent, avoids the problems of the other one. A defense of the consistency of Mill's distinction, even based on traditional interpretations is to be found in Norman O. Dahl, "Is Mill's Hedonism Inconsistent?" in *Studies in Ethics*, American Philosophical Quarterly Monograph Series, No. 7 (Oxford: Basil Blackwell, 1973), pp. 37–54. See also Rex Martin, "A Defense of Mill's Qualitative Hedonism," *Philosophy* 46 (April, 1972), 140–151.

12. In fact, Mill's discussion virtually *begs* for such an analysis, as his use of the language of desire and pleasure is freighted with ambiguities. Sometimes (as was most often the case with his father), he used the term "pleasure" to refer to an aspect of a sensation, or to an internal sensation itself. At other times, he speaks of desiring *that* which *is* a pleasure, e.g., intellectual activity, money, and virtue. Moreover, the latter use tends to predominate in *Utilitarianism*, and it is that use which is most consistent with the present interpretation. He does appear to have been confused, however.

13. If one reads the essay in this way, it is evident that Mill did not give his *final* definition of happiness until *after* this discussion.

14. *CW*, X:210–211.

15. Ibid., pp. 211—212.

16. Ibid., p. 214.

17. Ibid., p. 212.

18. Ibid., pp. 250—251. It is worth noting that the points made in this passage would help provide a rationale for an aspect of our moral life noted by Philippa Foot. If one distinguishes between positive duties (to *aid* someone), and negative duties (to avoid *harming* others), it would appear that, in general, the latter are stricter, and carry greater weight (cf. Philippa Foot, "Abortion and the Doctrine of Double Effect," *The Oxford Review* 5 [1967], 5 — 15). This would be explained if security is central to happiness in the way Mill described, and observance of negative duties is the primary guarantee (open to human endeavor) of security.

19. Ibid., p. 255. Mill's theory of rights and justice is rarely taken seriously. I believe, however, that the essay *On Liberty* can best be understood as an application of his theory of justice. In particular, I believe the essay on liberty is a defense of the claim that everyone who meets certain conditions has a right to individuality. In his autobiography, Mill described *On Liberty* in these very terms. This, however, is a subject for the chapters which follow.

20. Ibid., p. 256.

21. Ibid., p. 237.

22. Ibid., p. 239.

23. *Logic*, *CW*, VIII:621—622.

24. *On Liberty*, *CW*, XVIII:224.

25. *Utilitarianism*, *CW*, X:231—232.

26. Ibid., p. 234.

27. Ibid., p. 238; *Logic*, *CW*, VIII:842.

28. See, *Utilitarianism*, *CW*, X:212—213. The argument Mill gave there is that the preferences people then have do not reflect truly *voluntary* choices. This does not appear to be the claim on which his defense ultimately rests, however.

29. This depiction is decidedly Aristotelian in certain respects. See *Nicomachean Ethics* 1097^{b}10-20.

30. His second characterization of the Greatest Happiness Principle refers to the distinction between the higher and lower pleasures. Thus, the happiness with which the principle is concerned favors the higher pleasures. See *Utilitarianism*, *CW*, X:214.

31. Ibid., pp. 213—214. He wrote: "I have dwelt on this point [his account of happiness], as being a necessary part of a perfectly just conception of Utility or Happiness, considered as the directive rule of human conduct. But it is by no means an indispensable condition to the acceptance of the utilitarian standard; for that standard is not the agent's own greatest happiness, but the greatest amount of happiness altogether; and if it may possibly be doubted whether a noble character is always the happier for its nobleness, there can be no doubt that it makes other people happier, and that the world in general is immensely a gainer by it. Utilitarianism, therefore, could only attain its end by the general cultivation of nobleness of character, even if each individual were only benefited by the nobleness of others, and his own, so far as happiness is concerned, were a sheer deduction from the benefit."

32. See, e.g., his statement in the *Logic* referring to happiness "in the higher meaning," which, he explained, is "such as human beings with highly developed faculties can care to have." *Logic, CW*, VIII:952.

33. "Utility of Religion," *CW*, X:409.

34. I think the two best full-scale defenses of Mill's proof have been: James Seth, "The Alleged Fallacies in Mill's 'Utilitarianism,' " *The Philosophical Review* 17 (September, 1908), 469—488; and Everett W. Hall, "The 'Proof' of Utility in Bentham and Mill," *Ethics* 60 (October, 1949), 1—18. Though I shall draw on these, there are details in both with which I disagree. Many of the more recent defenses address small points, and in many cases the interpretations are extremely unconvincing.

35. I have not taken up the objection that Mill committed the so-called "naturalistic fallacy," for the following reasons. First, not all philosophers would agree that there really is a fallacious mode of inference that that expression designates. Also, it is perfectly clear that Mill was *not* involved in *defining* "good"; the interpretation and criticism that has him doing this displays gross ignorance of his objectives and of his views on the role of definitions in inference. There is, however, one interpretation of the alleged "fallacy"—that of deducing an evaluative conclusion from a nonevaluative premise—on which one of the points I discuss does have some bearing.

36. See, letter to Theodor Gomperz (the German translator of *Utilitarianism*) in *Later Letters, CW*, XVI:1413—1414.

37. "Bentham," *CW*, X:111.

38. "Remarks on Bentham's Philosophy," *CW*, X:6

39. *Utilitarianism, CW*, X:230.

40. See "Textual Introduction," *CW*, X:cxxiii.

41. The points made here are similar to an account given by Michael Stocker. Stocker's explanation of the proof, however, analyzes "X is approved by A" as "A believes X is pleasurable." As we have seen, this is not entirely correct. One may approve of X because the *idea* of it is pleasant, without thinking of X itself as a source of pleasure. See, Michael Stocker, "Mill on Desire and Desirability," *Journal of the History of Philosophy* 7 (1969), 199—201.

42. *Utilitarianism, CW*, X:239.

43. "The Gorgias," *CW*, XI:150.

44. *Utilitarianism, CW*, X:234.

45. *Later Letters, CW*, XVI:1414.

46. *Logic, CW*, VIII:812n.

47. "Remarks on Bentham's Philosophy," *CW*, X:15.

48. *Utilitarianism, CW*, X, p. 217. In a letter to Henry S. Brandreth, he held such a sacrifice is sometimes a *duty*, e.g., in the case of a soldier in the performance of military duty. See, *Later Letters, CW*, XVI:1234.

49. "Remarks on Bentham's Philosophy," *CW*, X:15.

50. "Utility of Religion," *CW*, X:420—422.

51. *Utilitarianism, CW*, X:233.

52. Ibid., p. 217.

53. James Mill, "Edinburgh Review and the 'Greatest Happiness Principle,' " in

Utilitarian Logic and Politics: James Mill's 'Essay on Government', Macaulay's critique and the ensuing debate, ed. Jack Lively and John Rees (Oxford: Clarendon Press, 1978), pp. 228–230.

3: THE GREATEST HAPPINESS PRINCIPLE AND MORAL RULES

1. The most influential account of the various utilitarianisms is in David Lyons, *Forms and Limits of Utilitarianism* (Oxford: The Clarendon Press, 1965).

2. See "The Interpretation of the Moral Philosophy of J. S. Mill," *The Philosophical Quarterly* 3 (January, 1953), 33–39. Not long after Urmson's article, John Rawls published an influential article ("Two Concepts of Rules," *The Philosophical Review* 64 [January, 1955], 3–32), in which he described two different conceptions of rules in utilitarian theory, which correspond with the views outlined in the text as act- and rule-utilitarianism. In the one view, rules "summarize" past experience, hence, are guides to future action. In the other conception, rules "define," and thus make possible actions of certain kinds, e.g., hitting a home run, kicking a field goal, etc. Actions falling under the concept defined are justified by appeal to the rules; thus, it makes no sense for a baseball batter to challenge an umpire's calling him out after a third strike by appeal to anything but the rule. Rawls maintained that there are certain moral "practices" in which rules define actions, e.g., promising and punishing, and that justification of acts falling within these concepts must appeal to the rules defining the practice. Though Rawls also said that there are not a great many moral "practices," many took him as being a rule-utilitarian. Rawls's later publications have, in fact, revealed him to be one of the leading and most effective opponents of utilitarianism; see, especially, *A Theory of Justice* (Cambridge, Mass.: Harvard University Press, 1971). Other important papers dealing with the interpretation of Mill's views on moral rules are: J. D. Mabbott, "Interpretations of Mill's *Utilitarianism*," *Philosophical Quarterly* 6 (1956), 115–120; Maurice Mandelbaum, "Two Moot Issues in Mill's *Utilitarianism*," in *Mill: A Collection of Critical Essays*, ed. J. B. Schneewind (Garden City, NY: Doubleday and Company, Inc., 1968); Brian Cupples, "A Defence of the Received Interpretation of J. S. Mill," *Australasian Journal of Philosophy* 50 (August, 1972), 131–137; John M. Baker, "*Utilitarianism* and 'Secondary Principles,' " *The Philosophical Quarterly* 21 (1971), 69–71; and D. G. Brown, "Mill's Act-Utilitarianism," *Philosophical Quarterly* 24 (1974), 67–68.

3. *Utilitarianism*, in *CW*, X:210.

4. Urmson, "The Interpretation of the Moral Philosophy of J. S. Mill," p. 37.

5. I have already said that Austin explicitly adopted it; I shall discuss Austin's theory subsequently. Consider the following quotations from John Gay and from James Mill: "The criterion of any thing is a rule or measure by a conformity with which any thing is known to be of this or that sort, or of this or that degree. And in order to determine the criterion of anything, we must first know the thing whose criterion we are seeking after. For a measure presupposes the idea of the thing to be measured, otherwise it could not be known, whether it was fit to measure it or no, (since what is the proper measure of one thing is not so of another). Liquids, cloth, and flesh, have all different

measures; gold and silver different touchstones. This is very intelligible and the method of doing it generally very clear, when either the quantity, or kind of any particular substance is thus ascertained" (John Gay, *Concerning the Fundamental Principle of Virtue or Morality* [1973] in *British Moralists*, Vol. II, ed. L. A. Selby-Bigge [Indianapolis and New York: The Bobbs-Merrill Co., 1964], 270).

"The word *criterion* commonly means something by which another thing is tried, or tested, and shown to be what it is. Thus chemists have a number of tests or *criteria* by which they determine what things are, one to test an alkali, another an acid; and so on. But what thing is it by which we test morality? And above all, because that is the previous question, what is morality? A test, is a test of a thing known, not of a thing unknown. When a man desires a touchstone, a test, or criterion of gold, he knows beforehand what gold is—he only knows not whether such a piece of matter be gold or not. The test does not show what gold is; so neither does a test of morality show what morality is" (James Mill, *A Fragment on Mackintosh* [London: Longmans, Green, Reader, and Dyer, 1870], p. 2).

There are numerous places in which John Stuart Mill implicitly uses such a distinction. A very clear instance occurs in his essay on "Nature," in which he points out that those who appeal to nature as a guide to conduct do not propose a verbal proposition which assigns a meaning to "nature" or to the words "what we ought to do," but, rather, propose a "criterion of what we should do," viz., what is in accord with nature (see "Nature," in *CW*, X:377).

6. The general problem of decision-procedures for validity is an illustration of some such distinction as we are getting at. We *know* that with respect to certain classes of arguments in the full first-order predicate calculus that though we can *define* the notion of validity for them there can be no complete effective test for them.

7. The examples display disparate logical features, e.g., truth-tables provide a *conclusive* test, while this is not true of the other examples. This is deliberate as I do not wish to fix on any one sort of example, and the utilitarians seem to have used the expressions "test," "standard," and "criterion" in all of these ways.

8. Though I believe the points made in this paragraph are almost always overlooked, they were certainly not invented by me. As Richard Arneson has reminded me, the essential points were made by J. J. C. Smart, who also pointed out that G. E. Moore appears to have been an act-utilitarian who believed, on strategic grounds, that one should never act on the basis of calculation of the consequences of the act that is contemplated (see J. J. C. Smart and Bernard Williams, *Utilitarianism: For and Against* [Cambridge: Cambridge University Press, 1973], pp. 43—44).

9. Jeremy Bentham, *A Fragment on Government and An Introduction to the Principles of Morals and Legislation*, ed. Wilfrid Harrison (Oxford: Basil Blackwell, 1960), p. 126. It is worth noting that this formulation does not say that every act is right or wrong, only that every act is approved or disapproved by the Principle of Utility. Indeed, a few paragraphs later, when speaking of "right," or "wrong," and "ought," he appears to leave open the possibility of tripartite classification: permissible, right, and wrong.

10. Ibid.

11. Ibid., p. 127.

12. Ibid.

13. Ibid., p. 189.

14. Strictly, Bentham points out, these next to last two are not indices of the value of the pleasure or pain, but are longer range consequences of the act. Thus, they must be added in computing the tendency of the act.

15. Ernest Albee, *A History of English Utilitarianism* (London: George Allen and Unwin Ltd., 1957), p. 320. Albee did recognize that the *Principles* was directed primarily at the establishment of general rules backed by the sanctions of the state. His interpretation seems to be based on another work, the Bowring version of the *Deontology*: "In the *Deontology*, however, where the object is to guide the individual agent in his moral life, computations in the particular case seem, not merely often, but generally, to be suggested, while there is no single passage in the book which insists upon the importance of general rules, as opposed to such particular computations" (Albee, p. 188). This is very weak evidence at best, especially as the examples Albee quotes are perfectly consistent with holding that where computation is not possible, appeal to general rules is permissible. Also, Bentham *did* say in the *Principles*: "It is not to be expected that this process should be strictly pursued previously to every moral judgment, or to every legislative or judicial operation" (*Principles*, p. 153).

16. *Principles*, p. 274.

17. This "strategy" has features in common with what is called a "maximin" principle of choice. See, e.g., Rawls, *A Theory of Justice*, pp. 153ff.

18. *CW*, I:185.

19. *Earlier Letters*, *CW*, XII:236. He quickly added, however, "but even that falls far short of what is wanted."

20. John Austin, *The Province of Jurisprudence Determined and The Uses of the Study of Jurisprudence*, ed. H. L. A. Hart (London: Weidenfeld and Nicolson, 1954), p. 37.

21. Ibid., p. 38.

22. Ibid., p. 41.

23. In a later passage, Austin wrote that "the Deity is perfectly good; and . . . since he is perfectly good, he wills the happiness of his creatures" (ibid., p. 87). This makes goodness logically independent of God's will, and independently defined. This was a point of importance to J. S. Mill, who, in reviewing Austin's *Province*, sought to clear him from a misinterpretation which would make goodness a function of God's power. Goodness is not *constituted* by the Divine Will, but "recognised and sanctioned by it" (*Dissertations and Discussions*, Vol. III [London: Longmans, Green, Reader, and Dyer, 1867], 224).

24. *Province*, p. 49.

25. Ibid., p. 40.

26. Ibid., pp. 52–53.

27. *Autobiography*, p. 211.

28. Mill, *A Fragment on Mackintosh*, pp. 162–163.

29. Ibid., p. 163. All quotations in this paragraph are from this page. The discussion I have summarized is to be found on pages 157–164.

30. Ibid., p. 246.

31. Ibid., p. 249. A similar view was expressed by Austin. (*Province*, pp. 41—42). It is not entirely clear, however, that Austin dismissed these from both of the classes— moral and immoral acts, though it is likely he did.

32. *Fragment*, p. 251.

33. It would seem that Mill had dismissed prudent acts from the class of moral acts. John Stuart Mill displayed a similar ambivalence toward prudence, sometimes regarding it as a portion of morality, sometimes as a coordinate branch of "the Art of Life."

34. *Fragment*, p. 253.

35. Ibid., pp. 255—256.

36. Ibid., pp. 257—258.

37. J. S. Mill, *Autobiography*, chap. 5.

38. Ibid., pp. 145—147. Though Mill wrote here of utility as the test of moral rules, this should not be taken as a departure from act-consequentialism. He had earlier described utilitarianism s "taking as the exclusive test of right and wrong, the tendency of actions to produce pleasure or pain" (ibid., p. 30). As we have seen, this was the formulation used by Bentham and James Mill. There is no reason to interpret this as committing one to utility as a test of rules only.

39. "Bentham," in *CW*, X:110—111.

40. "Remarks on Bentham's Philosophy," *CW*, X:7.

41. Ibid.

42. Ibid., p. 8. One can only speculate as to why Mill added the phrase "if practised generally, would itself lead." Richard Arneson has suggested to me that it shows Mill was confused about the difference between an act- and rule-consequence utilitarianism. This is surely reasonable, though rendered somewhat less so by his response to John Venn, who (apparently) *did* formulate it for him (see *The Later Letters*, *CW*, XVII:1881—82). This would still leave unexplained why he would attribute to Bentham a formulation that the latter never gave. My own speculation is that Bentham's applications were within the realm of lawmaking, where it is the general practice that is enforced. It may be argued, then, that in practice, he employed something like Paley's formulation.

43. This essay was written during the period 1830—1831, and rewritten in 1833. It was published as an article in 1836, and later combined into a book with other essays as *Essays on Some Unsettled Questions of Political Economy*. Mill was unable to gain a publisher's acceptance, however, until after his *Logic* had attained success, and thus the book did not appear until 1844. See "Editor's Note to *Essays on Some Unsettled Questions of Political Economy*," in *Essays on Economics and Society*, *CW*, IV:230.

44. An excellent treatment of Mill's views on social science and ethology is in chaps. 9 and 10 of Alan Ryan's *The Philosophy of John Stuart Mill* (London: Macmillan, 1970).

45. John Stuart Mill, *A System of Logic*, *CW*, VII:317—318.

46. Ibid., *CW*, VIII:869—870.

47. Ibid., *CW*, VII:444.

48. Ibid., p. 445.

49. This formulation is neutral with respect to a controversy which has arisen (and which is not germane to my concerns) over the ontological status of tendencies in Mill's view. On the one hand, Mill referred to tendencies as fully operating even *when* counteracted; events, then are the resultant of occurrent forces which, at the very least, one must refer to in explaining the events. Mill's use of a *realist* vocabulary in describing tendencies has led one commentator to hold that Mill's view was Platonistic: "Mill postulates an abiding reality of forces beneath the flux of appearances so as to provide objects of which we can have certain and systematic knowledge" (R. P. Anschutz, *The Philosophy of J. S. Mill* [London: Oxford University Press, 1963], p. 119).

On the other hand, Alan Ryan has argued that Mill's realist statements are wrong to begin with. When Mill states that a counteracted force has had its full effect, he is simply saying what is wrong. When a body remains in place, having ben subjected to opposing forces, "the correct statement of the situation is that neither force had any effect because of the opposing force. . . . In terms of what visibly happened, the answer is that nothing visibly happened" (Ryan, *The Philosophy of John Stuart Mill*, p. 66). In Mill's defense, Ryan points out first that in some cases at least, Mill was willing to say that a tendency of something just *is* its atomic or molecular structure. The explosive tendency of gunpowder, he observed, consists "in a collocation of particles." In other cases, he stated that a capacity is *not* a real thing in the object, but our reference to it merely reflects our confidence that the thing will act in certain ways under certain circumstances. Ryan thus suggests an interpretation devoid of realist connotations: statements about operative tendencies which are counteracted can be translated into statements which assert that the object, event, etc., displays the result as if all the tendencies have had their full effect. The body in place is where it would be had the first force operated fully, followed by the second.

Mill did, indeed, express himself as Ryan suggests. Moreover, the most central theme in Mill's discussion is not ontological, but epistemological. It is his insistence that for the purposes of predicting, calculating, and explaining how an effect is produced, one must suppose all tendencies operative (see, *CW*, VII:444). Still Ryan's argument is not quite right. If I push on an object and it does not move, something observable *has* happened—it remains in place despite being pushed. It *was* exposed to a force. This is an observable effect of the operation of the opposing force. This effect is not its "full effect" in one sense, since the body did not move. On the other hand, it did exert its full *force*, else the body would have moved somewhat in the opposite direction. The net effect, then, really *is* a resultant of operative forces. Need we interpret these as occult, platonic realities with no empirical features? I think not. Properties of things, according to Mill, are just "permanent possibilities of sensation." The powers, tendencies, and capacities, of things, events, etc., are as readily describable in such terms as any other kind of property. The theory is Platonistic only to the extent that "permanent possibilities" are thought of as occult realities themselves. There is no reason to think that Mill thought of them in this way.

50. *CW*, IV:337.

51. *CW*, VIII:944−945.

52. Ibid., p.898.

53. Ibid., p. 945.

54. Ibid., p. 946.

55. "Carlyle's *French Revolution*," in *Mill's Essays on Literature and Society*, ed. J. B. Schneewind (New York: The Macmillan Company, 1965), p. 200.

56. *CW*, IV:338−339.

57. *The Later Letters 1849 to 1873*, *CW*, XVII:1881−1882. To the evidence afforded by the letter to Venn, we can add a passage written with John Grote in "Taylor's Statesman": ". . . if we once admit as the supreme test of right and wrong in an act, the balance of all its consequences, by what approach to omniscience can we pretend to predict that such balance must always be on one side, in every conceivable diversity of cases? . . . To admit the balance of consequences as a test of right and wrong, necessarily implies the possibility of exceptions to any derivative rule of morality which may be deduced from that test" (*CW*, XIX:638).

58. *CW*, X:181.

59. Ibid., p. 182.

60. Whether or not Mill's analysis of the causal process is *correct* is a difficult matter, indeed. It is certainly *not* true that all violations have an *equal* effect (consider secret ones, for example). Nor is our ignorance of likely effects always of equal degree, so as to justify the *attribution* of equal effects. To a great extent, the answer will turn on the criteria by which one identifies and individuates actions. For a lengthy treatment of this issue, see Lyons, *Forms and Limits of Utilitarianism*, chaps. 1−3. For Mill, the issue is complicated even more by the fact that he held that an action consists in an intention, followed by "an effect" (e.g., the moving of an arm) (*CW*, VII:55). Presumably, classes of acts are to be picked out (in part, at least) by the occurrence of the same, or similar, intentions. Moreover, there is the problem of secret violations in which the bad tendencies consist primarily in tendencies to affect the *agent's* character and behavior.

61. *CW*, X:220.

62. Ibid.

63. *CW*, VIII:943−944.

64. Ibid., p. 1154.

65. In an excellent discussion of these points, Maurice Mandelbaum presents an account of the changes which would explain Mill's dropping the last paragraph, while still in agreement with them. See Mandelbaum, "Two Moot Issues in Mill's Utilitarianism," pp. 214−221.

66. *CW*, X:101−102.

67. *CW*, VIII:1154−1155.

68. *CW*, X:259. In these cases, "some other social duty" justifies the violation.

69. "Taylor's Statesman," in *CW*, XIX:640. Apparently, it was the practice in jointly authored works for each author to write a different part. It is not known if Mill actually wrote the paragraph quoted. On the other hand, it makes the point so graphically that it seems implausible that Mill could ever have held some other view

without feeling called upon to explain what is mistaken in the theory stated. It would also require explanation as to why he would publish as joint author something on which he held a radically different view.

70. *CW*, VII:952.

71. Ibid., p. 898.

72. J. M. Robson "surmises" that Mill did not consider it a major work (J. M. Robson, *The Improvement of Mankind: The Social and Political Thought of John Stuart Mill* [Toronto: University of Toronto Press, 1968], p. 158).

73. D. P. Dryer, "Mill's Utilitarianism," in *CW*, X:xcvi, and "Justice, Liberty, and the Principle of Utility in Mill," in *New Essays on John Stuart Mill and Utilitarianism*, *Canadian Journal of Philosophy*, Suppl. Vol. V (Ontario, 1979), 64. See, also, Urmson, "The Interpretation of the Moral Philosophy of J. S. Mill," pp. 33–39. Urmson goes on to maintain that Mill held that moral issues arise only when the general welfare is "more than negligibly affected." Though he is not entirely clear on this point, he seems to hold that Mill marked that line with his distinction between self-regarding and other actions. I shall argue that Mill indeed held that self-regarding acts do not pose issues of moral assessment. This, however, hardly yields the conclusion that these are cases in which the general welfare is only negligibly affected. Self-regarding acts may, Mill admitted, "affect" others in significant, though "indirect" ways. These issues will be discussed in chapter 5.

74. *CW*, X:206.

75. A similar response is made in Cupples, "A Defense of the Received Interpretation of J. S. Mill," pp. 131–137.

76. *CW*, X:224–225.

77. J. D. Mabbot, "Interpretations of Mill's Utilitarianism," p. 115–120.

78. One textbook describes the Almanac as follows: "In 1776 the Royal Astronomer of Great Britain began publication of the *Nautical Almanac*, a book of astronomical calculations that can help a sailor determine his position at sea. A tremendous amount of calculation was required to produce this book. Most of the work was done by retired clergymen who did all their work by hand and made many errors; it is known that ships were wrecked due to errors in the *Almanac*" (Charles D. Miller and Vern E. Heeren, *Mathematical Ideas: An Introduction* [Glenview, Ill.: Scott, Foresman and Company, 1968], p. 227).

79. *CW*, X:226.

80. Ibid., p. 225.

81. Ibid., p. 214.

82. "Taylor's Statesman," in *CW*, XIX:638–639.

83. *CW*, X:210.

84. D. G. Brown, "What is Mill's Principle of Utility?" *Canadian Journal of Philosophy* 3 (September, 1973), 1–12.

85. Ibid., p. 3.

86. Brown, "Mill's Act-Utilitarianism," pp. 67–68.

87. *CW*, X:246.

88. See, especially, David Lyons, "Mill's Theory of Morality," *Nous* 10 (May, 1976), 101–120; and "Human Rights and the General Welfare," *Philosophy and Public Affairs* 6 (Winter, 1977), 113–129.

89. Lyons, "Mill's Theory of Morality," p. 107.

90. Lyons, "Human Rights and the General Welfare," p. 122.

91. Lyons, "Mill's Theory of Morality," p. 109.

92. David Copp, "The Iterated Utilitarianism of J. S. Mill," in *New Essays on John Stuat Mill and Utilitarianism*, *Canadian Journal of Philosophy*, Suppl. Vol. V (Ontario, 1979), 75–98.

93. Dryer, "Justice, Liberty, and the Principle of Utility in Mill," pp. 63–73.

94. John Gray, *Mill on Liberty: A Defence* (London: Routledge & Kegan Paul, 1983), p. 31. (I note that in places, Gray appears to slip, and make it a necessary condition for the rightness of an act that it be "maximally expedient" as well as punishable; see pp. 29, 31.)

95. L. W. Sumner, "The Good and the Right," in *New Essays on John Stuart Mill and Utilitarianism*, *Canadian Journal of Philosophy*, Suppl. Vol. V (Ontario, 1979), 99–114.

96. Ibid., pp. 107–109.

97. I owe the example to Professor Bruce Russell.

98. *CW*, X:225.

99. David Lyons, "Benevolence and Justice in Mill," in *The Limits of Utilitarianism*, ed. Harlan B. Miller and William H. Williams (Minneapolis: University of Minnesota Press, 1982), p. 70 n. 11.

100. Gray, *Mill on Liberty*, pp. 31–32; Sumner, "The Good and the Right," pp. 111–112.

101. Though I do not think this is entirely clear from the text, Gray does not think the theory he attributes to Mill permits direct appeal to the Principle of Utility. In his version, a mature moral code will contain within it elements that indicate how to resolve conflicts, and so on, without requiring direct assessment of the consequences of the act. In discussion, he has conceded that this will create an unresolved tension between the requirements of utility and those of morality, in cases where the best consequences will be produced by acting immorally (as defined by the code), and where this is known.

102. Sumner, "The Good and the Right," p. 108.

103. Ibid., pp. 113–114.

104. *CW*, VIII:949.

105. *CW*, X:213.

106. Ibid., p. 7.

107. *CW*, X:182.

108. Ibid., p. 225. (Emphasis added.)

109. *CW*, XIX:640. (Emphasis added.)

110. *CW*, V:659.

111. *An Examination of Sir William Hamilton's Philosophy, CW*, IX (see p. 454 for a statement of the proportionality criterion; p. 460 n. for an endorsement of the punishability discussion in *Utilitarianism*).

112. *CW*, V:651, 659.

113. *The Later Letters, CW*, XV:649.

114. James Mill, *Analysis of the Phenomena of the Human Mind, Vol. II*, ed. John Stuart Mill (London: Longmans, Green, Reader and Dyer, 1869), 298–299, n. 56.

115. *CW*, X:249. Mill's discussion here is specifically concerned with the "sentiment of justice." In *Analysis*, however, the account is cited as an elucidation of the sentiments expressed by judgments of *duty* in general.

116. Ibid., p. 250.

117. *Analysis* II:324.

118. "Auguste Comte and Positivism," *CW*, X:338.

119. *CW*, X:249.

120. David Hume, *A Treatise of Human Nature*, ed. L. A. Selby-Bigge (Oxford: Oxford University Press,1960), p. 472.

121. *Analysis* II:326.

122. Sumner, "The Good and the Right," p. 110.

4: THE THEORY OF JUSTICE

1. Major exceptions are to be found in the work of Professors David Lyons and John Gray. I refer below to work of both that give great weight to Mill's views on justice. Both have kindly allowed me to read unpublished work of theirs on Mill, have given me the benefit of their criticisms of and suggestions for my own work, and have discussed these issues with me at length.

2. John Rawls, *A Theory of Justice* (Cambridge, Mass.: Harvard University Press, 1971), p. 26. Robert Nozick carries the point a step further and maintains that utilitarianism permits the total sacrifice of persons for the greater good of all. See Robert Nozick, *Anarchy, State, and Utopia* (New York: Basic Books, Inc. 1974), pp. 30–33.

3. H. L. A. Hart, "Are There Any Natural Rights?" *The Philosophical Review* 64 (1955), 185. A similar view is maintained by Rawls (*A Theory of Justice*, p. 112). Later in his book, Rawls elaborates important qualifications, and distinguishes the principle of fairness from a "natural" duty to support and further just institutions (pp. 333–335).

4. I have based the example on an actual case in which an "artist" arranged a "show" of a mentally retarded man sitting unmoving in a chair. I mention this in case the reader should think the suggestion too bizarre to be worth taking up.

5. There are claims of this sort to be found in Rawls, *A Theory of Justice*, pp. 22–27, and in Nozick, *Anarchy, State and Utopia*, pp. 30–33.

6. *Utilitarianism, CW*, X:240.

7. In this respect, Mill was following the method of philosophical clarification he had outlined in his *A System of Logic, Ratiocinative and Inductive, CW*, VII:150–154; also

37–40. I shall return to consider Mill's view on philosophical clarification later in this chapter.

8. *CW*, X:245–246.

9. Ibid., p. 246.

10. Ibid., p. 247. Mill also remarked that some ethicists mark the distinction between perfect and imperfect duties in an imprecise way—the latter leave to our choice the particular occasions for fulfilling the obligation. I shall discuss some problems with this formulation later in this chapter.

11. Ibid., p. 248.

12. Ibid.

13. Ibid., p. 249.

14. Ibid.

15. Ibid., pp. 249–250.

16. Ibid., p. 250.

17. James Mill, *Analysis of the Phenomena of the Human Mind*, Vol. II, ed. John Stuart Mill (London: Longman's Green Reader and Dyer, 1869), 325.

18. *CW*, X:251.

19. *The Later Letters*, *CW* XV:762. The quotation lends some support to David Lyons's rule-related interpretation of Mill's moral theory, which is discussed in chapter 2. It is also consistent with the interpretation for which I argued, especially in light of the qualifying clauses "in most cases" and "generally." Also, the utilities cited seem to follow from recognized rules, not merely ideal ones, as Lyons's view would seem to require obligations to be tied to. Finally, it should be remembered that Grote and Mill had jointly authored the review of Taylor's *Statesman* in which they had written that "philosophy commands" that all circumstances of an act be considered, and that if one willfully ignores bad consequences, "he cannot discharge himself from moral responsibility by pleading that he had the general rule in his favor" (*CW*, XIX:640).

20. Most notably in chapter 5 of *Utilitarianism*, which I have been discussing, and in his review, "Thornton on Labour and Its Claims," *CW*, V:631–668.

21. To cite just one example, Pedro Schwartz has discussed various of Mill's principles of justice in the area of economics. See Pedro Schwartz, *The New Political Economy of J. S. Mill* (London: Weidenfeld and Nicolson, 1968).

22. In a way, this is surprising, as Mill himself emphasized that the "real character of any man's ethical system depends not on his first and fundamental principle, which is of necessity so general as to be rarely susceptible of an immediate application to practice" ("Blakey's History of Moral Science," *CW*, X:29). What constitutes the essence of one's theory, he held, are the secondary principles adhered to.

23. An excellent discussion is found in Alan Ryan's "Introduction" to Mill's book on Sir William Hamilton; see *CW*, IX:lix–lxvii. I should add to my remarks in the text that although I do not believe the determinist can provide a satisfactory account, I am not convinced that there *is* an intelligible notion of "free will" with which to flesh out the concept of responsibility. In this respect, I am a skeptic.

24. Alan Ryan, *The Philosophy of John Stuart Mill* (London: Macmillan, 1970), p. 229. Ryan does not quite give the argument my text indicates; his concern in the passage was with the failure of the putative analysis to bring in any notion of the agent having acted freely. It is clear from the quotation later in this paragraph that Ryan *also* accepts the criticism as I have framed it. See also, H. J. McCloskey, *John Stuart Mill: A Critical Study* (London: Macmillan, 1971), pp. 92–93.

25. Alan Ryan, *J. S. Mill* (London and Boston: Routledge & Kegan Paul, 1974), p. 121.

26. *An Examination of Sir William Hamilton's Philosophy*, CW, IX:462.

27. Ibid., p. 454.

28. Ibid., pp. 454–455.

29. *Utilitarianism*, CW, X:228; and "Remarks on Bentham's Philosophy," CW, X:12–13.

30. *Sir William Hamilton's Philosophy*, p. 458.

31. Ibid., p. 459 n.

32. Ibid., p. 460 n.

33. Ibid.

34. *Utilitarianism*, p. 228.

35. Ryan, *The Philosophy of J. S. Mill*, p. 114.

36. *Sir William Hamilton's Philosophy*, p. 462.

37. "On Punishment," *Monthly Repository*, 8 (1834), p. 735.

38. Ibid.

39. *Sir William Hamilton's Philosophy*, p. 460 n.

40. In a letter describing *Utilitarianism*, Mill wrote: "I derive most of the peculiar characters of the moral sentiment from the element of vindictiveness which enters into it" (*Later Letters*, CW, XV:825).

41. *Analysis*, II:323 n.

42. Joel Feinberg, "The Expressive Function of Punishment," in *Doing and Deserving: Essays in the Theory of Responsibility* (Princeton: Princeton University Press, 1970), p. 100.

43. Joel Feinberg, "Noncomparative Justice," in *Rights, Justice, and the Bounds of Liberty* (Princeton, N.J.: Princeton University Press, 1980), p. 288.

44. Ibid.

45. It would appear that Feinberg *does* restrict the notion of an injustice in this way. For example, he maintains that not all cases of wrongful promise-breaking are also cases of injustice because one can "mistreat a person without being particularly unfair to him" (ibid., p. 269). He goes on to argue that, in fact, most cases of promise-breaking *are* unfair, hence, injustices.

46. H. L. A. Hart, "Punishment and the Elimination of Responsibility," in *Punishment and Responsibility: Essays in the Philosophy of Law* (New York: Oxford University Press, 1968), p. 183.

47. Ibid.

48. Herbert Morris, "Persons and Punishment," in *On Guilt and Innocence: Essays in*

Legal Philosophy and Moral Psychology (Berkeley, Los Angeles, London: University of California Press, 1976), pp. 31–88.

49. P. F. Strawson, "Freedom and Resentment," in *Studies in the Philosophy of Thought and Action*, ed. P. F. Strawson (London: Oxford University Press, 1968). pp. 71–96.

50. Ibid., p. 96.

51. I have argued for this analysis in my paper, "Gratitude," in *Ethics* 85 (July, 1975), 298–309.

52. *On Liberty*, *CW*, XVIII:279–280.

53. "On Punishment," p. 735.

54. Graham Hughes, "Should Alfie Be Let Off?" *The New York Review of Books* 27 (November 20, 1980), p. 47.

55. See Berger, "Gratitude," p. 305.

56. Thus, James Mill wrote: "Acts are performed, not for their own sake, but for the sake of their consequences. A voluntary act has no other meaning than that it is an act performed as the means to an end" (James Mill, *A Fragment on Mackintosh* [London: Longmans, Green, Reader, and Dyer, 1870], p. 310). But, I should note that in the sentence preceding the one quoted, he referred to "the act itself, the muscular contraction," whereas he indicated elsewhere, and throughout the book, that he regarded an act as a set of movements *together with* an intention. Earlier, he had agreed there are acts we like and seek for their own sakes; but, he added: "That is to say, the acts; for the outward act, detached from the mental part, is not an object of liking, or disliking" (ibid., p. 85).

57. Useful discussions are to be found in the following works: John M. Robson, *The Improvement of Mankind: The Social and Political Thought of John Stuart Mill* (Toronto: University of Toronto Press, 1968), pp. 245–271; Graeme Duncan, *Marx and Mill: Two Views of Social Conflict and Social Harmony* (London: Cambridge University Press, 1973), pp. 238–248; Alan Ryan, *J. S. Mill*, pp. 183–189; Pedro Schwartz, *The New Political Economy of J. S. Mill*, pp. 221–226.

58. "Civilization," *CW*, XVIII:122.

59. *Principles of Political Economy*, Vol. II, *CW*, III:794–6.

60. "The competition of the market may represent a practical necessity, but certainly not a moral ideal" ("Auguste Comte and Positivism," *CW*, X:341).

61. John Stuart Mill, *Autobiography*, *CW*, I:239.

62. "Chapters on Socialism," *CW*, V:748–749.

63. Fred R. Berger, "John Stuart Mill on Justice and Fairness," in *New Essays on John Stuart Mill and Utilitarianism*, *Canadian Journal of Philosophy*, Suppl. Vol. V (Ontario, 1979), pp. 115–136. I borrow from this paper below.

64. "Utilitarianism," *CW*, X:251.

65. Though the point is a bit sophistical, we can claim that Mill could have consistently made the point that society should interfere only with harmful conduct, and still have argued that it should institute a "rule of the road." The antecedently harmful conduct is unsystematic or unregulated behavior.

66. In a letter to John Venn, Mill discussed the importance of violations of useful rules in endangering security: "And that this mischievous tendency overbalances (unless in very extreme cases) the private good obtained by the breach of a moral rule, is obvious if we take into consideration the importance, to the general good, of the feeling of security, or certainty; which is impaired, not only by every known actual violation of good rules, but by the belief that such violations ever occur" (*The Later Letters, CW*, XVII:1881–1882).

67. *Principles of Political Economy, CW*, III:956.

68. Ibid., p. 957.

69. Ibid., p. 959.

70. H. L. A. Hart, *The Concept of Law* (Oxford: Clarendon Press, 1961), p. 193.

71. *On Liberty*, p. 289.

72. H. L. A. Hart, "Are There Any Natural Rights?" *The Philosophical Review*, 64 (April, 1955), 155.

73. Rawls, *A Theory of Justice*, p. 112. Later in the book, Rawls elaborates important qualifications, and distinguishes the principle of fairness from a "natural" duty to support and further just institutions (pp. 333–355). I shall not be concerned with these finer points here.

74. John Rawls, "Legal Obligation and the Duty of Fair Play," in *Law and Philosophy: A symposium*, ed. Sidney Hook (New York: New York University Press, 1964), p. 10.

75. Nozick, *Anarchy, State, and Utopia*, pp. 90–95. Nozick's examples are directed at the formulations of Hart and Rawls of a principle of fairness. I believe these examples are adequately defended against by A. John Simmons in his extremely well-argued book, *Moral Principles and Political Obligations* (Princeton, N.J.: Princeton University Press, 1979), pp. 118–136.

76. Some of the problems to be faced in framing an acceptable principle are canvassed in David Lyons, *Forms and Limits of Utilitarianism* (Oxford: Clarendon Press, 1965), pp. 161–177. Lyons's basic point is that utilitarian considerations will not suffice to deal with the complex difficulties, and that only by considering the agent's "motives or reasons" can the notions of fairness and unfairness be fully captured. Utilitarians, he held, are concerned only with actual, not intended effects, hence, are unconcerned with *how* the act is performed, or with what intentions. This is, historically speaking, almost the opposite of the truth. *All* the classical utilitarians—Bentham, James Mill, John Austin, and John Stuart Mill—held that motives *or* intentions can play an important role in the morality of an act. John Mill (as well as his father and Bentham) *defined* an act as an intention along with a physical movement, and held that where there are different intentions, there are different acts. Both he and his father insisted that the morality of an act *depends* on the intention, as the intention can product different effects. If, indeed, it is important to us *how* someone has acted (e.g., "sought to get something for nothing," "wanted to consume without contributing"), if we *are* affronted by the *reasons* for acting, then noncompliance will have the effect in these cases of producing ill-will, a sense of affront to our dignity, and so on. Now Lyons claims that our

repugnance to the way someone has acted in these cases presupposes a moral judgment of unfair behavior. I do not see any reason to suppose this. It may reflect only a sense that there is a heightened threat to security by such blatant displays of uncooperativeness, or it could reflect a primitive, "natural" sense that all should abide by the same rules, or the affront could be an instinctual response to the making of exceptions for self.

Another useful discussion of the complexity of duties of fairness is to be found in Simmons, *Moral Principles and Political Obligations*, pp. 101–142.

77. *Considerations on Representative Government*, CW, XIX:567.

78. *Utilitarianism*, p. 256.

79. Ibid.

80. Ibid., p. 247.

81. *The Later Letters*, CW, XV:762.

82. *Utilitarianism*, p. 220.

83. "Auguste Comte and Positivism," CW, X:338.

84. *On Liberty*, p. 276.

85. Ibid., p. 225.

86. *Utilitarianism*, p. 256.

87. Schwartz, *The New Political Economy of J. S. Mill*, p. 194.

88. Ibid.

89. "Vindication of the French Revolution of February 1848, in Reply to Lord Brougham and Others," *Dissertations and Discussions*, Vol. II (London: John W. Parker and Son, 1859), 395.

90. R. J. Halliday, *John Stuart Mill* (London: George Allen & Unwin Ltd., 1976), p. 101.

91. Ibid., p. 136.

92. Ibid., p. 137.

93. John Gray, "John Stuart Mill on the Theory of Property," in *Theories of Property: Aristotle to the Present*, ed. A. Parel and T. Flanagan (Waterloo, Ontario: Wilfred Laverier University Press, 1979), p. 268.

94. Ibid.

95. *Utilitarianism*, p. 257–258.

96. "Civilization," pp. 123–125. The same points are made in his essay on *Democracy in America*, where he argued that de Tocqueville had mistakenly attributed these consequences to advancing democracy, rather than to the greater degree of civilization in modern life ("De Tocqueville on Democracy in America [II]," CW, XVIII:192).

97. "Civilization," p. 129.

98. "De Tocqueville on Democracy in America [II]," p. 163.

99. "The Savings of the Middle and Working Classes," CW, V:419.

100. "Coleridge," CW, X:134.

101. Ibid., p. 123.

102. "Centralisation," p. 591.

103. Ibid., p. 591.

104. "De Tocqueville on Democracy in America [II]," p. 166.

105. *Principles of Political Economy*, pp. 766—769.

106. "Taylor's Statesman," p. 636—637. These bad effects on the judgment of wielders of power were reiterated in *Considerations on Representative Government*, pp. 444—445.

107. "Use and Abuse of Political Terms," *CW*, XVIII:12.

108. *The Subjection of Women*, in *Essays on Sex Equality*, ed. Alice S. Rossi (Chicago: The University of Chicago Press, 1970), p. 165.

109. Ibid., pp. 163—164.

110. Ibid., p. 213.

111. "The Spirit of the Age," in *Essays on Politics and Culture*, ed. Gertrude Himmelfarb (Garden City, NY: Doubleday & Company, Inc., 1962), pp. 25—27.

112. "Centralisation," p. 610. A similar point about different conceptions of freedom is made in *The Subjection of Women*, p. 175, should any one mistakenly think the quotation in the text represents the "other," conservative, Mill.

113. "Auguste Comte and Positivism," p. 339.

114. "Vindication of the French Revolution," p. 395.

115. *Considerations on Representative Government*, p. 449.

116. *The Later Letters*, *CW*, X:421.

117. "Utility of Religion," *CW*, X:421.

118. *The Subjection of Women*, p. 174.

119. "Auguste Comte and Positivism," p. 339.

120. *Utilitarianism*, pp. 231—233.

121. *The Subjection of Women*, p. 174.

122. *Utilitarianism*, p. 232.

123. Mill's economic theories have been canvassed by Schwartz in *The New Political Economy of J. S. Mill*. See also, Samuel Hollander, "Ricardianism, J. S. Mill, and the Neoclassical Challenge," in *James and John Stuart Mill/Papers of the Centenary Conference*, ed. John M. Robson and Michael Laine (Toronto and Buffalo: University of Toronto Press, 1976), pp. 67—85. The essential features of Mill's theories on government are brought out well in Dennis F. Thompson, *John Stuart Mill and Representative Government* (Princeton, NJ: Princeton University Press, 1976). Thompson also has an excellent assessment of Mill's views on the trend toward equality (pp. 158—173). A capsule summary of the views Thompson attributes to Mill can be found in my review of Thompson's book in *The Philosophical Review* 87 (April, 1978), 322—325. For less than book-length critical summaries of Mill's economic and political theories, there are excellent discussions by Alan Ryan in *J. S. Mill*, chaps. 6 and 7.

124. "Vindication of the French Revolution," pp. 388—389; also: *Autobiography*, p. 239; and "Newman's Political Economy," *CW*, V:443; *Principles of Political Economy*, pp. 207—208.

125. *Autobiography*, p. 239.

126. "Newman's Political Economy," pp. 443—444.

127. *Autobiography*, p. 239. The same point is made in "Newman's Political

Economy," p. 443. For Mill's discussion of what I have called "the private property principle" and its implications, see *Principles of Political Economy*, pp. 217–218.

128. "Newman's Political Economy," p. 443.

129. "Coleridge," pp. 157–158.

130. Ibid., p. 154.

131. "De Tocqueville on Democracy in America [II]," p. 166.

132. "Centralisation," p. 591.

133. *Principles of Political Economy*, p. 808.

134. Nozick, *Anarchy, State, and Utopia*, pp. 235–236.

135. The point that "natural disadvantage" is not an expression that is neutral with respect to social context is extremely important in a variety of contexts. Richard Wasserstrom has pointed out that we can so construct our physical environment that people who cannot walk can nevertheless lead a normal life involving access to buildings, seating at concerts, movies, lectures, and so on. The effect of natural features of persons depends on how we structure the natural and social environment. Wasserstrom uses this point to argue that natural differences between the sexes need not be a basis for imposing social disadvantage (see "Racism and Sexism," in *Philosophy and Social Issues* [Notre Dame, Ind.: University of Notre Dame Press, 1980], pp. 32–33).

136. Actually, Nozick acknowledges some force to the claim that there is a duty on society to make the competitive aspects of economic life fairer. He provides two counterexamples to such a principle, however (both of which seem to me irrelevant to any formulation of such a principle for which anyone wants to argue). His major objection, however, is that rights to "equality of opportunity, life, and so on," require material things and actions to which others may have rights. This "substructure of particular rights," Nozick contends, forms a barrier against the assertion of any general rights of the kind needed for equalizing the competition; "no rights exist in conflict with this substructure of particular rights" (Nozick, *Anarchy, State, and Utopia*, p. 238). Mill would reject this notion that such rights are inviolable, especially when they *avowedly* do not turn on desert or merit. There is little by way of argument by Nozick for his extraordinary claim, anyway. I shall discuss one aspect of what I take to be his argument when I discuss Mill's view that wages of certain sorts may be taxed.

137. *Considerations on Representative Government*, p. 387.

138. In the *Chapters on Socialism*, for example, he canvassed the various sorts of desert bases that might be claimed in a communist economic arrangement, using the points made as a basis for holding that there would be need of a "dispensing power" or authority for apportioning work. He thought that competition would spring up for the management positions, which could result in dissension (*Chapters on Socialism*, pp. 743–745). A similar discussion of the difficulties of determining desert bases is found in *Principles of Political Economy*, pp. 206–207.

139. *Principles of Political Economy*, p. 880. The point is repeated in *The Later Letters*, *CW*, XVII:1739–1740.

140. "Vindication of the French Revolution," p. 389.

141. *Principles of Political Economy*, p. 223.

142. Ibid., p. 207.

143. *Chapters on Socialism*, p. 753. Were it not impossible, one might otherwise have taken Mill, in the quotation, to have been rejecting Nozick's position as quoted in n. 136. Of course, to *reject* a view is not the same as to *refute* it.

144. *The Later Letters*, *CW*, XVII:1740.

145. "Use and Abuse of Political Terms," p. 12.

146. *Principles of Political Economy*, pp. 224−225.

147. Ibid., pp. 960−962.

148. Ibid., p. 980. The point Mill made here seems to be an acceptance of something like one of John Rawls's principles of justice—the "difference" principle (Rawls, *A Theory of Justice*, p. 83). Rawls himself cites a *different* passage in Mill as evidence for Mill's having accepted the *desire* to act from the difference principle. He says that Mill failed to realize that this would mean acting from a desire *other* than to act on the principle of utility (*A Theory of Justice*, p. 502). The confusion here is Rawls's, however. Mill had made clear that his theory did *not* require always acting from the immediate desire to maximize utility. (I have shown this at length in chap. 1, in the section on "Motives.") A criterion of right and wrong action need not also be a criterion of appropriate motivation. Utility, he held, can best be maximized by adopting the rules of justice in practical affairs; hence, acting from the desire to do justice is more likely to result in right action. Elsewhere in his book (pp. 181−182), Rawls maintains that, for the utilitarian, to adopt his principles of justice as governing society would be to give up utilitarianism. This seems to follow, however, only on his own idiosyncratic and historically inaccurate definition of "utilitarianism." I shall have more to say on this later.

149. *Principles of Political Economy*, p. 811.

150. Alexander Bain, *John Stuart Mill. A Criticism: With Personal Recollections* (London: Longmans, Green, and Co., 1882), p. 89.

151. *Chapters on Socialism*, p. 736.

152. *Principles of Political Economy*, pp. 231−232.

153. "Coleridge," pp. 157−158.

154. Ryan, *J. S. Mill*, pp. 171−172.

155. *Principles of Political Economy*, pp. 806−807.

156. Ibid., p. 808.

157. "Thornton on Labour and Its Claims," *CW*, V:654−655.

158. Ryan, *J. S. Mill*, p. 171.

159. *Principles of Political Economy*, p. 810.

160. "Civilization," p. 130.

161. James Mill, " 'The Greatest Happiness Principle,' " in *Utilitarian Logic and Politics: James Mill's 'Essay on Government', and Maccaulay's critique and the ensuing debate*, ed. Jack Lively and John Rees (Oxford: Clarendon Press, 1978), p. 149. Mill wrote: ". . .the greatest aggregate of happiness must always include the happiness of the greatest number. For the greatest number must always be composed of those who individually possess a comparatively small portion of the good things of life; and if any

thing is taken from one of these to give to the others, it is plain that what he loses in happiness, is greater than what the others gain. . . . It is the avowal that half-a-crown is of more consequence to the porter that loses it, than to the Duke of Bedford who should chance to find it."

162. In a letter to the economist, John Elliot Cairnes, he wrote: "I agree in what you say about equality of sacrifice, but in estimating this, I only exclude necessaries. I do not think a distinction can be fairly made between comforts and luxuries, or that I am entitled to call my tea and coffee by the one name, and another person's melons and champagne by the other" (*The Later Letters, CW*, XV:976).

163. *Principles of Political Economy*, p. 809.

164. Ibid., p. 814 ff; also, "The Income and Property Tax," *CW*, V:553.

165. *Principles of Political Economy*, p. 819.

166. Ibid., pp. 819–820.

167. Ibid., p. 828.

168. Ibid., pp. 810–811.

169. Ibid., p. 811.

170. Nozick, *Anarchy, State, and Utopia*, p. 168. I think Nozick is right to point out in places that his argument may show only that taxation of income from labor is "like" forced labor. For, given appropriate conditions, e.g., limits on such taxation, a democratic polity in which citizens have a voice in *whether* they are to be taxed, how much, and for what purposes, it is also significantly *un*like forced labor and having property in others. I note also that Professor John Gray seems correct in claiming that Nozick's view that original appropriation of natural resources generates a duty of compensation to those who will suffer a decrease in well-being as a result *also* entails "conferring a partial title to the labour of each man upon all the rest in virtue of the fact that part of the value of the originally appropriated resource is now locked into transformed objects" (Gray, "John Stuart Mill on the Theory of Property," p. 276). Part of the argument I shall attribute to Mill relies on this very point. I note also that as I was writing this section an article was published by Professor Lawrence C. Becker, arguing that people have an *obligation* to engage in socially useful work. Some of his arguments parallel ones that play a role in the argument I give in the text. Becker *opposes* enforcing the obligation to work via penalties on those who do not, but he does not consider the propriety of mandatory taxation (Lawrence C. Becker, "The Obligation to Work," *Ethics* 90 [October, 1980], 35–49).

171. *Principles of Political Economy*, p. 938.

172. Ibid., pp. 803–804.

173. Ibid., pp. 947–971.

174. Ibid., pp. 938–939.

175. Ibid., p. 828.

176. Ibid., pp. 199–200.

177. *The Later Letters, CW*, XVI:1443.

178. *Principles of Political Economy*, p. 112.

179. "Thornton on Labour," p. 656.

180. *Principles of Political Economy*, pp. 31—44.

181. Ibid., p. 47.

182. Ibid., pp. 102—115.

183. Ibid., p. 49. Were he inventing his *own* technical language, however, he *would* include these qualities in the concept.

184. Ibid., p. 41 (emphasis mine).

185. Ibid., pp. 829—830.

186. *Chapters on Socialism*, p. 727.

187. *Principles of Political Economy*, p. 209. The same point is made in *Chapters on Socialism*, p. 710.

188. *Principles of Political Economy*, p. 766n. The passage was left out of the 1852, and subsequent editions. Schwartz suggests several explanations (see *The New Political Economy of J. S. Mill*, p. 293, n. 38). I note that in his remarks on the nature of wage-labor, Mill seems to have captured a part of Marx's concept of "alienated labor."

189. "De Toqueville on Democracy in America [II]," p. 166.

190. *Chapters on Socialism*, p. 710.

191. *Principles of Political Economy*, p. 960.

192. Ibid., p. 962.

193. Ibid., p. 961.

194. "Vindication of the French Revolution," pp. 385—387.

195. *Utilitarianism*, p. 247.

196. Two excellent treatments of Mill's views on social dynamics are: Ryan, *The Philosophy of John Stuart Mill*, chaps. 8, 9 and 10; and Thompson, *John Stuart Mill and Representative Government*, chap. 4. The most extensive treatment of the role of class divisions in Mill's thinking is to be found in Duncan, *Marx and Mill*, especially chap. 6. The latter book, of course, provides materials for the comparison of Marx and Mill. Some further comparison of Mill's views with those of socialists is to be found in, Graeme Duncan and John Gray, "The Left Against Mill," *New Essays on John Stuart Mill and Utilitarianism, Canadian Journal of Philosophy*, Suppl. Vol. V (1979), 203—229.

197. I have inserted the phrase "prima facie" as the phrase "concern" has important limitations. Moreover, even when appropriately restricted, Mill did not hold the individual can never act solely for his or her own concerns. I shall argue in the next chapter that his principle was that freedom must be respected except when the actor threatens interests to which others have a right to protection.

198. "Thoughts on Parliamentary Reform," *CW*, XIX:322.

199. See "Coleridge," p. 154. A similar point is made as a warning that if the masses are *not* represented a "convulsion" could occur, in "Civilization," p. 127. Further, he endorsed the claim that the "positive political morality" determines who really wields power, but that that must be in accord with the actual distribution of power, in *Considerations on Representative Government*, pp. 422—423.

200. "Taylor's Statesman," pp. 636—637. The point is made even more strongly in *Considerations on Representative Government*, pp. 445—446.

201. *Considerations on Representative Government*, p. 467.

202. "Thoughts on Parliamentary Reform," p. 324.

203. *Considerations on Representative Government*, p. 447.

204. "Thoughts on Parliamentary Reform," p. 322.

205. *Considerations on Representative Government*, p. 400.

206. Ibid. The theme is repeated on p. 469.

207. Ibid., pp. 467—469.

208. Ibid., p. 469. The point is also made in "Thoughts on Parliamentary Reform," p. 324.

209. *Considerations on Representative Government*, p. 470.

210. *The Later Letters*, CW, XV:600.

211. *Considerations on Representative Government*, pp. 488—495.

212. Ibid., p. 488.

213. Ibid., p. 489.

214. Ibid., p. 488.

215. *The Later Letters*, CW, XV:608.

216. See, for example, "Thoughts on Parliamentary Reform," pp. 331—339. Excellent critical points (with which I agree) are made against Mill's views in Ryan, *J. S. Mill*, p. 213.

217. "Thoughts on Parliamentary Reform," p. 323.

218. Ibid., p. 327.

219. Ibid., p. 324.

220. Ibid., p. 327.

221. Ibid., p. 324.

222. "Recent Writers on Reform," *CW*, XIX:354.

223. Ibid. It is possible that Mill had a better sense of what the English workers would consent to than I suspect. In his autobiography he wrote of an experience he had when he was a candidate for Parliament: "In the pamphlet 'Thoughts on Parliamentary Reform' I had said, rather bluntly, that the working classes, though differing from those of some other countries in being ashamed of lying, are yet generally liars. This passage some opponent got printed in a placard, which was handed to me at a meeting, chiefly composed of the working classes, and I was asked whether I had written and published it. I at once answered 'I did.' Scarcely were these two words out of my mouth, when vehement applause resounded through the whole meeting. It was evident that the working people were so accustomed to expect equivocation and evasion from those who sought their suffrages, that when they found, instead of that, a direct avowal of what was likely to be disagreeable to them, instead of being offended they concluded at once that this was a person whom they could trust. A more striking instance never came under my notice of what, I believe, is the experience of those who best know the working classes—that the most essential of all recommendations to their favour is that of complete straightforwardness; its presence outweighs in their minds very strong objections, while no amount of other qualities will make amends for its apparent absence. The first working man who spoke after the incident I have mentioned (it was Mr. Odger) said, that the working classes had no desire not to be told of their faults; they

wanted friends, not flatterers, and felt under obligation to any one who told them of anything in themselves which he sincerely believed to require amendment. And to this the meeting heartily responded" (*Autobiography*, p. 168). The story is retold in Michael St. John Packe, *The Life of John Stuart Mill* (New York: Capricorn Books, 1970), pp. 450–451.

224. "De Tocqueville on Democracy in America [I]," p. 71.

225. *Considerations on Representative Government*, p. 510.

226. "De Tocqueville on Democracy in America [I]," p. 72.

227. *Considerations on Representative Government*, p. 449. In the very next chapter, unfortunately, he argued for differential votes for the better educated. There is no obvious inconsistency, however. That one is better qualified *does*, he thought, give a basis for greater weight. That one happens to be in a minority gives no basis for no further influence.

228. Ibid.

229. See Bain, *John Stuart Mill*, p. 89.

230. See Packe, *The Life of John Stuart Mill*, pp. 495–503; Eugene August, *John Stuart Mill: A Mind at Large* (New York: Charles Scribner's Sons, 1975), pp. 208–211. The range of reaction is canvassed in Josephine Kamm, *John Stuart Mill in Love*, (London: Gordon & Cremonesi, 1977), pp. 195–203. Julia Annas has written that it "became at once unpopular and neglected," and that it was his only book to lose his publisher money (Julia Annas, "Mill and the Subjection of Women," *Philosophy* 52 [1977], 179n). Though reaction tended to be hostile, it certainly was not *immediately* neglected, nor can I find evidence that it lost money. Annas cites Alan Ryan, *J. S. Mill*, p. 125, where this claim is made. But Packe writes that two editions "were rapidly exhausted," and that it was translated into German, French, and Polish. He further reports that Mill had his speech in Parliament on female suffrage reprinted, along with Harriet's *Enfranchisement of Women*, together with an article by her daughter, Helen Taylor. Of *this* publication, Packe writes: "It was the only occasion he ever lost money on his publications" (Packe, *The Life of John Stuart Mill*, pp. 496–497).

231. See, e.g., Kate Millet, "Mill versus Ruskin," in *Sexual Politics* (New York: Doubleday and Company, Inc.: 1970), pp. 126–151; Alice S. Rossi, "Sentiment and Intellect, The Story of John Stuart Mill and Harriet Taylor Mill," in *Essays on Sex Equality*, ed. Alice S. Rossi (Chicago: The University of Chicago Press, 1970), pp. 1–63; and Susan Brownmiller, "Introduction," in John Stuart Mill, *On the Subjection of Women* (Greenwich, Conn.: Fawcett Publications, Inc., 1971), pp. 5–11.

232. *The Subjection of Women*, p. 125.

233. Ibid., p. 217.

234. Ibid.

235. In a letter to a Belgian economist he wrote: "Vous savey combien je condamne les iniquités de la position actuelle des femmes dans la familie et dans la société, mais cette habitude de les traiter comme des enfants me semble contraire á leur dignité et vértitible intéret" (*The Later Letters*, CW, XVII:1736). Mill's argument for equality as a fulfillment of our social natures is found in *The Subjection of Women*, pp. 173–175; and in *Utilitarianism*, pp. 231–233.

236. *The Subjection of Women*, p. 146.

237. Ibid., p. 218.

238. Ibid., p. 220.

239. Gertrude Himmelfarb, *On Liberty and Liberalism: The Case of John Stuart Mill* (New York: Alfred A. Knopf, 1974), p. 171.

240. Ibid., p. 171.

241. Himmelfarb, *On Liberty and Liberalism*, p. 172.

242. *The Subjection of Women*, p. 144. It is too bad that Professor Himmelfarb did not give greater attention to this passage. Its language, with reference to "rights" of others as limiting liberty, is paralleled in *On Liberty* (*CW*, XVIII:276). It shows that Mill's theory of liberty cannot be completely understood without reference to his theory of justice, and it shows that he did *not* hold "an unmodified, unqualified individualism in social affairs," as she has claimed elsewhere, or that he "made the freedom of the individual the sole aim of social policy," as she held in the book I have been citing (see *Essays on Politics and Culture*, p. xviii; and *On Liberty and Liberalism*, p. 91.) Instances such as this show how important sound philosophical understanding is to sound historical scholarship. Professor Himmelfarb maintains strong historical claims based on interpretive claims about Mill's works, but her interpretive claims strike me as largely false.

243. *The Subjection of Women*, p. 235–236.

244. Ibid., p. 236.

245. Ibid., p. 222.

246. Ibid., p. 239.

247. Ibid.

248. Ibid., p. 241.

249. Annas, "Mill and the Subjection of Women," p. 191.

250. Ibid., 189.

251. "Auguste Comte and Positivism," p. 339.

252. *The Subjection of Women*, p. 238.

253. I am reciting part of the list of legal disabilities given by Eugene August (*John Stuart Mill: A Mind at Large*, pp. 207–208). I have been advised that some of these statements may not be entirely accurate, (I have not been able to confirm or disconfirm this); nevertheless, that severe legal restrictions of the kind noted here were placed upon the women of Mill's day is beyond question.

254. Annas, "Mill and the Subjection of Women," p. 191.

255. Ibid., p. 192.

256. *The Later Letters*, *CW*, XVI, p. 1098–1099.

257. Ibid., p. 1099.

258. Ibid., p. 1066.

259. Ibid.

260. Ibid., p. 1165. I should note that citing Mill's views on the treatment of the property rights of ex-slaveholders does not unequivocally support the claim that he would favor strong measures in support of remedial justice. He appears to have held that the southern slaveholders had forfeited all legal rights by declaring war (see *The Later Letters*, *CW*, XVI:1100).

261. For example, there is a current debate over the defensibility of any theory of rights such as Mill appears to have held—that a right is intended for the benefit of the rightholder. See the discussion of the issues involved in the editor's introduction to *Rights*, ed. David Lyons (Belmont, CA: Wadsworth Publishing Company, Inc., 1979), pp. 8–11. Mill discussed this matter, and the chief objection to the "beneficiary" theory in "Austin on Jurisprudence," *Dissertations and Discussions, Vol. III* (London: Longmans, Green, Reader, and Dyer, 1867), 229–231.

262. D. P. Dryer, "Mill's Utilitarianism," *CW*, X:ciii.

263. Anthony Quinton, *Utilitarian Ethics* (London: The Macmillan Press Ltd., 1973), p. 74. Others who have criticized Mill on similar grounds are: Lyons, *Rights*, p. 8; and David Miller, *Social Justice* (Oxford: Clarendon Press, 1976), pp. 57–58. Lyons argues that Mill was also mistaken in holding that all questions of justice and rights are interchangeable. A nasty person may deserve bad luck, but does not thereby have a right to it. I am not sure why this is relevant, since no questions of *duty* are involved; Mill's analysis of justice does not seem to be involved at all. Perhaps more importantly, Mill did *not* conflate statements about desert into statements about rights. Desert can be a *basis* for rights, but it does not follow that there is a right. His treatment of the Poor Laws, as discussed above, shows that *need* can also be a basis for rights. Again, he did not conflate the concepts. Miller concocts a case designed to show that failure to reward desert may be a wrong, but does not imply a right. He imagines a nurse who sacrifices years of her life caring for someone sick, but who gets no part of the inheritance when the person dies. The nurse is wronged because treated worse than she deserved, but she had no right to any of the inheritance. Though seductive, the example is not totally convincing. The full details may matter. On the one hand, the failure may be one of benevolence or gratitude. We should display benevolence to others, and especially toward those who help us. Thus, though the sick person *owed* the nurse nothing, though she had no moral *claim* on the deceased, the latter displayed an uncaring attitude in not writing her in for a share. However, the argument from *desert* is thus weakened, and the claim she was *wronged* is undercut *along with* the claim she had a right. On the other hand, if she literally *sacrificed* her life in care, and *devoted* her energies to the well-being of the other, who continued to accept the aid and succor, then a return (at least in gratitude) was owed. One can question if this need have been a share in the inheritance, but if that was the only appropriate response possible for the deceased, it becomes *far* more plausible to claim that not giving a share *wronged* the nurse. Consequently, as *that* becomes more plausible, it increases the plausibility of the claim that she had a *right* to it. Thus, to whatever extent it is plausible that it was *that* failure that wronged her, it is plausible that she had a right to the act omitted. I should also note that Mill held that gratitude *is* a duty of justice (*Utilitarianism*, p. 247).

264. *Logic*, p. 39.

265. Ibid., p. 151.

266. Rawls, *A Theory of Justice*, p. 31.

267. Ibid., p. 188. Rawls gives a more elaborate argument for this conclusion, based on an "impartial sympathetic spectator" interpretation of utilitarianism. I do not

believe any significant distortion of his view is introduced by my truncated summary, however.

268. Ibid., pp. 181—182.

269. Ibid., pp. 262—263.

270. For example, in summarizing his "ideal observor" argument that utilitarianism conflates all desires into one system, he says that the ideal spectator imagines himself with the various desires of the persons. Maximizing utility then becomes a matter of desire—or want-satisfaction; see *A Theory of Justice*, p. 27.

271. Ibid., pp. 395—587.

272. There are at least three ways these general facts of human nature are important to Rawls's own theory. In the "original position," those who are to select principles of justice to govern their institutions are ignorant of their own eventual place in the scheme, but they *do* know the general facts of human society, including the "basis of social organization and the laws of human psychology" (ibid., p. 137). Second, Rawls assumes there are certain "primary goods," i.e., "things that every rational man is presumed to want" (ibid., p. 62). These include rights and liberties, opportunities and powers, income and wealth, though one of the most important is a sense of one's own worth, or self-respect (ibid., p. 92, 397). In choosing principles, then, the persons in the "original position" will be concerned with safeguarding the primary goods such as liberty and self-respect, which, as rational people, it is supposed they are likely to want in society. In this respect, at least, Rawls's theory does *not* subordinate the theory of the good to the theory of the right. Finally, the principles of justice selected must be "stable" in the sense that people *can* come to desire to abide by them, and not generate "disruptive inclinations" (ibid., p. 454). To show his theory would be stable, he must appeal to facts about human nature, but this means that *his* theory is susceptible to undermining by a showing that he has got the "facts of human nature" wrong, just as is Mill's theory.

273. *Utilitarianism*, p. 232.

274. In writing on the subject of wealth in people, he stated: "In propriety of classification . . . the people of a country are not to be counted in its wealth. They are that for the sake of which its wealth exists. The term wealth is wanted to denote the desirable objects which they possess, not inclusive of, but in contradistinction to, their own persons" (*Principles of Political Economy*, *CW*, II:9).

275. Rawls, *A Theory of Justice*, pp. 181—182. I have throughout ignored possible complications engendered by Rawls's reference to "average" utility. In any event, he interprets Mill as an "average" utilitarian (ibid., p. 162).

276. Ibid., p. 182.

277. The extent to which Mill would have found Rawls's principles of justice acceptable, along with the priority ordering adopted by Rawls, is explored more extensively by Professor Bruce Russell in his doctoral dissertation. See Bruce Russell, "Rawls and Utilitarianism: A Comparison and Critique" (Ph.D. dissertation, University of California, Davis, 1977). The issues are also given careful consideration, in light of an interpretation of Mill very like the one I have given in this book, by Tim Roche.

See Timothy D. Roche, "Utilitarianism versus Rawls: Defending Teleological Theory," *Social Theory and Practice* 8 (Summer, 1982), 189—212. Despite the reservations I have indicated in the text, I have noted earlier that Mill appears to have accepted something like Rawls's second principle—the "difference" principle. *On Liberty* could be interpreted as an extended argument for something like Rawls's first principle, that guarantees the most extensive system of basic liberties for all. This is especially so if one emphasizes Mill's theory that *certain* things are crucial to human well-being. In addition, the "strategy" view of rules has aspects that are amenable to a hypothetical contract analysis; a passage in Mill cited in the previous chapter employs something like Rawls's "maximin" principle in the choice of rules—a guarantee that the worst possible results are avoided. ("We must seek our objects by means which may perhaps be defeated, and take precautions against dangers which possibly may never be realized" [*A System of Logic, CW*, VIII:898].) I shall also point out later some passages in which Mill appears to endorse the priority ordering between the two principles for which Rawls argues.

278. Rawls, *A Theory of Justice*, p. 25.

279. *Utilitarianism*, p. 246.

280. Ibid., pp. 247—248.

281. Ibid., p. 247.

282. Ibid.

283. Ibid., p. 246.

284. *Auguste Comte and Positivism*, p. 338.

285. *An Examination of Sir William Hamilton's Philosophy*, pp. 459—460.

286. David Lyons, "Benevolence and Justice in Mill," in *The Limits of Utilitarianism*, ed. Harlan B. Miller and William H. Williams (Minneapolis: University of Minnesota Press, 1982), p. 47.

287. Ibid.

288. Dryer, "Mill's Utilitarianism," p. xcix.

289. Ibid., p. c.

290. *The Later Letters, CW*, XVI:1319. I am not claiming that he *said* there that this is a duty of justice. The context leaves that point perfectly ambiguous. Moreover, in *Utilitarianism*, p. 259, he seems to be *contrasting* the duty to save a life with duties of justice, though that is not perfectly clear either. I am only claiming that this would be an enforceable duty owed a *particular* person, who would have ground for complaint, and that, given his analysis of rights, it would follow that there is a duty of justice.

291. *On Liberty*, p. 289.

292. Ibid.

293. *Principles of Political Economy, CW*, II:956—960.

294. *Utilitarianism*, p. 259.

295. I have made the same mistake, if it *is* a mistake, in claiming that the duty to show gratitude requires no particular acts; see Berger, "Gratitude," p. 306.

296. *The Later Letters, CW*, XVI:1319.

297. "Utility of Religion," *CW*, X:411.

298. *On Liberty*, p. 279.

299. Ibid.

300. "Thornton on Labour and Its Claims," pp. 659—660.

301. *Utilitarianism*, p. 259.

302. I should reiterate that I have accepted Lyons's claim that it is the *rights* criterion of perfect duties that is crucial. Lyons points out that though Mill did not accept that there are duties to oneself, the concept is not *logically* empty, but in such a case, there is no right involved. I am not sure that Mill would accept the conceptual possibility of *moral* duties to self, but he certainly *did* recognize that the *law* may impose them. In "Austin on Jurisprudence" (pp. 227—228), he contrasted "absolute" with "relative" duties. The former, he held (perhaps it was Austin's view; it is not entirely clear), do not have correlative rights; they are not to be done "towards or in respect to a definite person." There were three such duties given: duties to oneself, duties "towards persons indefinitely, or towards the sovereign or state," and duties to animals or religious duties. This may not, however, be the theory of perfect-imperfect duties in *Utilitarianism*, as *most* of the perfect duties of justice cited there are "towards persons indefinitely," in one sense of that expression.

5: The Theory of Freedom

1. John Stuart Mill, *Autobiography*, *CW*, I:259.

2. Among those who have contributed to this recent development in the Mill literature, I would cite J. C. Rees, Isaiah Berlin, Richard Wollheim, Alan Ryan, D. G. Brown, C. L. Ten, and John Gray. The latter two have produced book-length works that center on Mill's theory of liberty. See C. L. Ten, *Mill on Liberty* (Oxford: Clarendon Press, 1980); and John Gray, *Mill on liberty: a defence* (London: Routledge & Kegan Paul, 1983). There is much to commend in Gray's book, but I especially recommend his discussion of Mill's theory of individuality and autonomy in chapter 4. His interpretation of Mill parallels my own, but I think he advances it in important ways.

I also believe that Joel Feinberg's discussions of Millean themes have helped clarify the relevant issues. See, especially, the first four chapters of his book, *Social Philosophy* (Englewood Cliffs, NJ: Prentice-Hall, Inc., 1973).

3. Maurice Cowling, *Mill and Liberalism* (Cambridge: Cambridge University Press, 1963). Illiberal themes in Mill are also stressed by Shirley Letvin in *The Pursuit of Certainty* (Cambridge: Cambridge University Press, 1965).

4. Gertrude Himmelfarb, *On Liberty and Liberalism: The Case of John Stuart Mill* (New York: Alfred A. Knopf, 1974). p. 91; also "Introduction," in *Essays on Politics and Culture*, ed. G. Himmelfarb (Garden City, NY: Doubleday & Company, Inc., 1963). She also maintains that *On Liberty* is at great variance with the bulk of his moral and political philosophy. As should be obvious from the chief arguments of this book, I believe this claim to be seriously mistaken.

5. See, for example, George H. Sabine, *A History of Political Theory*, (3d ed. rev.; London: George G. Harrop, 1963), pp. 705—715.

6. C. L. Ten, in *Mill on Liberty*, is especially effective. Cowling is also effectively criticized in Graeme Duncan, *Marx and Mill: Two Views of Social Conflict and Social Harmony* (Cambridge: Cambridge University Press, 1973), pp. 276–280. Useful criticisms of Himmelfarb are to be found in Ronald Dworkin, *Taking Rights Seriously* (Cambridge, Mass.: Harvard University Press, 1977), chap. 11.

7. *On Liberty*, *CW*, XVIII:219.

8. Ibid., p. 220.

9. Ibid., p. 221.

10. Ibid., p. 222.

11. Ibid., p. 220.

12. *Autobiography*, p. 259.

13. Ibid., p. 260.

14. See, for example, Richard Taylor, *Freedom, Anarchy, and the Law* (Englewood Cliffs, NJ: Prentice-Hall, Inc., 1973), p. 60.

15. *Utilitarianism*, *CW*, X:212.

16. Ibid., p. 255.

17. *On Liberty*, p. 224. The People's Edition has the sentence read "of a man," rather than "of man" as in the final Library Edition (see "Textual Introduction," *CW*, XVIII:lxxxv). This alternative reading has been made much of by some philosophers unaware of the Library Edition version. Rawls, for example, cites the definite article as showing that Mill did not have in mind the historical development of mankind (see John Rawls, *A Theory of Justice* [Cambridge, Mass.: Harvard University Press, 1971], p. 209n). If the interpretation I give is correct, Rawls is wrong here; although for Mill, it would not matter a great deal *which* formulation is employed.

18. *On Liberty*, p. 260. See, also, his views on "solicitation" for gambling, prostitution, etc., ibid., pp. 296–297.

19. Ibid., p. 226, 299–301.

20. Ibid., p. 260.

21. R. P. Anschutz, *The Philosophy of J. S. Mill* (London: Oxford University Press, 1963), p. 25.

22. Ibid., p. 24, 26–27. Richard Arneson makes a similar claim, and concludes that "Mill clearly has in mind a variety of ill-sorted-out ideals." See Richard J. Arneson, "Mill versus Paternalism," *Ethics* 90 (July, 1980), 480. At least one of the three that Arneson picks out seems to me *not* a conception of individuality at all, and he makes no attempt to see if there *is* a conception of individuality or self-development of which the various characterizations Mill gave are an aspect.

23. *Autobiography*, p. 260.

24. *On Liberty*, p. 267.

25. In a letter to a French law professor, he referred to the central principle of the book as that of the autonomy of the individual ("celui de l'autonomie de l'individu"). See "Letter to Emile Acollas," in *The Later Letters*, *CW*, XVII:1831–1832.

26. *On Liberty*, p. 261.

27. Ibid.

28. Ibid., pp. 264–265.

29. See, for example, Herbert Marcuse, *One Dimensional Man: Studies in the Ideology of Advanced Industrial Society* (Boston: Beacon Press, 1964); and "Repressive Tolerance," in R. P. Wolff, B. Moore, and H. Marcuse, eds., *A Critique of Pure Tolerance* (Boston: Beacon Press, 1965), pp. 81–123.

30. *On Liberty*, p. 270.

31. Ibid., p. 262.

32. *CW*, X:212.

33. Arneson refers to this passage as picking out a *separate* conception of individuality that contrasts with "mediocrity." It is hard to see the motivation for this, since Mill gave no reason to think this, nor does there seem to be any ordinary notion of individuality with that meaning (see Arneson, "Mill versus Paternalism," p. 479). Robert Ladenson is led to conclude that for Mill, the development of individuality just is the cultivation of reason (see Robert F. Ladenson, "Mill's Conception of Individuality," *Social Theory and Practice* 4 [Spring, 1977], 167–182.) If the account in my text is correct, this confuses a *condition* for being and acting autonomously, and a *result* of being autonomous with individuality itself. To *be* individual requires the use of these faculties, and living an autonomous life further develops them. Moreover, Ladenson's claim would leave out as important in itself the development of what is unique to the individual. It seems clear, however, that Mill *did* think that development of the *individual's* nature is requisite to happiness, and *did* think of this as central to his doctrine of individuality.

34. *On Liberty*, p. 263.

35. "De Tocqueville on Democracy in America [II]," *CW*, XVIII:169.

36. *Considerations on Representative Government*, *CW*, XIX:403.

37. Arneson, for example, contrasts a version of autonomy that he attributes to Mill with "autonomy as a character ideal, something that persons might achieve or fail to achieve." Such an ideal would be part of the tradition he says stems from Rousseau and Kant that regards a person as autonomous if the person's behavior conforms to self-chosen laws or principles. Arneson correctly notes that such an ideal can be achieved even by a person straightjacketed and in prison (see Arneson, "Mill versus Paternalism," p. 475). While this seems right to me, all that appears to follow is that Mill's conception of autonomy is not exhausted by *that* character-ideal. I shall discuss Arneson's notion of autonomy later, for, though I am not convinced it was Mill's, I do not think Mill would have been inconsistent to adopt it.

38. *On Liberty*, p. 264.

39. In this connection, I note that Bain criticized Mill for not taking sufficient account of differences among people's happiness, and he held that Mill had overestimated the role of "energetic" character (see Alexander Bain, *John Stuart Mill. A Criticism: With Personal Recollections* [London: Longmans, Green, and Co., 1882], p. 107).

40. "Civilization," *CW*, XVIII:121–126.

41. "Thoughts on Parliamentary Reform," *CW*, XIX:335.

42. It is of some interest to compare Mill's account with that of a contemporary philosopher. See Sharon Bishop Hill, "Self-Determination and Autonomy," in *Today's Moral Problems*, 2d ed., ed. Richard Wasserstrom (New York: Macmillan Publishing Co., Inc., 1979), pp. 118–133. The argument of the essay that the right of self-determination implies that women not be given restrictive sex-role training in youth is implicit in Mill's conception of the right of autonomy.

43. *The Subjection of Women*, in *Essays on Sex Equality*, ed. Alice S. Rossi (Chicago: The University of Chicago Press, 1970), p. 222.

While I do not want to repeat the arguments given in chapter 4 for the claim of a mutual implication of freedom and equality, the claim has generated reactions of surprise at this point in the text, so further comment is in order. I note first that the theme of an interconnection has become common in liberal thought. Ronald Dworkin, for example, argues that equality—the right to equal concern and respect—implies the right to basic liberties (see Ronald Dworkin, *Taking Rights Seriously*, esp. chap. 12). Amy Gutmann, on the other hand, has recently argued that freedom cannot be achieved without equality (see Amy Gutmann, *Liberal Equality* [Cambridge: Cambridge University Press, 1980], pp. 9–10). The theme should not arouse surprise, then; respectable arguments for it have been given by others, in addition to Mill.

Richard Arneson has objected that a powerful monarch who does not exercise that power and respects and encourages his citizens' autonomy has unequal status, but that this does not interfere with their autonomy. I am not sure that some imaginable counterexamples undercut the *general* theme, anyway, but this case seems to me to reinforce the theme. The autonomy of the citizens is preserved by the monarch *not* exercising his power, i.e., by his treating the citizens *as* moral equals. Further, to the extent that his legal status looms in the background to be invoked, they must always act in fear of provoking his paternalistic powers, and that does interfere with their free choice.

44. Ibid., pp. 235–239.

45. Ibid., p. 173. In chapter 4, I quoted a passage from his essay "Centralisation," that also makes the point that through its opposition to the "love of power over others," liberty implies status as equals (see "Centralisation," *CW*, XIX:610–611).

46. *On Liberty*, pp. 223–224.

47. Ibid., pp. 224–225.

48. Ibid., p. 292. Professor Himmelfarb has made much of the (alleged) fact that Mill was seeking a "single, simple, and absolute" principle to govern social life, when the rest of his philosophy sought to eschew such a simplistic devotion to any one end, even freedom (see Himmelfarb, *On Liberty and Liberalism*, esp. chap. 1, "One Very Simple Principle"). In light of the implicit and explicit evidence that Mill did not think of his doctrine as *that* singular, simple, or absolute, he would have done better to have avoided the overstated language of the passage that has so captured Professor Himmelfarb's attention.

49. I take it that this is the implicit claim of Lord Devlin in his essay on "Morals and the Criminal Law" (see Patrick Devlin, *The Enforcement of Morals* [London: Oxford University Press, 1965], p. 14).

50. Ten, *Mill on Liberty*, chap. 2.

51. *On Liberty*, p. 281.

52. Ibid., pp. 283–284.

53. Ibid., p. 283.

54. Devlin, *The Enforcement of Morals*, p. 14.

55. David A. Conway, "Law, Liberty and Indecency," *Philosophy* 49 (April, 1974), pp. 135–147.

56. The work criticized is H. L. A. Hart, *Law, Liberty, and Morality* (New York: Random House, 1966).

57. Conway, "Law, Liberty and Indecency," p. 143.

58. Ibid., p. 143n.

59. Ten, *Mill on Liberty*, p. 27.

60. *On Liberty*, p. 283.

61. I am a bit unclear as to what extent Professor Ten would accept my two-part account as answering the objection that he posed in the earlier quotation. In a later section of his book, he discusses the utilitarian theories of Professors Sartorius and Hare that are similar in important ways to the "strategy" conception of rules I have attributed to Mill. He criticizes their theories on the grounds that rules so conceived can establish only rebuttable presumptions. He then adds that the assumption that Mill was being consistently utilitarian in adopting the principle of liberty is itself questionable, for, "by excluding some pleasures and pains, and some satisfactions, as irrelevant, Mill altered the content of the notion of utility or happiness" (Ten, *Mill on Liberty*, p. 39). Thus, Ten held, it must be shown further that this conception is genuinely utilitarian. In a later chapter, he considers a theory of happiness like the one I attribute to Mill, and I find it unclear whether he accepts or rejects the theory as genuinely "utilitarian." Since the last part of his chapter appears to outline and develop further a conception I find indistinguishable from the one I think Mill held, I am inclined to think that Ten would find my defense acceptable (see Ten, *Mill on Liberty*, chap. 5).

62. I shall not be concerned with the claim of Professor Ronald Dworkin that certain kinds of preferences of people cannot be consistently considered at all by the utilitarian. He distinguishes "personal" preferences for a person's own enjoyment of goods and opportunities from "external" preferences for providing goods and opportunities to others. He argues that utilitarianism is indefensible if external preferences are counted at all (Dworkin, *Taking Rights Seriously*, pp. 234–238). Mill *did* rule out *certain* external preferences; his prohibition against consideration of indirect effects entails the rejection of associated preferences people may have; but he would surely *permit* consideration of *other* kinds of external preferences. I cannot see, however, that Dworkin's arguments show anything more than that *some* external preferences cannot be considered. The argument for the stronger claim seems to me defective, and to have been decisively shown to be so by H. L. A. Hart (see H. L. A. Hart, "Between Utility and Rights," 79 *Columbia Law Rev.* 828–846 [1979]). I also believe the criticisms given by Professor Ten are effective (Ten, *Mill on Liberty*, pp. 30–33).

63. *On Liberty*, p. 283ff.

64. Ibid., pp. 292–293.

65. The literature on this issue is voluminous. Two of the more important sources to consult are: Isaiah Berlin, *Four Essays on Liberty* (London: Oxford University Press, 1969); and Gerald C. MacCallum, Jr., "Negative and Positive Freedom," *The Philosophical Review* 76 (1967), 312–334. Other useful discussions are to be found in: Feinberg, *Social Philosophy*, chap. 1; C. B. Macpherson, *Democratic Theory: Essays in Retrieval* (Oxford: Clarendon Press, 1973), chap. 5; and William A. Parent, "Some Recent Work on the Concept of Liberty," *American Philosophical Quarterly* 11 (July, 1974), 149–167.

66. *On Liberty*, p. 294.

67. Ibid., p. 293.

68. One place where this seems especially convincing is in *The Subjection of Women*, in a passage in which he contrasted the "love of freedom" of the ancients and in the Middle Ages that consisted in a sense of "the dignity and importance" of one's own person, with his conception of a freedom grounded in "a cultivated sympathy" among all. The former conception is consistent with dominating others, whereas the latter conception is that of self-developed equals (see *The Subjection of Women*, pp. 173–175). While Mill *did* seem to regard these as competing conceptions of *freedom*, it is not clear he was right in this regard, or that he consistently thought in these terms. It is also of some interest to note that he also recognized *as* a conception of freedom that which defines freedom as consisting in the attainment of human perfection—a conception insisted on by *some* advocates of positive freedom (see *An Examination of Sir William Hamilton's Philosophy*, *CW*, IX:458; in a footnote, he quotes a paper by M. Albert Reville: "La liberté, complète, réelle, de l'homme, est la perfection humaine, le but à atteindre"). There is no reason to think, however, that Mill accepted this conception.

69. Dworkin, *Taking Rights Seriously*, pp. 268 ff.

70. *Principles of Political Economy*, *CW*, III, 937–939.

71. H. L. A. Hart, for example, wrote: "Is the fact that certain conduct is by common standards immoral sufficient to justify making that conduct punishable by law? Is it morally permissible to enforce morality as such? Ought immorality as such to be a crime? . . . To this question John Stuart Mill gave an emphatic negative answer in his essay *On Liberty* one hundred years ago" (Hart, *Law, Liberty, and Morality*, p. 4).

72. D. G. Brown, "Mill on Liberty and Morality," *The Philosophical Review*, 81 (April, 1972), 133–158.

73. *On Liberty*, pp. 224–225.

74. Brown, "Mill on Liberty and Morality," pp. 145–146.

75. David Lyons, "Liberty and Harm to Others," in *New Essays on John Stuart Mill and Utilitarianism*, *Canadian Journal of Philosophy*, Suppl. Vol. V (1979), 1–19.

76. Ibid., p. 6.

77. Ibid., p. 11.

78. *On Liberty*, p. 224. Mill wrote that it must be "calculated" to produce evil, and some readers have thought Mill meant that it must have been *intended* to cause harm, but this hardly seems the right reading. It is more likely that he meant that after calculating the good and bad effects, the score comes out in favor of bad ones.

79. Mill's discussion is in *Utilitarianism*, pp. 248–256.

80. *On Liberty*, p. 276.

81. *An Examination of Sir William Hamilton's Philosophy*, p. 459 n. I am not sure to what extent this sort of point counts against Brown's claim, as his formulation of the Principle of Enforcing Morality contains two "prima facie" clauses, one after "ought" and one before "morally wrong." He does, however, explain the principle as follows, making it vulnerable to my objection: "The principle relates prima-facie judgments, and says in effect that the moral grounds for interfering with the liberty of action of the individual are precisely the same sorts of thing as tend to make his conduct wrong" (Brown, "Mill on Liberty and Morality," p. 148).

82. *On Liberty*, p. 299.

83. David Copp, "The Iterated-Utilitarianism of J. S. Mill," in *New Essays on John Stuart Mill and Utilitarianism*, *Canadian Journal of Philosophy*, Suppl. Vol. V (1979), 75—98. The relevant passage in Mill is in *Utilitarianism*, p. 246.

84. Copp does acknowledge a passage in J. S. Mill's footnotes to his edition of his father's *Analysis of the Phenomena of the Human Mind*, in which he summarized his conception of moral duty without mentioning conscience. He remarks that "what is said in *Utilitarianism* must take priority over what is said in a note to someone else's work" (see Copp, "The Iterated-Utilitarianism of J. S. Mill," p. 87 n.). However, it *is* intended as a summary of the theory in that work, and the fact that it was in a footnote does not seem important, since *all* of J. S. Mill's views were expressed in the footnotes (and the Preface) of that book. Furthermore, the surrounding passages in *Utilitarianism* suggest that he thought a violation of moral duty always *deserves* social punishment, even if it is not expedient to apply it in the particular case.

85. Devlin, *The Enforcement of Morals*, chap. 1.

86. Ibid., p. 17.

87. Ibid., p. 15.

88. See, for example, the essays in Richard A. Wasserstrom, ed., *Morality and the Law* (Belmont, CA: Wadsworth Publishing Company, Inc., 1971).

89. Hart, *Law, Liberty, and Morality*, p. 50.

90. Devlin made two points in response to Hart. The first was that he did not mean that *any* deviation from the moral code threatens a society's existence, only that deviations *can* do so, just as not every treasonable act in fact poses a real threat. His second point was that whether or not a society has disappeared is a matter of the degree of change that takes place. This is consistent with holding that a society *can* undergo *some* change; of course, *if* it does, the law can change also (Devlin, *The Enforcement of Morals*, pp. 13—14n). The first point, especially with its analogy to treason, suggests that it is the social disorder conception of "disintegration" he had in mind, whereas the second point seems to presuppose that the existence of a society is identified with the existence of a given moral code, with there being a range of variation before one can say *that* society no longer exists. However, this latter conception of "disintegration" still trivializes the connection between a change in the moral code and the disintegration of society. Devlin simply reasserted the two versions of the thesis that his original statements ambiguously suggested.

91. Devlin, *The Enforcement of Morals*, p. ix.

92. Ibid., p. 111. Later, he concludes that the line between acceptable and improper intervention cannot be drawn by the private-public distinction. It is a matter of what can safely be tolerated, public or private, and this may vary with circumstances (ibid., p. 113).

93. *On Liberty*, p. 295.

94. Ibid., p. 294–295.

95. Ibid., p. 294.

96. Ibid. Note that it was a bridge declared unsafe, not one that was *missing*. There is a *danger* of falling in, not a certainty.

97. It must be noted, however, that his position on the *taxation* of such articles appears to be inconsistent with this interpretation (and every other one I have seen). Mill conceded that taxing a product in order to make it less accessible to those who desire it is different only in degree from outright prohibition. However, taxation for revenue purposes is necessary to government, and what is taxed will inevitably result in making the product less accessible to some. It thus becomes the *duty* of the state to judge what things people can best spare, and "to select in preference those of which it deems the use, beyond a very moderate quantity, to be positively injurious" (*On Liberty*, p. 298). So long as the state needs the revenue, it can thus tax at whatever level is otherwise justified.

98. *On Liberty*, p. 298.

99. Ibid., p. 300.

100. Gerald Dworkin, "Paternalism," in Wasserstrom, ed., *Morality and the Law*, pp. 107–126.

101. Joel Feinberg, "Legal Paternalism," *Canadian Journal of Philosophy*, 1 (1971), 105–124.

102. John D. Hodson, "The Principle of Paternalism," *American Philosophical Quarterly* 14 (January, 1977), 61–69.

103. Arneson, "Mill versus Paternalism," p. 474.

104. Hodson, "The Principle of Paternalism," pp. 65–66.

105. Arneson, "Mill versus Paternalism," p. 475.

106. Ibid., p. 482.

107. *On Liberty*, p. 299. Hodson's position is argued for in "Mill, Paternalism, and Slavery," *Analysis* 41 (January, 1981), 60–62. I have not taken up some of his detailed arguments, as they seem to me to confuse the question of whether the state's refusal to enforce a contract or relationship is an interference with freedom, and the different question of whether people have a *right* to *have* the state provide enforced statuses or contracts of certain kinds. His *main* point is that the state *merely* refuses enforcement, thus not requiring behavior of people. The argument of the text attacks that point.

108. "Civilization," p. 122; and *Considerations on Representative Government*, pp. 394–396.

109. *On Liberty*, p. 224.

110. Ibid., p. 294.

111. Ibid., pp. 299–300.

112. Ibid., p. 291. Mill's *general* position was that irrevocable contracts (contracts "in perpetuity") should not be permitted, ranging from the marriage contract to employment contracts. Part of Mill's argument was that people may *not* know what is best for themselves in the long run, especially when they lack experience and are incompetent to judge (see *Principles of Political Economy*, pp. 953–954). Arneson holds that Mill has here permitted the state to overrule the individual's own judgment on the grounds that the state is more competent (Arneson, "Mill versus Paternalism," p. 486). However, this is not clearly the case, as all that Mill seems concerned with is that agreements in these cases be limited in *time*, allowing the parties to revoke the agreement if they choose later, but, presumably, to continue or renew them if they choose. I note also that Mill's condemnation of the treatment of Mormons shows that he recognized that the state, in refusing to recognize their marriage contracts, does *not* simply stand by; that it is committed to acting *against* their practices.

113. An extremely useful exchange on Mill's theory is found in H. J. McCloskey, "Liberty of Expression: Its Grounds and Limits (I)," *Inquiry* 13 (Autumn, 1970), 219–237; and D. H. Monro, "Liberty of Expression: Its Grounds and Limits (II)," *Inquiry* 13 (Autumn, 1970), 238–253. These essays are reprinted in my book, *Freedom of Expression* (Belmont, CA: Wadsworth Publishing Co., 1980). McCloskey presents a critical view, countered by Monro, that stresses the "strategic" elements in Mill's theory.

114. C. L. Ten, *Mill on Liberty*, p. 127.

115. Ibid., p. 130.

116. *On Liberty*, p. 243.

117. Ibid.

118. Ronald Dworkin has argued that freedom of expression is grounded in the right of all persons to be treated as equals, and he thinks that a suitably restricted version of utilitarianism (which he thinks was Mill's in *On Liberty*) can be made consistent with this approach (see "What Rights Do We Have," in *Taking Rights Seriously*; the essay is reprinted in *Freedom of Expression*, pp. 71–81). While I do not think Mill's theory was restricted in quite the way Dworkin suggests, it does seem to be restricted in ways that meet Dworkin's arguments against an unrestricted view (Mill *did* rule out consideration of *certain* kinds of "external preferences"). Furthermore, if I am correct in assuming that being self-determining for Mill requires status as equals, then the right of self-determination would be consistent with deriving *a* ground for freedom of expression from a right to status as equals. *That* right, however, could, in turn, have part of its basis in the right to be self-determining. (It had an independent status also for Mill, as I argued in the last chapter.)

119. To a limited extent, I have given a Millean argument against censorship of poronography in my essay, "Pornography, Sex, and Censorship," in *Social Theory and Practice* 4 (Spring, 1977), 183–209.

120. *Utilitarianism*, p. 231.

121. "Utility of Religion," *CW*, X:410.

122. Ibid., pp. 410–411.

123. *On Liberty*, p. 282.

124. Ibid., pp. 282–283.

125. "Utility of Religion," p. 411.

126. *On Liberty*, p. 241.

127. "De Tocqueville on Democracy in America [II]," p. 177.

6: A Critical Assessment

1. "Utilitarianism," p. 208.

2. Ibid., p. 207. Mill claimed that Kant had failed to show any contradiction in rational people adopting "the most outrageously immoral rules of conduct," and that he had only shown that the *consequences* of their adoption would be so bad no one would choose to do so. Since Kant (and many other philosophers) thought he had done something else, a detailed attack would be needed. Moreover, Mill did not ever acknowledge either Kant's grounds for claiming that morality *must* be based in *a priori* concepts of pure reason, or his arguments against a teleological basis for ethics.

3. There is *some* discussion in *A System of Logic* of the role of analytic considerations in a philosophical theory in general (see bk. 4, chap. 4, "Of the Requisites of a Philosophical Language, and the Principles of Definition," in *CW*, VIII:668–685).

4. *The Later Letters*, *CW*, XV:751.

5. R. M. Hare, *Freedom and Reason* (New York: Oxford University Press, 1965), pp. 113–136.

6. *Utilitarianism*, p. 217.

7. "Utility of Religion," p. 409.

8. *On Liberty*, p. 262.

9. John Gray first pointed this out to me.

10. The distinction derives from Brian Barry, *Political Argument* (London: Routledge & Kegan Paul, 1965), pp. 38–41. I have not used the terms in precisely the way Barry does; this is of little consequence for present purposes, however.

11. *On Liberty*, p. 224.

12. "The Claims of Labour," *CW*, IV:375.

13. "Vindication of the French Revolution of February 1948, in Reply to Lord Brougham and Others," in *Dissertations and Discussions*, Vol. II (London: John W. Parker and Son, 1859), 398.

14. *Considerations on Representative Government*, *CW*, XIX:445.

15. The chief exception is his essay "Use and Abuse of Political Terms," *CW*, XVIII:1–13; but this discussion is also incomplete, and it is not clear it is entirely consistent with his general theory of rights in *Utilitarianism*.

16. *On Liberty*, p. 276.

17. *Utilitarianism*, p. 212.

18. *Autobiography*, *CW*, I:147.

19. "On Marriage and Divorce," in *Essays on Sex Equality*, ed. by Alice S. Rossi (Chicago: The University of Chicago Press, 1970), p. 69.

20. David Lyons, "Liberty and Harm to Others," in *New Essays on John Stuart Mill and Utilitarianism*, *Canadian Journal of Philosophy*, Suppl. Vol. V (1979), 14.

21. *On Liberty*, p. 276.

22. Ibid., p. 225.

23. "Auguste Comte and Positivism," *CW*, X:338.

24. *On Liberty*, p. 289. Also, *Principles of Political Economy*, *CW*, III:956—958.

25. *On Liberty*, p. 289.

26. Paris Adult Theatre I v. Slaton, 413 U.S. 49 (1973). Bickel's quote is from "On Pornography: II—Dissenting and Concurring Opinions," *The Public Interest*, 22 (Winter, 1971), 25—26.

27. For an important critical discussion of this notion, see Samuel Scheffler, *The Rejection of Consequentialism: A Philosophical Investigation of the Considerations Underlying Rival Moral Conceptions* (Oxford: Clarendon Press, 1982). This interesting book became available to me too late to be able to take account of it in the present text.

28. See the contribution of Bernard Williams in J. J. C. Smart and Bernard Williams, *Utilitarianism: For and Against* (Cambridge: Cambridge University Press, 1973).

29. See my essays, "Gratitude," *Ethics* 85 (July, 1975), 298—309; and "Love, Friendship, and Utility: On Practical Reason and Reductionism," in *Human Nature and Natural Knowledge*, ed. A. Donagan, A. Perovich, and M. Wedin (forthcoming).

30. See John C. Harsanyi, "Morality and the Theory of Rational Behaviour," *Social Research* 4 (Winter, 1977), 625—656; and Amartya Sen, "Utilitarianism and Welfarism," *Journal of Philosophy* 76 (September, 1979), 463—489. (Harsanyi's essay is reprinted in the volume cited in n. 31 below.)

31. Amartya Sen and Bernard Williams, eds., *Utilitarianism and Beyond* (Cambridge: Cambridge University Press, 1982), p. 13. This collection of essays became available too late to take account of in the present text.

32. Amartya Sen, "Rights and Agency," *Philosophy and Public Affairs* 11 (Winter, 1982), 3—39.

33. Sen is clearly aware of the broader current usage among philosophers of the term "utilitarianism." He cites David Lyons as one who holds such an interpretation (corresponding with my own; see "Utilitarianism and Welfare," p. 463). That two *distinct* usages are becoming hardened in the writings in the field is a matter to be regretted.

34. I have in mind especially the University of Oxford thesis of Mr. Jon Riley, a student of Amartya Sen and John Gray, on "Collective Choice and Individual Liberty: A Revisionist Interpretation of J. S. Mill's Utilitarianism" (1983). I hope that this work

will be made available in more accessible form, and I am grateful to Mr. Riley for allowing me to read it in manuscript form.

35. A recent, important book that seeks to grapple with this problem, and which is inspired in part by Mill's views, is Amy Gutmann, *Liberal Equality* (Cambridge: Cambridge University Press, 1980).

36. Rawls, who interprets Mill accurately but defines "utilitarianism" narrowly, regards Mill as a liberal, but *not* as a utilitarian (see John Rawls, "Social Unity and Primary Goods," in *Utilitarianism and Beyond*, pp. 159–185).

BIBLIOGRAPHY

This list includes only works cited in the text, in the editions used there. More complete bibliographies are to be found in *Bibliography of the Published Writings of John Stuart Mill*, ed. Ney Mac Minn, J. R. Hainds; and James McCrimmon (Evanston, Ill.: Northwestern University Press, 1945); and in each issue of *The Mill News Letter* (Toronto: Toronto University Press, 1965—).

The listings of Mill's works refer to the *Collected Works* (abbreviated as *CW*), under the general editorship of John M. Robson, published by the University of Toronto Press, 1963—, and, in the remainder of the British Commonwealth, by Routledge and Kegan Paul.

The complete titles for the volumes in the *Collected Works* are as follows:

Vol. I: *Autobiography and Literary Essays*, ed. John M. Robson and Jack Stillinger.

Vols. II, III: *Principles of Political Economy: With Some of Their Applications to Social Philosophy*, ed. John M. Robson.

Vols. IV, V: *Essays on Economics and Society*, ed. John M. Robson.

Vols. VII, VIII: *A System of Logic: Ratiocinative and Inductive*, ed. John M. Robson.

Vol. IX: *An Examination of Sir William Hamilton's Philosophy and The Principle Philosophical Questions Discussed in his Writings*, ed. John M. Robson.

Vol. X: *Essays on Ethics, Religion and Society*, ed. John M. Robson.

Vol. XI: *Essays on Philosophy and the Classics*, ed. John M. Robson.

Vols. XII, XIII: *The Earlier Letters, 1812–1848*, ed. Francis E. Mineka.

Vols. XIV, XV, XVI, XVII: *The Later Letters, 1849–1873*, ed. Francis E. Mineka.
Vols. XVIII, XIX: *Essays on Politics and Society*, ed. John M. Robson.

WORKS OF MILL

Auguste Comte and Positivism. In *CW*, X:261–368.
Autobiography. In *CW*, I:1–290.
"Bain's Psychology." In *CW*, XI:339–373.
"Bentham," in *CW*, X:75–115.
"Blakey's History of Moral Science," in *CW*, X:19–29.
"Carlyle's *French Revolution*," in *Mill's Essays on Literature and Society*, ed. J. B. Schneewind. New York: The Macmillan Company, 1965. Pp. 183–206.
"Centralisation," in *CW*, XIX:579–613.
"Chapters on Socialism," in *CW*, V:703–753.
"Civilization." In *CW*, XVIII:117–147.
"Coleridge." In *CW*, X:117–163.
Considerations on Representative Government. In *CW*, XIX:371–577.
Dissertations and Discussions. 4 vols. London: Longmans, Green, Reader, and Dyer, 1859, 1867, and 1875.
The Earlier Letters of John Stuart Mill, 1812–1848. *CW*, XII, XIII.
Essays on Some Unsettled Questions of Political Economy. In *CW*, IV:229–339.
An Examination of Sir William Hamilton's Philosophy. *CW*, IX.
"The Gorgias." In *CW*, XI:97–150.
The Later Letters of John Stuart Mill, 1849–1873. *CW*, XIV–XVII.
"Nature." In *Three Essays on Religion*. *CW*, X:373–402.
On Liberty. In *CW*, XVIII:213–310.
"On Marriage and Divorce." In *Essays on Sex Equality*, ed. Alice S. Rossi. Chicago: The University of Chicago Press, 1970. Pp. 67–87.
"On Punishment." *Monthly Repository* 8 (1834), 734–736.
"Recent Writers on Reform." In *CW*, XIX:341–370.
"Remarks on Bentham's Philosophy." In *CW*, X:3–18.
"The Savings of the Middle and Working Classes." In *CW*, V:405–429.
"Sedgwick's Discourse." In *CW*, X:31–74.
"The Spirit of the Age." In *Essays on Politics and Culture*, ed. Gertrude Himmelfarb. Garden City, NY: Doubleday & Company, Inc., 1962. Pp. 1–44.

"The Subjection of Women." In *Essays on Sex Equality*, ed. Alice S. Rossi. Chicago: The University of Chicago Press, 1970. Pp. 123–242.

A System of Logic: Ratiocinative and Inductive. CW, VII, VIII.

"Taylor's Statesman" (co-authored with George Grote). In *CW*, XIX: 617–647.

"Thornton on Labour and Its Claims." In *CW*, V:631–668.

"Thoughts on Parliamentary Reform." In *CW*, XIX:311–339.

Three Essays on Religion. In *CW*, X:369–489.

"De Tocqueville on Democracy in America [I]." In *CW*, XVIII:47–90.

"De Tocqueville on Democracy in America [II]." In *CW*, XVIII: 153–204.

"Use and Abuse of Political Terms." In *CW*, XVIII:1–13.

Utilitarianism, in *CW*, X:203–259.

"Utility of Religion." In *Three Essays on Religion. CW*, X:403–428.

"Vindication of the French Revolution of February 1848, in Reply to Lord Brougham and Others." In *Dissertations and Discussions*, Vol. II. London: John W. Parker and Son, 1859:335–410.

"Whewell on Moral Philosophy," in *CW*, X:165–201.

OTHER WORKS CITED

Albee, Ernest. *A History of English Utilitarianism*. London: George Allen and Unwin Ltd., 1957 (1st ed. 1901).

Annas, Julia. "Mill and the Subjection of Women," *Philosophy* 52 (1977), 179–194.

Anschutz, R. P. *The Philosophy of J. S. Mill*. London: Oxford University Press, 1963.

Aristotle, *Nichomachean Ethics*.

Arneson, Richard J. "Mill versus Paternalism." *Ethics* 90 (July, 1980), 470–489.

August, Eugene. *John Stuart Mill: A Mind at Large*. New York: Charles Scribner's Sons, 1975.

Austin, John. *The Province of Jurisprudence Determined and The Uses of the Study of Jurisprudence*, ed. H. L. A. Hart. London: Weidenfeld and Nicolson, 1954.

Ayer, A. J. *Language, Truth and Logic*. 2d ed. New York: Dover Publications, Inc., 1946.

Bain, Alexander. *John Stuart Mill. A Criticism: With Personal Recollections*. London: Longmans, Green, and Co., 1882.

Baker, John M. *"Utilitarianism* and 'Secondary Principles.' " *The Philosophical Quarterly* 21 (1971), 69–71.

Barry, Brian. *Political Argument*. London: Routledge & Kegan Paul, 1965.

Becker, Lawrence C. "The Obligation to Work." *Ethics* 90 (October, 1980), 35–49.

Bentham, Jeremy. *A Fragment on Government and An Introduction to the Principles of Morals and Legislation*, ed. Wilfred Harrison. Oxford: Basil Blackwell, 1960.

Berger, Fred R., ed. *Freedom of Expression*. Belmont, CA.: Wadsworth Publishing Co., 1980.

———. "Gratitude." *Ethics* 85 (July, 1975), 298–309.

———. "John Stuart Mill on Justice and Fairness." In *New Essays on John Stuart Mill and Utilitarianism. Canadian Journal of Philosophy*. Suppl. Vol. V (Ontario, 1979), 115–136.

———. "Love, Friendship and Utility: On Practical Reason and Reductionism." In *Human Nature and Natural Knowledge*, ed. A. Donagan, A. Perovich, and M. Wedin. Forthcoming.

———. "Mill's Concept of Happiness." *Interpretation* 7 (Fall, 1978), 95–117.

———. "Mill's Substantive Principles of Justice: A Comparison with Nozick." *American Philosophical Quarterly* 19 (October, 1982), 373–380.

———. "Pornography, Sex, and Censorship." *Social Theory and Practice* 4 (Spring, 1977), 183–209.

———. Review of *John Stuart Mill and Representative Government. The Philosophical Review* 87 (April, 1978), 322–325.

Berlin, Isaiah. *Four Essays on Liberty*. London: Oxford University Press, 1969.

Bickel, Alexander. "On Pornography: II—Dissenting and Concurring Opinions." *The Public Interest* 22 (Winter, 1971), 25–26.

Bradley, F. H. *Ethical Studies*. 2d ed., rev. London: Oxford University Press, 1927.

Brown, D. G. "Mill on Liberty and Morality." *The Philosophical Review* 81 (April, 1972), 133–158.

———. "Mill's Act-Utilitarianism." *Philosophical Quarterly* 24 (1974), 67–68.

———. "What is Mill's Principle of Utility?" *Canadian Journal of Philosophy* 3 (September, 1973), 1–12.

Brownmiller, Susan. "Introduction." In *On the Subjection of Women*.

Greenwich, Conn.: Fawcett Publications, Inc., 1971. Pp. 5–11.

Conway, David A. "Law, Liberty and Indecency." *Philosophy* 49 (April, 1974), 135–147.

Copp, David. "The Iterated Utilitarianism of J. S. Mill." In *New Essays on John Stuart Mill and Utilitarianism. Canadian Journal of Philosophy.* Suppl. Vol. V (Ontario, 1979), 75–98.

Cowling, Maurice. *Mill and Liberalism.* Cambridge: Cambridge University Press, 1963.

Cupples, Brian. "A Defence of the Received Interpretation of J. S. Mill." *Australasian Journal of Philosophy* 50 (August, 1972), 131–137.

Dahl, Norman O. "Is Mill's Hedonism Inconsistent?" In *Studies in Ethics.* American Philosophical Quarterly Monograph Series, No. 7. Oxford: Basil Blackwell, 1973. Pp. 37–54.

Devlin, Patrick. *The Enforcement of Morals.* London: Oxford University Press, 1965.

Dryer, D. P. "Justice, Liberty, and the Principle of Utility in Mill." In *New Essays on John Stuart Mill and Utilitarianism. Canadian Journal of Philosophy.* Suppl. Vol. V (Ontario, 1979), 63–73.

———. "Mill's Utilitarianism." In *CW*, X:lxiii–cxiii.

Duncan Graeme. *Marx and Mill: Two Views of Social Conflict and Social Harmony.* London: Cambridge University Press, 1973.

———, and John Gray. "The Left Against Mill." In *New Essays on John Stuart Mill and Utilitarianism. Canadian Journal of Philosophy*, Suppl. Vol. V (Ontario, 1979), 203–229.

Dworkin, Gerald. "Paternalism." In *Morality and the Law*, ed. Richard Wasserstrom. Belmont, CA.: Wadsworth Publishing Co., Inc., 1971. Pp. 107–126.

Dworkin, Ronald. *Taking Rights Seriously.* Cambridge, Mass.: Harvard University Press, 1977.

Feinberg, Joel. "The Expressive Function of Punishment." In *Doing and Deserving: Essays in the Theory of Responsibility.* Princeton: Princeton University Press, 1970. Pp. 95–118.

———. "Legal Paternalism," *Canadian Journal of Philosophy* 1 (1971), 105–124.

———. "Noncomparative Justice." In *Rights, Justice, and the Bounds of Liberty.* Princeton: Princeton University Press, 1980. Pp. 265–306.

———. *Social Philosophy.* Englewood Cliffs, NJ: Prentice-Hall, Inc., 1973.

Foot, Philippa. "Abortion and the Doctrine of Double Effect." *The Oxford Review* 5 (1967), 5–15.

Gay, John. *Concerning the Fundamental Principle of Virtue or Morality (1731)*. In *British Moralists*. Vol. II. Ed. L. A. Selby-Bigge. Indianapolis and New York: The Bobbs-Merrill Co., 1964. Pp. 267–285.

Gray, John. "John Stuart Mill on the Theory of Property." In *Theories of Property: Aristotle to the Present*, ed. A. Parel and T. Flanagan. Waterloo, Ontario: Wilfred Laverier University Press, 1979. Pp. 257–280.

———. *Mill on liberty: a defence*. London: Routledge & Kegan Paul, 1983.

Green, T. H. *Prolegomena to Ethics*. New York: Thomas Y. Crowell Co., 1969.

Gutmann, Amy. *Liberal Equality*. Cambridge: Cambridge University Press, 1980.

Hall, Everett M. "The 'Proof' of Utility in Bentham and Mill." *Ethics* 60 (October, 1949), 1–18.

Halliday, R. J. *John Stuart Mill*. London: George Allen & Unwin Ltd., 1976.

Hare, R. M. *Freedom and Reason*. New York: Oxford University Press, 1965.

Harsanyi, John C. "Morality and the Theory of Rational Behaviour." *Social Research* 44 (Winter, 1977), 625–656.

Hart, H. L. A. "Are There Any Natural Rights?" *The Philosophical Review* 64 (April, 1955), 175–191.

———. "Between Utility and Rights." 79 *Columbia Law Review* 828–846 (1979).

———. *The Concept of Law*. Oxford: Clarendon Press, 1961.

———. *Law, Liberty, and Morality*. New York: Random House, 1966.

———. "Punishment and the Elimination of Responsibility." In *Punishment and Responsibility: Essays in the Philosophy of Law*. New York: Oxford University Press, 1968. Pp. 158–185.

Hill, Sharon Bishop. "Self-Determination and Autonomy." In *Today's Moral Problems*, 2d ed., ed. Richard Wasserstrom. New York: Macmillan Publishing Co., Inc., 1979. Pp. 118–133.

Himmelfarb, Gertrude. "Introduction." In *Essays on Politics and Culture*, ed. Gertrude Himmelfarb. Garden City, NY: Doubleday & Company, Inc., 1963. Pp. vii–xxiv.

———. *On Liberty and Liberalism: The Case of John Stuart Mill*. New York: Alfred A. Knopf, 1974.

Hodson, John D. "Mill, Paternalism, and Slavery." *Analysis* 41 (January, 1981), 60–62.

————. "The Principle of Paternalism." *American Philosophical Quarterly* 14 (January, 1977), 61–69.

Hollander, Samuel. "Ricardianism, J. S. Mill, and the Neoclassical Challenge." In *James and John Stuart Mill/Papers of the Centenary Conference*, ed. John M. Robson and Michael Laine. Toronto and Buffalo: University of Toronto Press, 1976. Pp. 67–85.

Hughes, Graham. "Should Alfie Be Let Off?" *The New York Review of Books* 27 (November 20, 1980), 47–49.

Hume, David. *A Treatise of Human Nature*. Ed. L. A. Selby-Bigge. Oxford: Oxford University Press, 1960.

Kamm, Josephine. *John Stuart Mill in Love*. London: Gordon & Cremonesi, 1977.

Ladenson, Robert F. "Mill's Conception of Individuality." *Social Theory and Practice* 4 (Spring, 1977), 167–182.

Letvin, Shirley. *The Pursuit of Certainty*. Cambridge: Cambridge University Press, 1965.

Lyons, David. "Benevolence and Justice in Mill." In *The Limits of Utilitarianism*, ed. Harlan B. Miller and William H. Williams. Minneapolis: University of Minnesota Press, 1982. Pp. 42–70.

————. *Forms and Limits of Utilitarianism*. Oxford: The Clarendon Press, 1965.

————. "Human Rights and the General Welfare." *Philosophy and Public Affairs* 6 (Winter, 1977), 113–129.

————. "Introduction." In *Rights*, ed. David Lyons. Belmont, CA.: Wadsworth Publishing Co., Inc., 1979. Pp. 1–13.

————. "Liberty and Harm to Others." In *New Essays on John Stuart Mill and Utilitarianism. Canadian Journal of Philosophy*, Suppl. Vol. V (Ontario, 1979), 1–19.

————. "Mill's Theory of Morality." *Nous* 10 (May, 1976), 101–120.

Mabbott, J. D. "Interpretations of Mill's *Utilitarianism*." *Philosophical Quarterly* 6 (1956), 115–120.

MacCallum, Gerald C., Jr. "Negative and Positive Freedom." *The Philosophical Review* 76 (July, 1967), 312–334.

Macpherson, C. B. *Democratic Theory: Essays in Retrieval*. Oxford: Clarendon Press, 1973.

Mandelbaum, Maurice. "Two Moot Issues in Mill's *Utilitarianism*." In *Mill: A Collection of Critical Essays*, ed. J. B. Schneewind. Garden City, NY: Doubleday and Company, Inc., 1968. Pp. 206–233.

Marcuse, Herbert. *One Dimensional Man: Studies in the Ideology of Advanced Industrial Society*. Boston: Beacon Press, 1964.

————. "Repressive Tolerance." In *A Critique of Pure Tolerance*, ed.

R. P. Wolff, B. Moore, and H. Marcuse. Boston: Beacon Press, 1965. Pp. 81–123.

Martin, Rex. "A Defense of Mill's Qualitative Hedonism." *Philosophy* 46 (April, 1972), 140–151.

McCloskey, H. J. *John Stuart Mill: A Critical Study*. London: Macmillan, 1971.

————. "Liberty of Expression: Its Grounds and Limits (I)." *Inquiry* 13 (Autumn, 1970), 219–237.

Mill, James. *Analysis of the Phenomena of the Human Mind*. 2 vols. Ed. J. S. Mill. London: Longmans, Green, Reader and Dyer, 1869.

————. "The 'Greatest Happiness Principle.' " In *Utilitarian Logic and Politics: James Mill's Essay on Government, and Macaulay's critique and the ensuing debate*, eds. Jack Lively and John Rees. Oxford: Clarendon Press, 1978. Pp. 131–149.

————. *A Fragment on Mackintosh*. London: Longmans, Green, Reader, and Dyer, 1870.

Miller, David. *Social Justice*. Oxford: Clarendon Press, 1976.

Millet, Kate. "Mill versus Ruskin." In *Sexual Politics*. New York: Doubleday and Co., Inc., 1970. Pp. 126–51.

Monro, D. H. "Liberty of Expression: Its Grounds and Limits (II)." *Inquiry* 13 (Autumn, 1970), 238–253.

Morris, Herbert. "Persons and Punishment." In *On Guilt and Innocence: Essays in Legal Philosophy and Moral Psychology*. Berkeley, Los Angeles, London: University of California Press, 1976. Pp. 31–88.

Nozick, Robert. *Anarchy, State, and Utopia*. New York: Basic Books, Inc., 1974.

Packe, Michael St. John. *The Life of John Stuart Mill*. New York: Capricorn Books, 1970.

Parent, William A. "Some Recent Work on the Concept of Liberty." *American Philosophical Quarterly* 11 (July, 1974), 149–167.

Quinton, Anthony. *Utilitarian Ethics*. London: The Macmillan Press, Ltd., 1973.

Rawls, John. "Legal Obligation and the Duty of Fair Play." In *Law and Philosophy: A Symposium*, ed. Sidney Hook. New York: New York University Press, 1964. Pp. 3–18.

————. "Social Unity and Primary Goods." In *Utilitarianism and Beyond*, ed. Amartya Sen and Bernard Williams. Cambridge: Cambridge University Press, 1982. Pp. 159–185.

————. *A Theory of Justice*. Cambridge, Mass.: Harvard University Press, 1971.

————. "Two Concepts of Rules." *The Philosophical Review* 64 (January, 1955), 3–32.

Riley, Jon. "Collective Choice and Individual Liberty: A Revisionist Interpretation of J. S. Mill's Utilitarianism." Doctoral Thesis, University of Oxford, 1982.

Robson, J. M. *The Improvement of Mankind: The Social and Political Thought of John Stuart Mill*. Toronto: University of Toronto Press, 1968.

Roche, Timothy D. "Utilitarianism versus Rawls: Defending Teleological Theory." *Social Theory and Practice* 8 (Summer, 1982), 189–212.

Rossi, Alice S. "Sentiment and Intellect, The Story of John Stuart Mill and Harriet Taylor Mill." In *Essays on Sex Equality*, ed. Alice S. Rossi. Chicago: The University of Chicago Press, 1970. Pp. 1–63.

Russell, Bruce. "Rawls and Utilitarianism: A Comparison and Critique." Ph.D. Diss., University of California, Davis, 1977.

Ryan, Alan. "Introduction." In John Stuart Mill, *An Examination of Sir William Hamilton's Philosophy*, *CW*, IX:vii-lxvii.

————. *J. S. Mill*. London and Boston: Routledge & Kegan Paul, 1974.

————. *The Philosophy of John Stuart Mill*. London: Macmillan, 1970.

Sabine, George H. *A History of Political Theory*. 3d. ed. London: George G. Harrap, 1963.

Scheffler, Samuel. *The Rejection of Consequentialism: A Philosophical Investigation of the Considerations Underlying Rival Moral Conceptions*. Oxford: Clarendon Press, 1982.

Schwartz, Pedro. *The New Political Economy of J. S. Mill*. London: Weidenfeld and Nicolson, 1968.

Sen, Amartya. "Rights and Agency." *Philosophy and Public Affairs* 11 (Winter, 1982), 3–39.

————. "Utilitarianism and Welfarism." *Journal of Philosophy* 76 (September, 1979), 463–489.

————, and Bernard Williams, eds. *Utilitarianism and Beyond*. Cambridge: Cambridge University Press, 1982.

Seth, James. "The Alleged Fallacies in Mill's 'Utilitarianism.' " *The Philosophical Review* 17 (September, 1908), 469–488.

Sidgwick, Henry. *Outlines of the History of Ethics*. London: Macmillan and Co., Ltd., 1931.

Simmons, A. John. *Moral Principles and Political Obligations*. Princeton: Princeton University Press, 1979.

Smart, J. J. C., and Bernard Williams. *Utilitarianism: For and Against*.

Cambridge: Cambridge University Press, 1973.

Spence, G. W. "The Psychology Behind J. S. Mill's Proof." *Philosophy* 43 (January, 1968), 18—28.

Stevenson, C. L. *Ethics and Language*. New Haven, Conn.: Yale University Press, 1944.

Stocker, Michael. "Mill on Desire and Desirability." *Journal of the History of Philosophy* 7 (1969), 199—201.

Strawson, P. F. "Freedom and Resentment." In *Studies in the Philosophy of Thought and Action*, ed. P. F. Strawson. London: Oxford University Press, 1968. Pp. 71—96.

Sumner, L. W. "The Good and the Right." In *New Essays on John Stuart Mill and Utilitarianism. Canadian Journal of Philosophy*. Suppl. Vol. V (Ontario, 1979), 99—114.

Taylor, Richard. *Freedom, Anarchy, and the Law*. Englewood Cliffs, NJ: Prentice-Hall, Inc., 1973.

Ten, C. L. *Mill on Liberty*. Oxford: Clarendon Press, 1980.

Thompson, Dennis F. *John Stuart Mill and Representative Government*. Princeton, NJ: Princeton University Press, 1976.

Urmson, J. O. "The Interpretation of the Moral Philosophy of J. S. Mill." *The Philosophical Quarterly* 3 (January, 1953), 33—39.

Wasserstrom, Richard, ed. *Morality and the Law*. Belmont, CA.: Wadsworth Publishing Co., Inc., 1971.

———. "Racism and Sexism." In *Philosophy and Social Issues*. Notre Dame, Ind.: University of Notre Dame Press, 1980. Pp. 11—50.

INDEX

Designer: U.C. Press Staff
Compositor: Trend Western
Printer: Braun-Brumfield
Binder: Braun-Brumfield
Text: Janson
Display: Palatino Bold

DATE DUE

MAR 2 8 1985		
DEC 1 2 1985		
APR 1 9 1991		
MAR 3 1 1995		
APR 1 7 2013		